Transformations of the State

Series Editors: **Achim Hurrelmann**, Carleton University, Canada; **Stephan Leibfried**, University of Bremen, Germany; **Kerstin Martens**, University of Bremen, Germany; **Peter Mayer**, University of Bremen, Germany.

Titles include:

Joan DeBardeleben and Achim Hurrelmann (*editors*)
DEMOCRATIC DILEMMAS OF MULTILEVEL GOVERNANCE
Legitimacy, Representation and Accountability in the European Union

Karin Gottschall, Bernhard Kittel, Kendra Briken, Jan-Ocko Heuer and Sylvia Hils
PUBLIC SECTOR EMPLOYMENT REGIMES
Transformations of the State as an Employer

Andreas Hepp, Monika Elsler, Swantje Lingenberg, Anne Mollen, Johanna Möller and Anke Offerhaus
THE COMMUNICATIVE CONSTRUCTION OF EUROPE
Cultures of Political Discourse, Public Sphere and the Euro Crisis

Achim Hurrelmann and Steffen Schneider (*editors*)
THE LEGITIMACY OF REGIONAL INTEGRATION IN EUROPE AND AMERICA

Achim Hurrelmann, Steffen Schneider and Jens Steffek (*editors*)
LEGITIMACY IN AN AGE OF GLOBAL POLITICS

Achim Hurrelmann, Stephan Leibfried, Kerstin Martens and Peter Mayer (*editors*)
TRANSFORMING THE GOLDEN-AGE NATION STATE

Lutz Leisering (*editor*)
THE NEW REGULATORY STATE
Regulating Pensions in Germany and the UK

Kerstin Martens, Alessandra Rusconi and Kathrin Leuze (*editors*)
NEW ARENAS OF EDUCATION GOVERNANCE
The Impact of International Organizations and Markets on Educational Policy Making

Kerstin Martens, Philipp Knodel and Michael Windzio (*editors*)
INTERNATIONALIZATION OF EDUCATION POLICY
A New Constellation of Statehood in Education?

Kerstin Martens, Alexander-Kenneth Nagel, Michael Windzio and Ansgar Weymann (*editors*)
TRANSFORMATION OF EDUCATION POLICY

Steffen Mau, Heike Brabandt, Lena Laube and Christof Roos
LIBERAL STATES AND THE FREEDOM OF MOVEMENT
Selective Borders, Unequal Mobility

Aletta Mondré
FORUM SHOPPING IN INTERNATIONAL DISPUTES

Christof Roos
THE EU AND IMMIGRATION POLICIES
Cracks in the Walls of Fortress Europe?

Heinz Rothgang and Steffen Schneider
STATE TRANSFORMATIONS IN OECD COUNTRIES
Dimensions, Driving Forces, and Trajectories

Heinz Rothgang, Mirella Cacace, Simone Grimmeisen, Uwe Helmert and
Claus Wendt
THE STATE AND HEALTHCARE
Comparing OECD Countries

Steffen Schneider, Achim Hurrelmann, Zuzana Krell-Laluhová, Frank Nullmeier
and Achim Wiesner
DEMOCRACY'S DEEP ROOTS
Why the Nation State Remains Legitimate

Peter Starke
RADICAL WELFARE STATE RETRENCHMENT
A Comparative Analysis

Peter Starke, Alexandra Kaasch, Franca Van Hooren (editors)
THE WELFARE STATE AS CRISIS MANAGER
Explaining the Diversity of Policy Responses to Economic Crisis

Silke Weinlich
THE UN SECRETARIAT'S INFLUENCE ON THE EVOLUTION OF PEACEKEEPING

Hartmut Wessler (editor)
PUBLIC DELIBERATION AND PUBLIC CULTURE
The Writings of Bernhard Peters, 1993–2005

Hartmut Wessler, Bernhard Peters, Michael Brüggemann, Katharina Kleinen-von
Königslöw, Stefanie Sifft
TRANSNATIONALIZATION OF PUBLIC SPHERES

Jochen Zimmermann and Jörg R. Werner
REGULATING CAPITALISM?
The Evolution of Transnational Accounting Governance

Jochen Zimmerman, Jörg R. Werner, Philipp B. Volmer
GLOBAL GOVERNANCE IN ACCOUNTING
Public Power and Private Commitment

Transformations of the State
Series Standing Order ISBN 978–1–4039–8544–6 (hardback)
978–1–4039–8545–3 (paperback)

You can receive future titles in this series as they are published by placing a standing order. Please contact your bookseller or, in case of difficulty, write to us at the
address below with your name and address, the title of the series and the ISBNs
quoted above.

Customer Services Department, Macmillan Distribution Ltd, Houndmills,
Basingstoke, Hampshire RG21 6XS, England

The Communicative Construction of Europe

Cultures of Political Discourse, Public Sphere and the Euro Crisis

Andreas Hepp

Monika Elsler

Swantje Lingenberg

Anne Mollen

Johanna Möller

Anke Offerhaus

First published 2016 by
PALGRAVE MACMILLAN

Palgrave Macmillan in the UK is an imprint of Macmillan Publishers Limited, registered in England, company number 785998, of Houndmills, Basingstoke, Hampshire RG21 6XS.

Palgrave Macmillan in the US is a division of St Martin's Press LLC, 175 Fifth Avenue, New York, NY 10010.

Palgrave Macmillan is the global academic imprint of the above companies and has companies and representatives throughout the world.

Palgrave® and Macmillan® are registered trademarks in the United States, the United Kingdom, Europe and other countries.

ISBN: 978–1–137–45312–9

This book is printed on paper suitable for recycling and made from fully managed and sustained forest sources. Logging, pulping and manufacturing processes are expected to conform to the environmental regulations of the country of origin.

A catalogue record for this book is available from the British Library.

A catalog record for this book is available from the Library of Congress.

Contents

List of Tables

List of Figures

Series Preface

Over the past four centuries, the nation-state has emerged as the world's most effective means of organizing society, but its current status and future are decidedly uncertain. Some scholars predict the total demise of the nation-state as we know it, its powers eroded by a dynamic global economy on the one hand and, on the other, by the transfer of political decision-making to supranational bodies. Other analysts point out the remarkable resilience of the state's core institutions and assert that even in the age of global markets and politics, the state remains the ultimate guarantor of security, democracy, welfare, and the rule of law. Does either of these interpretations describe the future of the OECD world's modern, liberal nation-state? Will the state soon be as obsolete and irrelevant as an outdated computer? Should it be scrapped for some new invention, or can it be overhauled and rejuvenated? Or, is the state actually thriving and still fit to serve, and just in need of a few minor reforms?

In an attempt to address these questions, the analyses in the *Transformations of the State* series separate the complex tangle of tasks and functions that comprise the state into four manageable dimensions:

- the monopolization of the means of force;
- the rule of law, as prescribed and safeguarded by the constitution;
- the guarantee of democratic self-governance; and
- the provision of welfare and the assurance of social cohesion.

In the OECD world of the 1960s and 1970s, these four dimensions formed a synergetic constellation that emerged as the central, defining characteristic of the modern state. Books in the series report the results of both empirical and theoretical studies of the transformations experienced in each of these dimensions over the past few decades.

Transformations of the State? (Stephan Leibfried and Michael Zürn (eds), 2005), *Transforming the Golden-Age National State* (Achim Hurrelmann, Stephan Leibfried, Kerstin Martens and Peter Mayer (eds), Palgrave Macmillan 2007), *State Transformations in OECD Countries: Dimensions, Driving Forces and Trajectories* (Heinz Rothgang and Steffen Schneider (eds), Palgrave Macmillan 2015) and *The Oxford Handbook of Transformations of the State* (Stephan Leibfried, Evelyne Huber, Matthew Lange, Jonah Levy

and Frank Nullmeier (eds), 2015) define the basic concepts of state transformation employed in all of these studies and provide an overview of
the issues addressed. Written by political scientists, lawyers, economists,
and sociologists, the series tracks the development of the post-World
War II OECD state. Here, at last, is an up-to-date series of reports on the
state of the state and a crystal-ball glimpse into its future.

1
Introduction

The euro crisis, as it is widely known, has been an important focus for media coverage both within Europe and beyond. Since 2009 we have been confronted with an ongoing discourse dramatising the crisis surrounding the euro in Europe and the EU. In 2003 *The Sun* was already writing about the 'EU in crisis' (12 December 2003) – a discourse that intensified when the financial crisis erupted. On 13 December 2008, for example, the German *Bild* talked of a 'crisis domino-effect', reflecting ongoing problems with the eurozone currency and financial politics in general. In Poland, one could read on 13 December 2008 that the member states of the EU should 'jointly struggle with the crisis' (*Dziennik Zachodni*). And in France, *Ouest France* called upon 'the state to rescue the crisis' (25 March 2008), while *Le Monde* anticipated that 'in Southern Europe, the crisis further weakens confidence in the state' (7 May 2013). More recently, on 4 November 2014 the Polish *Gazeta Wyborcza* agreed with politicians that 'the euro crisis has not been solved', asking what could be done. The German *Spiegel Online* calculated on 6 January 2015 that the euro crisis had 'destroyed 3.8 million jobs'. All in all, this throws up more questions than answers. Is the EU really under so much pressure? Do we risk the derailment of European integration? And is a process of re-nationalising Europe taking place, with the state acting the part of a trouble shooter? How can we interpret the various forms of Euroscepticism?

Questions like these are also the subject of intellectual debate – and some of Europe's best-known public intellectuals became involved. For example, Anthony Giddens (2012) argued in the *Guardian* that 'stabilising the euro should be a bridge to longer-term change' of Europe and the EU. In his book *Turbulent and Mighty Continent* (2014) Giddens imagines a different kind of Europe. He argues that the EU is a 'community

1

of fate' (2014: 18), in which the dominance of (German) austerity policy is problematic. Instead of being a centralised top-down polity, the EU should become more devolved, with the initiative being taken at the bottom: 'Citizens must at this point become more deeply involved in the process of European reform – the bottom-up element must be strong and persuasive, not confined to occasional consultations or even elections.' (2014: 46) In parallel, and also as a reaction to the euro crisis and the related politics of the German government, in 2014 Ulrich Beck published *German Europe*. Here he criticises the increasingly dominant position of Germany in the EU and the related 'national view' upon Europe. For him, this perspective weakens the originally transnational and partly cosmopolitan orientation of the European project. Spurred on by his conviction, Beck became politically active in building an initiative for a 'bottom-up Europe' – together with other politicians and intellectuals, such as Zygmunt Bauman, Jacques Delors, and Richard Sennett (cf. Delors et al. 2012). Jürgen Habermas (2012) also published various interviews and articles about the present situation of the EU, many of which were translated into English and as a consequence became part of the wider European debate. His book *On the European Constitution* (Habermas 2011) adds two academic essays to some of these newspaper articles, outlining the possibility of a post- or supranational Europe in a worldwide society. Besides calling for a deepening of European integration, these intellectual statements coincide with two arguments: first, that Europe and the EU should be considered a *transnational* rather than a *national* project and, second, that the euro crisis should stimulate a rethinking of Europe from a *citizens' perspective*.

Our research questions

This is the debate in which we want to position our book. We want to temper the emotionalism surrounding this debate by grounding it in empirical analysis drawn from a 12-year comparative research project that was conducted from 2003 to 2014. The overall project, 'The Transnationalization of Public Spheres in the EU', was part of the Collaborative Research Centre 597 'Transformations of the State' at the University of Bremen. Being funded by the German Research Foundation (DFG), we had the opportunity to investigate the media coverage of Europe from 1982 to 2013 in the quality, tabloid, and regional press, studying the practices of journalists producing this media coverage as well as the online activities of citizens and their media appropriation. This allowed us to present the European public realm as a communicative space. About half way through the project, what is now called the euro crisis blew up. It became an important reference point for our research. We had four principle research questions: First, is there such a thing as a European public sphere and, if so, what is its character? Second, how can we explain the character of such a European public sphere through the production practices of journalists? Third, how do citizens relate to the European public sphere and react to its character? Finally, did the subsequently revealed patterns undergo change in the context of the euro crisis?

In pursuit of answers to these principal questions, we conducted our research in and across six countries: Austria (AT), Denmark (DK), France (F), Germany (GER), United Kingdom (UK) and Poland (PL). We wanted to include the economically strongest founding member states of the EU including two EU-positive members (France and Germany) and one EU-sceptical member (UK), two smaller member states of which one is pro-EU (Austria) and the other EU-sceptical (Denmark), and one of the eastern latecomers to the EU (Poland). Our argument for selecting this sample was to focus our research on a varied selection of the countries that build the economic core of Europe and are main actors in constructing Europe as a society and the EU as its political institution. From today's perspective one might argue that at least one Southern European state is missing, partly because of differences in media systems (Hallin/Mancini 2004: 89–142; Hepp 2015: 51–59) and partly because of the deeper impact of the euro crisis on Southern European states, resulting in a different kind of media coverage and public discourse (Breeze 2014; Kaitatzi-Whitlock 2014). Such a criticism would have been justified if the aim of our study had been to draw comparisons of the Europeanisation of national public spheres in Europe with reference to their differences of media systems or if our research had been occupied with comparing the different consequences of the euro crisis on national public spheres. However, our interest is another one, namely, to investigate the communicative construction of Europe during the course of the euro crisis. Having such a research objective, it is much more appropriate to focus on those countries which are the dominant actors within this process of construction. And the Southern European states are present in our data at least indirectly as a topic of media coverage and online discourse, and thus also reflected in citizens' media appropriation.

Methodologically, we worked according to what we call a 'transcultural perspective' (Hepp 2009; Hepp/Couldry 2009). By this we understand an approach that does not take the 'nation state' and its 'national culture' as the unquestioned unit of comparison, structuring all the data from the very beginning in 'national containers' – something that has been widely criticised (cf. Beck 2000; Wimmer/Glick Schiller 2002). Instead, we analysed the data set in total, looking for transcultural patterns of similarity and difference across all the researched countries, including national differences where they are significant. At the level of newspaper coverage, our data in all six states is based on a quantitative content analysis of the media coverage during two artificial weeks of the years 1982, 1989, 1996, 2003, 2008, and 2013, including quality, tabloid, and regional newspapers. At the level of journalists, in the autumn of 2008 we conducted 216 interviews with EU and foreign news editors, chief editors, and foreign correspondents of 23 quality, tabloid, and regional papers. We also undertook participatory observations in two newsrooms per country and documented this in research diaries. This data was analysed according to the standards of grounded theory research (Glaser/Strauss 1967).

The same analytical approach was applied to our data gathered at the level of audiences: We carried out 182 in-depth interviews, qualitative network maps (interviewees' drawings of their communicative networks), and media diaries (interviewees' documentations of their media use over a period of one week). This fieldwork was undertaken from September to December 2011, a period when discourses surrounding the euro crisis initially peaked associated with a possible withdrawal of Greece from the Eurozone.

Finally, we completed a WebCrawler analysis of hyperlink networks for each of our research countries as well as on a transnational European level, and conducted an interaction analysis of 125 comment threads from 28 online comment forums, encompassing European as well as national forums. These comment forums were selected from blogs, mainstream news media, and the Facebook pages of political news media. The comments for the analysis were then sampled from these forums during a week of the so-called European Crisis Summit – the summit of the European Council – in June 2012.

All in all, these data offer a deep insight into what we have chosen to call the 'communicative construction of Europe'. The European public sphere is first of all a communicative space in which the joint transnational construction of Europe takes place. Of course, there are also further issues related to the social construction of Europe, for example, institution-building as it takes place in Brussels or policies like the Erasmus programme which motivate and facilitate European mobility. These are means of social construction familiar from the advent of the nation state (cf. Anderson 1983). However, the joint *communicative* construction is as important as are these other means, because it is through communication that we build our *understanding* of what the 'European society' (Vobruba 2012) is or might be. As this European society is still emerging, and as its communicative construction is an ongoing process, all research faces the problem of determining what already can be identified as European, and what cannot. In the ensuing process, we must reconstruct this specific European character through careful empirical analysis (cf. Neverla/Schoon 2008: 20). Our analysis will show that the euro crisis cannot be seen as causing a collapse of this communicative construction. Nonetheless, it might be a 'tipping point' (Eder 2014: 221), or at least a point of increased 'politicisation' (Risse 2015b: 12). Maybe Ulrich Beck and Anthony Giddens are right: The euro crisis has unleashed a clear desire for a 'Europe from below' (Beck 2014: 7), in which citizens' uncertainty, anxiety, and indignation should become a prime point of reference for politics.

Some basic concepts

For our analysis we need to clarify some interrelated but nevertheless distinct concepts. First, there is the difference between Europe and the European Union (or EU). When we use the term 'Europe', it refers to Europe as a society that is still in emergence, and that has borders less clear than those of the EU. Here we are rather at the beginning than at the end of a long-term process of social construction (cf. Vobruba 2012). Europe as a society is more than institutionalised politics. It has very much to do with everyday social relations, with partly conflicting understandings of what Europe is (or might be), and with varying attitudes towards it. In a certain sense Europe as a society is the everyday dimension of this unfinished project. In contrast, we reserve the term 'European Union' or 'EU' for the evolving political institutions of a European society. In this sense, the term is more specific and focused, not covering all aspects of the (communicative) construction of Europe, but only those related to political institutions. As Peter Golding (2008: 25f.) points out, this terminological distinction 'between the EU and Europe as objects of perception and aspiration' is of great help for any empirical analysis.

For both Europe and the EU, the European public sphere is a fundamental communicative space. The next chapter discusses in detail our understanding of the public sphere. However, at this point we need to provide at least a rough outline. In our view, a public sphere is best understood as a 'thickened space of political communication' (Hepp et al. 2012: 25).

As communicative spaces, public spheres are not exclusive phenomena in the sense that involvement in one precludes involvement in another. Rather, various public spheres 'overlap and interconnect' (Risse 2015b: 9) – and they are partly articulated through each other. The latter is especially the case for the European public sphere, which is a thickened communicative space articulated mainly through certain patterns of transnationalisation within local, regional, issue-related, and especially national public spheres (Koopmans/Statham 2010b; Wessler et al. 2008). Based on our previous distinction between Europe (the European society) and the EU (its political institutions) we can say that the European public sphere is the space in which a dual communicative construction takes place: On the one hand, it is the space in which the European society is communicatively constructed in its political dimension; on the other hand, it is the space in which the communicative construction of the legitimacy of EU politics takes place.

By means of such a definition of the public sphere we indicate that not every form of public communication – understood as generally accessible mediated communication – should be considered as constitutive for a public sphere. In parallel to recent reflections by others (cf. Lunt/Livingstone 2013), we argue that public communication becomes constitutive for a public sphere when it is related to common issues and related decision-making – in the case of the European public sphere, the common issues of an emerging European society. Hence, from the perspective of audience and user studies, the issue of to what extent everyday people have a 'public connection' (Couldry et al. 2007b: 5) to the European public sphere becomes an important question – how far they are involved in common European issues, and how controversial those issues might be. Only through an involvement with these issues do the various 'media audiences' in different European states become a European 'citizen audience' (Lingenberg 2010b: 45), and thus part of the European public sphere.

If we follow the present public discussion, one of the most-used words in relation to Europe is 'crisis'. Again, some analytical precision is necessary here if we are to avoid misinterpretation. In general, discourse about crises seems to be a constitutive moment of Europe and the European public sphere (cf. Triandafyllidou et al. 2009). This is not a new phenomenon, but an ongoing European narrative. To recall other recent crises: At the beginning of the 1990s there was a crisis of European foreign and security policy during the so-called Balkan conflict. In general, the eastern enlargement of the EU was understood as a process of ongoing smaller crises. And there was a crisis when the constitution for a pan-European institution was rejected in 2005 through referenda in France and the Netherlands. When in the following sections we talk in general about crises as one moment of the communicative construction of Europe, we point to the various crisis events which were and are a reference point of communicative construction within the EU. In a narrower sense, we use the term 'euro crisis'. By this, we understand the crisis we have witnessed since 2008 in the eurozone, an outcome of the financial crisis of 2007 caused by the breakdown of the US housing market and the consequent collapse of Lehmann Brothers. The euro crisis is not one single crisis but a multilevel phenomenon, including at least a banking crisis, a sovereign debt crisis, and a market crisis (Vobruba 2014b). That's why the euro crisis has no single meaning; it is – as our analyses will show – a signifier for various financial and economy-related phenomena, and open to different interpretations. As a signifier, the euro crisis is an important point of reference for the present communicative construction of Europe, and of the EU within the European public sphere.

An overview

Based on these fundamental analytical considerations, we develop the argument of this book in eight chapters. Chapter 2 outlines what we call a communicative constructivist perspective on Europe and the EU. Such a perspective does not mean that we want to reduce Europe and the EU to a semiotic phenomenon. European integration is a complex, multilevel social, cultural, economic, and political process that has to be theorised as such. Instead, the idea of communicative constructivism argues that the everyday meaning of such processes of integration becomes articulated in an ongoing process of communication, resulting in further processes of institutionalisation and social objectivation. To understand this communicative construction of Europe, we have to analyse both the European public sphere in which this process takes place and the different cultures of political discourse that are the fundament of this process of communicative construction, explaining its multi-segmentation. In the same way, the public discourse surrounding the euro crisis has to be understood as a phenomenon of communicative construction.

Chapter 3 presents the results of our newsroom studies of cultures of political discourse. Through our qualitative newsroom research, first, we demonstrate the stability of national cultures of political discourse as they are re-articulated in journalists' practices; second, we determine that transnational cultures of political discourse are related to certain modes of addressing audiences and reflect at least in part a stratification-related segmentation of Europe; and third, we decipher the emergence of a European discourse culture, which manifests itself in the way transcultural European references and patterns of European coverage become a daily routine within the journalists' practices.

Chapter 4 links the newsroom studies with our content analysis of political news coverage in the press. Here we take a long-term perspective and look back at the way this coverage has been transformed from 1982 to 2013. We demonstrate that a European public sphere emerged across all the nation states studied: The European public sphere manifests itself as an increasingly transnational coverage of EU political activities and an increased discussion that takes place across national borders. European identity references are sparse, but visible. However, this European public sphere remains quite segmented. On the one hand, it is grounded in national cultures of political discourse in which countries differ in their news coverage, thereby creating national segmentation. On the other hand, we see transnational segmentation by types of newspapers. In general, our research demonstrates that the euro crisis did not result in a breakdown of the European public sphere. Considering the entire timeframe of our analysis, it became obvious that while the euro crisis year 2008 has gained special prominence for political institutions, trends towards Europeanisation that were already apparent had been consolidated, there being only a small degree of instability, if any.

In chapter 5, we present our research on the way in which citizens take part in the discussion of the euro crisis in online comment forums, taking one euro crisis summit of the European Council in 2012 as an example. Overall, we analysed 125 comment threads from 28 political online forums from mainstream news media, political blogs, and political news media's Facebook accounts, four from each country in our sample, as well as four from the transnational European level. By first analysing hyperlink structures, we isolated main online forums where citizens can discuss political matters. From forums isolated in this way, we then selected 125 articles and posts that dealt with European issues during a week of a so-called European crisis summit and conducted an interaction analysis of citizens' online comments in reaction to these articles and posts. In this way we could identify different forms of interaction in citizens' online activities. Overall, our research demonstrates that the euro crisis creates a context for citizens' online engagement in a process of common European communicative construction. Discussion of the euro crisis can, for example, trigger conflict in citizens' interaction, but it can just as well evolve into expressions of mutual solidarity. Transnational forums provide a central context for the expression of conflict and solidarity in terms of national belonging. But at the same time, we see lines of conflict in the user bases of national forums.

Chapter 6 presents the qualitative audience research undertaken in late 2011. This research is based on 182 in-depth interviews on media appropriation, the EU, and its legitimation, on media diaries kept by the interviewees, and on a qualitative analysis of the interviewees' communicative networks. We can demonstrate that having a public connection to Europe is a common ground: Through their media use, but also everyday interaction, almost all interviewed persons have access to current events in Europe, especially in relation to the euro crisis. Across all countries, this chapter shows different forms of European public connections characteristic for particular types of people. These different forms of public connections cannot simply be understood as national patterns; they intersect with other factors (age, class, education, mobility, biography, etc.) and provide a more complex picture that goes beyond a simple causal model. This can be shown across the patterns, and also in how the euro crisis activates the public connection of European citizens.

Chapter 7, the final empirical chapter, focuses on one particular aspect of our qualitative audience research: How do European citizens construct the euro crisis differently? We undertake a dual-level analysis: First, we identify the constructions of the euro crisis and how citizens make sense of 'what's going on in Europe'. This process of making sense is marked by perplexity, anxiety, and speculation. These patterns relate to concerns about how it all began and what is now going on, worrying about possible effects on both personal lives and the future of Europe and, finally, speculating about the complex nature of the euro crisis. Then we analyse different solutions that citizens propose for solving the euro crisis. These solutions point to citizens' constructions of what a future EU, both legitimate and capable of overcoming the euro crisis, might look like. Here we can distinguish four anticipated solutions, or 'legitimation constructions': Firstly, an EU made up of national cultures, involving national solutions for the euro crisis that treat the different European nation states as the main agents for overcoming the euro crisis. Accordingly, each national government should first of all solve its own financial problems. Secondly, an EU of economic cooperation, highlighting the need for intensified economic cooperation between the EU member states in order to prevent and overcome economic crises such as the euro crisis. Thirdly, an EU of welfare and solidarity, pointing to European solutions for the euro crisis. Here the euro crisis itself is understood mainly as a European problem, and can therefore only be resolved through European action and solidarity. And fourthly, the United States of Europe, promoting the idea that it is only by fostering a European integration process corresponding to the US model that the EU can become a real Union of Europeans and solve its current and future economic problems. In sum, this chapter shows what a legitimate EU might look like from a citizens' perspective. The euro crisis represents an activating moment in citizens' communicative constructions, so that citizens begin questioning and renegotiating the legitimacy of the EU.

The conclusion reintegrates our various research results in an overarching understanding of the communicative construction of Europe. While this process is rooted in different cultures of political discourse as they take shape in journalists' practices, communicative construction as such takes place as public political communication orientated to common issues, political decision-making, and its legitimation – in short, within the multi-segmented European public sphere and the public connection that citizens have. As our research shows, the euro crisis continues to challenge this process of communicative construction. But it does not signify its end; rather, the euro crisis has a catalysing influence.

In addition, this book has an appendix with further information on our methodology. While each chapter includes sufficient guidance for a critical reading of our empirical analysis, we provide further details about our newsroom research, content analysis, online interaction analysis, and audience studies in this appendix. We wish our work to be as transparent as possible, without interrupting the argumentative flow of the chapters.

Acknowledgement

This book is the outcome of joint research and as a consequence we share intellectual responsibility jointly. However, each chapter had different lead authors who wrote first drafts which were then discussed and revised several times. The lead author of the introduction, chapter 2, and the conclusion was Andreas Hepp, and the lead author of chapter 3 was Swantje Lingenberg, supported by Johanna Möller. Chapter 4 was written under the lead of Anke Offerhaus. Anne Mollen was the main author of chapter 5. The principal responsibility for chapter 6 was with Johanna Möller, Swantje Lingenberg, and Monika Elsler and for chapter 7 with Swantje Lingenberg, Monika Elsler, and Johanna Möller.

However, while certain persons were responsible as lead authors, the whole book is based on the common research of our team, and each chapter is rooted in this common research. Thus, the overall argument of the book is a shared intellectual outcome of our team.

It would have not been possible to realise such a project without support and help from several sources. First of all, we would like to thank the DFG for having funded our project over 12 years until its third and final phase, and our committed reviewers who critically supported the project over such a long time. We are especially grateful to Stephan Leibfried and his tireless commitment to the Collaborative Research Centre, as well as to Dieter Wolf for his constant support, help, and cooperation. Without Bernhard Peters' essential work (Forst 2015; Peters 2008) in having initiated this research and that of Hartmut Wessler in continuing and further conceptualising Bernhard Peters's, the project would have never been realised. Furthermore, we profited from a mutual and ongoing exchange with our sister project, 'Legitimating States, International Regimes, and Economic Orders', especially in conversation with Frank Nullmeier, Dominika Biegon, Jennifer Gronau, Sebastian Haunss, Falk Lenke, Tanja Pritzlaff, Henning Schmidtke, and Steffen Schneider.

Chapters 3 and 4 are in particular based on work that was conducted in two previous research phases. Katharina Kleinen-von Königslöw and Michael Brüggemann, who left the project after its second phase, took a central position in conceptualising and conducting the content analysis and the newsroom studies in these previous phases. Furthermore, we want to thank Sune Blicher, Gabriel Moreno, and Stefanie Trümper who supported the research team in conducting the newsroom observations and journalists' interviews. An earlier version of chapter 7 was published as '"I just hope the whole thing won't collapse": "Understanding" and "overcoming" the EU financial crisis from the citizens' perspective' in the book *Money Talks: Media, Markets, Crisis* (Gripsrud and Murdoch 2015). We would like to thank Jostein Gripsrud and Graham Murdock for permission to develop chapter 7 from that essay.

For their helpful comments and recommendations on the results of our last phase during the Collaborative Research Centre's concluding conference on 'Transformations of the State', we would like to thank Jostein Gripsrud, Barbara Pfetsch, and Kim Christian Schrøder. In 2008 we held a workshop in which Peter Golding, Risto Kunelius, Paolo Mancini, Juan Diez Medrano, Barbara Pfetsch, and Hartmut Wessler provided valuable feedback, especially regarding our newsroom studies. And we would especially like to thank Daniel Smith and Keith Tribe for their brilliant proofreading and suggestions for stylistic improvement.

Our work is, furthermore, embedded in the ZeMKI (Centre for Media, Communication and Information Research) at the University of Bremen and, therein, especially in the research lab 'Media Culture and Globalisation'. Several – also former – members have supported our work with valuable comments, suggestions, and advice. We are especially thankful to Matthias Berg, Çiğdem Bozdag, Julia Gantenberg, Marco Höhn, Sigrid Kannengießer, Leif Kramp, Sebastian Kubitschko, Katharina Lobinger, Cindy Roitsch, Monika Sowinska, and Laura Suna. For organisational and administrative support we are grateful to Heide Pawlik.

Finally, all this would not have been possible without the help of numerous student assistants. For their essential help in coding the newspapers, for the transcription of the interviews with citizens across Europe, for the support in sampling users' comments from central online comment forums across Europe, as well as for general project administration tasks, we thank Elodie Bergot, Sara Blass, Jérémy Caro, Cécile Duparfait, Lara Gahlow, Ulrike Gerhard, Patricia Glabischewski, Alicja Grabowska, Katharina Gronemeyer, Ole Hammersland, David Heidenreich, Maria Heine, Martin Helbich, Helene Hoffman, Jeanne Hoffmann, Jakob Hörtnagl, Kathrin Hövel, Susann-Carmen Huff, Lisa Jürgensen, Dorra Kassem, Kira Kettner, Lukas Klose, Agniezska Kowalska, Eva-Katrin Landscheid, Marit Langheim, Susann Lukas, Martyna Malak, Simone Michel, Alexandra Mondry, Insa Müller, Ana Niederer, Charles Noirot, Gerda Marie Notholt, Michal Palacz, Sarah Pauly, Johanna Pawlik, Ramona Reichel, Johanna Reimers, Mareike Remus, Franziska Römer, Sophia Schulze, Eva Schurig, Linda Siegel, Svenja Steenken, Emilia Szczypior, Catalina Vazquez, Anna-Lena Vinke, and Nele Wolter. Some of these students worked on our project for more than two years, providing essential support for our research work.

2
Approaching the Communicative Construction of Europe: Cultures of Political Discourse, European Public Sphere and the Euro Crisis

In this chapter, we outline a communicative constructivist perspective on the European public sphere, Europe and the EU. As already emphasised in the introduction, this perspective does not mean that we reduce Europe and the EU to a semiotic phenomenon. Other processes of social construction are also taking place and are of great importance. Beyond any reductionism, the idea of communicative constructivism proposes that the everyday meaning of a European society is articulated in ongoing processes of communication. These communication processes are increasingly mediatised: mediated by and related to the institutions and technologies of the media, and also moulded by them. Furthermore, communication processes such as these are rooted in different cultures of political discourse: the culture producing a certain kind of political discourse, both national and transnational. The latter involves the various transnational cultural patterns of media communication which mark the transnational stratification of an emerging European society. We also suggest that something like a European culture of political discourse emerges. Considered in a long-term perspective, the euro crisis seems to be not so much a collapse of the communicative construction of Europe, but a potential 'tipping point' (Eder 2014: 221) in the practice of communicative construction. It has been observed that the euro crisis has brought about a 'politicisation' (Risse 2015b: 3) of the European public sphere: a general shift to a public sphere in which more citizens find their voice.

To substantiate this overall approach – which is the theoretical frame of our subsequent analysis – we argue as follows. First we outline a concept of the European public sphere which goes beyond its understanding as a space of functional legitimation. In contrast, we regard the European public sphere as 'a complex, thickened space of communicative construction'. In studying this social space we have to consider how people – the citizens of an emerging European society – become involved in this European public sphere and hence in the process of constructing Europe communicatively. However, the European public sphere remains 'multi-segmented' in various ways. Following on, we secondly discuss how far the European public sphere is rooted in different cultures of political discourse. This idea offers the chance of explaining the multi-segmented character of the European public sphere. Finally, we discuss to what extent the euro crisis as a 'mediatised conflict' might mark a kind of tipping point in the process of communicatively constructing Europe and the EU – a tipping point which possibly does not result in the breakdown of this process, but in its change of character. Here increasing political activity might alter the manner in which the legitimation of Europe and the EU is constructed.

2.1 Theorising the European public sphere: from functional legitimation to communicative construction

Today the discussion surrounding media, communication and Europe is greatly influenced by Jürgen Habermas' idea of the public sphere as *Öffentlichkeit*, an understanding which has a normative dimension. Habermas was originally interested in the transformation of the 'bourgeois public sphere' (Habermas 1989; cf. for a critical discussion Calhoun 1992; Fraser 1993), but later refined the concept of the public sphere into one of a communicative space that 'can best be described as a network of communicating information and points of view' (Habermas 1996: 360). Within this public sphere the 'streams of communication are, in the process, filtered and synthesised in such a way that they coalesce into bundles of topically specified *public* opinions' (1996: 360, italics as in the original). The public sphere is 'reproduced through communicative action' and it is 'tailored to the general comprehensibility of everyday communicative practice' (1996: 360). This concept of the public sphere has an obviously normative dimension; it is not just any space of communication. It is a space of political communication which is plural, contested and sustained by various institutions (Lunt/Livingstone 2013: 92). At the same time, this space of communication remains oriented towards certain ethics of deliberative communication and, in consequence, towards the production of a legitimate and therefore legitimating public opinion (Fraser 2007).

This understanding of the public sphere builds on democratic theory (Habermas 1996: 356; Peters 2008: 33–67; Risse 2010: 107–120): Public spheres are integral parts of late-modern liberal democracies. In these democracies there are legal and political institutions that ensure the deliberative quality of public political discourse (Kantner 2004: 46). These institutionally secured procedures of deliberation serve to ensure 'at least two normative requirements for a public sphere in liberal democracies' (Risse 2010: 115): first, openness to participation; and second, the possibility of demanding that public authorities legitimise their decisions.

This sense of the public sphere represents how the general understanding governing discussion about the European public sphere was (and is) positioned. Work on this started in the 1990s, with the fundamental question: Would the constitution of the EU as a supranational political institution be accompanied by the emergence of a European public sphere that would fulfil democratic functions at a European level (Meyer 1999)? To a certain degree, this work was stimulated by various media policies on the part of the EU which aimed at the 'production' of this public sphere in order to avoid any possible 'democracy deficit' in the EU (Brüggemann 2008; Lodge/Sarikakis 2013; Sarikakis 2007). In particular, there were three sceptical arguments against the existence of a European public sphere that might perform this function (Gerhards 1993, 2000). First, due to the absence of European media, a European public sphere would have no institutional foundation. Second, the lack of a common European language would make common understanding and reasoning impossible. And third, even if there were such an understanding, the dominance of national perspectives on Europe and the EU would work against any shared deliberation.

Criticism of this kind involves a normatively framed 'national ideal' of the public sphere which is then more or less applied directly to Europe and the EU (cf. Gerhards 2000: 288–292; Schlesinger/Deirdre 2002). This ideal falls short, however, when we consider multilingual nation states in Europe. Switzerland, for example, has no common native language (Kantner 2015: 86). This ideal applies even less at the European level (Mihelj 2007). Research has demonstrated that a European public sphere – understood as a thickened transnational space of political communication (Hepp et al. 2012: 22) – emerges through the transnationalisation of national public spheres that were formerly more strictly separated. Therefore, we cannot describe the European public sphere by employing criteria relating to a national ideal. Instead, we have to find criteria by which it becomes possible to describe the European public

sphere through processes of transnationalisation. At this point, it is possible to distinguish analytically at least four dimensions of European
transnationalisation (cf. Wessler et al. 2008: 11). While these criteria
were originally developed with mass media – and especially newspapers –
in mind, they can also be applied to other kinds of mediated communication, as, for example, in public internet forums (Bennett et al.
2015: 115). The four dimensions are:

1. *Europeanisation by vertical transnational connectivity:* The vertical dimension of transnationalisation means a Europeanisation of national
   public spheres through intensified 'communicative linkages between
   the national and the European level' (Koopmans/Erbe 2004: 101;
   Koopmans/Statham 2010a: 38). Transnationalisation takes place
   through a shared intensified 'monitoring of governance' (Wessler et
   al. 2008: 11) from Brussels. As political decision-making at the level of
   the EU gains in relevance in the various nation states, this results in
   intensified coverage and discussion about European politics across the
   nation states. This takes place in mass media coverage, for example,
   newspapers. But today there are other kinds of media – increasingly,
   online media and the various ways in which people are involved in
   online communication.
2. *Europeanisation by horizontal transnational connectivity:* Together with
   the vertical axis, horizontal transnationalisation means intensified 'communicative linkages between different member states'
   (Koopmans/Erbe 2004: 101; Koopmans/Statham 2010a: 38). Across
   the different national public spheres there is an increasing amount
   of mutual observation and mutual discursive exchange. In addition, we might also notice increasing references between different
   national actors (other members of the EU), resulting in intensified
   mutual recognition as part of the EU – the horizontal dimension of
   Europeanisation. Again, this is currently not just a matter of media
   coverage – it is also a matter of communicative connectivity of the
   internet, as, for example, in online forums.
3. *Europeanisation by transnationally converging discourse:* A third dimension of transnationalisation is 'discourse convergence' (Wessler et al.
   2008: 11, 15f.). This means that there is not only vertical and horizontal connectivity of the different national public spheres; in addition,
   we notice a certain rapprochement in the discourse that constitutes
   these public spheres. This happens, for example, through shared
   'frames' of media coverage (Kantner 2015: 97–105); 'not only [. . .]
   the same themes are discussed at the same time transnationally

but [. . .] the same frames of reference are available and in use in the various public spheres in Europe' (Risse 2010: 119; cf. also critical Downey/Koenig 2006). But it also occurs, for example, through converging forms of interaction, converging constructions of Europe in online forums, or even converging constructions of Europe, the EU and its legitimacy in everyday talk. Therefore, transnationally converging discourse implies that, hand-in-hand with increasing horizontal and vertical connections, the character of this discourse converges upon Europe and the EU.

4. *Europeanisation by transnational collective belonging:* A fourth dimension of transnationalisation is the expression of a sense of European collective belonging. In media coverage and online discourse, this means, for example, shared references to 'us as Europeans' or other expressions of a shared European identity. With regard to audiences and media users, this means that they understand themselves to be members of Europe, define the consequences of EU politics as meaningful for them, and through that become 'citizen audiences' (Lingenberg 2010b: 45). At its best, this results in what Thomas Risse calls the emerging 'European community of communication': 'when "foreigners" are no longer treated as such, but actively participate in debates about issues of common concern' (Risse 2010: 157).

Across these four dimensions, research demonstrates that there is a Europe-wide process of transnationalising public spheres, i.e. Europeanisation. This process has brought about a multilingual and transmedial European public sphere: a thickened space of political communication layered across other public spheres – national, regional, local or thematic – which is at the same time centred on European politics and European political decision-making. This is demonstrated by studies which can only be briefly reviewed. They cover such different areas as media coverage (for example Adam 2007; AIM 2006; Gripsrud 2007; Kantner 2015; Koopmans et al. 2010; Pfetsch/Heft 2015; Wessler et al. 2008), media events (for example Bolin 2006; Eder 2000; Hahn et al. 2008), citizens' communication through the digital platforms (for example Bennett et al. 2015; Rasmussen 2013; Trenz 2009; Wodak/Wright 2006), the manner in which journalists are involved in the transnationalisation of the public sphere (for example Heikkilä/Kunelius 2006; Offerhaus 2011; Raeymaeckers et al. 2007; Sarrica et al. 2010; Statham 2010a), as well as the related audiences (for example Lingenberg 2010b; Scharkow/Vogelgesang 2010).

In our own research, we call the resulting public sphere a 'multi-segmented European public sphere' (cf. Hepp et al. 2012). 'Multi-segmented' for the moment means that the transnationalisation of public spheres remains uneven across Europe. On the one hand, it remains nationally segmented, with remaining differences at the national level. On the other hand, it remains segmented across nation states – for instance, in relation to various forms of social inequality. This becomes evident, for example, in different types of media outlets ('tabloid' versus 'quality' media), where journalists address people as different kinds of 'imagined audiences' (Heikkilä/Kunelius 2006). These imagined audiences have no direct equivalent, but only an indirect relationship to the segmentation of real audiences, where, for example, education and age make a difference transnationally (cf. Herzog/Zingg 2007; Nielsen/Schrøder 2014; Paus-Hasebrink/Ortner 2010; Schrøder/Phillips 2007). At least in part, we face what Heinrich Best has called an 'elite-population gap' (Best 2011: 1008); in our case this is not related to the general formation of identities in Europe, like Best had in mind, but in relation to media appropriation. This is to some extent manifested in the different kinds of media outlets and forms of their appropriation (Corcoran/Fahy 2009; Risse 2010: 63–86).

Research such as this is of great importance since it has demonstrated two things: firstly, that a European public sphere emerges with the process of European integration; and secondly, there is something different about a European public sphere compared to national public spheres.

This said, most of the aforementioned research remained wedded to an understanding of the European public sphere as a space of functional legitimation of EU politics. We do not really have in mind here the discussion about legitimation that takes place in political science. This is often more concerned with questions of 'input and output legitimation' (Scharpf 1999). Input legitimation points to legitimation through the chains of (democratic) legitimacy; for example, by election or other forms of democratic representation (cf. Böckenförde 1991). Output legitimation refers to perception of the extent to which governance acts 'in the interest' of the governed people (Scharpf 2009). This is typically measured by people's attitudes towards a political entity and its government, such as, for example, the attitude to the nation state or to the EU and its government (Hix 2008; Thomassen 2007). In contrast to these kinds of legitimation analyses, media and communication research investigates the promotion of certain political institutions as legitimate within media discourse (Trenz/Eder 2004: 21).

One of the most sophisticated examples from the research noted above shows how this works. Paul Statham concludes the empirically rich study on which he collaborated, 'The Making of a European Public Sphere' (Koopmans/Statham 2010b), with a 'map of public sphere development'

(Statham 2010b: 278) that evaluates an emerging European public sphere against four possible types of Europeanised public politics and so reflects the political functionality of the European public sphere. Elaborating this map, Statham works with two analytic dimensions: first, the degree of 'public inclusiveness' in European decision-making and second, the degree of 'public visibility' of European decision-making. A matrix of four types of Europeanised public politics based on these two dimensions can be constructed. First, there is 'executive bargaining' with sparse media coverage and weak civil society access; second, 'corporatist interest group politics', with sparse media coverage but significant access for civil society. Third, 'elite-dominated public politics', with dense media coverage and weak civil society access; and fourth, 'inclusive public politics', with dense media coverage and strong civil society access.

This analytical distinction is helpful in a dual sense. On the one hand, it offers a reference point reflecting the historical development of EU politics and their relation to public communication. This began with 'executive bargaining' – for which a working European public sphere is of less relevance – and moved on to a kind of 'public politics', for which a European public sphere is a fundamental requirement. On the other hand, when contrasting weak and strong civil society access, this analytical distinction makes possible the analytical description of the current European public sphere: Is it rather a 'public sphere "lite"' (Statham 2010b: 283) of an elite-dominated European public politics? Or is it a well-developed European public sphere of 'inclusive public politics' (Statham 2010b: 278)? Recent research on the European public sphere identifies something in-between which, in the course of recent 'politicisation' (Risse 2015b: 3) through the euro crisis, has become more inclusive than it had been.

Analysis like this is of considerable importance, since it reminds us of the significance of the European public sphere to European politics and EU institutions. However, we wish to add to this approach a further perspective which limits the role of the European public sphere not just to its function for political institutions, but asks more broadly: *What role does the European public sphere have for the construction of a European society?*

This perspective helps us rethink questions of the European public sphere in a social theory framework. Georg Vobruba recently reminded us why it is worthwhile to investigate the process of European integration within a broad social approach. As he wrote, this process 'presents an excellent opportunity for analysing the social construction of a society under modern conditions' (Vobruba 2012: 264). Vobruba argues against putting forth a ready-made sociological idea of a European society, since this blocks an appropriate understanding of its emerging form in relation to the nation state. Rather, one should investigate the different definitions of (European) society in their relations to the various 'observer positions' of the actors involved (elites, politicians, citizens and so on) and their power positions. This makes it possible to investigate in a quite open manner the social construction of European society – without defining in advance its definitive character.

It is a help to transfer this idea to the question of the European public sphere. Here the task is to investigate its role for the construction of a (possible) European society. If we adopt a position of observing politicians, certainly one important question is how far a European public sphere functions to legitimise both their political action and EU institutions. However, this is only one such 'observer position' in the process of social construction. For other positions, different questions might be of greater importance – and we should not exclude them from the start by restricting our study to one functional perspective. Other such positions might be, for example, the observer position adopted by regional journalists who consider emerging European society with respect to possible support for regional problem-solving. Or it can be the observer position of citizens who themselves question what an appropriate idea of Europe and its institutions might look like.

Irene Neverla and Wiebke Schoon (2008: 20) argued that the challenge of theorising Europe is to understand it as a space which is 'mainly constructed communicatively', as we would say, through and within its public sphere. Public spheres – whether local, regional, national or issue-specific – are spaces of communicative construction in the true sense of the word. The reason for this is that they 'do not preexist outside communication, but are created precisely when people speak to one another, be it in the interpersonal setting or through media' (Risse 2010: 110).

A shift of focus to the role of the European public sphere for an emerging European society places us in the middle of a discussion about communicative constructivism. In essence, communicative constructivism is an approach that studies 'communicative action as the basic process in the social construction of reality' (Knoblauch 2013: 297). This should not be taken to mean that all social construction is communication. However, when 'joint meaning making' is under consideration, communication is involved. And since the general construction of society is based on the production of shared meaning, communicative construction is central to social construction.

Communicative constructivism explores these processes of communicative construction and thereby relates them closely to the media. The argument for this is that our present societies are marked by a high degree of mediatisation (Couldry/Hepp 2013; Hepp 2013; Hjarvard 2013; Krotz 2009; Lundby 2014). Technological communication media are constitutive for our societies in their present form, as also in relation to politics and political decision-making (Esser/Strömbäck 2014; Kepplinger 2002; Landerer 2013). We have therefore to investigate processes of communicative construction as *mediatised* processes – which requires consideration of the specificity of various media for each communication process. This is also the case for the European public sphere, if this is studied as a fundamental communicative space for the construction of a European society.

To understand this thickened communicative space adequately, we need to develop a deeper understanding of the main actors involved in its articulation: the journalists who are the professional producers of this communication, but also the people who have a connection to the European public sphere. With digital media especially, people also find their voice in the European public sphere and react as citizens in so doing.

In relation to the European public sphere, we understand journalists to be professionalised 'cultural intermediaries' (Bourdieu 2010: 360; Negus 2002). As such, they are not the 'leading forces in the field of public sphere nor representatives of "the ordinary people"', as Heikki Heikkilä and Risto Kunelius (2006: 67) put it. Rather, journalists are 'modern professionals, whose daily practices deploy, reproduce and recreate social imaginaries on the modern social order' (Heikkilä/Kunelius 2006: 67). This kind of professionalisation is a general feature of journalists, also for journalists who are involved in communication about Europe. This communication is not just reporting; it also involves commenting and other forms of contextualising and classifying politics. Therefore, journalists play an active role in the process of constructing Europe communicatively. This active character can reach the point where they have a certain 'advocacy role' (Statham 2007: 468) in promoting a European society. As Paul Statham remarks based on his own empirical research, 'even journalists on the tabloids and popular newspapers are mostly informative-educative about Europe, raising awareness for understandings within their own established editorial line, rather than being partisan ideologues over Europe' (Statham 2007: 473).

Discussion in media and communication research linked to the idea of a European public sphere has raised the question of the prospects of a 'European journalism'. Firstly, this kind of journalism was thought to be located in Brussels, where the European correspondents of the various national media outlets work (Offerhaus 2011). This has been described as a 'microcosm' and 'small world' (Baisnée 2002: 109) centred on the daily EU Commission Midday Briefing as 'the heart of the matter' (Baisnée 2006: 32). Here, a certain milieu for EU reporting developed, with fairly close links between the journalists and an increasing expertise in the journalists' roles and work practices (Offerhaus 2011: 278–282).

While the work of these correspondents is of great importance for the European public sphere and therefore for the communicative construction of Europe, European journalism cannot be generally equated with that. Stephan Russ-Mohl (2003: 206) reminds us that 'in the larger European countries, most journalists are "localists"', being orientated to their own language and the audience region of a given media outlet. Correspondingly, Paolo Mancini (2005) applies the concept of European journalism not to the Brussels correspondents, but to the (for him open question of a) shared history and tradition of journalist's working practices across the different (central) European nation states (cf. also Golding 2008; Örnebring 2009). Following this line of argument, Irene Neverla and Wiebke Schoon (2008: 19) define European journalism as 'a form and tradition of journalism which is rooted in European history and connected with the present European society in its specific formations in economics, law, culture and ideology'. As such it is related to a certain 'journalistic professionalism, recognisable by role models and ethnic codices as well as practices and routines of action' (2008: 19). In short, European journalism is the journalism of an emerging European society. As such, it is still in the process of becoming; we can find it in the shared European patterns of journalistic practices across the nation states, as well as in the 'small world' of Brussels.

The people form the second kind of actors we have to consider with reference to the European public sphere. We are here faced with a question comparable to the one in the case of journalists: Under what circumstance does the people become a relevant actor in relation to the communicative construction of Europe? Or put differently: When are the people not just *general* media users, but active participants in the *European* public sphere? Referring to her own audience research (Lingenberg 2010a), Swantje Lingenberg introduced the concept of the 'citizen audience' (2010b: 53). Referring back to Peter Dahlgren (2006), she made a distinction between 'media audiences' and 'citizen audiences'. While media audience more or less means the group of people who consume a certain kind of media (content), the idea of a citizen audience is more specific. It involves a media audience which feels affected by media coverage in some way, 'a feeling that can arise from the perception, interpretation and assessment of indirect consequences as well as from relating them to personal lifeworlds, ideas, experiences and beliefs' (Lingenberg 2010b: 54). This kind of involvement is crucial for entering into public discussion and thereby becoming engaged in public communication either as interested listener, viewer or reader, or as someone who himself or herself has spoken out. With regard to the European public sphere, involvement can be provoked by common problems, by the perceived impact of EU political decisions, as well as by the perceived interdependencies shared with other EU countries – or, for example, involvement with the euro crisis. As a consequence, our study is concerned with the 'European citizen audience as the audiences of a European society – and not with the various national audiences across the different European states.

However, we have to reconsider the meaning of audience in the light of the last wave of mediatisation – the wave in the development of digital media. With the emergence of internet-related media, mobile phones and other digital media devices, people can play a much more active role in public communication. It is argued they should therefore rather be understood as 'users', or even as 'produsers', instead of audiences (cf. Bruns 2008). As Elizabeth Bird puts it, convergent media 'have transformed the traditional "audience" experience, especially in the West, where even many people who are not really produsers are still taking advantage of multiple media platforms to extend their mediated practices' (Bird 2011: 510). With good reason, arguments like these emphasise the increasing complexity of a media environment which also offers new everyday possibilities of communicative practice, for example, in the so-called social web and through other kinds of digital platforms. However, we have to be careful not to overemphasise the possibilities of increased communicative participation (Nielsen/Schrøder 2014). They are far less widespread in everyday life than one might expect, and we need to develop a very detailed overview of how and when people participate through media (cf. Livingstone 2004, 2013). This said, public citizens' expressions of their own standpoints in relation to Europe and the EU lend insight into their everyday processes of communicative construction.

To properly understand this multiplicity, one should not consider European citizens as an audience for one kind of media, but as users of a variety of different kinds of media through which, in certain contexts and certain situations, they become part of the European public sphere. Therefore we need a three-level understanding of the European citizen audience: based first on their media appropriation; secondly, on their relation to the European public sphere; and thirdly, on their (possible) voice in it.

At the first level, it is not a single medium that matters for European citizens in relation to the European public sphere, but a variety of different media, a whole 'media repertoire' (Hasebrink/Domeyer 2012; Hasebrink/Popp 2006). Media repertoire as a concept involves all the media a person regularly uses. The conceptual basis of this understanding of media repertoire is threefold. First, it is a user-centred perspective, moving the variety of media appropriated by one person into focus. Second, it stresses the need to consider together the entirety of appropriated media by a person to avoid misinterpretations resulting from single media analysis. Third, the media repertoire approach is relational. That means it seeks interrelations of specific media and their content within a certain media repertoire. Having in mind that it is not only technically mediated communication but also direct communication that matters, we also might think about the communication repertoires of persons, including their individual media repertoire and the repertoires of different forms of direct communication. At the present stage of mediatisation, the communication repertoires through which citizens become part of the European public sphere are increasingly complex and manifold. It is cross-media communicative networking which is of importance here, since we live in times of 'polymedia' (Madianou/Miller 2012b: 169) and the 'media manifold' (Couldry 2012: 44).

This refers to the second level of understanding of the European citizen audience: the level of 'public connection'. Originally, Nick Couldry, Sonia Livingstone and Tim Markham (2007a, b) used this term to describe the access people enjoyed to (national) public matters. Public connection is an analytical concept to 'capture an orientation to *any* of those issues affecting how we live together that require a common solution' (Couldry et al. 2007b: 6, italics as in the original). In parallel to our argument, they emphasise that 'public' refers to more than social belonging and expressions of identity. It also implies being affected by problems that need collective action and require a common solution. As they put it: '"Public connection" is an orientation to a space where, in principle, problems about shared resources are or should be resolved, a space linked, at least indirectly, to some common frame of collective action about common resources' (Couldry et al. 2007a: 7). In this sense, a European public connection is a public connection being related to the European public sphere as a communicative space in which 'problems' that matter for European society are discussed. Today, people's public connection to this European public sphere is articulated not by one kind of media, but through the aforementioned complex communication repertoire, including a variety of media (cf. Schrøder 2011: 14–16; 2014: 6), and also through various forms of direct communication, as we will demonstrate for European public connection (cf. chapter 6).

On a third level, we have to take the voice of the citizens into account. Referring back to general discussion about media participation (Carpentier 2011; Livingstone 2013), here we do not use this term for any kind of media-related action, for example, on digital platforms. In a narrower sense, we reserve this term for active participation within the European public sphere through the use of one's own 'voice' (Couldry 2010; Flew 2009; Hirschman 1970). This is a kind of media practice that goes far beyond the practices of listening, watching, hearing or chatting – which are nevertheless fundamental for any European public connection. The possibilities for this kind of participation in the European public sphere have increased with the digitalisation and the emergence of various internet platforms (cf. Dahlgren 2013). For example, online forums offer citizens the chance of articulating their political opinions in public, of becoming engaged in a public discourse on European matters and problems. While the speaker role for citizens in these forums remains different to that of professional journalists – whose voice also has a different position online – they can nevertheless articulate their position as part of what we call the European public sphere. Changes such as these brought about a new level of complexity for voices in the European public sphere. We will come to this point later, when discussing the euro crisis as a possible tipping point in the process of the communicative construction of Europe.

In this perspective the European public sphere is a thickened space in which Europe as society and the EU as its political institutionalisation are constructed communicatively. It is the space where different actors articulate their (conflicting) understandings, where they argue for certain positions, where they mock others, where they communicatively gather and socially act in various other different ways. The emerging European public sphere – this space of transnational political communication – is where we communicatively construct Europe.

2.2   Cultures of political discourse: explaining the multi-segmented European public sphere

Understanding public spheres as spaces of communicative construction does not mean theorising them as situative or volatile media phenomena. As Bernhard Peters put it: 'public spheres have a social and cultural foundation that extends well beyond the framework of media markets and media organisations' (Peters 2008: 246). We understand 'cultures of political discourse' as this foundation. They are the *Unterbau* – as Bernhard Peters originally called this – of public spheres, and give them a certain stability and sustainability. This sustainability, based on cultures of political discourse, helps to explain the multi-segmentation of the European public sphere; a 'national segmentation' in relation to nation states and a 'stratified segmentation' in relation to social inequalities across Europe. But it also offers the chance of discussing whether it might be possible that a European culture of political discourse as a potential foundation for a European public sphere could emerge.

Our concept of cultures of political discourse aims to integrate the approaches of political culture, international and transnational media and communication research (cf. Hepp/Wessler 2009). Present approaches do not in themselves seem to provide a satisfactory description of the foundation of (trans-)national public spheres. Although research on 'political culture' has demonstrated how differences in political systems can be explained culturally (Almond/Verba 1963; Pye 1968; Wilson 2000), it has yet not been sufficiently attentive to processes of media communication and the public sphere. The literature on international media and communication research has been subject to a significant cultural turn and is now developing an understanding of political communication culture and journalism culture (Hanitzsch et al. 2011; Mancini 2008; Pfetsch/Esser 2012; Weaver/Löffelholz 2008). However, it remains too heavily centred on the national institutional actors in politics and journalism. The field of transnational media and communication research has developed an elaborated transcultural approach that integrates the entire range of media cultures' communicative processes (Curran/Park 2000; Hepp/Couldry 2009; Kraidy 2005; Thussu 2009). However, it has remained relatively underdeveloped where issues of political communication are concerned. Integrating these three strands of research into a comprehensive approach thus seems a promising avenue of work.

How then can these strands help us define cultures of political discourse? First of all, cultures of political discourse are a specific kind of 'culture'. Situating ourselves particularly in the tradition of transcultural media research (Hepp 2015; Kraidy 2005), we understand cultures as specific thickenings of classificatory systems and discursive formations. Members of an identifiable group refer to them in their conflicting practices of communication to create meaning (Hall 1997). This said, culture is an everyday phenomenon – articulated in the everyday life of the people (Tomlinson 1999: 22–27). Cultures do not have to be territorially bound, as the cases of diaspora cultures or popular cultures demonstrate (Nederveen Pieterse 1995; Welsch 1999). However, 'territorialisation' – that is, constructing culture with reference to an imagined territory – has been fundamental for the articulation of national cultures (Anderson 1983). This is also the case for constructing European culture: understood as the thickening of culture within Europe and related by that to its imagined territory. The latter is not fixed, but shifts according to different understandings of what Europe is.

The proximity of this concept of culture to that of discourse is evident in the fact that discursive formations are understood to be a central aspect of culture. 'Discourse' itself has made great headway recently within the empirical social sciences. It is widespread in structuralism and post-structuralism, where under the influence of Michel Foucault (1970) discourse encompasses the totality of all practices that constitute knowledge and epistemological structures. It is well established in linguistic approaches, where discourse is understood to be a thematic connection that goes beyond individual texts, often being investigated in a critical manner (Fairclough 1995; Wodak/Meyer 2009). It is part of the conceptual inventory of a sociology of knowledge and of communicative constructivism (Keller 2012). And finally, normative understandings of discourse are also well established; for example, the normative concept within the work of Jürgen Habermas (1984) discussed above, which defines discourse as an organised discussion process of argumentative debate, that is, as deliberative practice (Wessler 2008).

Given our empirical interest in cultures of political discourse, we limit ourselves here to a non-normative concept of discourse. Discourse is for us a 'symbolic universe' (Keller 2012: 58) produced in communicative practice and itself producing a certain knowledge. This can be deliberative, as in accordance with a normative discourse theory of political communication, but it is not necessarily so. A specific discursive formation predefines (but not causes) what can usually be communicated in a specific cultural context – for example, what representations of politics are possible. It is obvious that discourses cannot be separated from issues of power. In any one culture, dominant discursive formations always refer to the prevailing fundamental patterns of political engagement and conflict.

Bringing both terms – culture and discourse – together and linking them to politics, a culture of political discourse for us is the culture of producing a certain kind of political discourse. We here employ a broad definition of the political, referring not only to institutional forms of politics (in government, parliament, political parties and so on), but also including what Ulrich Beck calls 'subpolitics' (Beck 1996: 94) – all forms of politics that are embedded in citizens' everyday practices beyond state institutions (cf. also Barry 2001: 7). Political in such a broad sense therefore also includes forms of (substantive) decision-making and the exertion of influence through everyday activity.

According to this definition, cultures of political discourse do not manifest themselves solely at the level of certain professional practices (for example journalism), as suggested by concepts of political communication culture and of journalism culture. As Paolo Mancini puts it, the latter have to be situated within a broader social context. Cultures of political discourse are 'part of the more general culture of the country [or Europe, the authors] and cannot be referred to and observed only in relation to the procedures of a specific field of social behaviour' (Mancini 2008: 159). This is exactly the move we want to make with our concept of political discourse culture. On the one hand it is a limiting concept, emphasising that we are only interested in that moment of culture that relates to political discourse. On the other hand, it is a contextualising concept emphasising that the culture of political discourse always has to be placed in a 'more general culture' – whatever this general culture might be.

To analyse cultures of political discourse we need to articulate two important points widely emphasised in cultural studies (cf. Du Gay et al. 1997; Johnson 1986). Firstly, cultures of political discourse are not harmonious phenomena. They are, as political cultures, marked by contradiction and conflict, also including struggle over their character. Secondly, they are multilevel phenomena that are not solely articulated at the level of production, as in the statements of politicians or the journalists reporting on them. Cultures of political discourse are also manifested at the levels of representation (political discourse in the media), appropriation (citizens making this discourse their own), various forms of identification (defining oneself as related to a certain public issue or part of a certain political unit) and their regulation (patterns of regulating this discourse). While it is practically impossible to investigate all these levels of political discourse culture as a whole, we need to keep in mind their comprehensive character.

For our analysis it is important that like thickening, the concept of political discourse culture is a relative one. We can empirically describe national cultures of political discourse. These are the typical patterns within certain national cultures. National discourse cultures seem quite stable, being related to long-standing national institutions and ways of political decision-making – together with media coverage of this, re-articulated in more or less stable everyday practices. However, there are cultures of political discourse that cut across these national cultures. At least two other kinds of cultures of political discourse are here of importance. First of all, there are cultures of political discourse characteristic for certain kinds of media outlets and their audiences across national cultures. Secondly, something like a European discourse culture seems to emerge: patterns of political discourse that are characteristic for Europe as a whole. If we want to understand the foundation of public spheres, we have to consider these overlapping cultures of political discourse. Consequently, we must avoid a purely 'binary comparative semantics' (Hepp 2015: 26), simply comparing one national cultures of political discourse with another national culture. Instead, we must move to a 'transcultural comparative semantics' (Hepp 2015: 27) comparing these various kinds of overlapping cultures of political discourse – in our case national and transnational cultures of political discourse.

If we make such a move, an investigation of overlapping cultures of political discourse helps to explain the multi-segmentation of the European public sphere: Each political discourse culture has a certain inertia, that is a tendency to remain. However, inertia is not an absence of change. According to Bruno Latour (2007: 35) no culture is socially inert as such. Patterns of culture are continuously re-articulated in everyday practices – and only in this ongoing process of re-articulation can they generate a tendency to remain. If we turn to ethnomethodology (Garfinkel 1967), we do not find a cultural explanation behind everyday practice – but within it. An understanding of inertia that is located in the habits of everyday practices offers us the chance to explain the multi-segmented character of the European public sphere.

First, we argue that *national cultures of political discourse* are the most stable ones. The nation state was the political unit within which modern democracy developed in Europe. This took place hand in hand with the emergence of 'produced media': first the mass media of the printed press (newspapers, books), later the broadcasting media (radio, television) and film (Thompson 1995: 44–80). The institutionalisation of modern states and of democracy took place in parallel with the emergence of national public spheres and cultures of political discourse in which the national became 'banal' (Billig 1995): the normal reference point for politics and political decision-making. For more than one century – from the second half of the nineteenth century to the second half of the twentieth century – the discussion of political problems and national decision-making became the norm within our cultures of political discourse, unproblematic and unquestioned. Continuously re-articulated as such, it seemed and still seems quasi-natural to us; not because the nation is part of human nature, but because of this long history of re-articulation (Heikkilä/Kunelius 2006: 69). As we will demonstrate in this book, this explains the residual stability of national segmentation in the European public sphere. The national has the 'trajectory of naturalness', a 'natural connection' (Heikkilä/Kunelius 2006: 77) continually re-articulated in the everyday practices of journalists and citizens in a transnational Europe.

Second, there are *stratification-related cultures of political discourse*. This is a very complex aspect of transnational cultures of political discourse and we must be careful to avoid simplification. There is a degree of social segmentation throughout Europe (Breen et al. 2010; Mau/Verwiebe 2010: 36–40). Published research on media and politics has long suggested that class differences are also related to political differences (cf. Parkin 1972). This was one reference point for the class-related distinction of different 'reading positions' in the encoding/decoding model introduced by Stuart Hall (1973). Apart from the idea that there were fixed ways of decoding that were more or less class-related – an approach that was soon abandoned (Brunsdon/Morley 1978; Morley 1992) – we want to broaden the argument, suggesting that something like stratification-related cultures of political discourse exist across Europe. As we have said, cultures of political discourse of this kind manifest themselves especially in relation to certain kinds of media outlets. These stratification-related differences have been dealt with in media and communication research using the dichotomy of 'quality press' and 'quality journalism' on the one hand, and 'tabloid press' and 'tabloid journalism' on the other. As historical studies indicate (Burke 1978; Williams 1978), there was a 'gradual separation of the upper and the lower classes in sixteenth- and seventeenth-century Europe, with popular culture becoming the domain of the latter group' (Dahlgren 1992: 5). As a consequence, tabloid journalism became part of a popular culture with 'clear working-class connotations' (Dahlgren 1992: 6) – in contrast to a more elite-oriented quality journalism. With the increasing individualisation of European societies (Beck 1987; Beck/Beck-Gernsheim 2001) these distinctions became less clear cut and popular culture a more general phenomenon (Storey 2003). However, distinctions like these are still present in journalistic practice when it comes to their 'professional imaginary' (Heikkilä/Kunelius 2006: 67). In this imaginary an 'educated audience calls for journalists as experts, and the uninterested for an educator' (Heikkilä/Kunelius 2006: 68). The increasing professionalisation of journalism does not only lead to a transnational 'professional culture' (Mancini 2008: 157), but also to transnational cultures of political discourse embodying a variety of journalistic practices, which represent a degree of stratified segmentation in European society (and societies). However, we should be cautious about relating tabloid journalism to the idea of a *separate* 'working class public sphere' (Negt/Kluge 1993) which could be positioned against a 'middle class public sphere' of quality journalism. In our empirical chapters, we will demonstrate that such a binary distinction is inadequate, because it oversimplifies. But throughout Europe, stratification-related cultures of political discourse have had a relatively long-lasting trajectory (Örnebring/Jönsson 2004). They help explain the transnational segmentation of the European public sphere: segmentation in relation to certain outlet types which relate to social inequality. This said, we need to bear in mind that, with real audiences, we encounter much more complex and contradictory transnational patterns, this complexity being rooted in the variety of media repertoires which offer different kinds of European public connection across the media. Bearing this complexity in mind, transnational segmentation remains important also at this point.

Third, a *European culture of political discourse* seems to be emerging – the political discourse culture of a European society that exists across all European states and characterises political communication as European. While the idea of Europe as a thickened communicative space is not absolutely new (cf. Kleinsteuber/Rossmann 1994), we are less used to thinking of Europe as a common political discourse culture. But this idea was already apparent when we discussed European journalism in the previous section. Considering the character of a 'European mode of journalism' (Mancini 2005: 77), Paolo Mancini mainly refers to European cultural patterns of political communication. In his view, the 'European model of journalism is much more partisan than the Anglo-American one' (Mancini 2005: 78). Because of the literary roots of European journalism it is 'very much oriented towards commentary and interpretation' (Mancini 2005: 83). In their comparative study of EU journalism, Heikki Heikkilä and Risto Kunelius (2006: 69) likewise suggest the existence of transnational cultural patterns, for example, the way in which European journalists construct Europe through a national lens. Irene Neverla and Wiebke Schoon (2008: 24, 28f.) also emphasise that emergent European journalism is marked by shared patterns and norms of communication. These kinds of studies are directed to what we want to call the European culture of political discourse. While this is only just emerging (or at least, becoming more embedded) and has a far shorter (or less dominant) history than national or stratification-related cultures of political discourse, we will find various manifestations of this kind of political discourse culture in our data. This emergent European culture of political discourse can be related to the increasing 'natural-ness' of the way in which journalists deal on a day-to-day basis with Europe and the EU, or the way in which citizens make use of online communication and everyday talk. We will argue in this book that a European culture of political discourse is emerging.

All three kinds of cultures of political discourse – national, stratifica-tory and European – matter in assessing the foundation of the European public sphere. Taken together, they enable an understanding and explanation of the multi-segmented character of the European public sphere. While economy might be a driving force in bridging national media systems and propelling them on to a converging commercial path (Chadwick 2013; Hallin/Mancini 2012), and while the process of European political integration might be a driving force for Europe-wide political communication (Eriksen/Fossum 2002; Koopmans/Statham 2010b), our analysis demonstrates the manifold character of the communicative construction of Europe.

2.3   The euro crisis: rethinking legitimation as communicative construction

'The crisis' is today central to any analysis of the multi-segmented European public sphere and its underlying cultures of political dis-course. Several European banking houses came under pressure follow-ing the bankruptcy of Lehmann Brothers in the USA, leading to a 'euro crisis' that resulted from the institutional deficiencies of the common European currency (cf. Preunkert/Vobruba 2011). However, beyond this particular case, crises are in general an important part of European inte-gration or the development of a European society. Paradoxically, some empirical studies confirm the idea that each European crisis leads to a higher level of European societalisation. The term 'societalisation' (*Vergesellschaftung*) refers back to the original writings of Max Weber (1972b [orig. 1921]: 21–23) and emphasises the *ongoing process* of constructing society, instead of understanding society as something 'just given' or 'being there' (cf. Walby 2007: 461f.). Making use of sociological studies, Martin Heidenreich transferred this idea of society to the field of economic and fiscal policy, arguing that from an institutional perspective we can understand the various crises in general and the euro crisis in particular 'as a chance for an incremental Europeanization' (Heidenreich 2014: 2): Again and again, the way 'out of the crisis' seem to have been deeper institutional societalisation. The same can be said when we not only focus on fiscal policy, but on communication and the public sphere. Each crisis tends to have resulted in an intensification of communication about Europe (Eder 2014; Triandafyllidou et al. 2009). The role this plays in the long-term process of communicatively constructing Europe is still an open question. As Mai'a K. Davis Cross and Ma Xinru put it: 'European actors seem to use crises as opportunities to further shape European order, enhance legitimacy, and increase integration, beyond what can be achieved incrementally' (Cross/Xinru 2013: 1). But is this always the case?

This question indicates the complexity of 'crisis' as a phenomenon in relation to the communicative construction of Europe. Whereas in everyday language crisis is framed as a 'critical point' or even 'catastrophe', from this analytical point of view it is a much more contradictory phenomenon. Building on the long-standing history of this term, Georg Vobruba (2014a: 185) noted that we should understand crisis as an 'open constellation'. Crisis then means a 'decision situation for institutions under pressure which is perceived as such by the involved actors' (Preunkert/Vobruba 2011: 2). Each crisis is 'socially open' (Vobruba 2014a: 185). Action in conditions of crisis cannot depend on established institutions; it requires an increased interpretation of the contexts and aims of action, and this opens up opportunities for actors. This is the reason why the outcome of any crisis is so difficult to predict and why each crisis is so ambiguous. This was always the case for previous European crises – and it has equally been the case for the euro crisis since 2008.

The openness of a social crisis is usually related to conflict; not only institutional conflict, but also conflict involving actors in and across institutions and their interpretation of the crisis. Each crisis is normally a conflict event. Conflicts, however, do not prevent societalisation. In his writings, Simmel (1950 [orig. 1908]) differentiates between two fundamental relationships in conflict: Being against one another and being for one another. Both can be contrasted with a third relationship, pure mutual indifference. His argument is that being against one another – i.e. conflict – is a more intense mode of societalisation than any mutual indifference. This is because participants in a conflict are in a defined antagonistic social relationship with each other, especially in situations of competition (cf. Fehmel 2014: 4; Vobruba 2014b: 25). Therefore conflict does not necessarily work against European societalisation; a conflict with a shared focus – provided, for example, by the European economy and currency – is a manifestation of European societalisation (cf. also Berkel 2006). We can also relate this general statement to conflictual communication in the European public sphere: Conflictual events like the euro crisis might be more important for the communicative construction of Europe than any consensual communication. As Thomas Risse puts it: 'the more contentious European policies and politics become and the more social mobilisation occurs on European issues, the more we actually observe the emergence of a European public sphere' (Risse 2010: 112). We would add to that, the more progressive are the processes of communicatively constructing Europe.

With this argument we come close to an approach of understanding the euro crisis as a 'mediatized conflict' (Cottle 2006). Media are here treated as integral to the articulation of conflict, having an 'active *performative* involvement and *constitutive* role within' it (Cottle 2006: 9). This applies to the euro crisis as a conflict event. As we will demonstrate, media are not simply the medium through which events are reported. By the intensive communication of a crisis and presenting certain images of the crisis, media have played an active role in the process of the communicative construction of the euro crisis and hence also in the communicative construction of Europe.

Klaus Eder has argued that the euro crisis is a kind of 'tipping point' (Eder 2014: 220) in the communicative construction of Europe, representing 'a "critical moment" in the evolution of a European society' (Eder 2014: 219), 'triggering people-making in Europe' (Eder 2014: 224). Using Albert Hirschman's (1970) terminology, it became more an event in which the people raised their 'voice' than an event which marks an 'exit' from a discourse about Europe, the EU and its futures (Eder 2014: 219ff.). Such a statement is based on an understanding of voice as 'any attempt at all to change, rather than to escape from, an objectionable state of affairs [. . .] through various types of actions and protests, including those that are meant to mobilize public opinion' (Hirschman 1970: 30).

This definition appears to correspond with our empirical research results, as well as with the research results of others: The euro crisis triggers a transnational and transcultural public discourse about Europe and its possible futures (Angouri/Wodak 2014; Breeze 2014; Joris et al. 2014), contrasting the possibilities of a more integrated or less integrated EU with varying models of the relationship of nation states to the EU. Within this discourse, various actors, including citizens, raise their voice and do not exit from this discourse. In a comparable line of argument, Thomas Risse (2015b) likewise indicates that the euro crisis stimulates intensified cross-border communication in Europe, as well as a politicisation of this discourse.

The euro crisis thus has *activating* consequences and not disabling consequences. In relation to the public sphere we take the term 'raising one's voice' quite literally, meaning participation in public discourse about Europe and the EU. This includes not only the voices of journalists and (political) elites within media coverage (cf. for example Möller 2013; Rafter 2014), but also normal citizens' voices on digital media platforms. At this point, digitalisation as the last wave of mediatisation is of relevance because it changed the prospects for user participation (Dahlgren 2013; Flew 2009: 987). Through digital media – especially platforms – citizens have new opportunities to become engaged in mediated discourse relating to Europe and the EU (cf. Baden/Springer 2014 and Georgakopoulou 2014, as well as our analysis in chapter 5). But voice is not just a matter of mediated public discourse on digital platforms and further media. As already argued in relation to the European citizen audience and also relating to what will be demonstrated empirically below, the euro crisis has also had an activating role in citizens' everyday encounters and discussions.

Klaus Eder framed this in a quite positive way when he concluded: 'the less voice, the lower the degree of loyalty' (Eder 2014: 227). As already indicated, we are more cautious about connections like these. In essence, we argue that loyalty implies legitimation. Someone is only loyal to a political entity and its government if the latter is in his or her view legitimate. But if legitimation is expressed by various forms of voice, it is not just a matter of agreement or disagreement. In addition, it is a question of the character of this legitimation. Which forms of legitimation are communicatively constructed by the people through their voice – through reciprocal media communication; for example, in online forums, but also through the direct communication in their daily encounters? And how does this relate to their European political connection? Questions like these offer the possibility of researching political legitimation in a more complex frame: Which forms of legitimation are communicatively constructed becomes an empirical question.

We want to substantiate this idea by reference to the classics of the social sciences. The types of authority outlined by Max Weber are far more sensitive to questions of social construction than first impressions might suggest. Fundamental for any 'legitimate domination' is something Weber calls 'belief in legitimacy' (Weber 1978 [orig. 1921]: 213). This is, more or less, the attribution of legitimacy by the dominated group. It is through these ideal types of belief in legitimacy that Weber differentiates his 'pure types of authority' (Weber 1978 [orig. 1921]: 215): The belief in the 'legality of enacted rules and the law' results in *legal authority*. The belief in the 'sanctity of immemorial traditions' results in *traditional authority*. The belief in the 'exceptional sanctity, heroism or exemplary character of an individual person' results in *charismatic authority*. While Weber's typology appears quite strict from today's point of view, his argument is remarkable for defining authority from the perspective of the legitimacy constructed by the governed groups of people.

The reflections by Peter L. Berger and Thomas Luckmann are also of interest here. For them, legitimation is an important process within the social construction of reality. It is a '"second order" objectivation of meaning', making existing institutions – first order objectivations themselves – 'objectively available and subjectively plausible' (Berger/Luckmann 1967: 92). This is the reason why a 'symbolic universe' is a manifestation of everyday discourse (cf. Keller 2012: 55). Legitimation in this sense is a complex process in which an institutional tradition is 'explained' and 'justified' (Berger/Luckmann 1967: 93). The highest level of this legitimation is that which occurs through what Berger and Luckmann call *symbolic universes*: 'bodies of theoretical tradition that integrate different provinces of meaning and encompass the institutional order in a symbolic totality' (Berger/Luckmann 1967: 95).

Today this understanding of symbolic universes seems too homogenising. Since legitimation is based on symbolic interaction – communication – it is a much more polysemic and open-ended process than Berger and Luckmann imply. In this sense, we are empirically confronted with *various* 'small symbolic universes', as in Benita Luckmann's 'small life-world' argument. Late-modern societies decompose into various 'sectors of everyday life', 'sub-universes of human existence' (Luckmann 1970: 580). Another problem in Berger and Luckmann is the idea that these (small) symbolic universes are 'second order' constructions, understanding this in a temporal sense. In late-modern societies, at least, their communicative construction takes place together with the 'first order' institutions: both are co-articulated.

However, Berger and Luckmann are right to emphasise that legitimation is in essence a communicative construction, a kind of narration which *explains* and *justifies* an institutional order – quite often in a
highly symbolic way. In media and communication research there is a
tendency to investigate this 'symbolic legitimation' at the level of discourse. François Foret, for example, analysed the 'symbolic legitimization of the European political order' through the changing meaning of
the 'European flag' (Foret 2009: 317). Or with reference to the present
euro crisis, Eero Vaara analysed the discursive legitimation of particular
political positions, understanding legitimation as the 'creation of a sense
of positive, beneficial, ethical, understandable, necessary or otherwise
acceptable action in a specific setting' (Vaara 2014: 503). However, with
Weber, as well as Berger and Luckmann, the analysis of legitimation as
an attribution on the part of the citizen is an important contribution to
our understanding.

These attributions are everyday communicative constructions of
legitimacy. They are citizens' attributions of legitimacy to a social entity
(in our case: Europe), its political institutional order (in our case: the EU)
and certain politics (in our case: EU politics and the politicians taking
action). Therefore, European constructions of legitimacy are a multilevel
phenomenon. They a) refer to certain everyday ideas of Europe which
are the foundation of these narrations of legitimation. On this foundation, they broach the issue of b) the EU as political institution. And
finally, they focus c) on EU politics and its politicians. It is an empirical
task to identify characteristic constructions of legitimacy across the various European countries using these three levels.

Our idea of communicative constructions of legitimacy is closely
linked to comparable work in political science. In a recent study,
Frank Nullmeier and his colleagues made an empirical evaluation of
legitimacy. Against normative theories of democratic legitimation and
empirical political attitude research, they argued (as we do here) that
legitimacy is a matter of attribution (Nullmeier et al. 2010: 31; cf. also
Barker 2001; Reus-Smit 2007). This attribution can be either a positive valuation, in which case it is legitimating. Or it can be a negative valuation, in which case it is delegitimating. The totality of these
valuations constitutes the overall legitimacy of a political institution.
Fundamental to this attribution of legitimacy is public discourse, which
is why Nullmeier et al. investigated the valuations of four different kinds
of political institutions in the press – the EU, besides others (Nullmeier
et al. 2010: 186–221).

The importance of this conception is its openness to various forms of
legitimation. The character of legitimation is not normatively predefined,

but open to empirical research. As a consequence, empirical investigation is able to describe different forms of 'precarious legitimation', that is legitimation in-between full democratic legitimation as anticipated by theories of democracy and the crisis of legitimation as a postulated characteristic of 'post democracy' (Colin 2004). Our move to communicative constructions of legitimacy is comparable to this undertaking, although more concerned with the detailed character of the communicative construction of legitimacy through the people as citizens.

This approach to communicative constructions of legitimacy – which is an additional level of analysis, especially when it comes to our audience studies – refers back to the question of legitimation that was a point of criticism at the beginning of this chapter. We hope that the underlying argument of this criticism is now more evident. Our point is not that questions of legitimation would not be important for an analysis of the European public sphere and its cultures of political discourse during the euro crisis. Rather, our argument is that we have to rethink legitimation in the frame of communicative constructivism. In this frame, legitimation is not just an 'outcome' of the 'functioning' of a European public sphere. Instead, progress in the communicative construction of legitimation is part of the process of communicatively constructing Europe. One moment of the communicative construction of Europe is the construction of its fundamental idea, institutions and politics as in themselves legitimate. Narrations of legitimation are then co-articulated with the further European society and its public sphere. The task of the subsequent chapters is to analyse this complex co-articulation.

3
Journalistic Practices: National and European Cultures of Political Discourse

As we have argued in the previous chapter, we consider the concept of cultures of political discourse helpful to understand the multi-segmentation of the European public sphere. By applying this concept to our analysis of the communicative construction of Europe and the emergence of a European public sphere, we assume that the multi-segmented European public sphere is shaped by different cultures of political discourse in Europe. Aiming at understanding the communicative construction of Europe within and across various European countries, our empirical analysis first of all focuses on journalistic production practices related to EU political issues. Our main argument is that journalists in their everyday work practice continuously re-articulate cultures of political discourse – national as well as transnational – so that differences between them become concrete in the ways journalists handle Europe and the EU.

Our qualitative newsroom research in the six EU countries under investigation highlights two contrary but intertwined phenomena. First, we notice a remarkable stability of national cultures of political discourse – national perspectives dominate the journalistic reporting of Europe. Second, journalistic practices differ transnationally across countries in relation to specific types of newspaper. In other words, in relation to different types of newspaper, journalists across countries address their audiences in specific ways. Here we see a link to what we called stratification-related cultures of political discourse in the previous chapter. With reference to this, the fundamental question we want to answer in this chapter is: How come, within the multi-segmentation of the European public sphere, national cultures of political discourse continue to exist, while at the same time new cultural forms of specific transnational political discourses emerge? Given this question, it becomes clear why we at first focus on journalists as part of the actor constellation of the European public sphere. Cultures of political discourse are re-articulated in an ongoing process through journalistic practices.

Our analysis in this chapter is based on 'ethnographic miniatures' of journalists' work practices and of newsrooms (cf. detailed information about the sample and the methodology the appendix, for a broader description of our analysis Lingenberg et al. 2010 and Hepp et al. 2012). Through interviews with journalists and foreign correspondents of quality, regional and tabloid papers, maps of their professional networks, as well as observations of on average three working days in two newsrooms per country, we investigated the practices of journalists who were responsible for the media coverage about Europe in the newspapers under investigation (cf. for an overview of our data Table 3.1). We conducted the newsroom research presented here in 2008, a point of time when the euro crisis had its first peak, but where the crisis did not dominate public discourse as a news topic as much as in the years following, when we also collected empirical data for audience research from online comment forums and for newspaper content analysis. This said, all of the following is based on an analysis of news production of EU-related content in journalistic practices. If statements about news content are made, these only represent journalists' perceptions of and reflections on it.

The following chapter is structured in two parts. First, we focus on the national segmentation of the European public sphere; that is, the re-articulation of national cultures of political discourse in journalists' practices in national newsrooms of quality, tabloid and regional papers in Austria (AT), Denmark (DK), France (F), Germany (GER), Poland (PL) and the United Kingdom (UK). More precisely, we analyse journalistic patterns of nationalisation – a set of practices that journalists in all the researched countries share and that we call 'doing nation'. While this doing nation as such is a European phenomenon, these practices differ from country to country, thereby pointing to different national cultures of political discourse. Second, we focus on the transnational segmentation of the European public sphere – a segmentation according to transnational types of newspaper characterised by specific ways of addressing audiences. This is the point where we see stratification-related cultures of political discourse at work. They do not point to the national, but to various moments of a European-wide social stratification which becomes manifest in journalists' images and their practices in addressing their audience. In all, we hope that this analysis offers a deep understanding of the 'foundation' (Peters 2008: 246) of the European public sphere in different kinds of cultures of political discourse.

Table 3.1 Newsrooms under investigation

Country	Newspapers	Interviews with journalists
Austria	*Die Presse* (quality paper)	– 5 editorial staff – 1 EU correspondent – 1 Germany correspondent – 1 Spain correspondent
	Der Standard (quality paper)	– 2 editorial staff – 1 France correspondent – 1 Germany correspondent – 1 UK correspondent
	Kleine Zeitung (regional paper)	– 3 editorial staff – 1 EU correspondent – 1 Italy correspondent
	Neue Kronenzeitung (tabloid paper)	– 2 editorial staff
Denmark	*Politiken* (quality paper)	– 4 editorial staff – 2 EU correspondents – 1 Czech Republic correspondent – 1 France correspondent – 1 Sweden correspondent
	Berlingske Tidende (quality paper)	– 2 editorial staff – 2 EU correspondents – 1 Germany correspondent – 1 Spain correspondent – 2 UK correspondents
	Jydske Vestkysten (regional paper)	– 4 editorial staff – 1 EU correspondent – 1 France correspondent – 1 UK correspondent
	Ekstra Bladed (tabloid paper)	– 10 editorial staff – 1 Germany correspondent
France	*Le Monde* (quality paper)	– 5 editorial staff – 2 EU correspondents – 1 Germany correspondent – 1 Italy correspondent – 1 Scandinavia correspondent – 1 UK correspondent
	Le Figaro (quality paper)	– 3 editorial staff – 2 EU correspondents – 1 Italy correspondent – 1 UK correspondent
	Ouest France (regional paper)	– 3 editorial staff – 3 EU correspondents
	Le Parisien (tabloid paper)	– 7 editorial staff – 1 EU correspondent – 1 Balkan states correspondent – 1 Germany correspondent

(*continued*)

Table 3.1   (continued)

Country	Newspapers	Interviews with journalists
Germany	Frankfurter Allgemeine Zeitung (FAZ) (quality paper)	– 6 editorial staff – 2 EU correspondents – 1 Czech Republic correspondent – 1 UK correspondent
	Süddeutsche Zeitung (SZ) (quality paper)	– 2 EU correspondents – 1 Czech Republic correspondent – 1 Italy correspondent – 1 Spain correspondent – 1 UK correspondent
	Westdeutsche Allgemeine Zeitung (WAZ) (regional paper)	– 2 editorial staff – 2 EU correspondents
	BILD (tabloid paper)	– 4 editorial staff
Poland	Gazeta Wyborcza (quality paper)	– 5 editorial staff – 1 EU correspondent – 1 Germany correspondent
	Rzeczpospolita (quality paper)	– 4 editorial staff – 1 EU correspondent – 1 Germany correspondent
	Dziennik Zachodni (regional paper)	– 5 editorial staff
	Fakt (tabloid paper)	– 7 editorial staff – 1 EU correspondent
United Kingdom	The Times (quality paper)	– 4 editorial staff – 1 Austria correspondent – 1 France correspondent – 1 Italy correspondent – 1 Spain correspondent
	Financial Times (quality paper)	– 6 editorial staff – 2 EU correspondents – 1 France correspondent – 1 Germany correspondent – 1 Poland correspondent
	Manchester Evening News (regional paper)	– due to legal constraints no interviews could be conducted
	Daily Express (tabloid paper)	– 3 editorial staff

Note: Newsroom observations were undertaken in the newsrooms of the underlined newspapers.

3.1   National cultures of political discourse: journalistic practices of nationalisation

In the following we focus on patterns of nationalisation. This is the main area of articulating national cultures of political discourse in journalistic practices, which also implies substantial national differences. Nationalisation as a set of journalistic practices describes the articulation of Europe-related news content in a way that a reader living in a given country will be able to relate to his own national experiences. Nationalisation thus refers to journalists' practices of embedding foreign issues in the context of one's own nation and thereby the ongoing re-articulation of its discourse culture.

The dominance of this pattern is also proved in research, which investigated nationalisation as an important journalistic production practice (cf. Deuze 2002; Hahn et al. 2006, 2008; Heikkilä/Kunelius 2006; Riegert 1998). Ulf Hannerz (2004), for example, examined how foreign correspondents living in different cities of the world stay connected with their countries of origin and their national readership. If we follow his line of argument, the maintenance of a link to the relevant (national) political discourse culture is of importance. Purposeful mobility strengthens that: Hannerz's research demonstrates that staff correspondents working in the political and economic power centres of the world only stay there for a couple of years and then move to other places, to prevent their view of the host country becoming routine and stale and thus staying connected with their national readership (Hannerz 2004: 84ff.). In the case of the journalists investigated by us, this link is made for the editorial staff by them living in their home countries.

Moments of nationalisation are of importance in Angela Dreßler's (2008) study as well. Her research involved an ethnography of 25 staff correspondents and freelancers working for different, primarily German, broadcasters and newspapers. She showed that the journalists' ideas of national readers' expectations form the fundamental horizon of the journalists' daily work. The practices of US correspondents are less oriented towards US public opinion than towards German opinion (Dreßler 2008: 164). Dreßler accordingly traces the emergence of a 'transatlantic sphere' of journalistic coverage. Hence we also find in transatlantic work practice an ongoing re-articulation of the national.

More specific in relation to our own study is research on EU correspondents in Brussels within the Adequate Information Management in Europe (AIM) project. This project ran from 2004 to 2007 (AIM Research Consortium 2007). Altogether, its results show that there are tendencies towards a homogenous professionalisation of correspondents' practices, something which is substantiated by further research (see also Baisnée 2002; Gleissner/De Vreese 2005; Offerhaus 2011). Basically, journalistic practices are marked by an explicit 'national demarcation', as Oliver Hahn, Roland Schröder and Stefan Dietrich (2008: 8) called it. According to these authors, national demarcations are divergent forces within the process of the emergence of a European journalistic culture (Hahn et al. 2008: 8). Against the background of our own research, the AIM-findings are indication for the fact that even for EU correspondents whose primary reference point is the EU, the re-articulation of national forms of work practice is important. Stephan Russ-Mohl (2003: 206) also supports this argument. He states that most journalists orient their work to national audiences. Regarding the concept of a 'European journalism', Paolo Mancini (2005) as well as Irene Neverla and Wiebke Schoon (2008) argue that this need not be related to Brussels correspondents' work, but rather to a shared history and tradition of journalistic professional practices in a European society (see also Örnebring 2009, 2011; Raeymaeckers et al. 2007).

Another research project dealing with the 'making' (Statham 2010a: 125) of European news coverage through journalistic practices is the Europub project. This research project carried out 110 interviews with chief editors, EU correspondents and journalists working on topics related to agriculture and immigration in France, Germany, Italy, the Netherlands, Spain, Switzerland and the United Kingdom. One of the project's main results is that the journalists perceived Europe as a difficult topic for reporting, since they had to frame it within established news values and norms – that is, values and norms that were mostly national (Statham 2010a: 132, 149). These findings indicate that journalists usually refer to the national as 'the established'.

If we try to locate a common thread in the aforementioned research, then it is in the demonstration that nationalisation in general and the nationalisation of Europe in particular are fundamental to journalists' working practices. Whilst this was investigated elsewhere, we regard three hitherto unexplored points in our investigation to be highly important.

First, our idea is not to research newsrooms as nationally separate work environments, but to look for national commonalities found across newsrooms in one country. Without understanding the national as something homogeneous, we aim at reconstructing national specificities. Therefore, we pay particular attention to the journalists working in newsrooms in their home countries, because they are the ones who eventually edit the foreign correspondents' articles for the printed newspaper. Nevertheless, we also interviewed selected foreign correspondents as well as the Brussels correspondents of these newspapers, so that we might integrate their perspective into our analysis (cf. for this Table 3.1 above). Second, in so doing our research aims to answer the question: How does doing nation become manifest in the journalists' everyday practices and how do journalists reflect this expression of national cultures of cultures of political discourse? Third, we do not consider national cultures of political discourse as something static. Rather, we consider them as elements of a work in progress which is at least partly related to change. An important aspect of this change is the Europeanisation of national cultures of political discourse. Hence we are confronted with a process in which Europe is seeping into the journalists' doing nation – that is: Europe is being routinised (*veralltäglicht* in the Weberian sense of the word) in the journalists' everyday practices. Citing Saskia Sassen (2008), we are confronted with the 'paradox of the national': Here, the national is not only globalised, but also Europeanised in the journalistic production of public discourses.

We can attach such moments of doing nation to typical journalists' practices and the orientations of practice across all our researched countries. These practices of nationalisation are the 'national embedding' and 'transnational contextualisation of the national'. While these are the two dominant practices of nationalisation, further journalists' practices have to be considered in a more general orientation of nationalisation, related to a hierarchisation of the national, a routinisation of the transnational and specific horizons of information seeking. As we will demonstrate, we are confronted here with an interplay of national and international references which in total support nationalisation. Analysing this substantiates the doing nation of the journalists, in which the national cultures of political discourse of Austria, Denmark, France, Germany, Poland and the United Kingdom become manifest.

National embedding

The journalistic practice of 'national embedding' relates Europe and the world back to national contexts, pointing out the relevance and consequence of foreign events to one's own nation. Hence, journalists locate foreign news in national contexts by linking them to national political, social or economic events and developments, as well as to experiences and problems with which the readers feel familiar in their given national contexts and everyday lives. In the process of news production, comprising news selection and news editing, journalists embed the EU and the world into the context of their own nation. National embedding does not, however, simply mean reference to one's own nation in a specific article. Rather, national embedding points to the reconstruction of the journalists' perspective onto the national as part of their daily work. Crucial is the fact that the practice of national embedding is a matter of everyday journalistic practice.

Analytically, we distinguish between *implicit* and *explicit* national embedding. In the case of implicit national embedding, journalists perceive the national relevance of the news issue to be given, so that the national relevance simply needs to be linked to in the work practice. In contrast, explicit national embedding is marked by the fact that the national relevance of an issue is not obvious from the journalists' perspective. The national relevance therefore needs to be communicatively constructed in a much more explicit way by the journalists, so that explicit national embedding requires a higher level of creativity in the journalists' work. Often, the perceptibility of obvious or given references to the own nation constitutes a criterion of selection. In this sense, the journalists speak about the 'Austria-reference' (EU editor, *Die Presse*, AT), about a topic that is 'directly related to the people's lives' (foreign news editor, *Dziennik Zachodni*, PL) or about an event that is 'for comprehensible reasons' relevant for an 'ordinary German citizen' (political editor, *BILD*, GER). Explicit embedding, by contrast, is often communicatively constructed by contextualising the news issue in national history. For instance, a Polish foreign news editor said that he introduced the German chancellor-candidate Frank-Walter Steinmeier in autumn 2008 as 'pro-Russian' due to his close connection to the German ex-chancellor Gerhard Schröder, who is well known in Poland for his friendship with Vladimir Putin. In so doing, the journalist constructed a link to historical associations with Polish sufferings following the German-Russian Alliance in World War II and accordingly presumed that this would 'attract interest among Polish readers' (foreign news editor, Dziennik Zachodni, PL). With regard to differences between the practices of journalists in the national newsrooms and correspondents working in Brussels, our analysis revealed certain conflicts. According to the news editors interviewed at home, the Brussels correspondents often tend to neglect the construction of national references when reporting about the EU. An economic editor of the German FAZ, for example, states that there is sometimes a gap, inasmuch as the 'Brussels correspondents are very appreciative of the EU, whereas we at home are far away and not very sympathetic to EU issues' (economic editor, FAZ, GER).

In all, our analyses show that implicit and explicit national embedding play a crucial role in journalists' re-articulation of their respective national cultures of political discourse. National embedding can thus be regarded as the self-evident foundation of journalists' working practice. Considerably stronger is the practice of national embedding in the EU reporting in Denmark and Poland. In these countries, the national embedding is foregrounded so much that Europe as the original cause for reporting almost disappears. Thus, while the practice of embedding EU and foreign news into the national context forms a constitutive part of journalists' work in all countries, we observe differences in *how* the national embedding is realised. Especially with regard to implicit embedding, there are national differences to be found.

Concretely, we find that the journalistic re-articulation of foreign events is related to the specific national space of identity, collective experience and history. This points to characteristically national accesses to the EU and to the neighbouring European countries in each country, through which a nationally historicising political discourse is constructed. In Poland, for example, reporting about European issues is often linked to communism and National Socialism and thereby to the Polish problematic of exiles and compensation. Using the example of Belarus, one of the interviewed Polish journalists states that 'issues related to Belarus [. . .] are interesting for Polish people, because there is a historical connection: Parts of Belarus once belonged to Poland' (foreign news editor, *Gazeta Wyborcza*, PL). In France, news reports about Africa are often linked to the French colonial era. Here, the interviewed journalists emphasise the fact that reports about North Africa are an important matter for France and French readers, because Africa is 'a region of full development and full transformation' (editor in chief, *Le Monde*, F) that has to be covered. Another characteristic of French journalists' national embedding are comparative references to neighbouring EU countries. For example, French journalists often compare political events or decisions in other EU countries with the French situation, or discuss current problems in France in the framework of political decisions taken in other countries. As the editor in chief of the newspaper *Le Parisien* states, these serve 'as foreign examples that can serve as thought-provoking impulses for French people' (editor in chief, *Le Parisien*, F). As in France, journalists' practices in Austria are characterised by historical references. Austrian journalists tend to construct historical links, especially when reporting on Eastern European countries with which Austria shares a common history. Accordingly, one of the Austrian interviewees states that locating a staff correspondent in Zagreb is regarded as 'a tradition, because the Eastern European region is of high importance for us' (political editor, *Kleine Zeitung*, AT). In British political discourse culture, the construction of humorous-satiric references as well as a more distant attitude towards the EU plays a crucial role. More precisely, British journalists tend to regard neighbouring European countries as a source of absurd and humorous stories that refer to the British national identity and a distanced attitude to the EU. In Germany, journalists tend to construct strong links to the politics of the day. The interviewed German journalists state that historical national contextualisation is not very often applied – unless a reference to World War II or National Socialism is on the table.

As our findings demonstrate, doing nation forms a fundamental part of journalistic practices in all researched countries. However, the understanding and thereby construction of the own nation differs from country to country – and so does the specific construction of explicit and implicit links to the own nation in journalists' reporting about the EU and Europe.

Transnational contextualisation

'Transnational contextualisation' is the inverse practice of national embedding. Hence, transnational contextualisation signifies the journalistic practice of using 'the transnational' (including Europe and the world) as a context of the nation, accentuating the importance of national events for the transnational context. Here we employ a very broad definition of the transnational: We understand transnationalisation as the 'extension of social spaces, which are constituted by dense interactions, beyond national borders without necessarily being global in scope' (Zürn 2000: 197). Additionally, we consider the nation as a persisting reference in the process of transnationalisation and define the journalistic practice of transnational contextualisation as follows: All journalistic references to political spaces beyond the own nation form the basic element of transnational contextualisation, with Europe as the central example of our analysis. As a journalistic practice, transnational contextualisation aims at reporting national events and developments against a transnational background, thereby locating the national in transnational contexts and making the national easier to understand. In contrast to the journalistic practice of national embedding, transnational contextualisation is about reporting the national in a (geographically) wider political space (for example the EU or NATO).

By 'context of the transnational' we do not only refer to the EU and EU member states, but also to other countries and regions of the world. Nevertheless, we always reflect on the relation of these other countries or regions to Europe. By Europe, we mean both the EU and EU countries – allowing for journalists' everyday talk and practices. The journalists locate themselves, their practices, and national events and developments in a broader social space. Thus, the question underlying their work practices is: How do we, as a nation, locate ourselves in the transnational?

In our analysis we find, once again, two basic forms of transnational contextualisation: applying *implicit* or *explicit* references. More precisely, national events can be contextualised explicitly in a transnational context, for example, by stressing the national contribution to certain transnational political developments. Alternatively, transnational developments can be reported either with or without implicit links to the own nation, so that the national relevance manifests itself only in the fact that the transnational is reported in a national political discourse. Both explicit and implicit transnational contextualisation point to the practice of locating the national in the transnational and thereby to the practice of communicatively constructing transnational spaces. However, the national remains the central point of reference, so that transnational contextualisation must be regarded as a journalistic practice of doing nation.

The case of Denmark shows that the construction of references to the transnational does not necessarily correspond to a transnational orientation or openness. Danish journalists tend to detach their own country from the transnational context. By constructing transnational news without referring to the own nation, they do not include Denmark as a natural part of the transnational. Furthermore, Danish journalists report political problems to the disadvantage of the EU by taking up a distanced position. Danish journalists do indeed report about the transnational, considering it to be something towards which they have to adopt a position, but with which they do not necessarily have to identify. The UN climate conference in 2009 is an example for this: In Danish reporting on the conference, Denmark was considered to be rather in the background as an actor and participant. In Austria and Germany, by contrast, transnational contextualisation is realised in a completely different way: The interviewed journalists consider themselves to be analysts of transnational developments, being privileged to observe and interpret them. An Austrian journalist calls the inner- and outer-European space the horizon for 'issues that are always attractive' (EU editor, *Die Presse*, AT). Similarly, a journalist working for the German *FAZ* states that especially with regard to 'developments in Europe and in the world' (foreign news editor, *FAZ*, GER) he would expect his readers to be interested in such issues. Austrian and German journalists seem to perceive their own nations as already being a self-evident part of transnational contexts, so that they do not have to emphasise the own nation's contribution. Finally, British journalists show a willingness to treat the transnational extensively, but as a separate phenomenon. A journalist working for the British *Times*, for example, states that having international news as a quality feature of the newspapers makes readers feel part of a transnational community.

Denmark, France and Poland are the countries in which transnational contextualisation is primarily realised in a direct form, so that national events and developments are explicitly located in the transnational context. Nevertheless, the communicative construction of transnational links is realised differently in each country. Whereas French journalists aim at portraying the own nation as part of an international or European political order, Polish journalists tend to emphasise the specific role and impetus of Poland. For example, a Polish journalist states that 'Poland's fate depends on who governs in Washington' (EU editor, *Gazeta Wyborcza*, PL). In Denmark, by contrast, journalists tend to report about transnational (and European) developments without referring to the own nation, emphasising a somewhat distanced position.

In all, we conclude that – no matter if the links are explicit or implicit – journalists perceive the transnational as a natural reference point for the own nation. By their way of reporting the transnational, however, they continuously re-construct the national, so that the journalistic practice of transnational contextualisation must be regarded as an important part of doing nation as well.

Hierarchisation

The journalistic 'hierarchisation' of work practices shows that more importance is placed on the own nation than on Europe and the world. Hierarchisation points to the relevance journalists attribute to national and foreign news within their everyday routines. Hierarchisation does not only manifest itself in the journalists' individual perspectives, but also in the daily work of the newsroom as a whole, what we could call the newspaper's tendency. The hierarchisation of national, European and other foreign news in journalistic practice does not address quantitative relations, the amount of relevant articles in relation to each other. Rather, our analysis aims at reconstructing the importance journalists attribute to the relation of national, European and other foreign news in their daily practices. Within these daily practices journalists continuously have to make decisions about which news they rank higher. Therefore, overall it represents a certain orientation of the journalists' practices.

Not surprisingly, our analysis indicates that throughout the whole sample, journalists tend to consider national issues as being more important than news from abroad. In corresponding news about the own nation against Europe and the world, journalists first select news that include a strong reference to the own nation, so that we observe a clear national prioritisation. Nevertheless, the intensity of national hierarchisation and the order of second priorities (Europe or the world) varies. Against this background, the national prioritisation is another moment of journalistic doing nation: Topics with a clear national reference are considered more important. In other words, the construction of a national political discourse has a higher 'cultural significance' (*Kulturbedeutung*, Weber 1949) than the construction of other political discourses. Exceptions, like pointing to a balanced hierarchisation of national and international news, are certain newspapers in Austria (*Die Presse, Der Standard*) and Germany (*FAZ*).

The order of secondary priorities following the national prioritisation in the journalistic practices is relevant to our research question.

Here we find significant differences in whether Europe or other regions of the world are considered secondary priorities. Nevertheless, European issues are considered more important than other foreign issues in most of the newsrooms studied. This is especially true for Germany, France and Austria. Striking is the fact that in Austria and Germany, the hierarchisation of journalistic practices is quite moderate – journalists consider foreign news to be nearly as important as national news. Moreover, Austrian and German journalists tend to prioritise Europe over the world on the grounds that news from Brussels is not really 'foreign politics [. . .] but the extension of national politics' (editor in chief, *Kleine Zeitung*, AT). In Denmark and Poland, by contrast, journalists' practices are characterised by an intense national hierarchisation. Furthermore, European news is ranked lower than other foreign news – especially news from the USA and Russia: 'The more international news, the less EU news – with regard to the last six years' (editor in chief, *Ekstra Bladed*, DK). In Great Britain, like in Denmark, news from the USA is consistently ranked higher than news from Europe.

Our distinction of a hierarchisation manifesting itself in the journalists' everyday practices on the one hand and a hierarchisation manifesting itself in the newsroom's organisational work flows on the other, is helpful in revealing national differences: whether a national culture of political discourse is characterised by tendencies of nationalisation or by tendencies of transnationalisation. In some countries (Austria, Denmark and the United Kingdom) we observe a clear coincidence, so that journalists do not regard their individual prioritisation of European and other foreign news as being in conflict with newsroom tendencies. Here, a high degree of stability in hierarchisation exists. Whereas in Denmark and Great Britain a stable hierarchisation is manifested by the consistent orientation towards an intense national prioritisation, we observe a rather moderate orientation of national prioritisation in Austria. Austrian journalists tend to rank national news as high as international news, so that we detect a tendency of transnationalisation. A greater degree of conflict persists in those countries in which the journalists' individual and the newsroom's organisational prioritisations diverge, so that there is a low degree of stability in hierarchisation. Crucial, however, is the direction in which inconsistencies between journalists and newsrooms point. In France, for example, we find intense national prioritisation on the level of individual journalists that often contrasts with the organisational level of the newsroom. As a consequence, the practice of reporting on national and international news can, in the end, be quite balanced. We find similar mechanisms in Poland. Here, journalists tend to prioritise the own nation intensely, but cannot always realise this prioritisation in their daily work practices in the newsroom. Even more than in France, journalists in Germany tend to rank international news equally with national news. With regard to Europe, however, the German journalists interviewed perceive a discrepancy in the political relevance of the EU and actual reporting about the EU in their newspapers, regarding the latter as not being sufficiently intense.

Routinisation of the transnational

'Routinisation' (*Veralltäglichung*) of the transnational as part of journalistic practices points, in the Weberian (1972a) sense, to the integration of Europe and 'the world' into everyday journalistic routines, resulting in a permeation of EU-related content that is no longer categorised as either foreign, economic or national news. In other words, Europe becomes an unproblematic part of journalists' daily practices, implying that European issues are treated by journalists across an increasing proportion of a newspaper's coverage. Together with Alfred Schütz and Thomas Luckmann (1973: 21), we assume that the everyday is the unquestioned sphere of the social world, so that routinisation does not only imply the loss of the *particular*, but also the loss of the *problematic*. In our field of research, we are confronted with a paradoxical moment of nationalisation. On the one hand, routinisation of the transnational means that Europe – the EU and the European countries – is imbued into journalistic routines, even routines not obviously referring to Europe, such as producing articles on health issues, reporting about local cultural events and so on. On the other hand, we are confronted with an ongoing journalistic practice of nationalisation, since Europe no longer involves an intrinsic value, but is a (natural) part of reporting about national or regional events and developments.

Hence by routinisation of the transnational we do not mean a quantitative rise in the importance of Europe in journalistic news reporting. Rather, we highlight a qualitative process in which Europe becomes a natural part of practices, as well as of the overall coverage of the newspaper. The orientations of journalists' practices change and Europe increasingly seeps into journalists' everyday horizons of meaning, resulting in a dispersal of references to Europe across the entire newspaper. This leads, in the long run, to a change in national cultures of political discourse, either pointing to a stronger transnational orientation and openness towards Europe or to a more intense shaping of the own national profile.

In our newsroom studies we find that routinisation of the transnational mainly occurs with regard to European, and not other foreign issues. For example, the editor in chief of the French *Le Monde* states that European issues have become a 'natural part' of his daily routines, so much so that he does not even think about it anymore: 'Every day we talk about Europe. [. . .] It's part of an actuality of proximity' (editor in chief, *Le Monde*, F). Across all researched countries, we are confronted with differences regarding the stage that routinisation of the transnational has reached. In detail, we find national differences in the intensity with which European issues are treated in different areas of a newspaper. In Austria, Germany and France the routinisation of the transnational – especially the routinisation of European issues – is quite advanced in journalists' practices. The EU and European countries have become a natural and unproblematic part of journalists' everyday practices. Furthermore, a growing diffusion of references to Europe across newspapers persists in these countries. For example, an Austrian interviewee states: 'The question is whether to publish a European topic in the economic or the EU section, but not whether to publish it at all' (editor in chief, *Die Presse*, AT). Journalists' practices in Great Britain are a special case. There is almost no routinisation of the transnational to be found, as British journalists do not regard Europe as a self-evident part of their daily routines. Europe remains a deviant phenomenon, and British journalists tend to refer to neighbouring European countries only to use them as a source for more or less cynical-humorous news stories. The findings for the Danish and the Polish cultures of political discourse are different again. Here, the routinisation of the transnational is only partly present. In Poland, we observe a slight routinisation of the transnational for European issues. Nevertheless, Europe cannot yet be regarded as being a self-evidently part of everyday journalistic practices. In Denmark, journalists ascribe an increasing importance to Europe in their practices, but at the same time they do not consider Europe to be unproblematic or completely integrated into their routines. Accordingly, reporting on Europe is treated as a duty: 'We report many EU issues only because we have to – as a quality paper' (GB correspondent, *Berlingske Tidende*, DK). Furthermore, Danish journalists consider boundaries between different areas of a newspaper to be firmly fixed, so that Europe is primarily treated as foreign news and only very rarely is dealt with by the economic or cultural pages.

Horizons of information seeking

Doing nation also involves the scope of information seeking. Among the journalists studied by us, there is a continuous review of other (national and foreign) media for background information or seeking material for specific articles – something that we have encountered in other research contexts (Reinemann 2003). Relevant to our own research framework is the fact that all journalists base their active search for information on a specific perspective, as well as on personal research networks. Both perspective and personal networks can be nationally or transnationally oriented.

By perspective, we understand the overall orientation of journalists when seeking information in other media. The question guiding our analysis is: Are these perspectives oriented towards the world, towards Europe or mainly towards the national?

Comparison of the respective countries shows that national cultures of political discourse are characterised by different focal points for journalists' information seeking practices. Whereas Danish journalists tend to focus on the USA, UK and the EU, Polish journalists focus on the USA, Russia and the former Soviet countries. In all, journalists' perspectives become manifest in three different practices: reading, observing and researching. The practice of reading points to the journalists' daily routine of intensively reading certain newspapers as parts of their 'communication repertoires' (Hasebrink/Domeyer 2012). The practice of observing, by contrast, points to a rather superficial media screening, aiming to stay up to date with the latest news within a broader information horizon. This practice employs a considerably broader media spectrum than the practice of reading. The practice of researching points to systematic information seeking and reading for a particular article on which the journalist is currently working.

At first sight it seems to be self-evident that journalists working for international newspaper sections permanently have an eye on international media coverage. Indeed, our data shows that they are very well-informed about political events and developments outside their nations. On closer inspection, however, we find that journalists in their home countries, as well as foreign or Brussels correspondents, primarily focus on national media content for information. This is especially true for the practice of reading; it is only rarely that international newspapers are read intensively. This national focus also applies to the practice of researching. It is only with the practice of observing that we get a different picture. Most of the interviewed journalists move in a somewhat transnational space, observing the international media landscape (cf. Sarrica et al. 2010: 417 for the relevance of the internet in this context). It is the actual space of observation that constitutes the key difference between the national cultures of political discourse studied here.

Altogether, we find a clear pattern characterising journalists' perspectives across all countries. Whereas the practices of reading and researching are strongly focused on national media, almost all journalists claim that they constantly observe the European (and US) media landscape.

The rather superficial practice of observing media coverage via the internet and subscribed newspapers primarily serves as a source of inspiration for the issues treated in their own work, but also as an information source for trends in European political discourse. Since the journalistic practices of reading and researching mainly refer to national media, a doing nation can also be identified in journalists' perspectives. Some of the journalists interviewed emphasise that they are not only interested in pure information about certain events and developments, but also in the *way* the information is presented – and thereby located – in the national culture of political discourse. This is not only true for cultures of political discourse that we have classified as being somewhat nationally centred, like that of Denmark or Great Britain. In countries where journalists' practices are more transnational, as in Germany and Austria, a pivotal role is played by the reconciliation of patterns of argument context in European and foreign news coverage. Where journalists' information repertoires include foreign media, these are mostly media from the same language area. For example, Austrian journalists tend to read German media and British journalists tend to read US media.

If we shift our analysis to the research networks of journalists, the sources that journalists regularly contact in order to receive work-related information are of importance. To maintain these contacts, journalists continuously engage in social networking – beyond their specific investigatory activities. In this sense, research networks are the human equivalent of perspectives oriented towards other media coverage. Similarly, we are interested in whether journalists' research networks are centred more on the national or open up towards the transnational. Beyond the in-depth interviews and newsroom observations, network maps of the professional contacts the individual journalists provided us with are an important element of the material we have used.

In order to arrive at an adequate understanding of journalists' research networks, we have to make several distinctions. First, we distinguish between impersonal contacts involving administration authorities, organisations and ministries, and personal research contacts. Second, we distinguish between editorial contacts and the personal contacts of individual journalists. Whereas editorial contacts arise simply out of newsroom membership, personal contacts have to be established and maintained by individual effort. However, editorial contacts become personal contacts when a journalist works in the same newsroom for several years. In sum, most of journalists' research contacts are personal contacts. Therefore the journalistic practice of professional 'networking' (Wittel 2006: 164) and keeping in touch becomes relevant for our analysis.

The research networks of journalists working in big newsrooms are characterised by lively communicative relationships with correspondents across the entire globe, so that at first sight they seem to be very transnationally oriented. For example, a French journalist considers himself to be a 'correspondent for the correspondents', since he stays 'in contact with our foreign correspondents all the time' (EU editor, *Le Monde*, F). By contrast, the research networks of journalists working in smaller newsrooms, only employing a few or even no correspondents, are usually a lot less transnational. In individual cases, however, personal contacts compensate for this. In order to grasp adequately the characteristics of journalists' research networks, it is important to consider their editorial or personal character.

In general, we observe across all countries that journalists' personal research networks are mainly centred on the national, so that networking practices form an intrinsic part of journalistic doing nation. Journalists usually stay in contact with persons living in their own country or of the same nationality. These contact persons are researchers, experts or journalists working for other (national) newspapers. Similarly, for more impersonal contacts with authorities or ministries on international and transnational levels, we find a national-centredness in journalistic practices. Journalists tend to contact representatives of their own countries, such as national MEPs or the national information offices of the European Commission. An EU editor of the Polish *Gazeta Wyborcza*, for example, clearly distinguishes between Polish and non-Polish research contacts: 'Information sources in the European Commission – Polish people and non-Polish people' (foreign news editor, *Gazeta Wyborcza*, PL).

We conclude from this that journalists' research contacts are mostly centred on persons and institutions in their own country. Contacts abroad are mostly persons of the same nationality. Hence an Austrian EU editor states that he would first of all contact the 'EU's representative office in Austria' (EU editor, *Die Presse*, AT) in order to obtain relevant information that has already been angled towards Austrian interests. Even in EU institutions, journalists tend to contact first of all their MEPs or their own national contact offices. It thus becomes clear that doing nation also manifests itself in the pattern of journalists' research contacts.

Doing nation in journalistic practices

Our findings concerning the articulation of national cultures of political discourse in journalistic practices demonstrate that doing nation is a basic and continuous part of journalistic practices in all countries. However, in each country, doing nation has distinct characteristics. In this transculturally shared practice of doing nation, the own nation is constructed as the centre of reporting and assessment in a quite specific way. As we have seen, national embedding points to the journalistic practice of relating Europe and the world back to one's own nation that is regarded as the political centre. Transnational contextualisation, by contrast, means that journalists' no longer perceive their own nation as isolated, but as part of a broader transnational space. The national is therefore shaped transnationally, but nevertheless remains the main reference point of communicative construction. The own nation also becomes evident in the scope of journalists' search for information and the way in which they hierarchise this. Here the national is prioritised over European or other foreign issues in journalists' practices.

More generally, considering the manner in which European issues are implied in journalistic practices, we found that routinisation of the transnational is quite advanced. As a consequence, Europe appears to be less something foreign than a natural reference point across the entire newspaper. Paradoxically, this contributes to the journalists' doing nation, inasmuch as the routinisation of Europe is a matter of national embedding and therefore national cultures of political discourse – Europe increasingly becomes a self-evident part of national reporting so that it may lose its transnational character.

According to our analyses, it is these practices of nationalisation that contribute to continuous and 'banal' (Billig 1995) doing nation in the newsrooms. Journalists locate Europe, the EU, political decision-making in Brussels and the EU member states, quite naturally within the continuous narration of the own nation. In this framework, we distinguish the journalistic practices and horizons of nationalisation according to different national cultures of political discourse (cf. Table 3.2).

In Austria, journalists tend to realise national embedding by referring to the country's history in relation to Eastern Europe. Transnational processes are regarded as intrinsic, so that the link to the own nation tends to be constructed implicitly. The routinisation of the transnational is quite advanced, inasmuch as journalists include transnational links even in regional news. Whereas journalists' research networks are quite national, perspectives appear more transnational, since Austrian journalists tend to use German-speaking media for close reading and researching.

In Germany, historical references to National Socialism form a characteristic aspect of national embedding. Transnational contextualisation realised through implicit links plays a crucial role in journalists' practices, whereas the journalists ascribe a special significance to the transnational as such. Hierarchisation in German journalists' practices involves

Table 3.2 Country-specific practices and orientations of nationalisation

		Austria	Denmark	France	Germany	Great Britain	Poland
Practices	*National embedding*	Regional references; historical references (Eastern Europe)	National references as criterion of selection	Comparative references to other EU countries; historical embedding (Colonialism)	Partly historical references (National Socialism)	Humorous-satiric references to other EU countries	Historical references (communism/National Socialism)
	Transnational contextualisation	Implicit national references (transnationalisation)	Implicit national references (dissociation/nationalisation)	Explicit national references (being part of the transnational)	Implicit national references (transnationalisation)	Implicit national references (being part of the transnational)	Explicit national references (emphasising the own specific role in the transnational)
Orientations	*Hierachisation*	Nation, Europe, world	Nation, world, Europe	Nation, Europe, world	Nation, Europe, world	Nation, world, Europe	Nation, world, Europe
	Ritualisation of the transnational	Advanced	Partly present	Advanced	Advanced	Not present	Partly present
	Horizons of information seeking	Observing: transnational European; Researching & Reading: German-speaking	Observing: transnational English-speaking; Researching & Reading: national	Observing: transnational European; Researching & Reading: national	Observing: transnational European; Researching & Reading: national	Observing: English-speaking, Researching & Reading: English-speaking	Observing: transnational, Researching & Reading: national
	Research networks	Nationally centred	Nationally centred	Nationally centred	Nationally centred	Nationally centred	Nationally centred

a ranking of Europe after the nation and ahead of news from the world. As in Austria, the routinisation of the transnational is quite advanced, whereas the range of information tends to be centred on the national.

In the case of Denmark, we are confronted with a completely different picture. National embedding is not simply applied as a common journalistic practice for locating news from abroad in the own national context. Moreover, the possible construction of links to the own nation forms an important aspect of issue selection. With regard to transnational contextualisation, the absence of explicit links to the own nation points to a distanced position with respect to Europe. Hierarchisation is characterised by the fact that Europe not only ranks behind the own nation, but also behind the world (especially the USA). Accordingly, journalists' perspectives focus more on English-speaking regions of the world than on Europe. There is only a partial routinisation of the transnational, so that Europe is treated as something separate in Danish journalists' practices.

In France, national embedding is often realised with reference to the French colonial era in North Africa; moreover, a comparison of the own nation with other (European) countries plays a crucial role in French journalists' practices. Transnational contextualisation is characterised by explicit links to the own nation and in journalists' hierarchisation practices Europe clearly ranks higher than the world. The routinisation of the transnational is quite advanced and journalists' perspectives tend to be transnationally centred on Europe.

In Great Britain, journalists' practices are characterised by a distanced attitude towards Europe. National embedding is often realised with the help of cynical-humorous references that emphasise the remoteness of Europe. This is also emphasised in journalists' transnational contextualisation practices, since these are realised by the application of implicit ironic references. In hierarchisation practices, Europe ranks lower than the own nation and the world (primarily North America). A routinisation of the transnational with regard to European issues cannot be found in British journalists' practices and journalists' perspectives are primarily oriented towards the English-speaking media.

In Poland national embedding through historical references is very important. Transnational contextualisation is primarily realised by implicitly negotiating the own nations' role in transnational space. Hierarchisation is characterised by the fact that Europe ranks lower than the own nation and the world. Routinisation of the transnational is only partly present in Polish journalists' practices. Information-seeking tends to focus on the own nation, but also includes the media landscapes of Russia and North America. Our overall impression for Poland is that journalistic production is undergoing an ongoing transformation. The increasing relevance of the EU in journalists' reporting has fostered a certain re-nationalisation.

The analysis presented in this chapter helps to arrive at a deeper understanding of journalists' modes of doing nation. The manner in which journalists realise practices of nationalisation points to the specifics of their national cultures of political discourse. The various implicit ways of constructing national political history show that discursive traditions play a crucial role in journalists' doing nation. By reflecting the own nations' history, both in explicit reporting on historic issues and in implicit references to national history, journalists constantly re-articulate their own national cultures of political discourse. In other words, established national patterns of journalistic practices are continuously reproduced in journalistic routines. The 'new' – in our case Europe and the EU – is integrated over and over again into the history of the 'old' national identity. Consequently, the national remains the central reference for the transnational – the national segmentation of the European public sphere is rooted in highly institutionalised journalistic practices that persist, despite political decisions and events that increase the EU's significance. This said, it becomes evident that journalists' doing nation represents a transculturally shared working practice. All journalists in the six EU countries under investigation realise nationalisation practices and have a national orientation in their daily work, even though these involve different nations and are therefore peculiar. It is exactly this finding that we link to the discussion of transnational or global professionalised journalism cultures outlined in the previous chapter. Whereas comparative research on an emerging global journalism culture emphasises the homogenisation of journalistic practices, our research points to shared practices which remain different from one national context to another. In this sense, we find not a global homogeneity, but transcultural patterns in the construction of national difference. Understanding this is an important step in explaining the persisting transnational segmentation of the European public sphere.

3.2   Stratification-related cultures of political discourse: transnational patterns of addressing audiences

The multi-segmentation of the European public sphere does not imply the existence of national cultures of political discourse. We also find transnational patterns of journalistic practices for different types of addressing audiences existing across our researched countries. For example, working practice in quality papers is distinct to that in tabloid or regional papers, a transnational segmentation of the European public sphere that relates to social stratification. By focussing on journalists' practices, we aim to reconstruct and explain these stratification-related aspects of cultures of political discourse. We thereby achieve a more sophisticated picture of the cultural foundation of a multi-segmented European public sphere. By developing this more elaborated picture, we overcome the rather simplistic distinction of quality, tabloid and regional newspapers. Cultures of political discourse do not refer to the nation, but to the specific character of outlet types based on specific imagined audiences related to social status. Referring to the different audiences the journalists conceptualise, we distinguish four modes of addressing audiences across the countries researched by us: the analyst, the ambassador, the reporter and the caterer.

Paolo Mancini (2008) has in a similar fashion distinguished two types of journalistic cultures: national journalistic cultures and a transnational journalistic culture involving 'a specialised or rather professionalised culture' based upon certain 'norms, procedures and traditions' of a 'super-national character' (Mancini 2008: 157f.). This transnational journalistic culture involves a field of research currently discussed in terms of 'global newsrooms' (Cohen/Kennedy 2000; Gurevitch et al. 1997; Reese 2008) or 'newsroom cultures' (Brüggemann 2011, 2012). Whereas the comparative study of national professionalisation processes builds upon an established tradition in media and communication research, our argument here is once more that we do not observe global homogeneity, but instead a segmentation quite closely linked to the stratificatory segmentation of European societies or European society itself. From this we obtain an understanding of how transnational segmentation of the European public sphere is produced through journalists' practices.

This approach resonates with other empirical studies on journalistic production and European reporting. The aforementioned AIM research consortium derived from their interviews with journalists in different EU countries 'three types of professional discourses about EU issues' (Heikkilä/Kunelius 2008: 382; Kunelius/Heikkilä 2007: 61). First there is a discourse of 'classic professionalism', second one of 'mundane discourse' and third a 'cosmopolitan discourse'. We distinguish these three types with regard to the locality of reporting, the anticipated relationship between journalist and audience, and the presumed problems of the EU. Journalists working in the discourse of classic professionalism assume the nation to be the locality of reporting and consider themselves neutral facilitators and critical commentators for well-informed national citizens, diagnosing a lack of efficiency and public support with regard to the EU. Mundane discourse implies that everyday life is the locality of reporting, journalists considering themselves to be 'service consultants' for individual consumers, criticising the dissociation of the EU from the everyday life of citizens. Cosmopolitan discourse, by contrast, assumes that journalists take the independent world of international politics to be the locality of reporting. They consider themselves to be experts in the service of multi-cultural and cultivated elites, and they criticise the EU for its lack of dynamism. Risto Kunelius and Heikki Hekkilä describe these three discourses as a specific feature of professional journalism in Europe (cf. Kunelius/Heikkilä 2007: 67).

While these research results provide a starting point for us, the AIM consortium did not analyse discourses as part of a transnational pattern of journalistic news production. The same applies to the project's differentiation of 'reporters' and 'ambassadors' (Heikkilä/Kunelius 2008: 390): Whereas reporters try to make complex and abstract EU topics understandable by translating them into a national and increasingly utilitarian vocabulary, ambassadors, by contrast, fight for understanding the logic and language of the castles and corridors in Brussels and sympathise with the more elite idea of transnational government. The analytical differentiation of both types remains at the level of the individual journalist. The broader context of the newsrooms is only discussed with regard to the 'cultural struggle' between the two types: 'If, then, a cultural struggle within a news organization takes place between reporters and ambassadors, it seems clear that ambassadors are being pushed to the margins' (Heikkilä/Kunelius 2008: 390).

At this point we detect parallels with the approach taken by the Europub project, another large research consortium that has recently explored journalists as actors in the European public sphere (Statham 2007, 2008, 2010a). The criterion for structuring empirical data here was the 'perceptions of readerships' demands', which partly involves stratification-related images of the readership (Statham 2010a: 131). This criterion involves the assumption that newspapers are commercial companies, so that media producers have to keep an eye on their (imagined) markets. Four types of journalistic advocacy were elaborated from interviews (Statham 2010a: 142). In the 'business as usual' approach journalists do not deem it necessary to adopt a position towards Europe. 'Educational advocacy' means that journalists consider Europe to be an important topic and aim to explain it to their readers. 'Partisan advocacy', by contrast, involves reporting on Europe, because a certain political interpretation of the EU is supported. Finally, 'ideological advocacy' involves a clear position for or against Europe. With respect to all four types of advocacy, Paul Statham states: 'Generally we found that journalists' experiences did not significantly vary much across countries, newspaper types, and journalistic types' (Statham 2010a: 143).

Such findings are relevant for our own research in a dual sense. First, they demonstrate that, despite the ongoing professionalisation of journalism in Europe, there is no homogeneous treatment of European issues to be found. Instead, there are different discourses about Europe and the EU within journalists' newsrooms, coupled with different journalistic attitudes and different forms of journalistic advocacy. Second, the studies cited suggest that the imagined or 'implied reader' (Statham 2010a: 131) is pivotal for transnational differences: Depending on ways in which journalists imagine their audience, the treatment of Europe and EU topics differs significantly.

This fundamental argument becomes even more evident if we link this EU-focused research to more general investigations of journalism. Quantitative (Weischenberg 2002) as well as qualitative (Wiedebusch 1989) data demonstrate the extent to which the average image of the audience among a certain group of journalists is of importance (similarly Firmstone 2008: 438; Hohlfeld 2005: 196f.). A widespread argument in this field is that audience orientation within media production is constantly increasing. Researchers tend to think of this increasing audience orientation as a process of tabloidisation (Meyen/Riesmeyer 2009). However, it makes a difference whether journalists say that the consideration of audience interests gains in importance (Blöbaum et al. 2010: 2) or whether these journalists perceive an 'increased audience orientation' as an influence in their everyday practices. Against this background it becomes evident that we must look at the way in which audience images manifest themselves in journalists' practices.

Empirical findings indicate that colleagues, friends and other professional contacts have more influence on journalists than 'real' information regarding the journalists' audience (Weischenberg 2002: 253–258). Journalists connect with their audiences only through readers' letters (Malik 2004: 300). Researchers who conceptualise media producers as 'cultural intermediaries' in the sense of Bourdieu come to similar conclusions (cf. Hesmondhalgh 2006; Negus 2002). They point to the distant relationship between producers and consumers in the field of cultural production. More crucial to journalistic decision-making in the production process are personal preferences and images of addressees, rather than factual knowledge about addressees and their interests.

We define 'audience image' as the journalist's conception of their audience, which is continuously re-articulated in their work practices. The sources of these conceptions are various. Direct contact with the

readers is, however, unusual. Nevertheless, the journalists' conceptions of their audience are highly important in the choice of form of
address. By 'modes of addressing audiences' we mean the ensemble of
specific journalistic practices of dealing with (European political) issues
for the imagined audience. Depending on the specific audience image,
we distinguish between characteristic forms of reporting or modes of
addressing. In conformity with the audience image, we observe a specific journalistic self-conception of how to communicate European and
foreign issues, that is to say a specific involvement with resources, and
a specific attitude towards Europe and the EU. As already mentioned
above, based on our newsroom studies in Austria, Denmark, France,
Germany, the United Kingdom and Poland, we found the following four
modes of addressing audiences:

1. The *analyst* presents an extensive analysis of political processes in
   Europe. Europe and the world are perceived as a relevant political
   and cultural framework which is continuously observed and critically
   discussed.
2. The *ambassador* approaches political processes in Europe pedagogically. Europe is explained in a supportive manner by linking political
   and cultural processes to readers' everyday lives.
3. The *reporter* addresses readers by providing them with a basic and neutral overview of European coverage. Economic constraints enforce a
   pragmatic approach to the coverage of international news.
4. The *caterer* places a strong emphasis on comforting readers, providing them with European content as soft news. International coverage is only of interest if it is shocking, sensational or allows strong
   emphatic comparisons.

The categories we have relied on to analyse the data from interviews and
newsroom observations with regard to our transnational typology are:
The journalistic image of the reader, journalistic self-conception, importance of and attitude towards the EU, the importance of EU countries,
and practices of nationalisation. The four types of address have to be
treated as complex cultural patterns that cannot be located at the level
of individual journalists. Instead they involve certain kinds of media
outlets and thereby specific moments of transnational, stratification-
related cultures of political discourse.

The analyst

The analyst is the journalist typical of *Die Presse* (AT), *Der Standard* (AT),
FAZ (GER), *SZ* (GER), *Le Monde* (F), *Le Figaro* (F), *Rzeczpospolita* (PL) and

The Times (UK), favouring an ambitious, extensive and in-depth analysis of political processes. They consider a differentiated, profound and diverse EU, and foreign coverage to be a key requirement within their daily journalistic routine. The imagined reader is here summed up by the term 'well-educated elite'. As one journalist says: 'We have an educational mandate, at least towards the elites' (EU correspondent, *FAZ*, GER). It is thus not surprising that analysts conceive their professional specialisation as well as their own in-depth interest to be significant; they underpin the importance of constantly keeping track of relevant and complex processes, presenting varied perspectives and background information. Structural constraints such as limited economic resources (for example little space, little time), as well as limitations in the reader's knowledge about EU and foreign affairs seem to have no relevant impact on this self-conception. In contrast, they emphasise the need for even higher demands in order to address their imagined well-educated and sophisticated audiences. Analysts describe their daily working routines with regard to the EU and foreign affairs coverage by clearly distancing themselves from other journalists who prioritise news values such as topicality and sensationalism. In sum, the EU and foreign affairs are characterised as 'extremely important' and 'essential' (London correspondent, *The Times*, UK). Both Europe and the world are perceived to be natural surroundings in which relevant political action and communication take place. Transnational political processes such as globalisation or European integration are objects of regular discussion and work practice. It is thus not surprising that analysts mainly refer to nationalisation, transnational routinisation and contextualisation. Since they perceive the transnational political environment to be a relevant and natural arena, it is merely a logical consequence to integrate transnational references into daily production routines. Analysts primarily realise transnational contextualisation in an implicit manner – references to national frameworks somehow merge into an integrative perspective upon transnational political processes.

The ambassador

The journalists of *Kleine Zeitung* (AT), *Politiken* (DK), *Ouest France* (F), *Le Parisien* (F) and *Gazeta Wyborcza* (PL) are ambassadors, deploying a pedagogical approach. As with analysts, journalists of the ambassador type seek to discuss political processes and favour background analyses rather than topicality and sensationalism. Their specific profile relates, however, to their emphasis upon the importance of being close to the everyday life of the reader, often within a national and local framework. The image of the reader held by the ambassador integrates people from all societal strata – in other words, everyman. One of the French journalists puts it as follows: 'In comparison to *Le Monde* [. . .] we admittedly address a readership somehow more at the grassroots level' (editor, *Le Parisien*, F); however, an Austrian journalist adds that coverage is also directed towards the 'elite stratum' (editor in chief, *Kleine Zeitung*, AT).

The ambassador typically seeks to deal with the challenge of creating a comprehensible coverage of issues arising in the EU and foreign affairs. The ambassador approaches his readers by trying to explain and facilitate understanding of political processes within transnational political contexts: 'We simply want the people to understand what we report on. [. . .] So, it's in a very pedagogical manner that we try to make the world more comprehensible' (EU and foreign editor, *Le Parisien*, F). This specific mandate is evident in the fact that they promote a constructive, sometimes even enthusiastic, image of the EU and the idea of European integration. The ambassador aims at meeting the reader's need to recognise the relevance of a particular story with regard to his everyday life. He does not necessarily feel obliged to follow the news agenda. The ambassador tends to report on issues that conform to his pedagogical mission (for example the building of a European civil society) in respect of his readers. Journalists of the ambassador type consequently place strong emphasis on national embedding. On the other hand, they have a tendency towards a European hierarchisation, in particular by favouring articles on European topics over coverage concerning the rest of the world.

The reporter

The reporter is dominant among journalists working in the newsrooms of *WAZ* (GER), *Berlingske Tidende* (DK), *Jydske Vestkysten* (DK) and *Dziennik Zachodni* (PL). When describing his daily working routines this type strongly supports a pragmatic perspective, presenting themselves as being subject to structural constraints such as resource restrictions in searching for background information on EU and foreign news issues or for writing articles. The reporter imagines an average citizen without any special demands to be representative of his audience: 'people without especially high education' (editor, *Dziennik Zachodni*, PL). From a reporter's point of view, this reader expects an overview of crucial political events rather than ambitious in-depth analyses of processes. His main task is thus to present issues in a manner that people easily relate to the local and national context in which they experience daily life. In so doing, journalists of this type emphasise the need to be objective, thus distancing themselves from a moralising style of reporting.

Altogether, this type is in favour of stories 'providing the people with a good experience' (editor, *Jydske Vestkysten*, DK).

Reporter-type journalists see their EU attitude as supportive, while avoiding any explicit enthusiastic or sceptical commitment. This attitude again results from their specific reader orientation: 'In sum, we have to be pragmatic and follow a pro-European line. [. . .] People are not stupid and understand the obvious advantages resulting from the European development' (editor, *Dziennik Zachodni*, PL). This statement indicates that coverage of EU countries is of only average importance for the reporter – and even less so in case of reporting on other European countries. Important and relevant events are mainly covered if they obviously relate to readers' imagined needs. It has thus become clear that journalists of the reporter type lay stress on the journalistic practice of national embedding. Their pragmatic perspective, mainly resulting from economic constraints, meets with their readers' image of an average citizen who is mainly interested in local news immediately related to his personal regional and national context.

The caterer

The caterer as a journalistic type of addressing audiences is characteristic mainly of the *Neue Kronenzeitung* (AT), *BILD* (GER), *Ekstra Bladed* (DK), *Daily Express* (UK) and *Fakt* (PL). The caterer's main quality is to place great emphasis on meeting readers' expectations in their reporting on surprising and shocking topics as well as on topics that easily relate to the everyday lives of people at the bottom of the social scale. The caterer thus imagines his reader to be someone from a lower, less educated class 'whose hand we need to take' (EU and political editor, *BILD*, GER). Especially with regard to EU-related topics, the caterer addresses those 'who are maybe not in favour of the EU, who are fighting a losing battle against constraining life conditions' (editor in chief, *Fakt*, PL). This type is mainly concerned with being the voice of the little man, especially with regard to research and writing routines on the EU and foreign affair topics. He neither aims to present ambitious analyses of political processes, nor to approach readers pedagogically. The question of whether and how he might write from the perspective of the reader, becoming the voice of the little man, is an integral part of the caterer's self-conception. The journalist's own evaluation of the EU's importance is subordinated to this service orientation.

Reporting on the EU and other European countries seems to be of significantly lower relevance than reporting on nationally relevant issues; in some cases it plays no role at all. Here journalists place a great deal of emphasis upon structural constraints such as limited space, personal resources and time. Beyond that, the caterer is characterised by a hypocritical attitude towards the EU. On the one hand, journalists of this type constantly present themselves as being in favour of the EU; on the other hand, they feel obliged to provide their imagined audience with sceptical, sometimes negative and in many cases sensationalistic coverage in this area. Against this background, it seems plausible that journalists of the caterer type place great emphasis upon the journalistic practices of national embedding and national hierarchisation, which seems to follow from very powerful images of the simple reader, who would only consider those issues to be relevant which relate to a familiar political context – the national.

3.3   Imagined audiences: transnational modes of addressing

Our findings on journalists' transnational modes of addressing audiences demonstrate the role of their imagined audiences. Journalistic modes of addressing audiences are patterns of profiling with regard to imagined audiences and related journalistic self-conceptions (cf. Table 3.3). Relating these modes of addressing audiences back to specific newspapers confirms their appearance in the context of different media outlets. It is not surprising that the *analyst* type is mainly present in quality papers, the *caterer* typically appears in tabloids and the *reporter* in regional newspaper frameworks. Interestingly, the *ambassador* type overcomes any typical attribution, appearing in all three types – quality, regional and tabloid papers.

In conclusion, we ask what these research results mean in relation to stratification-related cultures of political discourse. As our analysis demonstrates, the four modes of addressing distinguish the respective journalists' audience image. This image is not just an individual one, but relates to the editorial office and its overall discourse and work practices, and has a great deal to do with the stratificatory segmentation of European societies. The analysts do address their coverage to what they understand to be the well-educated elite citizen, an image which could typically be related to what is called upper-middle and upper class. They understand this citizen to be well-informed and they perceive themselves as being able to align their work practices with an extensive analysis of political processes. The ambassador and reporter seem to be more oriented to the middle classes, having in mind more or less stereotypical images of the everyman and average citizen. Differences exist in the

Table 3.3 Modes of addressing audiences

	Analyst	Ambassador	Reporter	Caterer
Journalistic readers images	well educated elite citizen	everyman	average citizen	little man
Journalistic self-conception	extensive analysis of political processes	pedagogic treatment of political processes	pragmatic view of political processes	little man's voice
Importance of/attitude towards EU	EU as relevant framework to be discussed critically	EU as complex project in need of support and explanation	EU as a duty, accepted as everyday reality	hypocritical: Pro European position/sensationalistic critique
Importance of EU countries and world	Europe and world as self-evident framework	Europe as illustrational moment for the national	Europe as marginal news resource	Europe as marginal boulevard resource
Practices of nationalisation	transnational contextualisation, routinisation of the transnational	national embedding, European hierarchisation	national and regional embedding	national embedding, national hierarchisation
Newspapers	*Die Presse, Der Standard, FAZ, SZ, Le Monde, Le Figaro, Rzeczpospolita, The Times*	*Kleine Zeitung, Politiken, Ouest France, Le Parisien, Gazeta Wyborcza*	*WAZ, Berlingske Tidende, Jydske Vestkysten, Dziennik Zachodni*	*Kronen Zeitung, BILD, Ekstra Bladet, Daily Express, Fakt*

way in which these journalists conceive the middle class, either seeing a need for a pedagogical approach or a more pragmatic one interested in 'pure facts'. Finally, the caterer seems to have someone from the lower (working) classes in mind and wants to be the voice of these people.

Research results like these are of interest because they partly differ from the more general discussion of the individualisation of European societies. Following sociological insights (Beck/Beck-Gernsheim 2001), societies in Europe are increasingly marked by processes of individualisation; something which should also be the case for Europe as a whole. Following this line of argument – and at the level of the people, their media appropriation and public connection to Europe, we substantiate this argument (cf. chapter 6) – class should be less dominant, as the data presented in this chapter suggests. But on the other hand, our data demonstrates quite well that journalists' ways of imagining and addressing audiences, and the work practices related to this, are based on a quite simple model of social stratification. This model is very close to a segmentation of societies into working, middle and upper classes – irrespective of the degree to which European countries, and therefore also Europe as a whole, is stratified in this way (cf. Mau/Verwiebe 2010: 36–41). The main point here is that the idea of stratification guides the work practices of journalists at the everyday level.

From our data, we note the existence of something like a stratification-related political discourse culture, at least at the level of journalistic working practices related to imagined audiences. This culture of political discourse helps to explain the transnational segmentation of the European public sphere, a segmentation in relation to the stratification of the various national societies in Europe and, as a consequence, also emerging European society. As we argued in the previous chapter, this stratification refers back to the stratification history of the various nation states, where for the last century political discourse was also embedded in social conflicts stemming from class differences. Journalists' perceptions also echo the character of their readership, which is substantiated by statistical data. Indeed, readers of the newspapers carrying material from journalists of the analyst type are typically people from the upper or at least well-educated classes. Readers addressed by the caterer type – mostly tabloid newspapers – are usually categorised as members of the lower or working class, with an average to low level of education (Axel Springer Media Impact 2015; Elvestad/Blekesaune 2008). This is not, however, the main argument here. Instead, we argue that the idea of a stratified society guides the practice of journalists in those European countries we have studied – and also, that we explain the transnational segmentation of the European public sphere through this.

4
Representing Europe in the Press: The Multi-segmented European Public Sphere

In this chapter, we focus on a specific mode of communicative construction: the European public sphere as constructed in newspaper coverage. Like in other mass media, public communication in and through the press is considered to be a *sine qua non* of a European public sphere, given the ongoing political integration of Europe and early discussion of the EU's democratic and public deficit during the 1990s (Gerhards 1993). Analysing the European public sphere, based on the content of mass media, involves empirical investigation of the manner in which, and extent to which, the EU and Europe are dealt with in different media, and assessing the reach of transnational communication within and across these media.

Empirical research has here increased substantially since the mid-1990s. Since then, there have been many studies of the content of national mass media news coverage. These vary in their focus on different media: While early research was almost exclusively on quality media with a strong bias towards the quality press (for example D'Haenens 2005; Meyer 2005; Trenz 2005, 2004; for television cf. for example De Vreese 2003; Esser 2002; Gripsrud 2007; Peter/De Vreese 2004), studies in recent years have also considered the tabloid and regional press (for example Downey et al. 2012; Gattermann 2013; Kleinen-von Königslöw 2010b; Lohner 2011; Offerhaus et al. 2014; Vetters 2007). Given the increasing relevance of online media, all kinds of public online platforms have gained further attention within the field (for example Bennett et al. 2015; Michailidou/Trenz 2010; Rasmussen 2013; cf. also chapter 5). Quality media outlets, used by small elite audiences, are considered to be the principal public vehicle for both political and social European discourse. It is likely that more frequent and more detailed articles about the EU exist in quality national newspapers than in regional papers or tabloids. Due to their orientation towards well-educated and well-informed citizens, quality newspapers have their own standards for selecting newsworthy issues, and are continuously observing and monitoring political processes at the EU and member state levels. However, this elite bias reduces the European public sphere to a political discourse of public debate between socially advanced people, and apart from these rational and well-argued debates ignores everyday public debate. To avoid this elite focus, during the 12 years of our research we gradually extended its scope. We have now arrived at a point where we are able tackle the stratification-related segmentation of different press outlets by a cross media exploration of quality, regional and tabloid newspapers, as discussed in the previous chapter.

Beside country specific studies, many content analysis studies focus on comparing countries in order to look for differences and commonalities of European news coverage. While there have in recent years been a number of collaborative research projects comparing a range of countries (for example AIM; EMEDIATE; EUROPUB; EUROSPHERE), these studies usually involve cross-country comparisons between only two European countries or a few more (for example Novy 2013; Rovisco 2010). That national cultures matters in the way that the EU and Europe are reported was demonstrated by Barbara Pfetsch (2008) and her colleagues (Pfetsch et al. 2008), who established that Europeanisation was more prominent in the news outlets of continental European countries that are fully involved in the European integration process than in the press of countries with a lesser degree of integration. Regarding the earlier empirical work, Machill et al. (2006: 67) identified an imbalance of research, with an overemphasis upon 'big' rather than 'small' European member states. Consequently, at the beginning of our research in 2003 we chose the broad sample of countries already outlined: France and Germany both represent major political actors in the EU, being among the largest countries by population and also being founder nations. Austria and Denmark are much smaller and also are more recent member states. Denmark and the UK are typically eurosceptic by attitude and are not part of the eurozone. Poland was included as one of the most recent and larger Eastern member states with a distinct history compared to the other countries studied, given its historical connection within the Eastern Bloc and with the USSR.

Studies also vary in their focus on news coverage. While some research is dedicated to routine coverage (for example Gerhards et al. 2009; Koopmans/Statham 2010b), most is event-oriented. Some investigate events related to the political routine of the EU, such as European parliamentary elections or European summits (for example Boomgaarden et al. 2013, 2010; De Vreese 2001; Gattermann 2013; Maier et al. 2011; Meyer 2010; Oberhuber et al. 2005; Peter/De Vreese 2004; Schuck/De Vreese 2011; Schuck et al. 2013, 2011; Wilke/Reinemann 2007). Others are case studies, related to special or unforeseen events and topics such as European enlargement, the introduction of the euro, the European constitution or EU scandals like the Haider case (for example Downey et al. 2012; Statham/Trenz 2013; Van de Steeg/Risse 2010). Unlike many other studies of the European public sphere, we have not chosen specific EU issues or policies as subjects for content analysis. Instead, we have included all kinds of issues and topics in order to present a more comprehensive picture of the (trans)nationalisation processes within public debates. By also taking a longitudinal approach covering 30 years of political reporting, we take the EU's long-term development into account. We have chosen six waves of article collection (1982, 1989, 1996, 2003, 2008 and 2013), the sample consequently stretching over different phases of the European integration process. It includes the main developments and tipping points of EU history, such as the programme to establish the single market during the late 1980s, the move towards political union in the 1990s, the introduction of the euro, the enlargement of the 2000s and the period up until the euro crisis in 2008, starting with the financial crisis of 2007.

Nonetheless, although we have not approached our material thematically, we may ask at this point of our research how Europe has been communicatively constructed during the euro crisis. This has been the focus of recent content analysis, addressing, for example, particularly the financial crisis, the Greek crisis, or crises during the European integration process and their relevance for the European public sphere in general (for example Breeze 2014; Cross/Ma 2015; Joris et al. 2014; Kaitatzi-Whitlock 2014; Meijers 2013; Post/Vollbracht 2013; Schranz/ Eisenegger 2011; Triandafyllidou et al. 2009; Tzogopoulos 2013; Wodak/ Angouri 2014). European crisis situations are relevant objects for media research devoted to the mediatised communicative construction of the crisis. The media frame the situation, define who is to blame, and disseminate narratives and scenarios about a crisis. Many studies are however limited to treating a crisis as a conflict event and correspondingly cover a short sample period. Using qualitative content analyses of several European crises Krzyżanowski (2009), for example, found that Europe has changed its role in news media discourse over time. From being an adversary or source of problems for the nation, Europe has become the bearer of common values for many, if not all, European nation states. Our quantitative longitudinal approach also enables us to trace the impact of the euro crisis on long-term patterns of a mediatised European public sphere. We place the Europeanisation of news coverage in a longer timeframe and ask whether these patterns and their current form have been changed by the situation of political crisis.

Using our cross-media, cross-country and longitudinal quantitative content analysis of political news coverage, this chapter displays the extent to which national and emerging European discourse cultures are articulated in the press. We firstly focus on vertical and horizontal processes of Europeanisation, especially with regard to the recent euro crisis, looking for signs of European identification visible in the news coverage of our whole sample. Referring to 'the ambassador' as a specific transnational and transmedial type of journalistic addressing, we then analyse the character of its writing by making comparisons with the other types. This is possible by relating each type of journalistic addressing of audiences back to its underlying newspaper. Thirdly, we concentrate on the case of the *Financial Times* as an example of a transnational European medium. Here again, we examine the characteristics of its news coverage as compared with that of other national quality newspapers. We conclude by interpreting emergent trends against the backdrop of the communicative construction of Europe and the impact of the euro crisis.

4.1   The European public sphere: stability in times of crisis

Our earlier research (Hepp et al. 2012: 63–84; Offerhaus et al. 2014; Wessler et al. 2008: 40–54) has shown that the European public sphere is multi-segmented with regard to the way that the press treats EU- and Europe-related matters. Multi-segmentation involves two separate forms of segmentation found in our analysis.

The first form is the 'national segmentation' of European public spheres. This segmentation is an obvious one, since the European public sphere is articulated through different levels of the transnationalisation of national public spheres. While there is a vertical Europeanisation – the increase of reporting about EU institutions and politics – over time, the horizontal dimension of Europeanisation, the observation of other EU member states, has remained fixed at a relatively high level. There is little collective identification with a European community. There are significant differences between countries (for example between the United Kingdom and France) in these general trends of Europeanisation.

Second, we argue that the European public sphere remains multi-segmented since we also noted the way in which there was 'segmentation according to newspaper types'. This segmentation is more striking, since it is transnational. Across all those EU member states that were studied, we found certain types of media outlets that – in spite of their different national backgrounds – share common patterns in their construction of the European public sphere. We found different degrees of Europeanisation at all levels when comparing quality, regional and tabloid papers. Tabloid papers follow different patterns. Here we discovered a lower level of Europeanisation that also began significantly later. Furthermore, no identification with Europe is expressed in their news coverage. Our findings show that debates on Europe remain predominantly national, and differ across countries and across newspaper outlet types.

But do all of the previously identified patterns remain stable in times of the euro crisis? And does the so-called euro crisis result in a rejection of the European idea? Or, by contrast, does it impel the European project forward, as proposed by some scholars (cf. discussion in chapter 2)? We have to consider different trend scenarios. First, we might consider a continuing trend of Europeanisation. Second, processes of Europeanisation could also be turned into trends of (re-)nationalisation at a particular point in time – a prognosis that is widely shared in the context of the euro crisis. Third, tendencies of Europeanisation could also stall and remain fixed at the plateau already achieved.

Following the distinction made in chapter 2, articles were analysed by focusing on vertical and horizontal Europeanisation, as well as on European identification. The *vertical dimension* was realised by monitoring the scope of EU politics. Vertical Europeanisation could be said to be taking place either when EU institutions became more visible within the longitudinal analysis or when an increasing focus on European policies as a principal topic characterised these articles. The *horizontal dimension* was realised by the scope of transnational exchange and the visibility of other countries through explicit reference in coverage. If there was considerable attention to other European countries, mentioning or directly and indirectly quoting actors from these countries, we could identify the existence of horizontal Europeanisation. A far more demanding indicator, going beyond the aforementioned processes of Europeanisation, is the process of collective identification as European. It measures whether objective communicative exchange across national borders is acknowledged by its participants subjectively as a common discourse. It defines Europeanisation in terms of the emergence of a common transnational 'community of communication' (Risse 2010: 109). Hence we coded the use of 'we-references' (for example 'We, the Europeans', 'We, the Brits') or the naming of collective identities (for example 'the Europeans', 'the French people') (cf. Table 4.1).

Table 4.1   Dimensions and indicators of Europeanisation

Dimension	Indicators
Vertical Europeanisation	Monitoring transnational politics: – Visibility of EU institutions (and its speakers) – Focus on EU policies
Horizontal Europeanisation	Transnational discourse: – Visibility of EU countries – Quotation of speakers from EU countries
European Identification	Level of Identification: – European we-references – References to Europe as a collective

Since there is no normative standard for what the 'good' and the 'weak' scope for a European public sphere might be, we can only measure and interpret Europeanisation processes proportionally. We compare newspaper reporting in several countries, in several media outlets and their respective developments over time. For the interpretation and evaluation of our data it is important to identify the baseline of these trends. The scope of 'Europeanness' as well as the trend and the level of Europeanisation are three important qualities of transnationalisation processes (Wessler et al. 2008: 22ff.). Using a data set of 38,758 coded articles, we study Europeanisation processes in different countries (Austria, Denmark, France, Germany, United Kingdom and Poland) and different press outlets (quality, regional and tabloid press) over time (1982, 1989, 1996, 2003, 2008 and 2013). (For further information about the newspapers coded, the selection of articles and coding procedure, cf. appendix).

Vertical Europeanisation

Starting from the European public sphere deficit noted above (Gerhards 2001), we examined the extent to which the shift of political power from the national to the European level was accompanied by increased public attention in the press. As regards the legitimacy of European governance, citizens should be aware of what is going on at the supranational European level. Monitoring European governance, measured by the visibility of EU institutions as well as the focus on EU policies within newspaper coverage, is therefore one important dimension of the Europeanisation of public spheres.

The first indicator (*visibility of political institutions*) names political institutions or cites its political representatives as speakers in news coverage. Both provide a rough idea of the significance of certain political institutions in public discourse. However, this indicator does not give any further information beyond simple naming; there is no information on the extent of reference. References to political institutions as represented by members cited is completely dominated by national institutions (96 per cent), whereas 3 per cent of the institutional references are linked to the EU and 1 per cent to the UN. This high percentage of national references might be because journalists prefer to cite national sources in their news coverage, given their supposed prominence and familiarity to the audience. It is also obvious that it is only a small proportion of articles (9,193 out of 38,758), where speakers are quoted at all. This might suggest that, within a sample of heterogeneous newspapers, not many speakers have the opportunity of being quoted by the press.

As for trends within the whole sample, we record in the last row of Table 4.2 the rising visibility of speakers from EU institutions, albeit from a low level of 1.5 per cent to 4.3 per cent for all papers. Given the segmentation of newspaper types, some of the patterns mentioned above become apparent. In comparison with other newspaper types, quality newspapers show the highest quantity of references to EU speakers. Tabloid papers show the lowest share, whereas regional papers are in between. If we consider the years of the euro crisis, between 2008 and 2013, we see in all papers only a minor decline of EU references (from 6.1 per cent to 5.9 per cent; 3.3 per cent to 3.2 per cent and 2.5 per cent to 2.3 per cent). With the wide variation in the number of articles in quality papers during 2008 and 2013 in mind, we are faced with contradictory signs of Europeanisation in this period, whether for the whole sample or for the analysis comparing media outlets. What becomes obvious, however, is that the euro crisis is not associated with renationalisation, as one might have expected in times of crisis.

In order to examine national segmentation in vertical Europeanisation in greater detail, Figure 4.1 concentrates only on one characteristic of the indicator 'references to transnational political institutions'. It disregards 'UN-institutions' and 'other international and transnational political institutions' as further characteristics, being focused only on 'EU institutions'. 'National institutions' were not coded in this variable, which leads in contrast to Table 4.2 having a higher percentage level. Based on a total of 6,373 references to transnational political institutions, we see a trend towards Europeanisation in all nations. The examples of Austria (joined the EU in 1995) and especially Poland (joined the EU in 2004) show what we have elsewhere called a 'pattern of catch-up Europeanisation' (Kleinen-von Königslöw/Möller 2009: 101). It shows increasing reporting on EU matters and issues at a later point of time

Table 4.2   References to speakers from political institutions

	1982	1989	1996	2003	2008	2013	References per paper (n)
Quality papers							
National political institutions (%)	98.1	97.3	95.7	94.2	93.9	92.7	4,179 (94.2%)
EU-institutions (%)	1.6	2.4	3.5	4.1	6.1	5.9	214 (4.8%)
UN-institutions (%)	0.3	0.2	0.8	1.7	0.0	1.4	44 (1.0%)
References per year (n)	*318*	*412*	*487*	*515*	*560*	*2,145*	*4,437 (100%)*
Regional papers							
National political institutions (%)	97.8	98.1	97.4	94.6	95.8	96.3	7,115 (96.5%)
EU-institutions (%)	1.5	1.4	2.3	4	3.3	3.2	200 (2.7%)
UN-institutions (%)	0.7	0.6	0.3	1.4	0.9	0.5	55 (0.7%)
References per year (n)	*992*	*1,086*	*1,217*	*1,224*	*1,582*	*1,269*	*7,370 (100%)*
Tabloid papers							
National political institutions (%)	97.2	99.1	96.6	96.6	97.5	97.1	3,632 (97.3%)
EU-institutions (%)	1.6	0.2	2.7	1.9	2.5	2.3	75 (2.0%)
UN-institutions (%)	1.2	0.6	0.7	1.6	0.0	0.5	26 (0.7%)
References per year (n)	*322*	*467*	*563*	*645*	*755*	*981*	*3,733 (100%)*
All papers							
National political institutions (%)	97.7	98.2	96.8	95.1	95.9	94.7	14,936 (96.0%)
EU-institutions (%)	1.5	1.3	2.6	3.4	3.6	4.3	489 (3.1%)
UN-institutions (%)	0.7	0.5	0.5	1.5	0.5	0.9	125 (0.8%)
References per year (n)	*1,632*	*1,965*	*2,267*	*2,384*	*2,897*	*4,395*	*15,540 (100%)*

Note: Multiple coding was possible; the table contains $n = 15,540$ references in $N = 9,193$ valid articles; references to speakers from 'other international and transnational political institutions' and 'non-political institutions' are excluded.

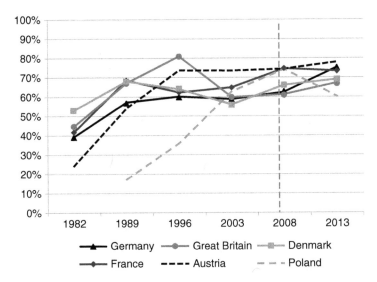

Figure 4.1 Vertical Europeanisation, based on the percentage of references to 'EU institutions' by country from 1982 to 2013

Note: Multiple coding was possible; the figure contains $n = 6,373$ references in $N = 4,211$ valid articles.

than in the old member states when they first joined. In contrast, newspapers in France, Germany, Denmark and the UK seem to have reported in quite a convergent fashion in recent years. This also includes the fact that the process of vertical Europeanisation was not fractured by the euro crisis. That said, there seem to be some consequences from the euro crisis, Poland being in a phase of decreasing, Germany and the UK in an increasing, and France in a stagnating phase of Europeanisation. Differences like these are expressions of national segmentation.

The second indicator (*political issues or the reach of policy*) is also distributed according to national policies. Some 75.3 per cent references are to national policy, faced with 5 per cent of references to EU issues, and 19.7 per cent to foreign and international issues. Table 4.3 shows that the years of the emergent euro crisis saw a broadening of the coverage of international issues (from 12.3 per cent to 16.6 per cent) compared to national issues (a decline from 82.2 per cent to 77 per cent) and it also shows that European issues remained unaffected (a rise only from 5.5 per cent to 6.4 per cent). The slight peak of EU issues in 2003 might have been related to the impending enlargement of the EU. For the complete period, we see a low but stable vertical Europeanisation related to

Table 4.3   References to political issues

	1982	1989	1996	2003	2008	2013	References per paper (n)
Quality papers							
National policies (%)	62.3	75.4	67.4	56.7	75	69.6	3,375 (67.9%)
EU policies (%)	2.6	5.0	5.9	12.4	7.9	9.5	390 (7.8%)
Foreign and international policies (%)	35.1	19.5	26.6	30.9	17.1	21.0	1,208 (24.3%)
References per year (n)	*567*	*635*	*728*	*857*	*832*	*1,354*	*4,973 (100%)*
Regional papers							
National policies (%)	74.7	78.9	82.8	76.2	85.5	82	4,978 (80.2%)
EU policies (%)	2.3	2.8	2.9	4.5	5.2	5.0	235 (3.8%)
Foreign and international policies (%)	23.1	18.3	14.3	19.4	9.3	13.0	996 (16.0%)
References per year (n)	*967*	*902*	*1,210*	*1,049*	*1,052*	*1,029*	*6,209 (100%)*
Tabloid papers							
National policies (%)	68.9	77.4	79.2	64.9	84.5	80.5	4,555 (76.5%)
EU policies (%)	1.7	1.0	6.3	4.8	3.9	4.6	240 (4.0%)
Foreign and international policies (%)	29.4	21.7	14.5	30.3	11.6	15.0	1,158 (19.5%)
References per year (n)	*646*	*711*	*993*	*1,091*	*1,108*	*1,404*	*5,953 (100%)*
All papers							
National policies (%)	69.7	77.4	77.8	66.5	82.2	77.0	12,908 (75.3%)
EU policies (%)	2.2	2.8	4.8	6.8	5.5	6.4	865 (5.0%)
Foreign and international policies (%)	28.1	19.7	17.4	26.7	12.3	16.6	3,362 (19.6%)
References per year (n)	*2,180*	*2,248*	*2,931*	*2,997*	*2,992*	*3,787*	*17,135 (100%)*

Note: Multiple coding was possible; the table contains *n* = 17,135 references in *N* = 15,727 valid articles; 'other social issues' are excluded.

successive enlargement of the Union, despite the developing euro crisis. But it remains multi-segmented; it is the quality press that not only covers foreign and international issues extensively, but also reports more frequently than average on European matters.

Comparing trends of vertical Europeanisation in the newspapers analysed in each country (cf. Figure 4.2), the 2003 peak becomes especially obvious in countries like France (11.1 per cent), the UK (8.3 per cent) and Poland (7.7 per cent). This peak is not maintained, as all shares drop again in the next wave of article collection, although in France and Poland they still remain at a high level. Newspapers from Germany and especially Austria show a constantly rising awareness of EU issues. In sum, not represented here, Austria (6.5 per cent) shows the highest level of Europeanness, followed by France (5.7 per cent) and Germany (5.3 per cent), countered by the coverage of the UK (3.9 per cent), which reports extensively on national, but also on foreign and international policies. Poland (4.9 per cent) and Denmark (4.1 per cent) are middling in their degree of Europeanness.

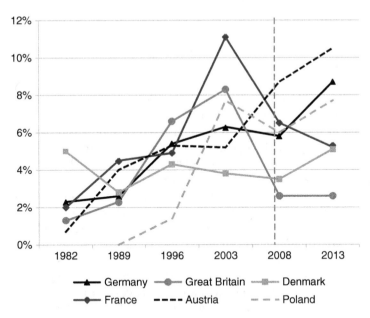

Figure 4.2 Vertical Europeanisation, based on the percentage of references to 'EU issues' by country from 1982 to 2013

Note: Multiple coding was possible; the figure contains $n = 17,135$ references in $N = 15,727$ valid articles.

Horizontal Europeanisation

Here we examine the extent to which national media are interested in and aware of what is going on in other countries. 'Mutual observation' and 'discursive exchange' are two indicators for the horizontal Europeanisation of public spheres. They focus on cross-border flows of opinions and arguments, and thereby show to what extent public debates in member states are integrated into a common European discourse. This dimension was measured by considering the range of countries mentioned in the articles, as well as the extent to which foreign speakers were quoted either directly or indirectly and the origins of those speakers. National references and national speakers are those explicitly named or implicit in the content of the article, and that relate to the domestic origin of the newspaper in question. References to speakers from 'European member states' and 'EU speakers' relate to European nations that are EU members and therefore part of the community at the time of reporting. Besides 'US references', references to all other foreign countries or to their speakers are included in 'other foreign countries'. 'Transnational speakers' are those who – like Ban Ki-Moon, the Secretary-General of the UN – represent international and transnational organisations, and are not explicitly connected to their national origin.

Using a total of 71,614 'references to countries' as a first indicator of horizontal Europeanisation, it becomes clear in Figure 4.3 that after a trend towards Europeanisation in the first half of the 1990s (from 15 per cent to 20.7 per cent), development has consolidated and is now quite stable at a level of around 21 per cent, independent of the Union's extent and the general political climate. Whereas reporting about the member states of the European Community in 1982 included 10 countries, reporting in the second half of 2013 potentially includes 28 member states of the EU. This integration process is dealt with by counting a reference to a country as a member or non-member at the time of publication. Results in the category 'European member states' have thus been calculated dynamically, that is country references were recoded from being non-EU member to being EU member depending on their status during the period of data-coding (Poland for instance was coded as a non-EU member in the years 1982 to 2003 and as an EU member ever since). Where national references and references to the US persist at a more or less stable level, we observe a stronger decrease of references to other, non-European countries, which is obviously the other side of the coin of Europeanisation. However, concentrating on the period of the

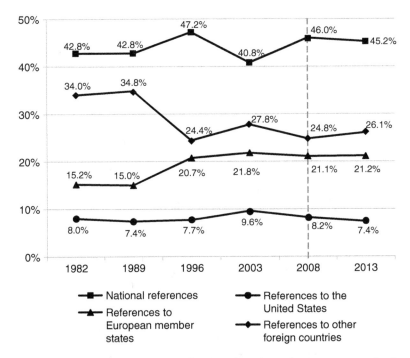

Figure 4.3 Horizontal transnationalisation, based on the percentage of references to 'countries' from 1982 to 2013

Note: Multiple coding was possible; figure contains $n = 71,614$ references in $N = 38,705$ valid articles.

euro crisis, none of the indicators' characteristics seems to be affected. In sum the overall distribution of country references links 44.2 per cent of national references to 19.5 per cent inner-European references, 8.1 per cent references to the United States as a special global player and 28.2 per cent of references to countries from the rest of world.

Figure 4.4 shows the transnational outlet-related segmentation of horizontal Europeanisation. This demonstrates the consistency of this development, manifest in equal trends of Europeanisation and its consolidation on a 'stable plateau' in 2003 for all papers, but at different levels. Again, quality newspapers are the most likely media type contributing to mutual observation, focussing attention on events in other European member states.

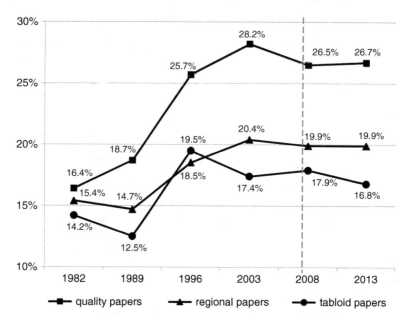

Figure 4.4   Horizontal Europeanisation, based on the percentage of references to 'EU member states' by newspaper type from 1982 to 2013

Note: Multiple coding was possible; figure contains $n = 71,614$ in $N = 38,705$ valid articles.

A second indicator of transnational discourse is the 'origin of the speakers' quoted within articles. If actors from other European countries, irrespective of their function in society, are directly or indirectly quoted, we might assume the existence of an integrated discourse culture among European member states. In contrast to the first indicator (but similar to the difference in percentages between 'speakers from political institutions' and 'political institutions' in section 4.1.1), it is noticeable in Table 4.4 that the share of references for the origin of speakers tends to a higher percentage for national speakers compared with those from foreign countries. Where in the overall distribution national speakers are quoted on average 76.7 per cent of the time, European speakers are only quoted on average 7.5 per cent of the time; speakers from other nations are quoted in 9.3 per cent of instances, American speakers in 5.1 per cent and transnational speakers in 1.4 per cent of the cases. These are on the whole rather low and slightly fluctuating trends in references to all non-national speakers, although we also detect a slight increase during the period of euro crisis between 2008 and 2013. Thus, we do not only have stable Europeanisation for the whole duration (from 7.6 per cent

Table 4.4   Origin of referred speakers

		1982	1989	1996	2003	2008	2013	References per paper (n)
Quality papers	National speakers (%)	50.6	51.1	56.9	58.0	64.5	55.5	5,659 (56.5%)
	EU speakers (%)	15.0	11.2	15.0	15.5	13.5	14.3	1,424 (14.2%)
	US speakers (%)	9.8	7.7	6.1	7.0	7.1	8.5	788 (7.9%)
	Transnational speakers (%)	0.8	0.9	1.2	2.5	0.5	3.9	258 (2.6%)
	Speakers from other nations (%)	23.8	29	20.8	17.1	14.5	17.8	1,895 (18.9%)
	References per year (n)	*593*	*847*	*1,038*	*1,223*	*1,300*	*5,023*	*10,024 (100%)*
Regional papers	National speakers (%)	79.7	82.2	85.5	81.8	85.9	85.4	19,365 (83.8%)
	EU speakers (%)	6.1	4.2	5.0	6.0	4.6	5.8	1,212 (5.2%)
	US speakers (%)	3.7	1.9	2.9	4.5	2.9	2.9	721 (3.1%)
	Transnational speakers (%)	0.9	0.8	1.3	1.7	1.8	1.4	321 (1.4%)
	Speakers from other nations (%)	9.6	10.8	5.2	6.0	4.9	4.6	1,488 (6.4%)
	References per year (n)	*2,786*	*3,106*	*4,026*	*3,908*	*5,074*	*4,207*	*23,107 (100%)*
Tabloid papers	National speakers (%)	78.4	74.6	80.2	77.9	81	81.4	11,908 (79.3%)
	EU speakers (%)	7.5	4.9	7.8	6.1	6.6	5.6	954 (6.4%)
	US speakers (%)	5.1	6.9	5.8	8.4	5.9	5.5	944 (6.3%)
	Transnational speakers (%)	0.3	0.3	0.3	0.7	0.4	1.4	97 (0.6%)
	Speakers from other nations (%)	8.7	13.3	6	6.9	6.2	6.0	1,110 (7.4%)
	References per year (n)	*1,533*	*1,893*	*2,645*	*2,666*	*2,683*	*3,593*	*15,013 (100%)*
All papers	National speakers (%)	75.8	75.2	79.8	76.7	81.4	72.6	36,932 (76.7%)
	EU speakers (%)	7.6	5.5	7.3	7.5	6.4	9.1	3,590 (7.5%)
	US speakers (%)	4.9	4.4	4.3	6.2	4.4	5.8	2,453 (5.1%)
	Transnational speakers (%)	0.7	0.7	0.9	1.5	1.2	2.4	676 (1.4%)
	Speakers from other nations (%)	11.1	14.3	7.6	8	6.6	10.2	4,493 (9.3%)
	References per year (n)	*4,912*	*5,846*	*7,709*	*7,797*	*9,057*	*12,823*	*48,144 (100%)*

Note: Multiple coding was possible; the table contains *n* = 48,144 references in *N* = 22,799 valid articles.

in 1982 up to 9.1 per cent in 2013), but also internationalisation in different directions during the euro crisis. Besides increasing references to speakers from European countries, speakers from other nations and American speakers are also quoted more frequently; transnational speakers even twice as much.

Regarding the segmentation of these trends in different newspapers, familiar patterns change and regional newspapers contrast with broadsheets over the proportion of some characteristics. For example, regional papers have more references to national speakers (a mean of 83.8 per cent) than tabloids (a mean of 79.3 per cent) and fewer references to European speakers (5.2 per cent compared with 7.5 per cent), to speakers from other nations (6.4 per cent compared with 9.3 per cent) and to American speakers (3.1 per cent compared with 6.3 per cent). In respect of the origin of speakers, tabloids seem to be more internationalised than regional papers. That is not so surprising, for it is not only political speakers that have been coded in this variable, but also international celebrities. All the same, quality papers have by far the lowest share of references to national issues (56.5 per cent) and the highest percentages of transnational references. Furthermore, it is only within quality papers that during the euro crisis there has been a noticeable internationalisation – at the expense of quoted national speakers (a decrease from 64.5 to 55.5 per cent). The frequency with which national actors have the opportunity of making themselves heard remains quite stable in the other papers. Here, tabloids increasingly refer to transnational actors (from 0.4 to 1.4 per cent), whereas regional papers cite speakers from European countries (from 4.6 to 5.8 per cent).

In Figure 4.5 we compare trends of horizontal Europeanisation across all countries. Firstly, it is obvious that from 1982 to 1989, references to speakers from European countries decrease, except in French and British newspapers. This is related to a generally higher share of references to international speakers during 1982–1989 not displayed here, which is probably caused by the political circumstances prior to the fall of the iron curtain. Secondly, the intermediate peak of references to European speakers in French and Polish newspapers in 2003 is in line with their peak of references to EU policies at that time. As already mentioned, this might be a pre-enlargement hint dealt with by one important old EU member and one of the accession candidates (cf. also Figure 4.2). Thirdly, there is a Europeanisation boost between 2008 and 2013, where references to European speakers increase in all countries. Average percentages, illustrating the degree of horizontal Europeanness, are identically

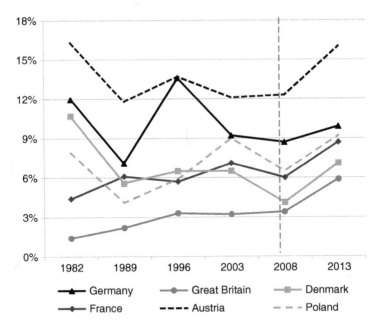

Figure 4.5   Horizontal Europeanisation, based on the percentage of references to 'speakers from EU member states' by newspaper type from 1982 to 2013

Note: Multiple coding was possible; the figure contains *n* = 48,144 references in *N* = 22,799 valid articles.

equal to the order in 2013 and also display, fourthly, a national segmentation. Austria (mean 13.8 per cent) and Germany (mean 10.0 per cent) show the highest proportions of direct and indirect quotations of speakers from other European countries. Newspapers from Poland (mean 7.5 per cent), France (mean 6.7 per cent) and Denmark (mean 6.5 per cent) follow on a slightly lower level; and finally references to European speakers within British newspapers bring up the rear with a mean of 3.6 per cent. Summing up and supplementing the results of the first indicator that reveal a constant awareness of other European countries, we conclude that the years of the euro crisis coincide with intensified discussion in and across the EU member states.

European identification

The third analytical dimension relates to the construction of communities as articulated in news coverage. European identity, for example the self-perception of being a part of the European community, is often considered a precondition for the legitimation of the European project (for example Bach et al. 2006; Bruter 2005; Herrmann/Brewer 2004; Kaina 2006; McLaren 2006; Risse 2004). European identity is a collective identity that is expressed in statements like 'we, the Europeans' or at least in the existence of a topos like 'the Europeans' within journalistic content. Hence we measured European identification within the indicators 'we-references' and collective identities as the 'significant others' in public discourse.

With regard to the first indicator (we-references) of the third dimension (based on a total of 28,859 we-references), we see, that European identification is still negligible. We differentiated between 'inclusive' and 'exclusive' we-references. The first refers to we-references that include the reader, for example, a 'national we' and a 'European we'. The latter means that the author of the article or an actor quoted in the article identifies himself or herself with a certain community, for example, 'we, the trade union' or 'we, the homosexuals'. News coverage seems to be quite reserved regarding reader-including references. As visible in Table 4.5, the overall distribution of we-references in the sample is dominated by 'exclusive we-references' (mean 76.3 per cent). References to a 'national we' follow with a mean of 22.9 per cent, while references to a 'European we' are barely visible and represented in only 0.8 per cent of cases.

Analysing we-references across time, it becomes obvious that exclusive we-references decrease continuously from 1996 (from 80.5 per cent to 74.1 per cent in 2013) to the advantage of national we-references, which increase from 18.9 per cent to 25.1 per cent at the same time. European we-references are at a minimal level, slightly growing until 2003 (from 0.2 per cent to 1.3 per cent) and stabilising since then (0.8 per cent).

Focussing exclusively on the level and trend of 'European we-references' in each newspaper type – although the sample size becomes quite small at that point – it becomes obvious in Figure 4.6 that if they can be found anywhere, it is most likely in the news coverage of quality papers. Taking into account the process of European integration, we only detect a peak in 2003 at 4.0 per cent, in advance of the eastward enlargement of the EU. Shares have continuously decreased since then (to 1.5 per cent in 2013). Regional papers show ups and downs, also including a peak in 2003 at 1 per cent but, also compared with tabloid papers, strongly decreasing towards the lowest proportion of 0.1 per cent in 2013. References in tabloid papers were quite volatile until the year 2008, but interestingly doubled their share in 2013 to 0.9 per cent.

Table 4.5 We-references

		1982	1989	1996	2003	2008	2013	References per paper (n)
Quality papers	National we (%)	48.9	47.4	38.7	41.6	34.4	34.8	2,161 (37.6%)
	European we (%)	0.7	1.4	2.2	4.0	2.6	1.5	114 (2.0%)
	Exclusive we (%)	50.4	51.2	59.1	54.4	63.0	63.8	3,468 (60.4%)
	References per year (n)	*274*	*492*	*543*	*678*	*925*	*2,831*	*5,743 (100%)*
Regional papers	National we (%)	20.4	19.1	16.6	14.7	20.8	14	3,018 (17.4%)
	European we (%)	0.1	0.9	0.3	1.0	0.5	0.1	82 (0.5%)
	Exclusive we (%)	79.5	80	83.2	84.3	78.7	85.9	14,206 (82.1%)
	References per year (n)	*1,996*	*2,251*	*3,079*	*2,897*	*3,746*	*3,337*	*17,306 (100%)*
Tabloid papers	National we (%)	19.1	15.1	15.3	26.9	28.6	29.6	1,421 (24.5%)
	European we (%)	0.5	0.3	0.5	0.2	0.4	0.9	33 (0.6%)
	Exclusive we (%)	80.4	84.6	84.2	72.8	71	69.6	4,356 (75.0%)
	References per year (n)	*413*	*610*	*941*	*913*	*751*	*2,182*	*5,810 (100%)*
All papers	National we (%)	23.1	22.5	18.9	21.2	24.2	25.1	6,600 (22.9%)
	European we (%)	0.2	0.9	0.5	1.3	0.8	0.8	229 (0.8%)
	Exclusive we (%)	76.7	76.6	80.5	77.5	74.9	74.1	22,030 (76.3%)
	References per year (n)	*2,683*	*3,353*	*4,563*	*4,488*	*5,422*	*8,350*	*28,859 (100%)*

Note: Multiple coding was possible; the table contains $n = 28,859$ references in $N = 12,928$ valid articles; 'We, the West' and 'We, the world/human mankind' are excluded.

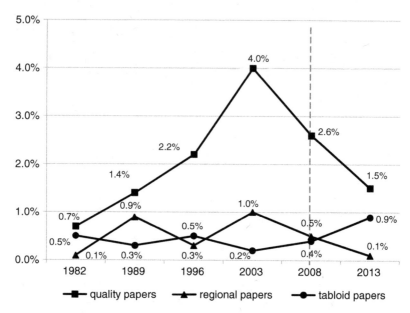

Figure 4.6   European identification, based on the percentages of 'European we-references' by newspaper type from 1982 to 2013

Note: Multiple coding was possible; the figure contains $n = 28{,}859$ references in $N = 12{,}928$ valid articles.

The second indicator (references to collective identities) for the third dimension is based on 9,231 items in total. In contradistinction to all other indicators, the overall distribution reveals a very small dominance of references to other nations (mean of 25.4 per cent) over references to the own nation (mean 24.4 per cent). Hence addressing significant others in public discourse seems to be as important as identifying oneself. Nonetheless, it has to be pointed out that this indicator does not record whether these collectives are negatively or positively connoted. In descending order, the other EU members are mentioned by 16.5 per cent individually, more than the other transnational collective identities that are other communities beyond the national frame such as religious or ethnic groups, mentioned in 14.5 per cent of the cases. The West as a community was named 7.2 per cent of the time, more often than the Americans at 6.8 per cent and lastly the Europeans with 5.2 per cent. It is remarkable that while the scope of references to the Europeans is insignificant, single European collectives like the Swedish or the Polish are relatively frequently addressed.

In Figure 4.7 it becomes evident that the trends of all references to collective identities fluctuate over time. Nonetheless, there are some notable tendencies. References to the own nation vary, but constantly increase in the long run (from 16.6 per cent to 34.7 per cent). References to the West as an identifiable collective fluctuate, but have constantly decreased since 1989 (from 13.8 per cent to 3.4 per cent). References to the community of the Europeans begin at a low level, fluctuate and finally decrease from 6 per cent to 3.8 per cent, whereas references to single European member states as collectivities are more frequent and increasingly addressed (from 13.1 per cent to 18.1 per cent). Similar to Figure 4.3 (references to the United States) and Table 4.4 (references to US-American speakers), we also observe here that references to the Americans are most frequently made in 2003, later falling back to the level of 1996. This peak might be explained by the involvement of the US in the Iraq war in 2003 and sustained attention to the US as a

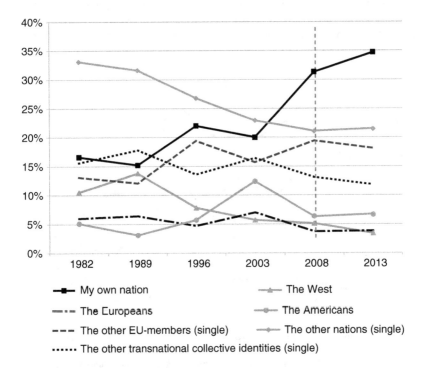

Figure 4.7   Transnational identification, based on the percentages of references to 'collective identities' from 1982 to 2013

Note: Multiple coding was possible; the figure contains $n = 9,231$ in $N = 4,714$ valid articles.

political player in the post-9/11 era. Regarding references to other foreign nations as collective identities, we detect a decrease from 33.1 per cent to 21.5 per cent. This tendency might be seen as complementing the decrease of references to other foreign nations that we have already seen for the country references in Figure 4.3. Here we have explained the decreasing interest in other nations as a consequence of the European integration process and the admission of more member states. In addition, we have to keep in mind the collapse of the USSR in 1989, resulting in the dissolution of the Western and Eastern spheres as closed political entities. References to other transnational collective identities fluctuate, but within a range of 11.8 per cent to 17.8 per cent.

Figure 4.8 directs attention to the trend of the characteristic 'the Europeans', where again clear patterns of transnational, outlet-related segmentation become obvious. The trends are nearly identical, but the level is different in a way typical for each newspaper type. All types of newspaper show that the pre-enlargement year of 2003 was very important for a collective European identity. References before and after were strikingly lower than in 2003, temporarily stopping a downward trend,

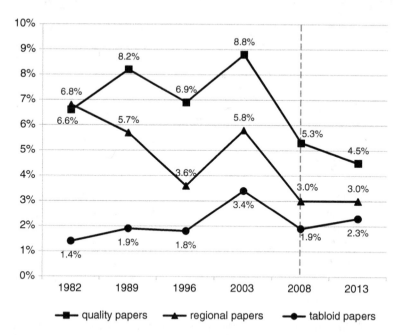

Figure 4.8   European identification, based on the percentages of references to the 'collective identity "The Europeans"' by newspaper type from 1982 to 2013

Note: Multiple coding was possible; the figure contains $n = 9,231$ in $N = 4,714$ valid articles.

with the exception of tabloid papers. The euro crisis does not seem to have had a direct impact, but it might support a more general trend of declining European identification.

Summarising the results regarding European identification within press coverage, we conclude that there is hardly any evidence of an explicitly expressed shared European identification: There is no growing common reference to 'We, the Europeans'. On the contrary, even the collective 'the Europeans' seems to lose weight in public discourse. Europe, however, is perceived in another way, namely identified by European countries that are increasingly addressed as single collective identities.

Reviewing these results regarding our three dimensions of Europeanisation and its six indicators, we detect a consolidation of Europeanisation trends. We have revealed a growing vertical Europeanisation up until 2003 and a more or less stable level until the present day. Horizontal Europeanisation has always been quite stable and to a considerable degree independent of the Union's extent. Purely European identification not only has an overall low level, but even decreases, from a temporary peak in 2003. Interestingly, only tabloids show a slight upward trend in European identification.

4.2 The ambassador: representing the idea of European middle-class audiences

As shown in chapter 3, we have detected different ways in which journalists address their imagined audience and shown how this refers to a stratification-related public discourse culture that we have derived from our newsroom studies and interviews. We distinguished four transnational modes of addressing audiences: the analyst, the ambassador, the reporter and the caterer, each characterised by particular journalistic practices and specific attitudes toward their professional self-conception, the EU and their audience. But what does their news coverage look like? Even if there is some research about journalists' working conditions and practices, it is rarely compared with the journalistic product (see for an exception Offerhaus 2012 on the EU scapegoating of journalists). When it comes to interviews and surveys with journalists, validity finds its limits in the lack of verifiability. The self-reporting of journalists might be inconsistent in respect of the professional standards expressed, claimed aspirations and actual professional practices. Despite knowing that these four modes of addressing audiences cannot be located at the level of individual journalists, we sorted our sample of newspapers corresponding to these four types. We move here beyond the common distinction of quality, regional and tabloid papers, and try to sketch the details of their news coverage against the backdrop of Europeanisation. By doing so we find how these specific modes of addressing audiences re-articulate certain stratification-related cultures of political discourse. We will especially focus here on the news coverage of the ambassador in comparison to the other types, since it addresses a rather middle-class audience by including journalists from quality, regional and tabloid newspapers (cf. Table 4.6).

As already stated, the ambassador follows an explanatory and clarifying, almost pedagogical approach in reporting on EU politics. From its pedagogical perspective, Europe seems to be a question of communication. Europe is communicated in a constructive and supportive manner, in close connection with the everyday life of the reader. We could expect a high proportion of European references, but we still need to assess empirically how Europeanised the ambassador's news coverage really is and what trends characterise this type of addressing audiences. We here focus on just one indicator per dimension, each time analysing the degree of Europeanness and the trend of Europeanisation as compared with other types.

Table 4.7 shows that the ambassador is ranked between the analyst (dominantly quality newspapers) and the reporter (dominantly regional newspapers), in respect of all characteristics. On the continuum from

Table 4.6   Newspapers behind the different modes of addressing audiences

Type of addressing	Newspapers	
Analyst	Die Presse (AT) Frankfurter Allgemeine Zeitung (GER) Le Monde (F) The Times (UK)	*Exclusively quality papers*
Ambassador	**Kleine Zeitung (AT) – regional newspaper** **Politiken (DK) – quality newspaper** **Ouest France (F) – regional newspaper** **Le Parisien (F) – tabloid newspaper** **Gazeta Wyborcza (PL) – quality newspaper**	*Includes all papers*
Reporter	Westdeutsche Allgemeine Zeitung (GER) Jydske Vestkysten (DK) Dziennik Zachodni (PL)	*Exclusively regional papers*
Caterer	Kronen Zeitung (AT) BILD (GER) Ekstra Bladet (DK), The Sun (UK)* Super Express (PL)*	*Exclusively tabloids*

Note: *Daily Express (UK) and Fakt (PL) were not part of the interview sample and were replaced by the above mentioned.

Table 4.7   References to speakers from political institutions

	Analyst	Ambassador	Reporter	Caterer	References (*n*)
National political institutions	93.8 (2,709)	95.8 (4,686)	96.4 (3,096)	97.1 (3,007)	13,498
EU institutions	5.3 (153)	3.3 (161)	2.8 (91)	2.3 (64)	472
UN institutions	0.9 (26)	0.9 (45)	0.7 (23)	0.7 (21)	116
All political institutions	*100%* *2,888*	*100%* *4,892*	*100%* *3,210*	*100%* *3,096*	*14,086*

Note: Multiple coding was possible; the table contains *n* = 14,086 references in *N* = 8,267 valid articles.

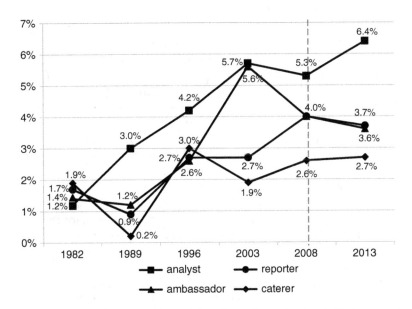

Figure 4.9   Vertical Europeanisation, based on the percentage of references to 'speakers from EU institutions' from 1982 to 2013
Note: Multiple coding was possible; the figure contains *n* = 14,086 references in *N* = 8,267 valid articles.

analyst to caterer, speakers from national political institutions are more frequently – and speakers from EU institutions decreasingly – addressed. UN institutions seem to lack attraction for all modes of addressing, there being hardly any references in news coverage.

In Figure 4.9, all modes of addressing start out at a quite similar level. From 1982 until 1996 the ambassador, reporter and caterer register hardly any differences in their percentage of references to speakers from EU institutions. However, in 2003 the ambassador moves up to the same level of Europeanisation as the analyst, although this then decreases immediately afterwards. Especially during the euro crisis period from 2008 to 2013, level and trend are again almost identical to that of the reporter. The ambassador seems to have played an important role in the early phases of eastward enlargement. Apart from that, the ambassador resembles the reporter in the trend of vertical Europeanisation.

In Table 4.8, with the exception of references to the US, the ambassador is again ranked between the analyst and the reporter for all characteristics. As regards horizontal Europeanness, the ambassador is positioned between the analyst and the reporter. Comparing percentages between analyst and caterer, it becomes obvious that the degree of Europeanness decreases, a pattern of segmentation in the European public sphere already sketched in the previous section. It is striking that with respect to trends in nationalisation and internationalisation, reporter and caterer obviously switch roles. The reporter has a higher level of national references (as expected) and the caterer, as compared with the reporter, has a higher proportion of US references and references to other, non-European countries.

What can we conclude about horizontal Europeanisation with respect to the ambassador? It also becomes clear in Figure 4.10 that all modes of addressing start in 1982 at a similar level, with only the reporter deviating slightly. Between 1989 and 1996 there is hardly any difference between the Europeanisation process on the part of the ambassador and the reporter. While the reporter continues on the same level for the next wave of data collection, the ambassador again registers the same level

Table 4.8   References to countries

	Analyst	Ambassador	Reporter	Caterer	References (*n*)
National	23.4	**39.4**	54.7	50.7	
references	(3,239)	**(7,139)**	(6,518)	(11,901)	28,797
References to EU	24.0	**21.9**	19.0	17.0	
member states	(3,321)	**(3,972)**	(2,271)	(3,992)	13,556
References to the	9.5	**7.0**	5.2	9.7	
United States	(1,320)	**(1,271)**	(620)	(2,269)	5,480
References to other	43.1	**31.7**	21.1	22.6	
foreign countries	(5,971)	**(5,718)**	(2,515)	(5,306)	19,510
All country	*100%*	***100%***	*100%*	*100%*	
references	*13,851*	***18,100***	*11,924*	*23,468*	*67,343*

Note: Multiple coding was possible; the table contains *n* = 67,343 in *N* = 35,740 valid articles.

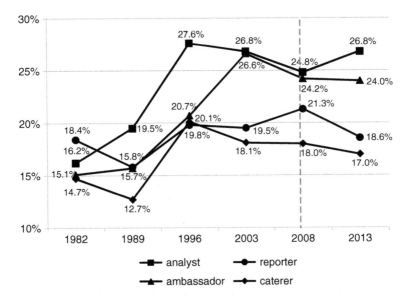

.*Figure 4.10* Horizontal Europeanisation, based on the percentage of references to 'EU member states' from 1982 to 2013

Note: Multiple coding was possible; the figure contains $n = 67,343$ references in $N = 35,740$ valid articles.

of Europeanisation as the analyst, but parallels their slowly decreasing trend until 2008. Despite the euro crisis, the Europeanisation level of the ambassador and of the caterer remains fairly constant, whereas the rate of European references on the part of the reporter decreases and the analyst's rate even increases slightly.

As visible in previous dimensions, the ambassador dominates (by three of seven characteristics) the analyst and the reporter in Table 4.9. We see again the segmentation patterns of increasing national references and decreasing references to the Europeans from analyst to caterer, whereas the ambassador tends more to the level of the reporter than to that of the analyst. Likewise, in section 4.1 there is a considerable degree of Europeanness if we consider attention to single European member states as collectivities, instead of all Europe as an entity.

In comparison with Figure 4.7 in the previous section, where we differentiated between the quality, regional and tabloid papers, we see some parallels in Figure 4.11, but also some differences. Decreasing references to Europeans as a collectivity in the reporter's news coverage, and the minimal and fluctuating references in the caterer's news

Table 4.9　References to collective identities

	Analyst	Ambassador	Reporter	Caterer	References (*n*)
My own nation	13.2	25.0	30.8	34.9	
	(350)	(755)	(603)	(491)	2,199
The West	10.3	6.2	7.0	3.3	
	(273)	(188)	(137)	(38)	636
The Europeans	9.3	4.0	3.8	2.0	
	(247)	(120)	(75)	(23)	465
The Americans	8.0	7.3	4.9	6.8	
	(213)	(219)	(95)	(83)	610
The other EU members (single)	14.1	16.4	18.7	15.8	
	(375)	(496)	(365)	(219)	1,455
The other nations (single)	24.8	28.7	22.6	25.7	
	(659)	(866)	(442)	(288)	2,255
The other transnational collective identities (single)	20.3	12.4	12.3	11.4	
	(540)	(373)	(240)	(125)	1,278
All references to collective identities	*100%*	*100%*	*100%*	*100%*	
	2,657	*3,017*	*1,957*	*1,267*	*8,898*

Note: Multiple coding was possible; the table contains *n* = 8,898 references in *N* = 4,657 valid articles.

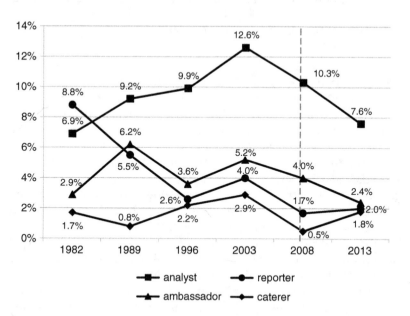

Figure 4.11　European identification, based on the percentages of references to the 'collective identity "The Europeans"' from 1982 to 2013

Note: Multiple coding was possible; the figure contains *n* = 8,898 references in *N* = 4,657 valid articles.

coverage remain unchanged. Characteristic of the ambassador are two peaks of European identification, one in 1989 and one at a lower level in 2003. But in the aftermath of enlargement, references to it are constantly decreasing – in parallel to the analyst, although at a lower level and not so severe. References to Europeans are also more prominent in 2003 than in 1989, but there is also the same strong decline after the last peak. Where there is segmentation, quality, regional and tabloid newspapers show clear and more or less similar trends at different levels, a categorisation by modes of addressing that reveals a greater distinction between analysts on the one hand and ambassador, reporter and caterer on the other. The latter is characterised by the lowest, but parallel, trend since 1996 and its convergence with the others at the same low level of European identification during last wave of data collection.

Summing up, we record that the ambassador is a transnational and transmedial mixed type, located between the analyst on the one side, and the reporter and caterer on the other. It has more similarity with the reporter and the caterer than with the elite-oriented analyst. Its pedagogy and its awareness promoting approach to Europe results in more Europeanised news coverage compared with other middle-class oriented reporters. This attitude was extremely visible in 2003, but later remained stable at a lower level and was not dramatically affected during the euro crisis.

4.3 The *Financial Times*: representing Europeans elite audiences

The fact that a European public sphere is not rooted in a genuinely European media because of existing national media systems directs our attention to transnational media. Transnational media are media that address audiences across national borders. Michael Brüggemann and Hagen Schulz-Forberg (2008) developed a typology of four different types of transnational media: national media with a transnational mission, international media, pan-regional media and global media. The *Financial Times (FT)*, part of the Pearson group, has a European edition and is a transnational newspaper that operates beyond the level of the individual member state. It is also an outstanding newspaper, being the newspaper of choice for all EU professionals. From interviews with these professionals, as well as with journalists familiar with Brussels, there is plenty of evidence that it has a privileged position in the Brussels press corps (Corcoran/Fahy 2009; Firmstone 2008; Offerhaus 2011: 113, 185, 215; Raeymaeckers et al. 2007). While only addressing elites, among scholars it is regarded as being influential in setting the agenda and framing EU coverage, and is a flourishing example of an evolving European discourse culture. Furthermore, it is assumed that it covers the EU in a style that is distinctively different from national newspapers. But how does the *FT* treat political news, given that it obviously has a transnational readership compared with other national quality press outlets? Could we expect a higher proportion of Europeanised news? The results of the following content analysis are based on a data set of 8,834 coded articles selected from one quality paper per country and *Financial Times Europe* ($N = 1,670$). It would certainly have been interesting to examine the development of news coverage during the present euro crisis; but since case numbers are too small, we will focus in the following only on a comparison of newspapers and use one indicator per dimension.

Exploring vertical Europeanness in 'references to transnational political institutions' reveals that the *FT* in fact has the lowest share of references to European institutions, 47.3 per cent (cf. Table 4.10). This goes along with the highest percentage of references to other international and transnational institutions such as NATO, OECD, EFTA, the World Bank and so on (39.6 per cent). It could be a question of journalistic style of news writing if in a written article an institution represents simply a named institution, or if actors representing political institutions are mentioned or quoted. However, while not displayed here, the *FT* has for the indicator 'speakers from transnational political institutions' also a higher, but still comparably low, share of EU references (57.8 per cent). Only *Gazeta Wyborcza*, from Poland (53.4 per cent) and the British *Times* (47.1 per cent) have lower shares. The German *Frankfurter Allgemeine Zeitung* and the Austrian *Die Presse* have a level of 80 per cent, and the French *Le Monde* and the Danish *Politiken* have at about 70 per cent a considerably higher proportion of references to institutional representatives of the EU. Additionally, it is important to note that on the other hand the *FT* and the British *Times* both have about 30 per cent of references to speakers from other international and transnational institutions.

We had to adopt a different approach when exploring horizontal Europeanness through references to countries. National references were counted as those referring to the country of residence of the newspaper in question. To assume that the *FT* is a European newspaper with no explicit domestic reference leads to an overestimation of references to other European member states within the *FT*, since all the EU references would end up in one category. Controlling by frequencies of the variable, which are those countries most often mentioned in the *FT*, it turned out that British references were the most frequent (20.3 per cent),

Table 4.10 References to transnational political institutions

	FAZ (GER)	Le Monde (F)	The Times (UK)	Die Presse (AT)	Politiken (DK)	Gazeta Wyborcza (PL)	Financial Times	References (*n*)
EU institutions	58.3 (350)	62.0 (419)	60.8 (236)	67.5 (407)	57.8 (273)	55.8 (410)	47.3 (416)	2,511
UN institutions	14.5 (87)	16.4 (111)	16.5 (64)	13.4 (81)	21.4 (101)	13.2 (97)	13.1 (115)	656
Other international/ transnational institutions	27.2 (163)	21.6 (146)	22.7 (88)	19.1 (115)	20.8 (98)	31.0 (228)	39.6 (348)	1,186
All references per paper	100% 600	100% 676	100% 388	100% 603	100% 472	100% 735	100% 879	4,353

Note: Multiple coding was possible; the table contains *n* = 4,353 references in *N* = 2,552 valid articles.

Table 4.11   References to countries

	FAZ (GER)	Le Monde (F)	The Times (UK)	Die Presse (AT)	Politiken (DK)	Gazeta Wyborcza (PL)	Financial Times	References (n)
National references	21.4 (857)	20.6 (692)	30.7 (1,020)	21.2 (670)	30.7 (872)	26.1 (1,189)	20.3 (1,013)	6,313
References to EU member states	24.0 (961)	22.8 (768)	20.2 (671)	29.1 (921)	21.8 (621)	27.8 (1,266)	20.9 (1,040)	6,248
References to the United States	9.1 (365)	8.7 (292)	11.7 (388)	8.7 (275)	8.8 (251)	7.5 (343)	15.2 (756)	2,670
References to other foreign countries	45.4 (1,814)	47.9 (1,611)	37.5 (1,246)	41.1 (1,300)	38.7 (1,100)	38.6 (1,762)	43.6 (2,175)	11,008
All references	100%	100%	100%	100%	100%	100%	100%	26,239
per paper	3,997	3,363	3,325	3,166	2,844	4,560	4,984	

Note: Multiple coding was possible; the table contains *n* = 26,239 references in *N* = 8,830 valid articles.

followed by the US (15.2 per cent), Germany (5.0 per cent), France (4.9 per cent) and then other countries (54.6 per cent). We therefore recoded British references as national references within the *FT*. As presented in Table 4.11, it becomes obvious that the *FT* shows the lowest portion of national, i.e. British references (20.3 per cent) – the British *Times* shows the highest (30.7 per cent), but horizontal Europeanness, at 20.9 per cent, is still quite weakly developed. This percentage is quite similar to that of the British *Times* (20.2 per cent) and the Danish *Politiken* (21.8 per cent). There are more references to other EU member states in the Austrian *Die Presse* (29.1 per cent) and the Polish *Gazeta Wyborcza* (27.8 per cent). Turning back to the *FT*, its news coverage shows, at 15.2 per cent, the highest percentage of US references (followed by the British *Times* with 11.7 per cent) and a quite high share of references to other foreign countries (43.6 per cent).

Exploring the degree of European identification based on references to collective identities, we refer to two characteristics in Table 4.12. Firstly, the share of references to 'the Europeans' as a collectivity; and secondly, the share of references to 'European members' as single collectivities, for example, 'the Spanish', 'the Italians' and so on. Regarding the first, the *FT* has at 4.6 per cent a below-average rate. Regarding the second characteristic, it has the lowest proportion (21.6 per cent) compared with the other European newspapers. Here the Danish *Politiken* (47.3 per cent), the Polish *Gazeta Wyborcza* (45.6 per cent) and the Austrian *Die Presse* (40.6 per cent) show a considerable degree of European identification although, as already remarked, we do not know whether these collectivities are negatively or positively attributed. Last but not least, as in the previous dimension the British *Times* (12.6 per cent) and the *FT* (14.3 per cent) address the Americans as a collective on an almost equal level. Furthermore, this newspaper has a highly transnationalised news coverage based on the outstanding proportion of references to other non-European countries (49.0 per cent). Other transnational collective identities seem to be of subordinate importance, the rate of 10.9 per cent compared with the other newspapers being also the lowest score.

Summing up, the news coverage of *Financial Times Europe*, European's elite medium by readership, is less Europeanised than expected. Its level is the same as a middle-range paper among the continental European quality papers. Instead, it has some parallels with the British Anglo-American political axis, indicated by the great attention paid to the United States. Furthermore, it is a newspaper that is much more focussed on international and global news beyond the European horizon.

Table 4.12   References to collective identities

	FAZ (GER)	Le Monde (F)	The Times (UK)	Die Presse (AT)	Politiken (DK)	Gazeta Wyborcza (PL)	Financial Times	References (n)
The Europeans	13.0 (115)	9.8 (76)	9.2 (43)	5.2 (16)	3.0 (11)	2.8 (37)	4.6 (22)	320
The Americans	9.6 (85)	7.9 (61)	12.6 (59)	3.9 (12)	7.5 (28)	8.2 (109)	14.3 (69)	423
The other EU members (single)	24.5 (216)	35.7 (277)	25.5 (119)	40.6 (126)	47.3 (176)	45.6 (607)	21.6 (104)	1,625
The other nations (single)	24.9 (220)	27.7 (215)	30.4 (142)	31.3 (97)	30.4 (113)	29.2 (388)	49.0 (236)	1,411
The other transnational collective identities (single)	28.0 (247)	18.9 (147)	22.3 (104)	19.0 (59)	11.8 (44)	14.3 (190)	10.6 (51)	842
All references per paper	100% 883	100% 776	100% 467	100% 310	100% 372	100% 1,331	100% 482	4,621

Note: Multiple coding was possible; the table contains $n = 4,621$ in $N = 2,367$ valid articles.

4.4   The European public sphere: a plateau of multi-segmented Europeanisation

Relating our empirical analysis back to the questions of how Europe is communicatively constructed within press coverage and how this construction might have changed during the euro crisis, the following result is striking: The multi-segmented European public sphere formed at the end of the 1990s did not break up under pressure from the euro crisis. It remained at the plateau achieved years before, despite the euro crisis. However, within this plateau, the euro crisis constituted an irritation within newspaper-based communicative construction of Europe.

Vertical Europeanisation took place in the 1990s and reached its plateau in 2003, in the run-up to European eastward enlargement. This involves a time frame during which the former European Community was deepened through several treaties, such as the Treaty of Maastricht (Treaty on European Union, 1992 signed, in force since 1993), the Treaty of Amsterdam (1997 signed, in force since 1999) and the Treaty of Nice (2001 signed, in force since 2003), then widened by the northern enlargement of the EU in 1995 (accession of Austria, Finland and Sweden) and the eastern enlargement in 2004 (accession of the Czech Republic, Estonia, Cyprus, Latvia, Lithuania, Hungary, Malta, Poland, Slovenia and Slovakia). Compared with national politics and monitoring of policies, the monitoring of the political institutions of the EU moves at a rather low level. Nonetheless, we found this development to be converging in all countries, with only slight differences among countries during the period of euro crisis. Vertical Europeanisation based on references to EU policies seemed to be more nationally shaped by individual members or groups of member states.

Integrating other European countries and their representatives into news coverage, described above as horizontal Europeanisation, has been on a higher level. Depending on choice of indicator, horizontal Europeanisation plateaued in 1996 (countries) or had a peak in 2003 (origin of speakers). While references to countries turned out to be quite stable over time, references to speakers from different countries fluctuate more greatly. Considering both indicators for the period of the euro crisis, the news coverage has to be seen in a wider context of internationalisation than renationalisation. If we focus exclusively on the development of speakers from European countries, we realise that public awareness is obviously more sensitive towards political circumstances. All countries showed a temporary reduction of references in 2008, but came back to an even higher level than before in 2013. Hence, in the time of the euro crisis, an intensified discussion among European speakers develops that also found the ear of journalists.

Indicators for European identification were weakly marked. European we-references are indeed constant over time, but nearly non-existent. There are references to the collective 'the Europeans', but they lose weight over time. However, what is obvious instead is that references to single EU members as collectivities are at a good middle-range level and increasing over time. This suggests at least the European motto 'united in diversity', acknowledged by the fact that increasingly European member states are recognised and addressed as associate societies, and not only mentioned political actors.

Regarding the national segmentation of the European public sphere, as also proved by other studies (for example Pfetsch et al. 2008), it is press outlets from the founder states France and Germany that show a considerable degree of Europeanisation. On the opposite side of the pole, it is the British press that has on all dimensions low shares relating to European institutions and actors, and many references to domestic institutions and actors, as well as in some cases comparably higher shares of references to the US. The Austrian and Polish press represent member states that joined the EU during the period of investigation. While Austrian news coverage demonstrates strong trends of Europeanisation and a rather high degree of Europeanness on nearly all dimensions, Polish papers, though representing a Europhile country, developed ambivalent trends of Europeanisation. One the one hand, Polish papers caught up very quickly with the political side of Europeanisation, referring to EU institutions and EU topics, but on the other hand they also show a declining number of references to the social project of European belonging. Finally, the Danish press is marked by a rather low degree of Europeanness on all dimensions. Regarding an outlet-related segmentation of the European public sphere, quality broadsheets favour the Europeanisation of news coverage, while regional and especially tabloid papers rarely report on European issues – and if they do, in a less Europeanised way. Nonetheless, trends towards Europeanisation could be traced for all papers until 2003, declining shortly afterwards.

An additional insight was offered by reconstructing the characteristics of news coverage from the ambassador, which has been identified as a specific transnational and transmedial type of addressing audiences among the journalists interviewed. Following a middle-class oriented and rather pedagogical approach, the ambassadors set their sights on communicating Europe in a constructive and supportive manner, and likewise relating it back the everyday life of their reader. News coverage of this type of addressing is fairly Europeanised. Admittedly, it ranks below the quality press; but it shows higher shares of European references than the regional and tabloid press. Also reviewed for its European qualities, the elite press outlet *Financial Times Europe* did not turn out to be as Europeanised as expected. Though read by the European elite, it does not necessarily represent an example of an evolving European discourse culture in the sense of representing an inner-European, self-referential and therefore identity-building media discourse. Instead the news coverage of the *FT* confirms its claim to being a global medium for highly internationalised and globalised news coverage, placing and contextualising Europe in world politics.

Notwithstanding that a longitudinal approach like ours is based only on very rough indicators of Europeanisation, it is stable across media outlets, its national peculiarities and its modifications in appearance over time. The period of the euro crisis could be placed in a wider time frame of transnational communication processes within different European press outlets. This multi-segmented European public press sphere has proved to be quite stable. However, what is written in the newspaper does not inevitably constitute popular opinion or active participation in the communicative construction of Europe.

5
Citizens' Online Engagement: The Euro Crisis in Online Forums

As we have seen, the euro crisis did not lead to a collapse of the European public sphere in our six research countries, at least not in the sense of either an increase or a decrease in reporting on European issues. However, as we will show in this and the following chapters, people across Europe do perceive the euro crisis as a major issue in their connection to a European public sphere. And so the question remains of what exactly happens in a situation like the euro crisis (cf. our definition in chapter 2). In this context, Klaus Eder reminds us that a '[c]risis is more than the discourse about it: It is a social process' (Eder 2014: 221). Focusing on crisis-related social processes necessitates a shift to the level of citizens and to their perceptions of the euro crisis.

The aim of this chapter is to identify how citizens as part of the actor constellation of the European public sphere are communicatively engaged in processes relating to the euro crisis. One way for such engagement to take place is via the internet; and, among other possibilities, through discussions of the euro crisis in online comment forums. In our analysis, we treat online comment forums narrowly, as communicative spaces that are accessible online (sometimes requiring registration) and embedded into websites offering or linking to journalistic content – either from traditional news media, or from professional, semi-professional or amateur bloggers – and in which users communicatively engage by writing and publishing comments. At the same time, we are aware that online comment forums appear in a multitude of different – also non-journalistic – settings. In our analysis, comment forums represent a connection between news media content through which many people realise elements of their public connection to Europe, and a communicative space where citizens possibly voice their thoughts and perceptions on issues like the euro crisis and contribute new perspectives, as the empirical evidence demonstrates

(Baden/Springer 2014). We can therefore here observe, analyse and follow *in situ* the way in which citizens supersede mere connection to a European public sphere by actively taking voice (cf. chapter 2) and communicatively engaging in social processes relating to the euro crisis, moving beyond news media discourse about it.

The internet, especially the social web, offers citizens a new position within the actor constellation of the European public sphere for two reasons. First, citizens as users can actively take part in communication about Europe and the EU. This enables users to engage in the communicative construction of the euro crisis, the EU and of Europe through their online practices. Second, because of its technological capabilities the internet provides an opportunity to communicate across national borders; therefore the communicative engagement of the citizens might be transnational. Here, an important question is how we might conceptualise online forums in relation to the European public sphere. We could understand them as a separated online public sphere – a space of communication mainly related to citizens' activities, where questions on the legitimacy of European institutions are being negotiated (Michailidou 2010: 67; Wright 2007: 1170). Alternatively, we could regard them as an integral part of the European public sphere, which means understanding the European public sphere as a thickened space of communication comprising both 'old' and 'new media'.

Our empirical data suggest that this latter position is more fruitful. The newspapers analysed in the chapter before are increasingly shifting to online publishing. A representative comparative analysis of online users' news habits covering all of our research countries except for Austria and Poland, demonstrated that, while TV remains a major source of news information across nation states, news media websites are almost equally often named as people's major source of information, especially among the younger generation (Nielsen/Schrøder 2014: 479). The comment forums analysed within this chapter are part of these online offerings. However, one also needs to acknowledge that commenting occurs to a much lesser degree. Around 8 per cent to 11 per cent of online users in the Nielsen and Schrøder study were found to comment on news stories on social networking sites and between 5 per cent to 8 per cent on news media websites during an average week. Users who comment on news stories are, therefore, not the majority of online users, but they represent a 'significant minority' (2014: 484). That is why the engagement in these online communicative spaces rather is an addition to peoples' public connection. The separation of printed media's European public sphere from an online European public sphere would, under modern conditions, be inadequate.

Online forums and other kinds of online media offer an opportunity for individuals to assume a specific actor role within the actor constellation of the European public sphere. This said, in online forums we are again confronted with the interplay of the national and the transnational, as highlighted in the previous chapter. As we will demonstrate, online forums are first of all segmented into national hyperlink structures, while there are very few transnational hyperlinks. However, as with the printed newspaper, the national or transnational range is not the main point of transnationality. Instead, our analysis reveals that users' communicative practices and the related processes of communicative construction are by and large transnationally shared, even when they occur in nationally segmented forums. The forums in our sample cannot really be distinguished according to their national embedding, but rather according to their dominance on either more 'relation-oriented' or more 'issue-oriented' interactions. Relation-oriented interactions involve users' interest in building and maintaining relationships with other users through their communication about the euro crisis and Europe. In issue-oriented interactions, users are more focused on the euro crisis as the main topic of discussion. Both orientations of interaction are relevant to communicatively constructing the euro crisis, the EU and Europe.

Reviewing the existing literature, there were high hopes for the internet in general and the social web in particular for supporting enhanced engagement of citizens with the European public sphere. In the context of their supposed democratic deficit, European institutions took up the social web as a way of involving European citizens in a direct communicative exchange, fostering their own legitimation on the basis of discursivity and deliberation (Michailidou 2010: 81; Michailidou et al. 2012; Sarikakis/Lodge 2013: 169). However, the high expectations for European democracy that were projected onto the social web proved to be over-optimistic, since online forums set up by EU institutions often implied an elite participatory bias (Wodak/Wright 2007: 402; Wright 2007: 1178), while those who did engage people in transnational online communication failed to live up to the anticipated high standards of rational public discourse and deliberation (Rasmussen 2013: 99; Trenz 2009: 44). Consequently, the expectation that the provision of online forums by institutions promotes democratic and legitimatory engagement with the EU on the part of citizens involves a purely technological perception of the prospects of online forums. The way in which users appropriated forums introduced by the EU shows that participants in online discussion have their own interests when communicating online, which possibly diverge from those of the institutions (Karlsson 2012: 65).

We developed our approach here in two stages. First we used a web-crawler to isolate the hyperlink networks of political websites for every research country in the sample, as well as for a transnational European level (Issuecrawler, cf. Rogers 2010, cf. appendix for details). These results enabled us to identify principal political websites for each country through which a connection to a political public sphere might be realised. We then drew a sample of online forums from the hyperlink networks of these political websites. During the week of a so-called European Crisis summit in June 2012, we then selected all user comments that were published on European issues within these forums. These comments were analysed with the help of an interaction analysis. Our aim here was to identify 'typical communicative practices' and the 'forms of interaction' in which citizens engaged when participating in online discussion of the euro crisis. These steps of the analysis also form the structure of this chapter. In the first section, we present the results of our hyperlink analysis and outline the main online forums so isolated. The second section presents the results of our interaction analysis for the online forums. Finally, we conclude by considering both stages of the analysis regarding citizens' online involvement in the communicative construction of Europe.

5.1   The political web across Europe: national segmentation and transnational websites

One way to assess where citizens make their connection to a European public sphere online and where they might potentially communicate about the euro crisis is to treat hyperlinks as the web's inherent reference structure from a network-analytical perspective. Here the focus was on hyperlink networks between political websites. This approach moves beyond the isolated treatment of news media in the context of European public spheres since hyperlink networks can cover a wide range of political websites, not only those involving news media but also websites established, for example, by civil society actors (Bennett et al. 2015: 111). What is initially a purely technological approach to hyperlinks can, therefore, be widened to incorporate a citizens' perspective, as we will show in the following. Furthermore, the resulting hyperlink maps allow assessment of the distribution of political websites within or across national boundaries.

Our analysis presumes national segmentation of the European public sphere, but transfers this idea to the internet. Most hyperlink networks of political websites remain within a national frame which segments the

European public sphere nationally. However, some transnational communicative spaces emerge across these networks of national hyperlinks. There are a number of distinct political websites from other nation states embedded in national hyperlink networks. These constitute select transnational links beyond the otherwise predominantly national frame. We, therefore, reveal the interplay between national and transnational political communicative spaces on the internet, although national segmentation is mostly dominant.

Our analysis does not demonstrate the general existence of a commonly shared communicative space across Europe via the internet. Overall, the results show that the networks of political websites are mostly made up of hyperlinks in a national frame. This corroborates empirical findings that, despite the internet's transnational potential, nationally based communication still dominates the World Wide Web (Curran et al. 2012: 10). Outgoing and incoming links were by and large to and from websites within the same nation state, established through the country-specific top-level domains. The German, French, Polish and UK networks especially have this national distribution of hyperlinks (cf. Figures 5.1, 5.2, 5.3 and 5.6). In nations that belong to a larger geopolitical space, such as Austria and Denmark and which are also among the smaller states in the sample, networks have rather more transnational linkage (cf. Figures 5.4 and 5.5). These are, however, mostly set within a common language area. There are, for example, some outgoing links towards German online news media in the Austrian hyperlink network and to Scandinavian websites in the Danish case.

For the national hyperlink networks, different web services (websites from mainstream news media, political blogs, political institutions and so on) are represented as central political websites in the network, which all remain in their respective national frame, with only some links to global websites such as *Google*, *Twitter* and *Facebook*. These websites, especially social networking sites and blogging platforms, indicate one limitation that we encountered in our approach to the webcrawler. Such platforms have an influence on the constitution of the hyperlink network, as, for example, in the French or Polish case (cf. Figure 5.2 and Figure 5.3). For the Polish blogosphere, a small number of different blogging platforms are important. The links between these platforms dominate the crawl. However, most of the time these links cannot be traced back to a conscious and individual user decision linking to a different website, but are instead set within the architecture of these platforms. The network is, therefore, constituted through a number of different clusters, mostly centred on one platform, with only some links to other

Figure 5.1   Hyperlink network for Germany

Source: Govcom.org Foundation (2015), Issue Crawler Software, Amsterdam, http://issue-crawler.net

websites outside of these clusters. When analysing the network of hyper-links we therefore need to keep in mind that not all hyperlinks are deep links and often do not go back to an individual user decision regarding a connection to the content of a different website. Having in mind the constitutive role that hyperlinks play in the architecture of the World Wide Web, this reminds us of the user's position in a constellation of different actors who all contribute to the emergence of hyperlink networks and possibly also to their national segmentation.

Even within the transnational European network of hyperlinks, it is possible to identify this national segmentation of political websites (cf. Figure 5.7). The websites of political blogs, mainstream news media and political institutions are grouped together, based on a combination of the topic they deal with and their geographical focus (blogs on UK domestic

Figure 5.2 Hyperlink network for France

Source: Govcom.org Foundation (2015), Issue Crawler Software, Amsterdam, http://issue-crawler.net

politics, UK blogs on European politics, European blogs on European politics, European institutions and so on). But a number of mainstream news media sites from the UK (*BBC, The Times, The Guardian*), France (*Le Monde*) or transnational sites (*Financial Times, The Economist*) appear throughout this European network.

The national segmentation of political websites on the internet partly confirms previous findings concerning online communication and the European public sphere. An early study by Ruud Koopmans and Ann Zimmermann investigated search engine results in order to map transnational tendencies on the internet. For queries relating to seven EU policy fields, they found that the content that they were led to was in large parts comparable to traditional national news media content (Koopmans/Zimmermann 2003: 18; 2010). Drawing on an analysis of hyperlink networks dealing with the issue of fair trade and climate

Figure 5.3　Hyperlink network for Poland
Source: Govcom.org Foundation (2015), Issue Crawler Software, Amsterdam, http://issue-crawler.net

change, Bennett et al. similarly conclude that websites from interest groups are firstly, not greatly involved in issue networks at the European level but remain nationally segmented; and secondly, are not concerned about engaging publics in the communication process (Bennett et al. 2015: 134). These findings correspond to the national segmentation that we found throughout our own hyperlink networks. But our analysis demonstrates that one also needs to consider single transnational communicative spaces emerging within these overall networks: Parallel to national segmentation, there are moments of transnationality in several of our national webcrawls, as well as in the European crawl. Across all of our research countries, major international news media are regularly found within the networks, like, for example, the *New York Times* in the Austrian crawl or the *Huffington Post* in the UK network. These

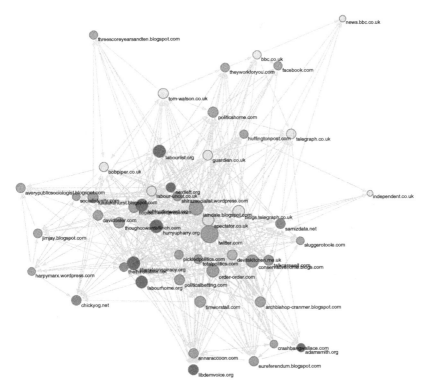

Figure 5.4   Hyperlink network for United Kingdom

Source: Govcom.org Foundation (2015), Issue Crawler Software, Amsterdam, http://issue-crawler.net

findings point to some singular moments of transnationality within the networks, despite a predominant national segmentation across all networks. Unsurprisingly, when it comes to transnationality, news media websites in English are of especial importance. We find hyperlinks going to and coming from news media like *The Guardian, The BBC, The Financial Times* and *Le Monde* across different webcrawls, which thereby play the part of transnationally relevant websites. Hence, our analysis also confirms the assumption that transnational political communicative spaces exist online. These transnational hyperlinking practices on the web therefore in part contribute to a European public sphere based on the transnational potential of technologies, something that Ingrid Volkmer equally discusses with respect to satellite technology in Europe (Volkmer 2008: 235; 2011: 6).

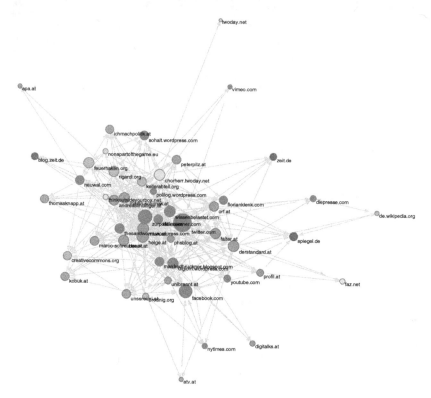

Figure 5.5   Hyperlink network for Austria

Source: Govcom.org Foundation (2015), Issue Crawler Software, Amsterdam, http://issue-crawler.net

From these findings regarding the analysis of hyperlink networks, people's public connection to Europe through the internet is likely to take place within a national frame. However, in the same way that the lack of a common Europe-wide media system does not signify the non-existence of a European public sphere, but rather points to fundamental differences between national and transnational public spheres (Gripsrud 2007: 483; Peters 2008: 192), the national segmentation of political websites likewise does not automatically imply that the internet fails to support the emergence of a European public sphere. Transnationality on the internet does not only manifest itself in the national or transnational embedding of specific websites, nor in a purely technical sense through hyperlinks. Rather, technological objects such as hyperlink structures have to be related to their wider embedment

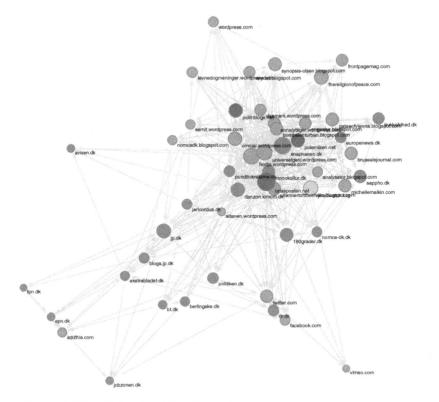

Figure 5.6 Hyperlink network for Denmark

Source: Govcom.org Foundation (2015), Issue Crawler Software, Amsterdam, http://issue-crawler.net

in people's actual communicative practices. In order to clarify some of the supposedly ambivalent observations concerning European public spheres online, this amounts to a re-conceptualisation of transnationality in online communication. Alongside technological structures, our study also addresses users' communicative practices, the content of their online communication and the related processes of communicatively constructing Europe, enabling us to assess the transnational dimension of a European public sphere online.

For this purpose our crawler analysis enabled us to isolate central online forums for each of our research countries as well as at the transnational European level. The analysis of the hyperlink networks revealed that a number of different political websites were important for every nation state in the sample. Using these results, news media,

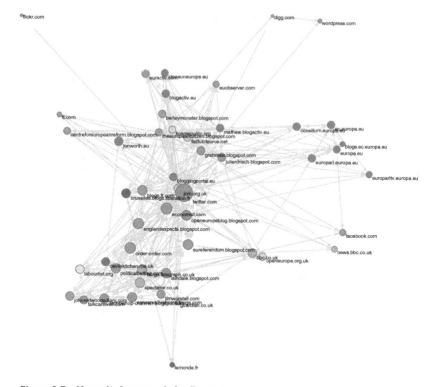

Figure 5.7   Hyperlink network for Europe

Source: Govcom.org Foundation (2015), Issue Crawler Software, Amsterdam, http://issue-crawler.net.

blogs and also *Facebook* as a social networking site were chosen as a preliminary filter for identifying forums for the second step of the analysis. Besides revealing the hyperlink networks, the crawler also delivers a 'per page ranking' listing of the most interlinked websites. From this list, we selected the first 20 news media and blogs that came up, confirmed their general political focus, selected those that had a comment forum which was freely accessible as well as actively used on a daily basis, and included further website ranking data. We based the forum selection of one news media and one blog for each country on this procedure (cf. appendix for a detailed description).

As regards sampling, one difficulty was that the network of hyperlinks did not allow us to differentiate websites into the webpages they contain. The appearance of websites like *Google*, *Twitter*, *Facebook* and similar platforms in the network demonstrates that they have some relevance, but we could not say which specific account or page is relevant as a political space. We therefore had to apply a different sampling technique for *Facebook*, which came up as the most important social networking site within the crawls. Here we referred back to the news media and blogs we had listed before. Since most bloggers did not have active *Facebook* accounts, we only sampled the *Facebook* accounts of the news media already included for every country and for the transnational European level, including a second news media account, which was sampled in the same fashion (cf. Table 5.1 for an overview of the forum selection).

5.2   Online practices: relation- and issue-oriented interactions on Europe

Transnationality in online communication on the topic of the euro crisis is articulated through the forms taken by users' communicative practices and the content of their online communication. We relate this to our distinction between vertical and horizontal connectivity in transnationalisation (cf. chapter 2). As vertical and horizontal dimensions of Europeanisation, they are often applied to traditional news media content. Citizens as online users communicate, however, not only about the supranational EU level or intergovernmental level relating to other EU member states (vertical and horizontal dimensions), but they also build communicative linkages in direct – sometimes even transnational – interactions (vertical and horizontal connectivity). Here it becomes obvious that the transnationally embedded websites we identified via our hyperlink analysis offer communicative possibilities for engagement in such transnational communication, as we will also show in the following.

Socio-linguistic studies have shown how users in online comment forums construct specific narratives and ideas about the euro crisis in their online communication (Angouri/Wodak 2014; Georgakopoulou 2014). The internet has the potential to involve people in the communicative construction of the euro crisis and thereby Europe. But to what extent do users share communicative practices and processes of communicative construction across nation states? While we have a dominant national segmentation at the level of hyperlink structures, it remains an open question as to how far this national segmentation is reproduced at the level of users' forms of communicative practices and the content of their communication.

Our analysis of users' communicative practices in their online interactions regarding the euro crisis is based on a sample of online comments selected from multiple online forums across the six nation states studied and at the transnational European level. Comments for the analysis were selected from the forums identified through our crawler analysis during the week of a so-called European Crisis summit in June 2012 (cf. appendix for details). The idea here was to deal with a transnational crisis situation as an important communicative event, offering citizens the opportunity of intensified communication about the euro crisis across nation states (cf. Cottle 2009; Hepp/Couldry 2010; Strömbäck et al. 2011; Vobruba 2014a: 185). If citizens are to become involved, then it is most likely during such an event of intense communication. In order to include the most diverse sample of comment threads, a matrix was designed for selecting primary inputs, that is, the news article, blog or *Facebook* post to which users were reacting with their comments as secondary inputs. The matrix considered the thematical variation of the primary input (Europe and domestic politics, supranational European politics, common foreign and security policy, EU and international relations and so on); the type of primary input (news item, commentary, interview, guest article and so on); the length of the comment thread (from a couple to several hundred comments); and the date of publication during the sampling week. In all, 125 comment threads were selected, from which 6,201 comments in total were analysed across all countries (cf. Table 5.1).

Our focus was the forms of users' communicative practices in these forums, as well as the content of their communication. We developed a method based on the principles of conversation analysis that we call interaction analysis (Antaki et al. 2006; Gibson 2009; Steensen 2014; Stommel/Meijman 2011); in addition, our approach takes into account the media environment where interactions take place – in our case, online forums. The analysis aims at identifying typical communicative practices in a given situation (cf. appendix). Users engaged in communication about the euro crisis, about Europe and the EU in a diversity of communicative practices that could be distinguished along the lines of relation-orientation, where social relations are paramount, and issue-orientation, where the content of communication is important. Through their online comments the forum users contribute to the discursive construction of the euro crisis and are engaged in expressions of meaning regarding a critical transformational political situation (Angouri/Wodak 2014: 542) within the EU. Comparing the different forums in our sample, our analysis does not reveal any fundamental differences between national and transnational forums. On national as well as on European levels, users are engaged in a variety of different forms of communicative practices. Our subsequent analysis will show that users deal with the euro

Table 5.1 Online forum selection

	Blog	News media	Facebook
AT	*FS Misik* 2 primary inputs/ 336 comments	*Der Standard* 8 primary inputs/ 590 comments	*Kurier* 7 primary inputs/ 14 comments *Der Standard* 4 primary inputs/ 11 comments
EU	*Charlemagne* 3 primary inputs/ 319 comments	*Financial Times* 5 primary inputs/ 388 comments	*Financial Times* 4 primary inputs/ 350 comments *The Economist* 11 primary inputs/ 269 comments
DK	*Berlingske Blogs* 6 primary inputs/ 143 comments	*Politiken* 10 primary input/ 167 comments	*Politiken* 1 primary input/ 50 comments *Ekstra Bladet* 1 primary input/ 18 comments
F	*Sarkofrance* 4 primary inputs/ 25 comments	*Libération* 6 primary inputs/ 483 comments	*Le Monde* 5 primary inputs/ 105 comments *Libération* 3 primary inputs/ 176 comments
GER	*Spiegelfechter* 4 primary inputs/ 330 comments	*Spiegel Online* 6 primary inputs/ 433 comments	*Bild* 1 primary input/ 242 comments *Spiegel Online* 5 primary inputs/ 194 comments
PL	*Stary Salon24* 2 primary inputs/ 96 comments	*Gazeta Wyborcza* 15 primary inputs/ 312 comments	*Gazeta Wyborcza* No primary input *Fakt* 1 primary input/ 3 comments
UK	*Guido Fawkes* 5 primary inputs/ 466 comments	*The Guardian* 5 primary inputs/ 572 comments	*BBC* 1 primary input/ 109 comments *The Guardian* No primary input

Note: Based on the analysis of hyperlink networks and contextual data as well as overview of data material.

crisis in different interactions and are – across nation states and forums – constructing images of the euro crisis and of Europe in diverse ways.

Relation-oriented interactions

Relation-oriented forms of interaction in the forums involve the production, maintenance and ordering of relations between forum users. For the constitution of the forums as communicative spaces and for the discussion of the euro crisis, users establish relations between each other by discussing European issues in a broad understanding. The euro crisis regularly springs up as a point of reference in interaction, users taking the opportunity to position themselves on the issue, establishing their position regarding the euro crisis, either in opposition to or in support of other forum participants. Three forms of interaction are typical for the relation-oriented forum communication regarding the euro crisis: 'small talk', 'amusement', and 'discrediting and arguing'. 'Articulating forum rules' was identified as a fourth relation-oriented form of interaction in this study. However, this does not primarily involve communication about the euro crisis and was therefore excluded from our results. In the three aforementioned forms of interaction, users are not so much concerned with communicating about the euro crisis in factual statements, but with using the euro crisis in their communication as a basis for building and articulating social relations, sometimes even across national borders.

In small talk, users create and maintain social relations between themselves and other users by giving information about themselves, their life, their everyday routine and their experiences. Especially in the transnational forums in the sample, these personal revelations often relate to their national background in the context of the euro crisis – ignoring questions of the authenticity of such revealed information. The hyperlink analysis revealed that in our sample only the *Financial Times, Charlemagne, The Guardian* and their respective *Facebook* pages could be described as being partly transnational communicative spaces. It is mostly here that users locate and situate other users in a national context. Some knowledge of other users' personality, mostly communicated within small talk interactions, is sometimes necessary for this purpose. Users hint at their nationality through their own user names, in their comments or are identified as belonging to a certain nationality by other users. In the transnational forums, users of different nationalities communicate with each other – even in direct communicative exchanges across Europe – on a horizontal level. The example in Figure 5.8 shows how in one comment from *The Guardian,* a user asks for another user's location in order to make sense of her or his comments in the discussion of the euro crisis.

	Recommend?(4)
	Responses (3)
	Report
	Link

Response to

what will work.. the only thing that can work is a system that will take the many along.. not the few.. this will not work.

Again, where are you writing from? Where are you based? If you go to the EZ you will quickly find out that the Euro has taken the many with it, the overwhelming majority of Europeans love the Euro and will stick with it. The few left that don't are bitter and disappointed and are writing whining pessimistic posts on this blog right now.

Figure 5.8 *The Guardian*, 29 June 2012, Eurozone crisis live, part I

This example demonstrates how far the relational dimension between users in a forum is supportive for political discussion of the euro crisis, and for understanding and contextualising other users' comments in a transnational discussion. By revealing information about oneself, users become tangible and can be addressed in terms of the image they project in the forums. Referring to the euro crisis as an important topic is not always necessary for that purpose. In Figure 5.9, two users are for instance communicating about questions of nationality and cultural points of references, such as country-specific food.

The users in this interaction know each other from previous encounters; they have some basic knowledge about each other, especially their national backgrounds. This makes it possible for them to relate to each other on this personal level. At the same time, this personal relation leads back to the users' respective positions regarding the euro crisis, which they express in a joking manner. In *The Guardian*'s partly transnational forum, users therefore express relations towards each other based on their different national backgrounds. However, one needs to keep in mind that questions of nationality are only addressed in a direct exchange, where users of different nationalities actually meet – therefore mostly in transnational forums.

Participants in small talk interactions sometimes also establish a topic not directly related to the euro crisis, but which has some relevance to their everyday lives in the broader context of Europe. During the period of our data collection, for example, the European football championship – the Eurocup – was taking place. The Eurocup as a shared event in Europe is a transnational point of reference to which many users in the forums commonly relate. That is why we find quite a few small talk as well as amusement interactions that relate to football, in which users of

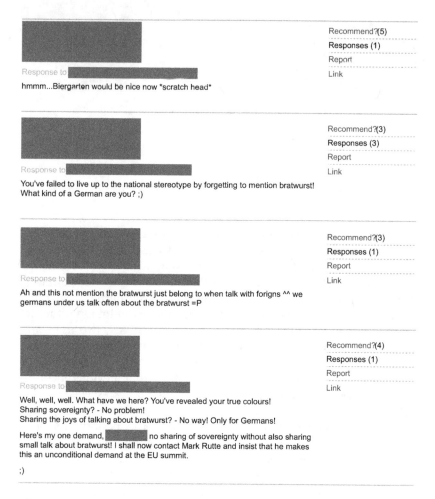

Recommend?(5)
Responses (1)
Report
Link

Response to
hmmm...Biergarten would be nice now *scratch head*

Recommend?(3)
Responses (3)
Report
Link

Response to
You've failed to live up to the national stereotype by forgetting to mention bratwurst!
What kind of a German are you? ;)

Recommend?(3)
Responses (1)
Report
Link

Response to
Ah and this not mention the bratwurst just belong to when talk with forigns ^^ we
germans under us talk often about the bratwurst =P

Recommend?(4)
Responses (1)
Report
Link

Response to
Well, well, well. What have we here? You've revealed your true colours!
Sharing sovereignty? - No problem!
Sharing the joys of talking about bratwurst? - No way! Only for Germans!

Here's my one demand,   no sharing of sovereignty without also sharing
small talk about bratwurst! I shall now contact Mark Rutte and insist that he makes
this an unconditional demand at the EU summit.

;)

Figure 5.9   *The Guardian*, 29 June 2012, Eurozone crisis live, part II

the forums often react towards each other in longer interactions. We find
these interactions both within our entire national as well as in the transnational forums. Users here often engage in amusement interactions by
constructing football-related metaphors in the context of the euro crisis
summit, stating in a humorous way, for example, that Germany let Italy
win the semi-final of the Eurocup in order to make more ground during the EU summit. Such joking comments do not signify a fact-based
political discussion of the euro crisis, but they offer a way for users to

teasingly articulate relations towards each other or create a narrative of the pervasiveness of the euro crisis within Europe.

Amusing comments and interactions often convey such specific euro crisis narrations. Sometimes users create fictional dialogues of politicians attending the euro crisis summit or describe fictional solutions. In the UK forum of the blog *Guido Fawkes,* some of these fictional scenarios even appear in a scenic form, since users here do not have to register for accessing the forum. That is why some of them repeatedly take the role of famous political actors and put words into their mouth in the context of the euro crisis. They ridicule these political actors and their supposed incapability regarding the euro crisis. Most amusement interactions are, however, descriptions of fictional political aims, statements, insinuations and so on. They often cross the line of reality, expressing irony and pointing out the euro crisis' perceived absurdities, as in Figure 5.10.

> ▬▬▬▬▬ hier j'ai vu un grec acheter de la nourriture
> (certes il n'avait pas mangé depuis 2 jours mais tout de
> même...) alors qu'il devait payer ces échéances! ces gens
> n'ont pas le sens des priorités!!!
> quel honte!!!!
>
> Übersetzung anzeigen
> Montag um 10:19   Gefällt mir   👍 26

Figure 5.10   Facebook Le Monde, 25 June 2012, Athens could have cheated by employing civil servants A

Note: Translation: 'Yesterday, I saw a Greek person buying groceries (sure, he had not eaten for two days, but still. . .) even though he has to pay his debts! These people have no sense of priority!!! What a shame!!!!'

Users also create amusing comments by decontextualising actors and events from the euro crisis context, often through references to popular culture. In one example from the German news magazine *Spiegel Online's Facebook* account, one user puts the euro crisis in the context of *Star Wars* and labels the German chancellor as 'Darth Angela Merkel' (*Facebook Spiegel Online,* 29 June 2012, 'Euro-Krise: Europas Mächtige treten an zum Streit-Gipfel') in order to create a humorous comment. In a similar way, a discussion emerges around the abbreviation 'QEII' (quantitative easing) in the Polish forum of the online newspaper *Gazeta Wyborcza,* where a couple of users are discussing the content and consequences of this monetary policy. Another user, who apparently does not know the term, jokes that he googled 'QEII' and found out that it stands for Queen Elizabeth II – a British ocean liner (*Gazeta Wyborcza*, 25 June 2012, 'Nikt nie bedzie zrzucal Europie dolarów z helikoptera'). This incident leads to some shared jokes on the topic. Through these amusing comments, users are bonding with other users or are creatively making their own narratives about the euro crisis. They position themselves with respect to current developments in the euro crisis and evaluate these through sarcasm, irony, fiction or mockery. To do so, they do not necessarily rely on rational and factual arguments, but express their opinions and images of Europe in humorous ways.

Just as with the small talk interaction, discrediting and arguing has a strong focus on the individual person. By criticising and insulting each other, users are positioning themselves towards each other. Contrary to the interactions mentioned earlier, this arguing about the euro crisis is mostly based on previous issue-related debates, in which the euro crisis was negotiated as a political issue, as Figure 5.11 demonstrates.

In this example, a user clearly disagrees with another user's previous comment on the euro crisis. As in this criticising comment, users are, therefore, concerned with evaluating and discrediting another user's comment based on their perceptions of the euro crisis. Sometimes such evaluations and criticisms are further explained in the comments, in that case often in combination with issue-oriented communicative practices (cf. for example Figure 5.12).

The user in this comment openly criticises another user for blaming the Greek people for their situation in the euro crisis. That user sees by contrast the banks at the centre of the euro crisis and blames them. Through these communicative practices, the user is therefore engaging in issue-oriented interactions, while equally expressing opposition to the other user.

A negative evaluation is expressed more aggressively than simple criticism when one user insults another, for example, through disparagement or even in the form of severe disagreement – especially when a user's statement is laced with hurtful, degrading and insulting comments aimed at a person and no longer at that person's statement. This

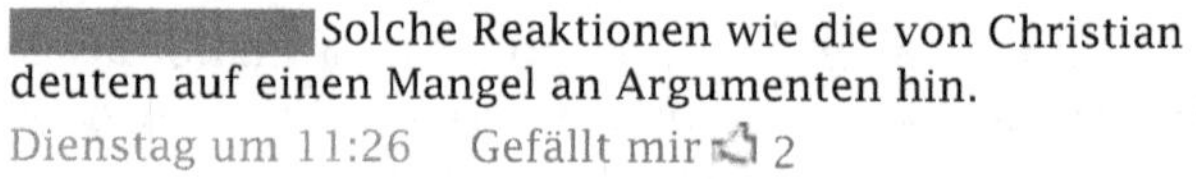

Solche Reaktionen wie die von Christian deuten auf einen Mangel an Argumenten hin.
Dienstag um 11:26   Gefällt mir 👍 2

Figure 5.11   Facebook Spiegel Online, 25 June 2012, Europe: Perfect solutions take a long time

Note: Translation: 'Reactions like the ones from Christian point towards a lack of argument'.

██████████████████ Ce qui est marrant c'est que je
parie qu'un type comme ████████████ ne bronche pas quand
il apprend que les gouvernements renflouent à coup de
milliers de milliards de NOS euros les banques qui sont à
l'origine de la crise financière. Par contre si les grecs (qui,
selon l'OCDE, sont les premiers travailleurs d'Europe en
heures par semaine) désobéissent aux plans de la troïka qui
les plongent dans la misère et ne règlent rien... Alors là ça
va plus ! Un bon bouc-émissaire bien misérable, on n'a
toujours pas trouvé mieux pour détourner la colère des
pigeons.

Übersetzung anzeigen

Montag um 10:28   Bearbeitet Gefällt mir   👍 11

Figure 5.12   Facebook Le Monde, 25 June 2012, Athens could have cheated by employing civil servants B

Note: Translation: 'What is funny, is that I would bet that a guy like fredo salsero would not flinch when he learns that the governments are bailing out the banks, which are the origin of the financial crisis, with millions and millions of OUR euros. But when the Greeks (who according to the OECD work the most hours per week in Europe) do not obey the plans of the troika, which would lead them into misery and would solve nothing . . . Well, that goes too far! (. . .)'

conflictual dimension often suggests users' differing constructions of the euro crisis and of Europe. The transnational forums directly addressing questions of nationality sometimes lead to such adversarial statements between users. In one example from the *Charlemagne* forum, two users insult another, whom they identify as being Northern European and whom they accuse of having posted racist comments (Charlemagne, 28 June 12, 'Europe on the rack'). Their derisive remarks about this other forum user suggest the other two users are expressing their solidarity with each other in their common disapproval of a third user and their take on the euro crisis. The analysis of the forum material thus shows that the question of nationality does not always lead to conflict in users' interactions. It also functions as a means of maintaining harmonious and supportive relations with other users. Often, though, conflict in transnational forums emerges in a direct exchange between users of different nationalities along the question of who is to blame for the euro crisis – often being a question of either the Northerners or the Southerners (cf. Figure 5.13).

Such interactions highlight users' fundamentally different constructions of the euro crisis, its causes and its solutions – even when one has to consider that a user might voice different opinions in online forums

The problem is in thinking that the entire Europe is a homogenous mix. It is not! In the North you have people who work harder and save more. In the South you have people who does the exact opposite. And you do not have a political framework to moderate both.It will allways be difficult to have a single monetary and political union. It is better to go back a decade and let individual countries and cultures set their own course.

Recommend 14   Reply

in reply to neil_dr

The only correct thing you said is that southern Europeans don't save money. You see the high inflation of the past meant that they had to invest their money into something if they didn't want it to lose value. Keeping it in the bank was stupid. Now working harder? Hahaha. The north having richer firms (and thus with better connections to exploit markets, better capital for investment, and better equipment) is the only thing that keeps the north richer.
The south works much more http://www.bbc.co.uk/news/magazine-17155304
But you wouldn't want to admit that would you? Cause you forgot that other major difference. In the north it's acceptable to be a racist if the tabloids justify it, right? Go read a book, it will help improve your character

Recommend 29   Reply

Figure 5.13   *Charlemagne*, 28 June 2012, Europe on the rack A

compared to a direct face-to-face exchange. In reflection on the euro crisis, one important assumption is often that a transnational crisis like this necessarily leads to conflict between nation states and their citizens. That is why studies of the press coverage of the euro crisis, which necessarily mostly rely on national news media, often focus on differences between the news media's reporting on the euro crisis in different nation states (Joris et al. 2014; Post/Vollbracht 2013). Other studies also find proof of national stereotyping in the news media's coverage, lending further emphasis to the national as a distinct dimension in the discourse on the euro crisis (Breeze 2014; Kutter 2014). There is a particular opposition set up in reporting between so-called crisis countries in Southern Europe and economically better-off countries in Northern Europe (Cross/Ma 2013: 32ff.). The same line of conflict exists in the aforementioned example from users' online interactions about the euro crisis in transnational forums. But these conflicting constructions do not only occur in transnational forums. We also find in national forums competing constructions, for example, when users are putting forward different ways out of the euro crisis, attributing blame or describing what led to the euro crisis. Conflict and opposition on the one hand as well as solidarity and support on the other are central elements in users' communicative practices when relating to each other. But it is important to note that nationality is only one among a number of reference points in relation to which users are positioning themselves when building these relations. In the forum data, we see that users' belonging to a specific political group, having a specific political affiliation or proposing a distinct political future scenario for the EU are just as important for articulating conflictual or supporting relations towards each other, even within nation states. These reference points, however, mostly emerge through users' issue-oriented interactions, which will now be described in more detail.

Issue-oriented interactions

In contrast to the relation-oriented interactions, the discussion of the euro crisis in its political dimension is the main focal point in issue-oriented interactions in the online comment forums. In the three issue-oriented forms of interaction – 'demarcating the euro crisis', 'interpreting the euro crisis' and 'discussing the euro crisis' – the prime concern is discussion of the euro crisis through description, explanation, evaluation and speculation. All patterns of interaction and communicative practices are defined by constant references to the euro crisis, Europe and the EU.

Many comments in issue-oriented forms of interaction deal with the demarcation of the euro crisis. These describe the current status of the euro crisis as the main issue. In so doing, users are often pointing out the problematic dimension of the current situation, as, for example, in Figure 5.14.

In their comments, users describe their individual perceptions of the euro crisis, which clashes with other users' perspectives. Users often integrate supposedly objective information into their comments to support their own arguments and descriptions of the current status quo, for example, through hyperlinks or by quoting external information. But users also support each other in their perception of the euro crisis. Moreover, users do not only describe a negative state of affairs, but also describe developments and achievements, either neutrally or positively. Attributions of responsibility and blame are also quite a common communicative practice in the interactions, which Jo Angouri and Ruth Wodak (2014: 542) also identified for online discussion of the Greek dimension of the euro crisis. In our sample, attribution of blame takes

The crisis has almost nothing to with deficits and debt levels. The balance of payments / debtor credit balance / current accounts and the lack of currency sovereignty among member states is what should actually be discussed and fixed. Structural reform, lack of competitiveness, relative wages rises since 2002 should be discussed secondarily.

Countries giving fiscal sovereignty away without some kind of democratic legitimacy is asking for trouble. Cuts etc being dictated from Brussels will increase resentment and tension making breakup a lot more likely in the near term.

No country in the Euro area wants to leave or breakup, the horrendous miss management and complete lack of understanding of what is actually going on from Europe's elite almost guarantees eventual breakup. It may take another 5 years of grinding depression and unemployment heading towards 20%+, this is exactly what is going to happen with the current policy response.

Figure 5.14   Financial Times, 26 June 2012, EU plan to rewrite eurozone budgets

the form both of having caused the euro crisis, as well as responsibility for solving it (cf. Figure 5.15).

In this example the EU and its supposed incompetence is identified as responsible for, firstly, having caused the euro crisis and, secondly, for not being able to solve it. Users either attribute blame or responsibility to particular political or economic actors, but also – especially in the context of the euro crisis – more generally to whole nation states. Besides these specific attributions, actors, developments and events in the euro crisis context are constantly evaluated in user comments, for example, through characterisations or value judgments. These might be

und was ist mit der Kontrolle?

Bankenrettung, Strafen für Schuldensünder, alles schön und gut. Aber der gesamte Kontrollapperat der EU hat komplett versagt: nichts wurde frühzeitig erkannt, keiner hat die schönten Zahlen durchschaut, niemand ist in der Lage Prognosen zu erstellen. Egal was beschlossen wird, es wird wieder scheitern - an er Inkompetenz der EU-Verwaltung.

Antworten / Zitieren

Figure 5.15   Spiegel Online, 25 June 2012, All hope rests on the plan of the four
Note: Translation: 'Saving banks, punishing debt sinners, all very well. But the whole control apparatus of the EU has failed completely: Nothing was recognised early enough, no one saw through the airbrushed numbers, no one is capable of giving a prognosis. It doesn't matter what will be decided, it will again fail – due to the incompetence of the EU's administration.'

quite blunt, even as insults or as more elaborate judgements in the context of the euro crisis when referring to current developments.

Such attributions of blame and evaluation in users' comments often form a foundation for users expressing the sense of a mutual relation. Attributions of blame can of course be with respect to nationality, for example, in a direct transnational exchange in transnational forums. But the focus on nationality also exists in national forums, as discussions about different nation states and their roles in the euro crisis, and expressing solidarity with these other nation states and their peoples. As regards attributions of blame to specific groups – either the Southerners or the Northerners – the analysis shows that such statements are quite common and that the same attribution of blame occurs across nation states and forums. In the German forum of *Spiegel Online*, for example, one user attributes blame to Germany itself, saying that Germany and Angela Merkel actually profit from the euro crisis and are preventing solutions for the Southern countries. A different user contradicts these statements and blames the Southern Europeans for their own situation (*Spiegel Online*, 28 June 2012, 'Merkel lässt Monti abblitzen'). In the *Charlemagne* forum we find a similar line of conflict and the same attributions of blame emerging between users (*Charlemagne*, 29 June 2012, 'Less disunion'). These two examples demonstrate that one cannot think of national and transnational forums as containers with clear conflict lines in terms of nationality. The central difference between national and transnational comment forums in our sample is that the users' nationality is only discussed in transnational comment forums, where users of different nationality actually get together.

When trying to form a complete picture of the euro crisis, users are sometimes also considering how the euro crisis has evolved, referring to past and also future developments. As in Figure 5.16, they are making causal connections between different events, integrating them into their own line of argument.

The traditional technological advantage is indeed important, but the institutional design is even more important because it sets the conditions to catch up or fall behind in terms of innovations or technology. It determines the cost of employment, of development etc. That is the reason why a lot of other countries have caught up compared to the "West" while some countries of the "West" are left behind, especially by Asian nations.

Figure 5.16   Charlemagne, 28 June 2012, Europe on the rack B

In this comment, a user brings different points into a causal connection ('sets the condition', 'determines', 'That is the reason') from which the euro crisis supposedly developed. The argumentative and explanatory character is clear in this example and becomes even clearer when a users poses a question regarding the euro crisis development, as in Figure 5.17.

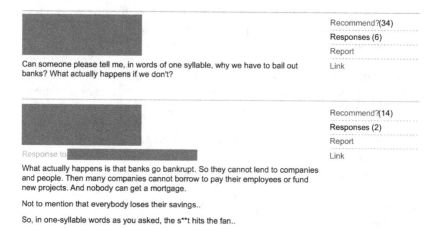

Recommend?(34)

Responses (6)

Report

Link

Can someone please tell me, in words of one syllable, why we have to bail out banks? What actually happens if we don't?

Recommend?(14)

Responses (2)

Report

Link

Response to

What actually happens is that banks go bankrupt. So they cannot lend to companies and people. Then many companies cannot borrow to pay their employees or fund new projects. And nobody can get a mortgage.

Not to mention that everybody loses their savings..

So, in one-syllable words as you asked, the s**t hits the fan..

Figure 5.17   *The Guardian*, 25 June 2012, Cyprus seeks eurozone bailout

When it comes to demarcating issues in online forums, users are constructing an image of the euro crisis by describing their perception of the situation, naming central actors, events and developments, and contemplating how the euro crisis has evolved. They deal with the euro crisis in a descriptive as well as an analytical manner.

While the demarcation of the euro crisis involves identifying the situation, users refer to very concrete developments in their interactions when they interpret the euro crisis. They try to make sense of new developments, generally described within an article or blog post as primary input. For that reason, references to primary inputs are very frequent in the comments. In this study, these new developments mostly relate to the European Council's Crisis summit that took place during the period that sampling was being done. The slow release of information on the summits' proceedings and the subsequent breakthrough at the end of the summit were heavily interpreted in users' comments. Users here express negative or positive evaluations concerning these new crisis developments and decisions, as in the Danish forum of the *Berlingske Blogs* (cf. Figure 5.18).

Skal vi tage et væddemål ? Denne redningspakke holder ca. 14 dage, så er vi tilbage dér hvor vi var før redningspakken. Som med de 27 foregående redningspakker. Inden Tour de France når Pyrenæerne, er Spanien i problemer igen.

Figure 5.18   Berlingske Blogs, 29 June 2012, Important Signal

Note: Translation: 'Should we bet? This safety package will last about 14 days, then we are back to where we were before the safety plan. Just like with the 27 previous safety plans. Before we will reach the Tour de Pyrenees, Spain will be right back in the problems.'

In this example, a user is referring to the safety plan agreed during the European Council summit. Next to an evaluative component, two further communicative practices in this pattern of interaction are already evident in this example: deciphering and deducting.

When users are deciphering information, they are describing the motives or ideas behind a political decision or statement. They translate information and explain what it 'really' means. These deciphering communicative actions appear in combination with a user's deductions, when for instance they are speculating about the implications of a political euro crisis decision.

In Figure 5.19, a user engages with Angela Merkel's 'cave-in' at the EU summit, and reconstructs step-by-step what this event means and where this will lead the euro crisis. In the comments, users are also deciphering the actions of politicians by imputing motivations, trying to make them comprehensible. A user in the forum of the Austrian blog *FS Misik*, for example, states that Angela Merkel's decision at the EU summit was based on her interest in representing German industry. The user implies that Merkel does not want the euro to stabilise, since this would

Report

The irony is that after this massive cave-in by Merkel to all the demands of the Spanish and Italians, Merkel will now inevitably lose the 2013 election and be replaced by an inflationist SPD/Green coalition, who are just like Hollande in supporting unlimited bailouts for the PIIGS.

The result will see Germany itself turn into a proto-PIG and opens the doors for multiple rounds of QE. I fail to see how this strengthens the Euro in the long run.

Figure 5.19   Financial Times, 29 June 2012, Europe agrees crisis-fighting measures A

harm German exports. That is why, according to the user, Merkel always gives in a little regarding other nations' demands, but will obstruct the prospect of long-term Eurozone stability (*FS Misik*, 01 July 2012, 'Angela Merkel – die gefährlichste Frau der Welt?'). These interpretations demonstrate how far users are constructing their own narratives of the origins of the euro crisis, its current development and possibly also its future.

The third form of issue-oriented interaction is the users' discussion of the euro crisis. Through responsive communicative acts they are mostly either expressing disapproval and rejection, or support and agreement regarding a previous comment on the euro crisis. Users are constantly positioning themselves with respect to another user's statements on the euro crisis. Longer threads of interactions, with occasionally large numbers of positive or negative comments, are the result. If users reject each other, this is mostly a repeated reaction, entering into a more extended discussion of the euro crisis. In such discussion further communicative practices such as deductions, deciphering, informing and positioning can play an equally important role. Positioning is quite central, since users are regularly discussing solutions for the euro crisis. They are consequently positioning themselves with respect to these proposed solutions, offering their own political opinion.

While such positionings as in Figure 5.20 are targeted on very specific euro crisis solutions, other users describe general conceptions of the EU's future (cf. Figure 5.20 and Figure 5.21).

Users often support their positioning with respect to a solution for the euro crisis with logically deductive statements. In one example from *The Guardian*, a user suggests the taxation of profits within a functioning monetary union as a political solution (*The Guardian*, 30 June 2012, 'David Cameron pledges referendum if EU demands more powers'). The user causally deduces how such an approach could contribute to a solution of the euro crisis in the current financial system. At the same time, discussion of such solutions is often also a discussion about the causes of the euro crisis. That is why many comments discussing ways out of the euro crisis also attribute responsibility.

It becomes clear that nationality is not the only or even the most prominent line of difference within the forums. When users propose euro crisis solutions, across all forums they adopt a mutual stance with respect to economic models, the conceptualisation of a future EU or with regard to opposing political and sometimes even ideological affiliation. In every forum, users envision different future scenarios for the EU, ranging from the United States of Europe to the dissolution of the EU. Equally, users' exchanges about the right way to solve the euro crisis

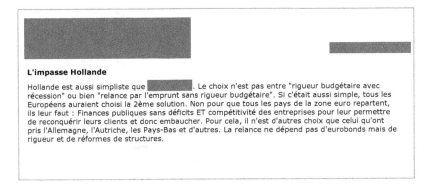

L'impasse Hollande

Hollande est aussi simpliste que ▓▓▓▓▓. Le choix n'est pas entre "rigueur budgétaire avec récession" ou bien "relance par l'emprunt sans rigueur budgétaire". Si c'était aussi simple, tous les Européens auraient choisi la 2ème solution. Non pour que tous les pays de la zone euro repartent, ils leur faut : Finances publiques sans déficits ET compétitivité des entreprises pour leur permettre de reconquérir leurs clients et donc embaucher. Pour cela, il n'est d'autres choix que celui qu'ont pris l'Allemagne, l'Autriche, les Pays-Bas et d'autres. La relance ne dépend pas d'eurobonds mais de rigueur et de réformes de structures.

Figure 5.20   Libération, 28 June 2012, 'Things are going well between the French and the Germans', Cazeneuve assures

Note: Translation: 'Hollande sees things just as one-sided as lucioledemai. The choice is not between "restrictive fiscal policy with recession" or "recovery through bonds without restrictive fiscal policy". If things were that simple everyone in Europe would choose the second solution. No, for every country in the Eurozone to get going again, we need: public financing without deficit *and* competitiveness of the enterprises so that they can win back their customers and start employing people again. For that, there is no other choice than to take the path that Germany, Austria, the Netherlands and others took. The recovery does not depend on Eurobonds, but on politics of austerity and structural reforms.'

Report

I can see many angry comments here by Euro-skeptics, that is a great sign to us Europeans pro EU who would like to see a EU united moving forward, competing against China, US, united can go much further, destroying the Euro could have been a total disaster for everyone including Germany and others. More regulations a common Central European Bank that would act like its counterparts in the US, Japan, etc.

Figure 5.21   Financial Times, 29 June 2012, Europe agrees crisis-fighting measures B

and the appropriate economic steps demonstrate that across all nation states, users debate along a fixed continuum of more austerity or more financially supported measures. Our analysis shows firstly, that it is not possible to draw a distinction between national and transnational forums with reference to the forms of interaction. The same construction processes take place across nation states and at the European level. Secondly, the results also show that users relate to each other through different points of reference, nationality being one of those. However, it becomes obvious that users communicate the same positions and opinions regarding these reference points across nation states, leading to similar lines of conflict and expressions of support throughout the forums – irrespective of national background. That is why commonalities between forums in different nation states and at the European level seem to be more striking than their differences. The diversity of the different constructions of the euro crisis and of Europe is, therefore, located within each forum, based on differences in use – as, for example, in their general (political) position against Europe and the euro crisis, rather than in between nation states or between the national and transnational level.

5.3   Online forums: national hyperlinks and transnational constructions

As we argued in chapter 2, in a situation of crisis people need to interpret the crisis. As a consequence, they intensify their observations of public events and of society in general. However, their multiple observations and different interpretations of current developments compete in critical moments of insecurity, which is why crises are conflictual events (Vobruba 2014a: 185). This is also plain in the competing definitions of the euro crisis in the forums investigated by us. Our results – across relation-oriented and issue-oriented interactions – point to this in three respects. First, users express their observations, their evaluations and their thoughts about the current euro crisis in their online comments in both relation- and issue-oriented interactions. These observations, secondly, can build the basis for users creating, expressing and maintaining relations towards each other on the grounds of their engagement with the euro crisis. These relations often take, thirdly, the form of conflict, especially when people's images of the euro crisis and of Europe conflict. However, supporting statements do also occur. And even the potentially conflictual dimension in users' communication on the euro crisis does not necessarily lead to any negative impact for European integration and the processes of social construction. Instead, the establishment of a common currency signifies a move away from a condition of indifference between nation states and their citizens, which in certain cases result in conflict. This, however, does not have to impede societal construction processes, first of all signifying an increasing engagement with each other (Vobruba 2014b: 28).

Our results demonstrate that in times of crisis we observe increasing engagement in online comment forums across Europe. However, comments made in the online forums also suggest that this engagement does not only happen between but equally across nation states and their people. If a conflictual dimension only occurred between people of different nationality, this line of national conflict would only be obvious in our sampled transnational forums. While users in transnational forums refer to the national in their interactions with other users, also in conflictual ways, this conflictual dimension is widespread also in nationally based forums. Furthermore, these conflict lines not only emerge regarding questions of nationality, but equally with respect to users' political affiliations, their ideas of adequate economic models, attributions of blame and responsibility, solutions to solve the euro crisis and so on. Users' positions on these aspects of the euro crisis similarly lead to conflict, or alternatively expressions of support, both within the national and the transnational comment forums in our sample. Noticing that these conflicts do not primarily run between different national forums or between national and transnational forums, we therefore conclude that users are commonly engaging in the communicative construction of Europe in online discussion of the euro crisis across all nation states and forums in the sample, albeit partly with quite different opinions and communicative practices.

With reference to the vertical and horizontal connectivity of European public spheres (cf. chapter 2), discourse about the euro crisis in all forums and nation states is a sign of strong discursive integration as a form of Europeanisation. But our hyperlink analysis of political websites demonstrated that the internet's transnational potential is only weakly realised. There are few transnational possibilities for communication in which users are engaging in direct communicative horizontal exchange. Online forums do not realise Klaus Eder's (2014: 221) call for more direct exchanges, for social relations between citizens across nation states in Europe as a prerequisite for the constitution of a European society. The differences between national and transnational forums seem to be limited to discussion of nationality in transnational forums, where users of different nationalities actually meet; the distinction between transnational and national forums is however only of limited relevance. Instead, there are common features in constructions of the euro crisis and of Europe. That is why there is reason to doubt that the national segmentation of online forums actually hinders the emergence of a European public sphere online and the communicative construction of Europe.

The identification of common reference points for users in the constructions of Europe indicates that the process of communicatively constructing Europe is shared to some extent by citizens across the six research countries and at the European level. There is no dominance of national conflict lines between nation states and citizens of different nation states. Rather, lines of conflict exist within citizenries and their differing perceptions of the euro crisis. Although transnationality is not strongly developed at the level of hyperlink structures or expressed in direct communicative exchange between citizens of different nation states, there is nevertheless a strong transnational potential in the communicative construction of Europe in citizens' online forums.

6

Appropriating Europe: Communication Repertoires, Citizens' European Public Connections and the Euro Crisis

In the previous chapters, we have discussed processes of communicatively constructing Europe with regard to journalistic production, media coverage and the interaction in online forums. We demonstrated that the multi-segmented European public sphere is rooted in different cultures of political discourse and that the related public sphere is characterised by a certain stability, even during the euro crisis. This chapter adds to this by investigating citizens' public connections with Europe and the EU. We will here focus on their media appropriation and their related involvement with the process of communicatively constructing Europe. Two research questions will be addressed: How do citizens approach Europe and the EU; and how are these approaches challenged within the context of the euro crisis? To answer these research questions, we carried out an audience study based on qualitative interviews, network maps and media diaries from a sample of 182 Austrian, Danish, French, German, British and Polish citizens (see the appendix for a detailed description of our methodology).

In so doing, we refer both to the concepts of 'communication repertoire' and 'public connection'. Communication on Europe is realised within a rapidly changing media environment, consisting both of traditional mass media, for example, television or the press, and so-called new digital media, like online newspapers or platforms. Direct communication interrelates with both. From an individual perspective, the concept of communication repertoire captures the totality of mediated and direct forms of communication (Hasebrink 2015; Hasebrink/Domeyer 2012; Hasebrink/Popp 2006). Using this as a general understanding of communication repertoire, our study is focused on what we call 'political communication repertoires': the part of the communication repertoire that is oriented towards public issues.

While the concept of political communication repertoire operates on the level of the individual, the main interest of our research is how these individuals relate to the European public sphere. Here the idea of public connection comes in or more precisely of 'European public connection'. European public connection correspondingly means the communicatively established link to the public affairs of Europe and the EU (Couldry et al. 2007a, 2007b). Although media are not the only means for communication on public issues, they do have 'an economically and socially privileged role in the organisation of popular knowledge' (Corner 2000: 394). Thus, in order to understand citizens' communicative involvement with Europe and the EU we have to investigate political communication repertoires on the one hand and forms of public connection on the other. Both offer empirical access to understanding citizens' contributions to the communicative construction of Europe.

The subsequent analysis is based on qualitative audience research in six European countries, generated from qualitative semi-guided interviews, media diaries and network maps. The data from the 182 individual cases was collected from October to December 2011. Our investigation was driven by a general interest in the citizens' media appropriation, their communication repertoires and their orientation towards Europe and the EU in a transculturally comparative perspective (Hepp 2015: 22–28; Hepp/Couldry 2009). According to the concept of highest possible variation (Glaser/Strauss 1967: 45–77), our sampling strategy was to conduct interviews with citizens from the most diverse backgrounds, varying with respect to gender, age, income and conditions of life, and living in rural or urban environments. Table 6.1 illustrates the overall sample, with subsequent lines structured regarding each of these dimensions. Besides a slight dominance of interviewees with a low income living in urban areas, the table demonstrates the relatively broad range of interviewees.

During our fieldwork in 2011, the euro crisis presented itself as a rich case for the study of European public connections. Typically, research on the European public sphere discusses citizens' role in relation to their communicative involvement within Europe and the EU, and its consequences for processes of legitimation (Fuchs 2011; Gerhards/Hans 2014; Risse 2010; for an overview Van de Steeg 2010). In the context of the crisis, therefore, key questions arise that refer to whether citizens take notice of leading political events and decision-making in the EU and, in consequence, whether the euro crisis impacts their engagement with the EU and Europe (Gerhards et al. 2014). Picking up this overall discussion, we want to go one step further by asking how these communicative

Table 6.1 Qualitative interview sample

N = 182		Austria 30	Denmark 30	France 31	Germany 30	UK 30	Poland 31
Gender	female	13	14	15	14	16	17
	male	17	16	16	16	14	15
Age	18–30	13	12	10	8	15	12
	30–50	8	9	12	15	7	7
	50–70	9	9	9	7	8	12
Income	low	12	13	8	17	11	13
	middle	8	10	12	10	15	14
	high	10	7	11	3	4	4
Life context	rural	11	13	4	5	4	9
	settlement	9	7	12	9	14	9
	town	10	10	15	16	12	13

connections are established and in which ways citizens are involved in the communicative construction of Europe, not least in times of crisis (cf. similar approaches Hepp et al. 2012; Ortner 2014; Paus-Hasebrink/ Ortner 2009; Risse 2010).

6.1 Europeanisation of media audiences: a European citizen audience

The above refers to three areas of research; namely European audiences, peoples' public connections and the concept of communication repertoires. While a brief review of empirical European audience research supports the argument for a bottom-up study of citizens' connection to Europe, the theoretical concepts mentioned provide an analytical starting point for such research. Whereas the notion of public connection helps to conceptualise a general orientation towards the communicative space of Europe and the political institutions of the EU, the concept of political communication repertoire provides a means of understanding how this orientation takes place in terms of appropriating and disseminating knowledge on Europe and the EU.

(1) From its beginning, research on the European public sphere has strongly emphasised the communicative link between Europe, the EU and its citizens as a key function of democratic legitimation, sustained by a European public sphere (Bohman 2007: 128ff.; Van de Steeg 2010: 31f.). Over the years, the academic perspective on this relationship has slightly

changed. For a long time, academic authors regularly highlighted the shortcomings of citizens' communicative inclusion (Koopmans/Pfetsch 2006: 134; Van de Steeg 2010). The generally negative assessment of peoples' inclusion has nevertheless been increasingly differentiated (elaborate discussion in Risse 2010). Academic discourse concerning a shared European identity serves as an illustrative example for this development. While in the beginning many studies discussed the subordinate, and thus problematic, role that Europe and the EU plays in citizens' communicative horizons (Fuchs 2011; Schlesinger 1993), researchers increasingly point to the '"new" social bond of diversity emerging in Europe' (Eder 2009: 433). Cultural diversity appears not as an obstacle, but as a resource for communicative interaction within Europe (Eder 2014; Risse 2010; Risse/Grabowsky 2008). Other discussion refers to the media that provide citizens with news about Europe and the EU. Whereas earlier studies with a focus on media content analysis have pointed to considerable shortcomings in communicating Europe, more recent publications argue that 'the institutional infrastructure for a public sphere [in the EU] is in place' (Van de Steeg 2010: 44). This is to say that citizens are *in principle* provided with the necessary possibilities for information about Europe and the EU. However, it remains an empirical question whether and how people appropriate such information.

With regard to discussions on constructing Europe communicatively, we nevertheless have to deal with arguments raised earlier on the stratification of cultures of political discourse and the related transnational segmentation of the European public sphere. From the perspective of most researchers, the European public sphere is a space dominated by elites or elite citizens. As Marianne van de Steeg wrote, 'the variety in backgrounds of the participants in most mediatized public debates on European issues is limited to politicians and other opinion-makers' (Van de Steeg 2010: 44; see also Corcoran/Fahy 2009; Preston 2009; Statham/Trenz 2013). The argument is that the vast majority of 'ordinary citizens' seems to be absent from the European project. If we transfer these questions to the study of appropriating mediated communication on Europe, we are nevertheless confronted with a different perspective. Klaus Eder (2014: 223f.), for instance, pursues an alternative viewpoint by pointing to the difficulties that arise when taking the imagined, fully integrated European society as a basis for evaluation (see a similar argument in Georgakopoulou 2014: 520). Eder argues that we should not judge the quality of citizens' involvement in the European public sphere on this basis, but instead ask questions about where we might 'find such capacities linking (critical) action and (critical) meaning in the ongoing processes of transnationalization of social relations in Europe' (Eder 2014: 228).

In relation to Europe and the EU, we notice the echo of a more general discussion about the lack of or even loss of interest, in politics – a familiar theme in national politics (Dahlgren 2004: 13; Neidhardt 2006: 49). However, much of this research is based more on general assessments of citizens as audiences, rather than on empirical studies. All the same, European audiences have so far not been in the centre of research on the European public sphere. Considering existing research in this field, we distinguish three strands: first, the analysis of media use with regard to the establishment of transnational media audiences (Bjur et al. 2014; Hasebrink/Herzog 2009; Hasebrink/Lampert 2012); second, empirical research investigating the influence of news reporting on citizens' approval of the EU (De Vreese/Boomgaarden 2006, 2009; Schuck/De Vreese 2006; Van Spanje/De Vreese 2014); and third, qualitative studies focussing on citizens' appropriation of EU political information in their everyday lives (Lingenberg 2006, 2010a, 2010b).

From a theoretical perspective, it makes sense to distinguish between 'media audiences' and 'citizen audiences' (Lingenberg 2010b: 54) in the public sphere. Media audiences consist of the recipients and users of media products. Concerning the Europeanisation of media audiences, one might ask whether media products reach transnational media audiences in Europe. More concretely, this can be realised by the Europe-wide use of transnational media products or the transnational use of national media products by citizens in different EU countries, especially by citizens living in neighbouring countries speaking the same language (Hasebrink/Herzog 2009). Citizen audiences, in contrast, do not consist of users of specific media products but of individuals and groups who feel affected by EU political decision-making and Europe in general, developing opinions, attitudes and actions (Lingenberg 2010b: 50ff.).

With regard to the 'Europeanisation of media audiences', the diversity of languages in Europe impedes the use of foreign media products. Therefore, the most frequently used television programmes in Europe are national programmes (Hepp 2015: 145–149). Only in smaller countries, where foreign language use is more common, is the use of television programmes also transnational. In Switzerland, for example, foreign television programmes have a market share of more than 50 per cent (Hasebrink/Herzog 2009). Here the use of entertainment programmes is more transnational than the use of information programmes. News from the own country or region is usually preferred, despite the availability of news in the same language from neighbouring countries. This said, it becomes obvious that the *segmentation* of media audiences in Europe is quite marked with regard to political information. Hence, we cannot speak of a European information media audience. And as we have argued above, we cannot speak of the Europeanisation of media audiences of transnational media products either.

Whereas Europeanised media audiences do not widely exist, we may still observe Europeanised citizen audiences. Such Europeanised citizen audiences emerge as a result of European citizens' use of national media products and the development of relatedness, attitudes and actions towards EU political decision-making. Empirical research focussing on the effects of media use points to the possible consequences of indifferent attitudes or low levels of information and knowledge on European politics. De Vreese and Boomgaarden (2006) demonstrate that the extent of media use and attention for the EU has positive effects on views concerning EU eastern enlargement – however, only if the extent of media reporting is not too low and its tendency quite explicit.

Hence research on media effects proves the influence of specific forms of media reporting on the disposition of opinions in large, anonymous and passive media audiences. However, this is just the top-down perspective on the formation of citizen audiences. In contrast, an understanding of active citizen audiences is necessary (Lingenberg 2010b). In this perspective the European public sphere emerges in a process of the appropriation of mediatised European public discourses by the people. As soon as individuals in the shared European space of political action perceive the impact of EU political decisions, as well as the interdependencies with other EU countries, a Europeanised citizen audience emerges in communicative interactions with others. Taking the example of the European constitutional debate with the failed referenda in France and the Netherlands in 2005, people in France, Germany and Italy did feel that there were interdependencies in the European constitutional process and therefore felt affected by the failed referenda (Lingenberg 2010a). Nevertheless, the topic has been discussed in Italy, France and Germany. Both the transnational spread of arguments and the nation-specific moulding of debates point to the existence of a Europeanised citizen audience that still remains nationally segmented.

(2) As this empirical audience research demonstrates, it is necessary to explore alternative theoretical concepts for the appropriation of Europe. This is the point where the concept of European public connection comes in. Fundamentally, this concept is related to the idea of analysing *how* people relate themselves to public issues, and what role media and communication play in this. The purpose of the concept is to ask, 'what *are* the practices that link private action to the public sphere' (Couldry et al. 2007a: 28 [italics as in the original]). The authors use

the notion of public connection to isolate a complex component of a working democracy; namely, that people establish a certain connection to the public as a precondition of involvement in democracies. Their underlying argument is that 'as citizens we share an orientation to a public world where matters of shared concern are or at least should be addressed: we call this orientation public connection' (Couldry et al. 2007b: 3).

This said, the concept of public connection sheds light on two key aspects regarding citizens' scepticism or lack of interest in political communication. First, it shifts the research focus from the provision of (valuable qualitative) political information by the media to 'the citizens' broader sense' of the news and only then to 'the role of the media in enabling it' (Couldry/Langer 2005: 238). Having a public connection does not necessarily imply agreement. It may imply support of a political system and politics, but also (sometimes heavy) criticism of politics and even the media (Couldry/Langer 2005: 250, 255; Kaun 2012: 106ff.; 2014). This goes hand in hand with ambivalent attitudes towards politics in general (Schrøder/Phillips 2007: 910). Second, the concept requires that the different ways of establishing a relation to public affairs within an increasingly complex and diverse media environment be investigated. This makes a 'unified "civic culture"' (Almond/Verba 1963; Couldry/Langer 2005: 239; Dahlgren 2005; see also chapter 2 of this book) less likely as there are numerous ways of integrating political information into everyday media consumption.

Couldry and Langer describe various types of public 'connectors', for example, 'old-style connectors, new style connectors, and time lackers, with a residual category of non-connectors' (Couldry/Langer 2005: 249ff.). We can explain differences between these types by education, age and, linked to that, understandings of duty (see in more detail Couldry et al. 2007b). In a study of young Estonians' public connections, Anne Kaun (2012) puts a stronger focus on young citizens' experiences of the political. Within this age group, she describes three forms of public connection: first, 'critical media connection'; second, 'playful public connection'; and third, 'historical public connection'. In other words, these notions embrace orientations towards the public that are characterised by, first, a fundamental distrust in the media's potential to support deliberation and differentiation, second, by 'joyful, voluntary ways of engaging with politics' (Kaun 2012: 123) and, finally, by the negotiation of historical conflicts between Estonian and Russian history. Thus, Kaun points to the media being an important, but not the exclusive context for civic experience.

In sum, the notion of public connection is instructive for the study of European audiences, since it moves our focus to the way in which people communicatively connect to the public affairs of the EU and Europe, and by virtue of this become a European citizen audience. Since our primary focus is not on citizens' general orientations towards public issues, but towards Europe and the EU, in the following we speak of European public connections. However, the question remains as to how we might describe these public connections with regard to the communicative means involved. This is the point where another concept comes in; namely, communication repertoires.

(3) The concept of communication repertoires extends the widely used concept of media repertoires. While the latter is limited to mediated communication, the former includes both mediated and direct communication. Current media and communication research mostly focuses on media repertoires. Following Taneja et al. (2012: 953), these are 'subsets of media from available media', or with reference to an earlier publication by Hasebrink and Popp (2006: 269) 'comprehensive patterns of exposure'. Researchers of media repertoires are therefore interested in 'how patterns of availability and individual traits influence repertoires of media use' (Taneja et al. 2012: 953). A key strength of all repertoire-related research is to overcome single-media approaches, since they cannot investigate media use as part of the present manifold media environment (Hasebrink/Popp 2006: 369). It is especially the growth in digital media that is seen in relation to new, hitherto insufficiently systematised, patterns of audiences' media appropriation (Hasebrink 2015; Hasebrink/Popp 2006; Taneja et al. 2012; Webster/Ksiazek 2012). This has consequences on different levels: for instance, the increasing economic importance of individual media users' choices have an impact on the media market, as Mirca Madianou and Daniel Miller (2012a, 2012b) argue. Although – as Hasebrink (2015) puts forward – it is helpful to understand media repertoires as a subset of communication repertoires, the latter remains the wider concept. The added value of the communication repertoire approach is that it reflects both the individual media appropriation within an increasingly diverse media environment and also the typical forms of communication used by this person, explicitly including direct communication.

Against this background, we understand communication repertoires to follow three core criteria (Hasebrink/Domeyer 2012: 795f.) that aim at integrating both environmental conditions and individual situatedness within them (Hasebrink/Popp 2006: 371; Taneja et al. 2012: 952). First, the concept is related to an individual perspective, focusing upon the individual as a media user and communicator. In contrast to a media-centric perspective, asking which audiences a particular medium reaches, this concept puts the emphasis on various forms of individual communication in direct and mediated ways. Second, the concept aims to record the entirety of relevant communications. The repertoire-oriented approach stresses the need to consider the complete variety of media and communicative forms regularly assembled by a person. In the case of our research, we focus on the subset of communications related to public affairs. And third, it is a relational approach. Within a repertoire perspective, the interrelations and specific functions of the components within this repertoire are of particular interest since they represent inner structure or coherence. Based on this, political communication means investigating the overall political communication of a person.

Given that we here explore citizens' orientations towards Europe and EU-related issues and seek to describe them in a meaningful way, it is necessary to consider the concepts of European public connection and political communication repertoire in their relation to each other. While political communication repertoires include a person's entire political communication, European public connection registers a person's existing or non-existing relations to EU- and Europe-related issues. It is through their political communication repertoires that people articulate their European public connection. Here it is important not to limit the investigation to the complexity and diversity of citizens' communicative practices (Schrøder/Phillips 2007: 893). Reaching beyond that, we have to question to what extent individual specificities of political communication repertoires are related to the social positioning of the individual, as well as to varying contexts. These have been mostly discussed with regard to media and communication repertoires in particular.

On an individual level, many researchers have noted the extent to which rhythms of everyday life shape communication repertoires. A number of scholars have highlighted 'situational affordances' (Schrøder/Kobbernagel 2010: 119) of media use, such as lack of time that might limit the range of media in use (Hasebrink/Domeyer 2012: 768; see also Couldry/Lange 2005: 255; Schrøder/Phillips 2007: 896). Taneja et al. (2012: 964) take this argument further by introducing a media repertoire typology that is oriented towards the rhythms of 'work, leisure, commute and sleep'. They distinguish between media repertoires that are valid during work ('computing for work'), free time ('television viewing' and 'media online') and while under way ('media on mobile')

(Taneja et al. 2012: 959). Following this typology, the authors make a strong case for the role of individuals' routines within everyday media use, depending on the availability of a given medium in a given situation. With reference to Anthony Giddens (1984), who points to the basic 'human need' to face the challenges of everyday life with the help of established routines, Taneja, Webster and Malthouse argue that different biographical experiences and phases of life-course result in stable patterns of media use. This becomes evident, for example, by contrasting working and retired persons.

On a positional level, researchers point to the significance of education, age and gender for explaining differences in communication repertoires. Schrøder and Phillips (2007: 869f.), for instance, develop a twofold typology of experiencing the media when searching for political information. While there is a general interest in getting an overview of regional and local news, citizens with higher levels of education prefer in-depth insights and tend to be more interested in international perspectives. In contrast, citizens with lower levels of education tend to stick to their more general interest in news, 'without unnecessary and irrelevant details' (Schrøder/Phillips 2007: 896). Similar arguments have been put forward in debates on the Europeanisation of public spheres, where the question of education has been broadly discussed in terms of an elite bias regarding participation in political communication (Favell/Recchi 2011; Risse 2010; Statham/Trenz 2013: 79ff.; Van de Steeg 2010: 44). Primarily, so-called quality media appear to provide users with ample and diverse information on Europe and the EU, and the main readership of newspapers like these comprises well-educated or elite European citizens (Axel Springer Media Impact 2015; Elvestad/Blekesaune 2008). What echoes here is our previous discussion of stratification-related processes of segmentation and corresponding cultures of political discourse.

Finally, there is a contextual level that means we have to understand communication repertoires as embedded in local, national and European political references. Explicitly, researchers have repeatedly pointed to the local embeddedness of audiences (Lingenberg 2010a, 2010b). Similarly, Nick Couldry and Ana Inés Langer (2005: 251) point to the paramount interest of citizens in local political affairs and their mainly local engagement when it comes to political activities (comparable research results Hepp et al. 2014: 227–246). In addition, we have to consider national embeddedness. Researchers have highlighted that citizens tend to refer to the media available in their national contexts and are confronted with media content that approaches Europe and the EU via national perspectives. And finally, a European embeddedness might also be of relevance. This contextual level at least partly finds its echo in national and European cultures of political discourse (see for both arguments Lingenberg 2010a, 2010b).

Hence, especially when studying citizens' European public connections, it is paramount to ask about the 'intersection' (Winker/Degele 2011) of the individual, positional and contextual level. With regard to these intersections, there is another complexity that needs to be considered in the following: the European public connection of citizens during the euro crisis. While the European character of this public connection introduces the dynamism of transculturation (Kannengießer 2012), reference to the euro crisis raises questions concerning the potentially activating role of this political event. Recent publications hint at various possible consequences of the euro crisis. At the individual level, citizens might find their habits of everyday media appropriation disrupted. That is not to say that this disruption would necessarily result in ignoring or neglecting the crisis, as Harsh Taneja and his colleagues (2012) might argue on the basis of their findings. Another possibility is the adaption of communication repertoires to crucial happenings like the euro crisis. This is what Uwe Hasebrink and Hanna Domeyer had in mind when generally speaking of media repertoires as '*relatively* stable trans-media patterns of media use' (Hasebrink/Domeyer 2012: 759 [italics as in the original]). With regard to the positional level, there are various possible consequences of the euro crisis. Paul Statham and Hans-Jörg Trenz (2013: 100f.) highlight an increasing tendency to contrast the elite and ordinary citizen brought about by the crisis. As frustration and disappointment might grow among those who feel increasingly socially excluded, European public connection might weaken. On a contextual level, in contrast, one finds contrary arguments; for example, by Klaus Eder (2014), who emphasises the politically activating role of the euro crisis, since this might make European embeddedness more accessible to a general public. His point is that nation states hardly provide citizens with answers to the global economic challenges they face. This said, the euro crisis, due to its transnational character, could be regarded as a chance to articulate a European *demos*.

Having this complexity of different levels, their intersection and further dynamics in mind, in the following we will present a three-stage analysis. First, we want to identify the different political communication repertoires we find in our data. Second, we want to ask about the typical kinds of European public connection across the six countries studied. Third and finally, we want to reflect on the specific role of the euro crisis.

6.2   Political communication repertoires: ranges and dominances

The diversity of the interviewees with respect to age, social position-ing and cultural background is steady across the variety of the three political communication repertoires that will be discussed in more detail in this section. When comparing these repertoires transculturally, we notice patterns with regard to two dimensions: first, with regard to their 'range', as encompassing those communicative means that are mobi-lised for the various moments of political communication, including Europe and EU-related issues; second, with regard to the communicative means that 'dominate' the given political communication repertoire (see for the analytical scheme Figure 6.1).

With regard to the range of appropriated communicative means, we do not simply have in mind the interviewees' references to a greater or lesser amount of media. It is instead a matter of the variance of appropri-ated communicative means. Within this range of communicative means we distinguish radio, television, newspaper, online and interpersonal communication. Thus, we mainly consider whether citizens combine different types of media. For instance, the appropriation of diverse quality media together with a local newspaper would only be discussed secondarily.

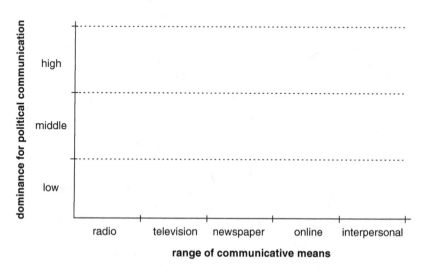

Figure 6.1   Political communication repertoires

With reference to dominance, as a second criterion, we have observed that each interviewee considers mostly one, sometimes more, communicative means as being indispensable or at least of basic importance for political information, including Europe and EU-related issues. Overall, we identified five political communication repertoires: a radio-dominated repertoire, a television-dominated repertoire, a newspaper-dominated repertoire, an online-dominated repertoire and, finally, an interpersonally dominated repertoire. These political communication repertoires are more or less digital. An interpersonal dominance, for instance, is based on direct communication or digital personal media communication. Similarly, the radio, newspaper or TV dominance refers to these media in their traditional or digital form. In contrast, a repertoire dominated by online media involves media that are 'originally' digital. Examples are the news on welcome pages of mail providers, social network sites or video platforms. Based on these terminological distinctions, it becomes possible to discuss the various communication repertoires in greater detail.

(1) First, there is a group of interviewees who have a radio-dominated communication repertoire. In other words, these identify radio as being indispensable for keeping oneself informed about political communication in general and with regard to European and EU-related issues in particular. An illustrative case is that of the Danish woman Lotte Lillebjerg, a storekeeper on parental leave, who is clearly oriented towards the regular consumption of radio news. She states: 'Well, mostly, I have the radio turned on. And there is radio news every hour, and there I hop on and off all the time' (Lotte Lillebjerg, 34, DK). However, as Lotte apparently struggles with writing and reading, an additional subordinate source is interpersonal communication. Conversations with her boyfriend, who is interested in politics, occasionally provide her with additional interpretations. Another illustrative case is that of the German gardener Simon Gärtner, who reports listening to the radio as much as possible during his daily work in the greenhouse. While he also refers to TV as well as online media use and intense political discussions with close friends as other means for political communication, it is the radio which is the source that he mostly trusts in and depends on: 'I actually find *Deutschlandfunk* [a quality radio station] provides quite comprehensive information and I am well satisfied with it.' He mentions that a programme called *Europe today* belongs to his favourites. In this context, Simon also explicitly points out that the radio dominance relates to his *political* communication repertoire, his remaining usage being dominated by the use of online media.

While these cases share a focus on radio as the basic communicative means for political communication, they vary significantly with respect to the range of communicative means. Lotte, the Danish storekeeper on parental leave, depends almost exclusively on the radio as her prime source of political communication. Simon, as implied above, has a more diverse repertoire. Finally, Cornelia Sucher, an Austrian 56-year-old learning counsellor, has a comparatively broad political communication repertoire. With regard to political communication, Cornelia places emphasis on both radio and her interpersonal network that functions via e-mail communication. Whereas the radio, namely the Austrian public programme *Ö1*, provides her with reportage that she especially appreciates, she uses e-mail to keep up with political events, for example, on unconditional basic income issues, which she regularly attends.

(2) Further, there is another group of citizens who have political communication repertoires with television dominance. In this case, it is the consumption of politics-related programmes that is thought the most salient means of providing content related to politics in general and Europe more specifically. For Edgar Davies, a 71-year-old retired engineer from London, for instance, the television is the most important news source: 'If I'm indoors I watch television. Mostly *BBC*.' Whereas Edgar refers to TV as an exclusive source for political communication, Kurt Binder's case points to a broader range. The former manager of a medium-size enterprise, now living on his private income, reports spending a considerable amount of time in front of the TV screen: 'For me the most important medium, media, for example the television. You see. That is where I get most information. And newspaper in the second place' (Kurt Binder, 60, GER). In case he does not manage to watch the programmes on TV he downloads them via the programmes' internet platforms. Nevertheless, as Kurt notes, the online versions are his second choice, only playing a role when he lacks the time for watching live TV. Poul Omegn represents a similar case, which is also illustrated by the impressive number of TV channels he lists in his network map (cf. Figure 6.2). Omegn, a currently jobless sales promoter, is well informed with regard to current political issues. He follows mostly public Danish TV on screens that are spread around his apartment. Other sources of political information, such as RSS feeds, play only a subordinate role. Irrespective of whether the interviewees have a political communication repertoire with a low, middle or high range, they share their orientation towards TV as a main source of political communication, not least on Europe.

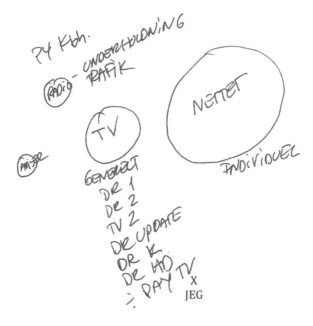

Figure 6.2 Media-related network map of the 44-year-old Danish Poul Omegn, Denmark

(3) There are also a number of illustrative examples for political communication repertoires that are dominated by newspapers. For instance, the Danish musician Mette Kongekjær Engholm, 24 years old, living in the suburbs of Copenhagen, focuses on freesheets as her almost exclusive source of political communication, including with respect to Europe. Occasionally, Mette also keeps herself updated via the main news on Danish public TV; this, however, remains of minor importance. Another case that illustrates a newspaper dominance of political communication repertoires is that of Arnim Pollmann (69, GER) whose habit is to access political information via a local newspaper. For as long as the retired fireman remembers, he has been a regular reader of the same newspaper his parents had read, the Berlin-related *Morgenpost*. In contrast to Mette, nevertheless, Arnim has a political communication repertoire including also radio and television as a means of political communication. The local newspaper, nevertheless, is the one that he considers a 'kind of a duty, even' (Arnim Pollmann, 69, GER) and which, despite his explicitly critical perspective on the media in general, he regards as a key source of political information.

Finally, the case of Lisa Harvey of Britain, a 58-year-old manager of a hair salon in Richmond, represents an example of political communication repertoires composed of a number of various means of communication. Within her political communication repertoire, newspapers are the dominant but by no means sole media reference. Besides her regular reading of dailies, the *Daily Telegraph* during the week and the *Sunday Times* on weekends, she consumes TV at home, radio in the car and beyond that occasionally the *BBC* app via her smartphone. Not least, she reports that from time to time she discusses economic issues at work.

(4) A fourth group concerns those interviewees whose political communication repertoires are dominated by the use of online media. As introduced earlier, in this case those media are of paramount significance that are *originally* digital. Thus, we see a difference with cases such as that of the Austrian Michael Mahdbauer, who uses an app to organise a transnational choice of e-papers where, however, the consumption of the *original* quality paper is the clear focus of interest. In contrast, the focus of Amina Zündler, another Austrian, 28 years old and a manager for cultural projects, is clearly on the use of online media. While, at first glance, her network map appears to list a high range of various media, a closer look shows that it is mostly online media that are listed. Her political communication repertoire is described by one statement that she clearly highlights: 'Internet, the world! [. . .] Forums, newsletter, [. . .]' (cf. Figure 6.3). The interview shows that it is mostly one medium, namely *orf.at*, the news page of the national public TV channel, that is used for 'getting a quick overview' (Amina Zündler, 28, AT) on what is going on in the world of politics.

In contrast to Amina's narrow political communication repertoire, Bogdana Kruczaj of Poland is an example of a broad range, dominated by the use of online media. Bogdana, a 56-year-old female lawyer from Cracow, regularly accesses various types of media. Her main focus regarding political information and communication is however on online media. Bogdana relates her interest in conservative politics and religious issues to the opportunities provided by digital platforms. She highlights here preference for choosing what and how she remains informed with regard to actual politics, including Europe. In consequence, she finds online media as to be the most indispensable. Nonetheless, she consumes numerous other media that are less significant, including TV, radio and newspapers. In this sense, the case of Bogdana highlights especially the fact that individual political communication repertoires are informed by the kind of public connections the respective interviewee pursues. This argument will be developed further in the following section.

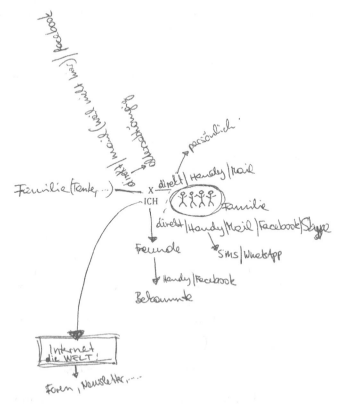

Figure 6.3   Media-related network map of the 28-year-old Amina Zündler, Austria

(5) Finally, there are the interpersonally dominated political communication repertoires. Here interviewees place the most confidence in information on and interpretation of actual political issues by friends, family members or other individual sources who are treated as experts. One illustrative case is that of Susanne Kramer of Germany, whose interpersonally dominated repertoire exclusively relies on regular conversations with her boyfriend. While she is a frequent internet and TV user, this does not play a role with regard to political information. She relies heavily on her boyfriend as her personal 'filter' (Susanne Kramer, 33, GER). Avoiding any political news as appropriated media content, she keeps politically updated through him. Oliver Cox, Britain, a 30-year-old waiter in a fish restaurant in Richmond, has a more extended political communication repertoire. While Oliver regularly checks breaking news on his mobile

phone in the morning, the key component that he explicitly highlights with regard to political information are the regular conversations with his French girlfriend in the evenings. Finally, an example with a political communication repertoire including a broad range of diverse media is that of the German-British Tamara Tannhäuser, a 30-year-old living in London, who, with regard to political communication, regularly consumes *BBC breakfast TV*, the websites of various German and British local and quality newspapers, as well as freesheets on her daily commute. Top priority, nevertheless, is given to talks with her father, living in Germany. Issues they discuss on the phone concern Germany and the UK, but not least, as she highlights, also Europe. In her political communication repertoire, these talks thus have a core orientation function in approaching the remaining political information that she considers.

Altogether, across this detailed overview, we want to discuss finally those criteria of difference that we referred to in the introduction to this chapter, namely potential differences regarding positional and contextual aspects. We have pointed to discussions related to income, age and gender, but also to living in rural or urban environments. Questions raised here concern whether specific dominances relate to specific, that is better, societal positions on the one hand or to a specific contextualisation on the other. Still, in this context it is important to keep in mind that the study presented in this and the following chapter serves only as a preliminary basis for the discussion of trends, since the qualitative sample was composed with these differences in view. In addition, the five political communication repertoires presented above have not been systematised according to quantitative, but rather subjective qualitative assessments from the interviewees' perspective. Repertoire dominances, as presented above, do not mainly refer to the frequency of use of a specific medium, but to the interviewees' assessment of whether the given communicative means has an anchor function in a given political communication repertoire.

Apart from this perspective and with regard first of all to positional aspects, the five dominances in political communication repertoires do not point to any specific trend. Yet, the data does reflect some well-known findings from audience research. We clearly find more quality newspaper readers and quality radio consumers among those with a stronger educational background and fewer among those with a weaker educational background. Another trend resonates with findings from the study of online communication dominance, namely that it is mostly young interviewees who refer to it. All the same, the case of Bogdana Kruczaj shows that there are exceptions. On the other hand, it is crucial to highlight that representatives of any social class, age and gender are found within any of the five political communication repertoires. In other words, newspaper, TV, radio, online or interpersonal dominance play a role for better and less educated, for elder and younger and, not least, for male and female. The latter is of special interest with regard to interpersonal dominances of a communication repertoire that might be characterised as a specific female feature. The examples discussed above point to a different finding. Both men and women depend on interpersonal communication as a main source for political information and interpretation.

Second, with regard to contextual aspects, one could discuss references to the uses of media across borders. Relating the local embeddedness of the interviewees in the sample and their educational or economic positions does not highlight any surprising finding. We find in the sample a considerable number of citizens whose well-educated self-positioning is accompanied by references to foreign media. All the same, we should note that there are singular contrasting examples. For instance, Oliver Cox, the British fish restaurant waiter mentioned above, is well informed of what is going on in French politics via his French girlfriend. Inversely, we also find cases of well-educated and well-off citizens who regularly travel across borders without developing any special interest in political communication across borders. Among these, one could mention the Polish Grzegorz Samochowiec, 54 years old, who for business reasons used to drive to Vienna. His political communication repertoire, however, remains focused on local and occasionally national media.

6.3   European public connections: centred, noticing and multi-perspective

Political communication repertoires, with their range of appropriated media and dominance for political communication, help us understand the variety of European public connections. A first, basic result of our research is that a fundamental European public connection is built up through all these five political communication repertoires, irrespective of their dominances and ranges of appropriated media. However – and this is our second, fundamental research result – these public connections vary in their character. We distinguish three basic European public connections: noticing, centred and multi-perspective ones. The noticing European public connection focuses on registering the most important issues on the media's agendas; the centred European public connection follows political communication through the perspective of an individual core topic; and finally, the multi-perspective European public connection puts emphasis on comparing various perspectives regardless of the issue.

The main point here is that there is little evidence that a specific European public connection relates to only one political communication repertoire. Citizens with a multi-perspective European public connection do not necessarily refer to a communication repertoire with a wide range of media and a preference of newspapers when it comes to political communication. In contrast, a multi-perspective European public connection can also be based on a television-dominated political communication repertoire with a limited variance of other media. We have to keep this point in mind when discussing segmentations on a positional or contextual level.

Noticing European public connection

With the noticing public connection, citizens emphasise their interest in 'what is up to date and what is on the agenda', as 35-year-old Austrian Michael Mahdbauer puts it. The focus here is on remaining informed about the most important ongoing issues in the (mediated) public realm. In particular, 'specific issues [. . .] are not of any further interest', says Markus Kleimann, a 37-year-old German logistics manager who is well-off and a family father. The reasons given are diverse. Some of the interviewees with a noticing European public connection emphasise the 'duty' (Anita Berger, 44, GER) of staying informed. Other interviewees, such as Megan Fraser, a 27-year-old British saleslady in a local bookshop, highlight the social dimension of being up to date: 'You never know when someone might come into it and you gonna go, oh, I didn't know that. And so it's kind of "I get the headlines" and that sort of thing.'

This underlines the fact that there are considerable differences in noticing public connections with regard to their respective political communication repertoires. The analysis of political communication repertoires suggests a great variety of dominances and ranges within the realm of the noticing public connection. For instance, many citizens focus on one central means of communication in order to realise their noticing public connection. A significant group, for instance, refers to a traditional focus. Often it is the local daily, sometimes the quality newspaper or, as in the case of many Danish interviewees, free papers that ensure a (quick) overview of what is actually on the agenda (for reflections on increase in significance of free dailies in Denmark see Schrøder/ Phillips 2007: 897). An illustrative example from the material is that of

24-year-old Polish student Janusz Ruchniewicz, whose communication repertoire is composed of various media (see Figure 6.4). With regard to political communication, however, his focus is clearly on the *Gazeta Wyborcza*, a left wing, pro-European quality paper (categorised as ambassador, see chapter 3), that he regularly buys every morning from a little kiosk in his street. Another source is Radio Agora, a news station that belongs to *Gazeta Wyborcza's* media enterprise. From Janusz's perspective the radio has a supplementary function, as it completes the political picture created via the *Gazeta Wyborcza*, while still referring to similar issues and interpretations. Although Janusz Ruchniewicz considers himself an 'enthusiastic European', Europe and the EU are not the issues that *guide* his media consumption. In fact, the newspaper provides him

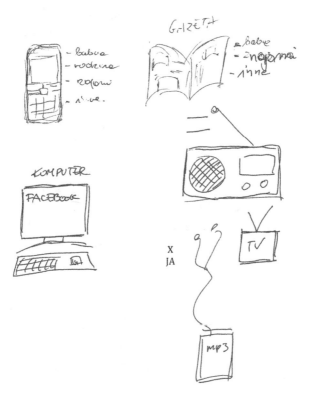

Figure 6.4 Media-related network map of the 24-year-old Polish student Janusz Ruchniewicz

with current information on politics and culture from a 'relaxed view of the world'.

In contrast to Janusz, Mette Kongekjær Engholm, the 24-year-old Danish musician introduced earlier, sustains her noticing European public connection by a newspaper-dominated political communication repertoire, reading three free newspapers on a regular basis. Even though she never commutes via the metro to the city centre, she periodically stops at a metro station to grab a free daily or asks her boyfriend to get her one. As illustrated in Figure 6.5, Mette disposes of a comparably broad communication repertoire. The media she refers to when gaining political information are, however, limited to free newspapers and occasionally the main TV news. It is these sources that keep Mette updated with the intention of 'just getting some impression of, let's call it the biggest things that have happened' (Mette Kongekjær Engholm, 24, DK). Via this approach, she is connected to European and EU-related issues. Her approach oscillates between criticising the EU for its intrusive role in Danish sovereignty on the one hand and perceiving Europe as part

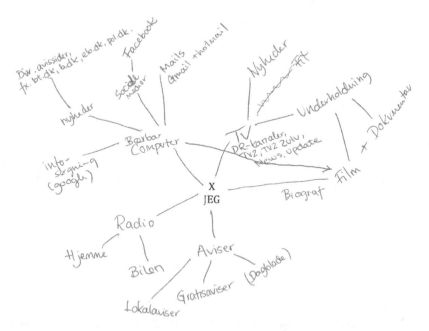

Figure 6.5 Media-related network map of 24-year-old Dane Mette Kongekjær Engholm

of Danish political reality on the other. Thus, she states that 'they make rules they themselves think are good, but they don't think about, ehm, we are some small countries that can think for themselves well enough', but also that 'the EU has been made with the intention, I think, that it shall be easier with regard to trade and travelling and there shall be some common regulation' (Mette Kongekjær Engholm, 24, DK). These quotes illustrate the core characteristics of Mette's noticing European public connection. By catching the most important issues from TV and free sheets, she mirrors key discussions related to the EU.

It is this way of viewing Europe and EU-related issues as a *given* ingredient of current political reality that is typical for the noticing European public connection. Citizens realise it with regard to varying media dominances in their political communication repertoire. Julien Hermès, a successful French dermatologist, focuses on TV news, updating during breakfast and watching the 'TV news spotlights, you see, that is very comfortable [. . .] I listen to the most important headlines' (Julien Hermès, 61, F). In contrast, Simon Gärtner, the 37-year-old gardener, clearly focuses on the radio that he listens to during his work in the greenhouse. Simon appreciates being regularly updated by a 'quality radio station' (Simon Gärtner, 37, GER) that he trusts to provide him with all the information he needs from a perspective that is as diverse as possible. He shares this focus on the radio with very many citizens from other European countries. Citizens talk of using regular commute times in the car to listen to the radio and keeping updated with regard to current political news in this way. An example is the Polish teacher and young mother Magdalena Gwosdek (33 years old) who catches up with political information while driving to the nearby city where she works in a school for disabled children.

There is also a small group of interviewees whose political communication repertoire is dominated by interpersonal communication. An interesting case is that of Susanne Kramer (33, GER), mentioned earlier, who consciously refuses to be in direct touch with political communication. Her relation to the media is problematic or conflicting, since she feels overwhelmed by information, especially political information, provided via the media. She thus depends on her boyfriend to inform her about current issues. A similar case is that of Marielle Gispon, a 30-year-old French woman working as a physics teacher near Montpellier. In her everyday life, Marielle concentrates on entertainment media (*Elle* magazine and *RTL radio* when commuting to work), while her main source of political information is her husband. It is this way that she keeps informed about the main public issues.

Finally, a number of interview partners pursue an online dominance. In this case, however, we can hardly speak of using less media. In the majority of the cases found across the interview sample, a digital focus appears to relate to a strategy of organising more media to realise a noticing public connection. In this context, an interesting case is that of Michael Mahdbauer, who aims at a transnational noticing European public connection. He gains an overview of various newspapers with the help of an app and reports going through the headlines to find out, for example, 'What is on the agenda in France? Simply, what is on the agenda' (Michael Mahdbauer, 35, AT). Similarly, he is interested in the agenda of his own and other countries. Michael Mahdbauer's political communication repertoire aims at a transcultural comparison of what is 'most important internationally', limited only by his language skills.

Likewise, the political communication repertoires of citizens who refer to more media can be characterised with regard to specific dominances. Here the focus involves the source that has a guiding function among other communicative means. Yvonne Rauch, a 22-year-old German who occasionally works as a cleaning lady, represents an example of a more media-related communication repertoire with a focus on direct communication. Yvonne is kept updated by regular talks with her father, be it face-to-face or by phone. While interviewees such as Julien Hermès or Simon Gärtner have a clear focus on one medium only, in their cases TV and radio, Yvonne also uses TV and the internet to gain more information or to confirm interpretations made by her father. All the same, her father and their conversations remain the key source for linking with the political. Altogether, it is important to keep in mind what these insights show: The noticing European public connection is realised across all types of communication repertoire.

Moreover, a noticing European public connection means that citizens have communicative linkages with the most salient current European and EU-related issues. While the interviewees that refer to it share this basic characteristic, a closer look brings to the fore a range of very diverse biographies and backgrounds, motives and strategies. While there are some interviewees that have more or less factual knowledge in this political field, others that realise a noticing public connection have an intuitive imagination of what is going on in Europe and work on constructing an understanding of what Europe means to them and their environments. Marianne Becker, a 40-year-old currently unemployed bakery sales assistant, claims that she is not very interested in Europe, 'because I do not live in Europe, I live in Germany, I live in Bremen'. Nevertheless, Europe exists and bothers her, via her noticing public connection. Marianne's main source for political information is her TV; she watches the news once or twice every evening on her favourite private channel (*VOX*). From her point of view, Europe 'is' (Marianne Becker, 40, GER) where European issues matter. In other words, Europe *is* in Greece at the moment inasmuch as it is going through a financial and euro crisis. Marianne relates Europe's significance to the representation of Europe in the news: 'totally unimportant I/ I would not say because one notices it. It is often present in the news. It is not. I am not part of it, as I said. But it is somehow, yes [. . .]'. Another case is that of the earlier mentioned Polish teacher for disabled children, the 33-year-old Magdalena Gwosdek. Even though she presents herself as a person who is not particularly informed, interested or engaged in politics, she strongly relates to traditional as well as the emerging European society as something Poland was and is part of, not least in relation to her identity as a Catholic.

Another extreme is 24-year-old Briton Jamie Plotter who recently finished his master's degree in political science and is engaged as a social worker while, at the same time, looking for a new job. Jamie pursues a noticing public connection with a digital focus, including the homepages of two quality newspapers:

> I hate not knowing what is going on in the world. So I always I, I either buy a newspaper or, ehm, check the internet, *BBC*, the *Guardian* for example, the newspapers is my homepage as well. [. . .] So that, or the *Independent* as well. My two favourite papers [. . .] [I read] most actually, usually, eh, you know, current affairs eh, I suppose, the culture sections, sports as well. (Jamie Plotter, 24, UK)

While different from Marianne Becker and Magdalena Gwosdek, Jamie pursues a broad-range political communication repertoire in a very similar way, the noticing European public connection is characteristic for his everyday dealing with Europe. This is how he appropriates his online media. Jamie is interested in 'breaking news [. . .] and then find out what's happening I suppose and that's why, that's why I check the internet first before anything else.' In contrast, he mentions that 'getting a newspaper is more of a leisure thing than let's say you know, maybe trying to find out, about something I guess' (Jamie Plotter, 24, UK).

Marianne and Jamie represent extreme cases in their comprehensive potential towards Europe, since Marianne hardly understands what the EU is and Jamie, both educated and analytical with respect to politics, pursues an unambiguously positive attitude towards Europe. Nevertheless, they both have noticing European public connections, keeping themselves updated with what is going on in Europe. Magdalena, in contrast, appears to have a better idea of Europe in general, but suffers from a lack of time to deepen her European public connection. Irrespective of these varying intensities, it is important to keep in mind that a noticing public connection refers to Europe and EU-related issues as something that is part of the most important political issues. There appears to be no question that one needs to deal with it. It is this basic insight that we gained across those interviewees with respect to a noticing European public connection.

Like other kinds of European public connection, the noticing public connection is articulated in a highly habitualised way. Anita Berger (44, GER), for instance, has organised her and her family's daily structure around the use of different media. There are specific media, such as a local radio station and a local newspaper that play a role in family time, while having breakfast and in the car when driving to school. And there are other media that play a role when she does the housework, for example, a national radio station. A different case is Anders Hansen, a 33-year-old homeless Danish street newspaper seller, who uses the time he spends on trains, buses or in public places to gain an overview of the news agenda:

> I read these freesheets a lot, *Metro* and *Urban* and *24 Timer*, in the trams and everywhere I go. And *Ekstrabladet*. Really depends on, well. Much up on Nørrebro (part of Copenhagen). And. There we used to sit, well, I can sit there or also at Østtorvet [another place in Copenhagen], when I'm on my way from A to B. So I can just, like, follow a little bit what's happening around. (Anders Hansen, 33, DK)

While these interviewees habitualise their noticing European public connection along well-established time schedules, there are other interviewees who emphasise the specific importance of one (single) trusted medium. One example is Sylvie Corona from France, who uses the radio all day long:

> I listen to the radio. The radio. I listen to the radio all day long when being at home. [. . .] It's *France Inter*, the channel. I wake up with this channel, and when I am at home it's on in the background. There is the flash news every hour, I listen really often to it. (Sylvie Corona, 25, F)

Similarly, Hilde Haltenberger (56, AT), an early-retired sales assistant, follows the *Euronews* during a specific time slot in the morning: 'My ritual is between taking a shower and, and quickly a coffee, and, and getting dressed, I do [. . .] the *Euronews*.' She emphasises that this update was especially important when she was still working as a sales assistant, as she 'then already got the most important issues a little bit'. While during that time she mostly watched *Euronews* while busy with other things, now she takes her time over it. Hilde Haltenberger's example also highlights the importance of biographical shifts for the adaption of political communication repertoires. A couple of mothers among the interviewees stress the need to adapt noticing strategies when time becomes a rare resource. This is the experience of 31-year-old Lara Bamberger, a European project manager in the German Ministry of Transport, who after having a family adjusted her noticing public connection by reducing it to a daily scan of the local newspaper.

Especially with reference to Hilde Haltenberger, but also to numerous other examples discussed above, we conclude that a noticing European public connection is characterised by a general phenomenon that we find in relation to very different individuals. Across our European sample, in parallel with the argument introduced by Harsh Taneja, James G. Webster and Edward C. Malthouse (2012), it becomes evident that individuals' political communication repertoires are highly habitualised, and that these media and communication related habits have an important structuring function within their daily lives.

Regarding the noticing Europe public connection, there is little evidence for correlation with 'social positioning'. The sample provides examples of various social classes and positions, including the early-retired and jobless Susanne Kramer, the Danish musician and middle class representative Mette Kongekjær Engholm, as well as the well-educated and well-positioned Austrian Michael Mahdbauer. In other words, there is no evidence that the noticing European public connection would dominate within a specific social stratum. However, it is striking that the interviewees articulate their different social positioning through and within their European public connection. This is illustrated by contrasting cases such as that of the Polish student Janusz Ruchniewicz, who talks of an ambitious bourgeois approach to Europe as a space of cultural openness, with that of the jobless Marianne Becker who explicitly sees herself at the bottom of the social ladder and, in consequence, as someone who can hardly change Europe's fate and influence on her life. Another illustrative example is that of Anita Berger (44, GER) whose key concern is the economic well-being of her family and, not least, of Germany. In relation to

Europe, Anita clearly articulates a middle-class social position by emphasising that Europe plays a key role in her political surrounding, although
she often understands little. In consequence, she sets herself the task of
being better informed so that she might be a responsible citizen.

Beyond that, the noticing public connection does not dominate
within a specific local or national *context*. On the one hand, interviewees living in both rural and urban contexts refer to noticing European
public connections. This has become clear across those living in Warsaw
(the student of history Janusz Ruchniewicz), London (the fish restaurant
waiter Oliver Cox) or in the French countryside (Marielle Gispon). On
the other hand, via these references to Europe, the interviewees also
express their local and national belongings. Again, this becomes especially apparent in the case of Anita Berger, who sees herself as a member
of her local-religious community and, beyond that, expresses her concern for the economic stability of Germany. Similarly, Anders Hansen,
the homeless Danish newspaper seller, highlights his interest in issues of
social justice, which should be solved by the Danish political responsi-
bles. Still, he does not consider poverty a problem that should be solved
on a global scale. From his point of view, it is not appropriate to spend
Danish money supporting Third World countries, but it is legitimate for
the EU to assist Greece in its current financially precarious situation.

In sum, the noticing European public connection is a pattern that
occurs across numerous individuals with varying political communication repertoires and attitudes towards Europe. However, the main common ground between all these cases is that the public connection is
neither centred on a certain topic, nor is there a deepened interest in
European politics. In this regard, the noticing European public connection clearly differs from the centred and multi-perspective European
public connection. A remarkable overlap among the three kinds, however, is the equally strong references to the habitualisation of political
communication repertoires. As we repeatedly argue, it is habitualisation
that substantiates the basic connection with Europe.

Centred European public connection

While the noticing European public connection is characterised by
remaining up-to-date with regard to current political issues, including
Europe and the EU, persons with a centred European public connection
are characterised by a thematic focus. This is a specific area of interest,
such as agriculture, family issues or economics that guide their approach
to Europe. In some cases, this goes hand in hand with the use of special-
interest media, like, for example, agricultural or family magazines. In all

cases, this is related to specific forms of media appropriation and communication. An example is the aforementioned Cornelia Sucher (56, AT), who has a focus on economics and intense communication about economy and money related issues within a group of friends. Also, Mikkel Poul Karstensen (32, DK), a vocational counsellor, claims to be mainly interested in two topics, 'that's partly politics and primarily what has to do with economic policy, and church related stuff'. Often issues that prove to be significant and are related to the job of the interviewees, such as common transport policy (as in the case of Gerhard Deichen, 62, GER, a retired director of the public transport system of a large German city), educational politics (Hubert Panzer, 50, AT, a secondary school teacher) or pharmacy (as in the case of Jacques Ardèche, 64, F, a manager in this field).

It is important to highlight that topics are often closely linked to specific worldviews. An example in our data that illustrates this is social injustice issues relating to power imbalances in societies. During her interview, Beata Szarek (58, PL), a cloakroom attendant at the University of Warsaw, repeatedly reconfirms the indissoluble contrast between 'the top brass' and 'we, down here'. Szarek, whose financial position is precarious, clearly identifies herself as belonging to the socially marginalised and expresses her general disappointment with the political elite. She contrasts poor Poland and rich Europe: 'We want the European only in Europe, because people earn money differently. And here, in Poland, are, well, unfortunately everything goes, as people say, to European costs, and they don't think of that there are people where income, in comparison to the European level, is significantly less' (Beata Szarek, 58, PL). A similar, but with regard to Europe rather inclusive, narration is put forward by a British homeless person who strongly relates his own personal situation to his vision of European solidarity:

Q: And who are your most important communication partners, so it's friends you mentioned, I think. And you're speaking to them about political, social things as well? A: No, usually it's about homelessness and trying to get a hostel. That's my main concern at the moment, trying to get a hostel. [. . .] Trying to get a roof over my head, that's what I'm concerned about at the moment. [. . .] Q: Ok, and is there anything specific coming into your mind when you're thinking about Europe, or politics? A: No, nothing specific. Well, I wonder how the country is being run. Q: In which sense do you wonder? A: For homeless people really. [. . .] Considering we're in Europe, we should all look after each other. I mean we're in Europe, aren't we? So look after each other, you know. (John Campbell, 58, UK)

Similarly, there are many cases where a centred European public connection occurs when political activism and interests overlap, as, for example, in the case of citizens with party membership of, for example, the 'social democrats' (Sigurd Birk Vandelmose, 65, DK) or in political activism for the protection of the environment (Jessica Price, 50, UK). Finally, it is worth mentioning that the interview sample provides no case where 'Europe' or 'the EU' was the guiding focus.

A closer look into the political communication repertoires found among citizens having a centred European public connection substantiates our findings in the previous section. Like the noticing, the centred European public connection is realised both by narrow and broader ranged communication repertoires, with a potential dominance of diverse communicative means for political communication. This will be illustrated by some contrasting examples.

On the one hand, there is a group of interviewees that grounds their centred European public connection within a political communication repertoire that is rather limited. One example is the case of Charlotte Miller (36, UK), whose European public connection has a thematic focus on social issues such as homelessness, while her political communication repertoire is dominated by interpersonal communication. While Charlotte discusses the most important issues with her local contacts, she also uses radio and freesheets along the way. In addition, there is the case of the 32-year-old Danish student of theology Mikkel Poul Karstensen. Mikkel, a family father, was not very successful in managing his own small construction company and now focuses on his studies. His Christian faith is a prime point of reference in his life, as is the centred European public connection, based on a fairly narrow communication repertoire with a dominance of radio and a quality newspaper (see Figure 6.6).

On the other hand, there are cases like the 56-year-old Pole Bogdana Kruczaj, whose European public connection, even though also oriented towards religious issues, is based on a much broader ranged communication repertoire. Bogdana is employed as a legal counsellor in a Cracow law company where she earns enough to live comfortably, owning a house and a holiday home in the nearby mountains. Her attitude – repeatedly emphasised within the interview we conducted with her – is that of a convinced Catholic and a political conservative. As represented by her network map (see Figure 6.7), Bogdana's centred European public connection is based on a broad political communication repertoire. As is visible at the top of her drawing, she is an extensive user of various internet platforms. Among the platforms she uses, there are general information platforms, such as the widely used *onet.pl* or *interia.pl* (both webmail interfaces with extensive news features),

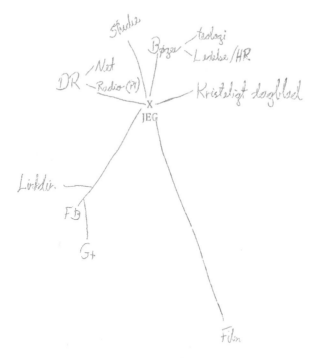

Figure 6.6 Media-related network map of 32-year-old Danish student of theology Mikkel Poul Karstensen

as well as platforms that pursue religious or conservative stances, for instance *wiara.pl* or the website of the former politician and publicist Stanisław Michałkiewicz. Nevertheless, she gets her European public connection in a thematically very centred way, as becomes apparent in the following quote:

> I don't buy newspapers [. . .]. Everything only via the internet. And, you know, although they spit and curse in these media, I don't pay attention, when I see that they said there that Jarosław Kaczyński [conservative politician, former prime minister of Poland the authors] should see a psychiatrist. I generally do not open that, what for? (Bogdana Kruczaj, 56, PL)

Two points are striking here. First, there is her use of special-interest media. Second is the appropriation of digital media, which acts as a supportive tool for gathering issue-specific information. However, both have to be discussed in context.

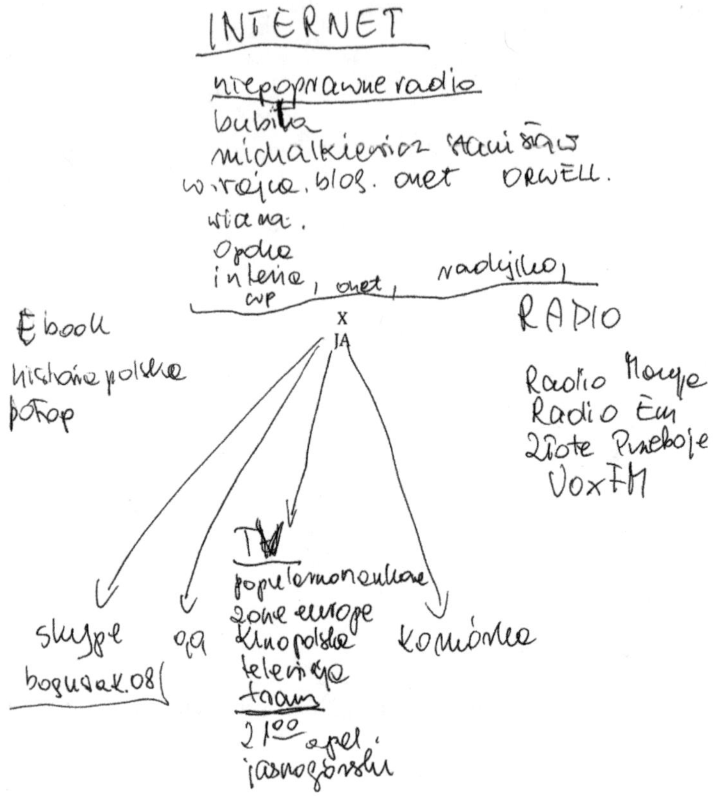

Figure 6.7   Media-related network map of 56-year-old Polish lawyer Bogdana Kruczaj

Regarding the first point, there is no evidence that the special-interest media are the only or primary sources of political information. This is not to argue however that issue-related media are in general of no importance for the European public connection. This appears to be proven by cases such as that of 62-year-old Briton Ismael Brooker. Ismael migrated to London in the 1960s, now runs a little internet café and is engaged in the anti-war movement, which also shapes his media appropriation and centres his European public connection. So searching for information he 'normally look[s] at *antiwar.com*.' (Ismael Brooker, 62, UK), which is also a main information source for him for further news. Here, the appropriated issue-specific media and the thematic centring of the European public connection go hand in hand. Nevertheless, issue specific media are often only one part of the political communication repertoire and centred public connection is articulated *across* a set of different media. In other words, there are cases where issue-specific interests relate to an intensified communicative involvement with Europe and the EU. Not least, we find numerous cases where a centred public connection is valid irrespective of the use of issue-specific media.

In fact, there are examples where our interview partners refer to specialised media. One case is the 33-year-old Polish farmer's wife Edyta Rolny, who gets her political information via a specific agricultural agency's website. Edyta Rolny is a young woman with two children and lives in rather simple conditions in a small village. The range of her political communication repertoire is quite low, consisting of agricultural magazines with information on EU politics and its impact on her survival as a farmer: 'here, still, it is the funding that we get, that is European money, and, yes, it is obviously what I associate with Europe – the EU [. . .], it would be tough without that for me [. . .]'. She considers her own situation to be paradoxical: Since Poland joined the EU, the prices for agricultural goods went down and living costs up. Against this background, she considers the EU funding as a necessary compensation, which is very welcome for her and her family since they heavily depend upon it. Edyta points to the internet as a key means of information. Here, her main source of information is the *Armir-Homepage*, the web site of the Polish Agricultural Agency, which distributes key information about changes in EU regulation and funding. As she puts it:

I always look up what is new, there [. . .] when do we have to hand in applications, what kind of money, it's mostly there. [. . .] Then, there is written, how much there is money from the national budget, how much is from the Union. How much or many people got it. [. . .] that seems so, I think, this is basic, not so much political. (Edyta Rolny, 33, PL)

Besides the fact that Edyta emphasises the economic rather than the political dimension of her interest, this quote highlights the extent to which she obtains insights into the EU's political decision-making through her centred public connection. A similar case is Constantin Zielke (25, GER), working in a bird reserve. He talks of his regular visits to websites and magazines dedicated to environmental issues and bird protection. While appropriating other media, such as the local daily and local radio stations, his highly specialised knowledge regarding EU environmental regulations and his advanced understanding of the underlying political structures is based on these specialised media.

Regarding our second point – digital media as a supportive tool for gathering issue-specific information – the case of Bogdana Kruczaj (56, PL) is once more striking. Her network map shows (see Figure 6.7) a range of different media. References to online media relating to political information dominate. She also uses both religious media, such as the broadcaster *TV trwam* (in English: *TV I persist*) or the famous orthodox Catholic *Radio Maryja*, as well as more general popular media, such as radio programmes from *VOX.fm* or internet platforms like *interia.pl* or *onet.pl*. Non-religious media are appropriated within a religious perspective – and the lack of this perspective she judges to be 'one-sided':

> And I don't listen to any discussion, because on TV, in the internet, because that is one-sided and it is, eh, I mean, there is this political correctness, from my point of view, and I take care to read, but what I want and not what they want me to. Nevertheless when I read, I don't watch any news on TV for years now [. . .]. I read in the internet. (Bogdana Kruczaj, 56, PL)

While this mainly confirms our earlier argument that a centred European public connection does not necessarily depend on special-interest media, it also hints at the role digital media play when gathering issue-specific information. For Bogdana, it is easier to find the kind of (religious) political information she is looking for online. Searching for specific information online is a general pattern we find in our data. Gerhard Deichen (62, GER), for example, an early-retired senior transport manager, continues his interest in transport policy by subscribing to the online press review provided by the public relations office of his former employer. In so doing, he continuously maintains an overview of the German-speaking media coverage in the field, including references to related developments at the European level.

However, we have in mind here that a centred European public connection does not necessarily imply online dominance of the political communication repertoire. Several of our interview partners build their centred public connection to Europe and the EU via communication repertoires of a quite different character. One example for this is Jacques Ardèche of France, who is 64 years old and has a special interest both in pharmacy and in art, especially architecture. Jacques' political communication repertoire is based on a wide range of media, with, however, a dominance of newspapers and magazines when it comes to political communication. Besides that, he listens to the radio and reads digital newsletters, neither being, however, his primary source for

European-related issues. Hand in hand with this newspaper dominance, he prefers reading books mainly about art and architecture in the variety of European cultures.

While Jacques' political communication repertoire is dominated much more by classical print media than online media, his European public connection remains a centred one. And like the other examples discussed in this section, this centring is related to a particular topic of general interest in his life. He approaches Europe and the EU from the perspective of this topic: His interest in art and architecture prompts a very specific way of understanding Europe as a culturally and intellectually rich space. The same pattern is characteristic for Bogdana Kruczaj, the Polish lawyer who has a focus on religious conservatism. Driven by her particular conservative stance, she has a deep knowledge of European history, the development of the EU and current European politics, and a specific understanding of Europe as a religious cultural entity:

> Every human being is important to Him, as to the Lord every human being is important, so for me this is also, that is why I also need to respect. That is why I have to, you know [. . .] appreciate other cultures. That is an incredible richness. [. . .] *That* is Europe. (Bogdana Kruczaj, 56, PL)

This brings us back to the three levels of analysis introduced at the beginning of this chapter: the individual, the positional and the contextual. On an individual level, we see once again the habitualised nature of political communication repertoires. There is no indication that people with an interest informed by a specific perspective attempt to deepen this perspective by adding new media to their political communication repertoires. There is also no indication that online media play an outstanding role. In contrast, just as with the noticing public connection, centred public connections are accompanied by well-organised and established habits of communication.

Again, Beata Szarek and Jacques Ardèche, serve as examples for this, albeit in different ways. Beata has two habits. On the one hand, she listens continuously to a Polish entertainment radio station during daytime work in the cloakroom. On the other hand, she regularly wanders around the rooms of the University building where she works to collect the newspapers left by students. Jacques' habits are based on a clear-cut daily structure. His working day encompasses periods of time-defined media use. As he describes it: 'from 5.45 to 6.30 am: *Europe 1*, radio, continues at 6.25 am: *Radio Classique*, for the weather [. . .], well, *Radio*

Classique up to 7 am and in the following in the office where via internet
I receive newsletters about a bunch of issues that deal with the confer-
ences that I organise' (Jacques Ardèche, 64, F). While the patterns in
both cases are different, they have in common the fact that their centred
European public connection is articulated by a highly habitualised individual communication repertoire.

   With reference to social positioning, our overall findings resonate with
what we argued in relation to the noticing public connection. Across the
countries studied by us and within them, citizens with various social
positions are apparently connected with Europe in a thematically centred way. This is not a matter of a particular social class. Their social
positioning ranges from individuals like Beata Szarek, the Warsawian
cloakroom lady with a special interest in social justice, to individuals
like Jacques Ardèche, director of a small company in the field of pharma-
ceutical congresses in Paris with a special interest in pharmacy and art.
Beyond that, however, this shared European public connection does not
involve the levelling of social differences. This becomes quite evident
in quotes like the following, in which Jacques is positioning himself
socially: 'Well, because, in fact, living in Europe one is always at the
heart of intellectual, cultural, artistic and passionate activity' (Jacques
Ardèche, 64, F). There are certainly relations between the topics citizens
are interested in, and their individual economic and social situations. In
the case of Beata Szarek, as well as the homeless man, these are concerns
of social injustice. Differences also remain within their political communication repertoires. While Beata represents an example of a citizen with
a rather narrow communication repertoire, focusing on radio and newspaper, Jacques profits from a broad range of varying media. While the
centred kind of European public connection does *not* depend on social
stratification, a different social positioning is re-articulated through the
detailed character of this public connection.

   Similar findings need to be highlighted with regard to the contextual dimension. Centred European public connections do not occur
without local and national references, but coalesce with a certain
local or national embeddedness. In other words, in and through this
European public connection, various different local and national contexts become re-articulated, in this case in a thematically centred way.
Again, two examples may illustrate this. Charlotte Miller, a 36-year-old
British nurse, interprets her local engagement against the background
of a broader mediated transnational context. Charlotte pursues a strong
interest in social issues and, beyond that, engages in local initiatives for
the support of homeless and sick people. This happens via *meetup.com*,
a networked organisation that acts locally but identifies itself via globally

shared problems. Charlotte explains: 'It started in New York and it's a pretty international thing and you can make, basically, whatever interests you've got, you can find a group [. . .]. And that sort of thing is real hands on, you can see a difference [. . .]. I'm not gonna get the troops out of Iraq so, you know, it might be a bit of a copout, but you know' (Charlotte Miller, 36, UK). While Charlotte sees her local engagement as part of a world movement, Herbert Sennenberger, retired from his job as a design draughtsman in Austrian public administration, maintains that 'one can absolutely be in the EU but nonetheless keep one's individuality' (Herbert Sennenberger, 65, AT). Herbert, whose focus is on both issues related to public administration and his conviction that 'money reigns the world' (Herbert Sennenberger, 65, AT), emphasises that his accepting perspective on the financial dilemmas of politics have a global, European and national dimension. His ideal is that Austria remains a sovereign player within this game – an issue that, among others, he articulates via letters to the editors of local newspapers.

What here becomes evident is the complexity of a centred European public connection. Characteristic for this kind of public connection is its approach to Europe and the EU through a particular thematically based point of view. The above has shown that social orientations and contextual aspects play a key role within this public connection. Beyond that and parallel to the argument introduced with regard to the noticing public connection, we have pointed out that the habits of various types of communication repertoires play a paramount supportive role in manifesting this dominant and centring thematic interest.

Multi-perspective European public connection

Finally, within our data we find a smaller group of people whose European public connection is multi-perspective. Citizens having this kind of public connection consider public issues something that necessarily should be discussed from various points of view. Therefore interviewees in the following are systematically looking for various and also contradictory political sources. The reasoning behind this comparative intent varies. A number of our interviewees keep an eye on different national viewpoints, others on different political positions or social positions. For example, Paul Unger points to the necessary deconstruction of social stereotypes rooted in his personal experiences as a gay man who has already lived in different European countries. Paul's ambition is to contribute to a European culture of diversity and acceptance: 'It would be great to get beyond [these stereotypes] and [. . .] consider the past nonetheless overcome all these clichés' (Paul Unger, 42, GER). One of the interviewees who highlight the significance of considering a number of different media and their political perspectives is Pierre Artis, who points to the 'advantage of reading several newspapers [since] this allows to have different opinions' (Pierre Artis, 56, F).

While in some cases the interviewees claim to simply distrust the media's coverage in general and therefore look for a multi-perspective access to media coverage, others point to the limitations of the media as a news organisation. Dennis Cooper, for example, reports that in the period of the 'Libya thing' he had subscribed to *Twitter* accounts both from Egypt and Libya 'just to get a sort of idea of what's going on in a different way than you get through the news. You know, regular news organisations' (Dennis Cooper, 29, UK). It is also worth noting that in many cases, the interviewees discuss the relation of the one-sidedness of any official political communication to their general distrust of politics and politicians. In addition, persons with this kind of public connection typically reflect on one-sidedness as an inevitable moment of communication per se – which can only be overcome by recognising opposite points of view. This results in a multi-perspective access to political communication in general, and European and EU politics in particular. Having a multi-perspective European public connection means, therefore, doing 'this comparison that you have, on the way different stories and political issues are simply presented, presented in a differentiated way' (Manuel Vechter, 19, AT).

Such an interest in different political positions might go hand in hand with a particular interest in questions of social equality. Théo Perrier, a teacher of French history, is concerned with 'how the lower classes receive the information, what kind of information do they give to them' (Théo Perrier, 29, F). Or Karl Autelberg, a 52-year-old Austrian writer influenced by Marxist ideas, who follows the people in his two favourite coffee shops – which he in the one case characterises as 'petty bourgeois of proletarian origin' and in the other case as 'bigoted bourgeois' – where he, by listening to their talk about politics, learns about their viewpoints. Bela Maschmann, a young artist from Berlin, keeps an eye on the, in his words, 'conservative' news and related forums, where he finds right-wing nationalist viewpoints. Bela has a special interest in 'what the people are like and this is a little bit more than consuming the *Tagesschau* [main public German TV news in the evening, the authors] or so' (Bela Maschmann, 32, GER). Bela's multi-perspective European public connection is characterised by his intention of contrasting what he thinks 'the people are like'. To him the media reflect what the people are like, and he contrasts it with his own critical worldview.

In many cases, multi-perspective European public connections are driven by the complexity of political decision-making. People with this public connection are critical of what they consider the necessary one-sidedness of political information and coverage. This critical standpoint can be routed in various political communication repertoires. However, while the dominant political information medium might vary, in tendency these repertoires are characterised by a wide range of different appropriated media. There are some examples that substantiate this: Inès Marquis (45), a French teacher, has a political communication repertoire that is dominated by references to the international quality press. Within this dominance, she reads several international newspapers: the German *ZEIT* and *Frankfurter Allgemeine Zeitung*, the Spanish *El País*, the British *Guardian*, and the Italian *Il Sole* and *La Repubblica*. Another example is German language teacher Paul Unger (42). His broad political communication repertoire is dominated by online and interpersonal communication. A third example is Dennis Cooper, whose political communication repertoire is dominated by online media. As he puts it: 'I live in the internet' (Dennis Cooper, 29, UK). This again goes hand in hand with the appropriation of various other media like television, radio and print (see his network map in Figure 6.8).

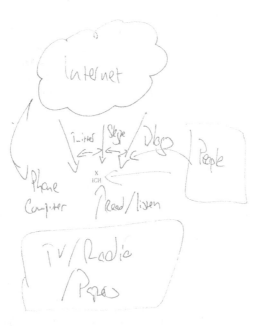

Figure 6.8 Media-related network map of 29-year-old British political science student Dennis Cooper

In our data, the only exception to a multi-perspective European public connection with a narrow political communication repertoire is Bela Maschmann. He is a 32-year-old German painter, living and working in a studio he shares with other artists in Berlin. Having a multiple European public connection, Bela almost exclusively relies on the internet (see Figure 6.9). Online he only reads articles and user's comments on *Welt online* in order to contrast their right-wing positions to his own left wing worldview. However, we have to have in mind that this is a marginal case of a multi-perspective European public connection.

It is not necessarily the reference to a variety of communicative sources that builds a multi-perspective European public connection. While having this kind of European public connection is mostly a reason for appropriating different media, the core of this kind of European public connection is awareness of the construction of political communication. Having a multi-perspective European public connection often means having a critical attitude to the media. Statements within our interviews that explicitly refer to Europe substantiate this. Gerhard Deichen, for instance, a 62-year-old former public transport company senior manager who retired early due to serious illness, refers to his distant attitude towards coverage on Europe as follows:

> I think that there is, ehm, ehm, also a lot of drama or also a lot on so-called European banks that is very targeted and consciously constructed. I am not even sure whether it is really so bad with the Euro, but within our united Europe I actually find it important, the most important, that we now, yes, really live together in Europe. (Gerhard Deichen, 62, GER)

INTERNET

X
ICH

HANDY

Figure 6.9 Media-related network map of 32-year-old German artist Bela Maschmann

Another case is Briton Daniel Weaver, 49 years old. Daniel works as a freelance financial trader and statistics trainer. He argues that it is hardly possible to understand what is going on via available communication platforms: 'we don't know much about what goes in Europe, I don't think so.' Daniel recalls the decision for a British engagement in the Iraq war: 'And I remember watching the debates, and then listening to the news, and I remember I couldn't believe they were talking about the same events. It does scare you a bit what, how you just get one perspective from the news, and it's not really good information if you listen to any political debate versus the headline news stories, there is a huge difference.' Bela Maschmann, the young artist from Berlin, also highlights the various approaches he could pursue with regard to Europe:

> I mean, I am not the rational type [. . .] but I understand it [Europe] and it is somehow progressive and modern and in no case mean or something like that to me, but it makes sense somehow [. . .]. Once you ask yourself whether Europe needs this progression, then, clearly, one also quickly thinks that there are these Third World countries are suppressed, whatever, you can look at it from here or there. But everything makes sense to me. (Bela Maschmann, 32, GER)

These examples highlight the awareness of the constructed character of political communication, characteristic of the multi-perspective European public connection.

Again, our analysis relates to the levels of the individual, to social positioning and to contextual embedding. On an individual level, we notice once more the habitualisation of public connection. This becomes evident especially on the basis of cases with a very wide political communication repertoire that involves a certain habitual organisation of this variety of appropriated media. This is demonstrated by Inès Marquis, a French woman with a broad, press-dominated political communication repertoire. She regularly buys various newspapers at a kiosk. Or Dennis Cooper, a 29-year-old student of political science and former think tank employee, who manages the high amount of political news only by a highly structured daily routine:

> I am woken up by the radio, I have the radio on a lot. And that wakes me up. [. . .] I listen to two radio channels, which is *Radio Four* and the *World Service*. [. . .] So I listen to that. I pick up a newspaper in the morning and read that. [. . .] I try to rotate. Usually it's

either the *Guardian* or the *Independent*. [. . .] there is the stereotype of a Guardianista, a typical *Guardian* reader who is sort of, you know, really a labour voter which to a large extent is what I am. [. . .] Ehm, so and then during, during the day I usually have my computer set up with *Twitter* open and maybe, you know, and I will just look at it from time to time. Q: And which, which I don't know which streams do you follow then or is it like. A: Oh, I have six hundred [. . .] I, I really like social media. Ehm, and I've got them divided into lists. So, I have got one which is UK media. [. . .] so that's *BBC, Channel Four News* and then the quality newspapers. [. . .] Ehm, and then I've got another one for defence and security which is professionally what I am interested in. Ehm, and then another one which is science and scepticism which is just what I am interested in. So I just look at the list and see. [. . .] And a lot of it is, if somebody I find interest in tweets something now and says this is worth looking at, I prob/ probably look at it, [lists names of *Twitter* authors he is interested]. [. . .] Ehm, there are o/, there is very few television programmes I'll tune in for. Most television news I think is crap to be honest. [. . .] Q: So in the evenings then? A: Yeah, yeah. That's all seven o'clock. Ehm, the, occasionally I watch *Newsnight*, which is ehm, the serious reportage programme at ten thirty on *BBC Two*. Ehm, the other I should have said is RSS feeds set up on my phone. [. . .] you know, where I am reading the headlines [. . .]. On Europe, ehm, it's a blog thing. I do mean I read blogs called *knowsmonkey*, ehm, *John works EU-topia*, [. . .]. Then I'll read about European, probably it's just what I see on *Twitter*. About Europe that looks interesting. And no, recently, there's another blog I that I really like. The guy who writes it is Chris Delow, ehm, who is, an economist, but actually I, he's an economist and he's quite good in explaining concepts and so to try to understand what is going on in Europe, in Greece, in the European crisis, I've been reading that quite a lot. Of course it's in general, it's, to be honest it's what what, a lot of it is what comes to, I didn't realize as much, but it's what comes up on *Twitter*. Ehm, what I hear in the morning on the radio programme. Ehm, I mean, what, to be honest, what's in the papers. The only thing is probably when I hear something, you know, if, if I read something in that paper and then I'm told about it on *Twitter* and or on the blogs, then I am much more likely to go back in order to look at it again and I'll go back to it again. So it's, you know. [. . .] I like producing videos. There I just talk about politics, usually if I've seen something that's making me angry then I go and make a video about it. (Dennis Cooper, 29, UK)

As demonstrated above, these habits might change. Bela Maschmann was an example. From time to time, he intentionally changes his systematically read a web page to gain a plural perspective. Similarly, Roberto Zero, a 25-year-old Italian-French agricultural engineer, reports that 'it depends on the period' which kind of media he regularly follows to substantiate his multi-perspective European public connection. Thus, people with a multi-perspective European public connection seem to be more likely to intentionally change their habits of media use when it supports their multi-perspective access to public affairs.

On a positional level, we are again confronted with questions of stratification. We could not relate the noticing and centred European public connection to a certain social position, while at the same time different forms of social positioning became re-articulated through these kinds of public connection. Having a multi-perspective European public connection is different in this regard. As the cases discussed in this section demonstrate, there is a much greater tendency that this European public connection is related to a higher level of education and middle-class self-positioning. We have to bear in mind that certain forms of multi-perceptivity presuppose, for example, language skills. Inès Marquis compares the various national and cultural perspectives on Europe based on her language skills, which she keeps active by reading newspapers. Such social positioning often is related to a certain sense of social responsibility, as the cases of Christine Hauschild (42, GER) and Théo Perrier (29, F) demonstrate. While Théo appears to be mainly interested in how ordinary citizens see the world, Christine highlights her missionary attitude towards people as follows:

> I read *Libération*, *Le Monde*, *Le Parisien* online. . . But *Le Parisien*, I love to buy the print version [. . .], because I like to have a rather populist approach to the news of the day. I like to see how the lower classes receive the information. What kind of information do they give to them? (Théo Perrier, 29, F)

Christine Hauschild works as a foreign language secretary and particularly emphasises the diversity of educational backgrounds in her social environment. While, however, she tends to 'explain' (Christine Hauschild, 42, GER) politics to those friends with lower education, she sees her more highly educated (and socially-established) friends as communication partners at her level. 'Those people I communicate a lot with', she explains, 'are more or less as I am, regarding educational background and knowledge.' Therefore, the multi-perspective European public connection is related to the re-articulation of social stratification in a double sense. On the one hand, in contrast to the two other European public connections under consideration, it is much more typical for well-educated and people in higher social positions. On the other hand, social differences are also re-articulated through this European public connection.

Finally, on a contextual level we do not find any local or national characteristics regarding the multi-perspective European public connection. People with this kind of public connection live in urban and rural areas across all countries studied by us. Also, the national becomes re-articulated through this European public connection. European matters are appropriated with relation to the own national situatedness and embeddedness. However, transnational references are more likely, while the level of reflexivity on the interplay of local, national and transnational references tends to be much higher. While the artist Bela Maschmann understands racism to be a transnational phenomenon that he also critically discusses with regard to Italy, he still believes that in Germany there is at least sort of a 'barrier' against its total takeover. Citizens, he claims, are at least confronted with what public media provide, 'only through this [. . .] public broadcasting' (Bela Maschmann, 32, GER). In contrast to Bela's rather narrow political communication repertoire, Peter Auermann, a 29-year-old business manager in the field of renewable energies, employs a diversity of communicative means. Each of these fulfils a different function with regard to his local, national and transnational self-localisation. After finishing his doctoral degree, the Austrian returned to his local community in order to live with his family. In this context, for instance with regard to a green local energy project he is involved in, interpersonal communication plays a paramount role whereas national and transnational contextualisation occurs with a focus on newspapers (digital) and radio. Obviously, Peter's strategy is highly reflexive regarding the different levels of contextualisation, numerous other interviewees referring to a multi-perspective European public connection.

Whereas the multi-perspective public connection is specific regarding related social positioning and its contextual embeddedness, it is comparable with the noticing and centred public connection regarding its habitual character. It is crucial to keep this in mind when we discuss the relation of European public connection to the euro crisis in the following section. As we will demonstrate, the euro crisis results in an activation of each of these European public connections – however, each in a different manner. In other words, the communicative construction of Europe has a reasonable chance of being renegotiated.

6.4 The euro crisis: activating European public connections

Up to this point, we have analysed three kinds of European public connections: the noticing, centred and multi-perspective. Each is rooted in habitualised everyday practices. This observation is consistent with findings on media and communication repertoires in the general field of political communication. Investigating the potentially increasing significance of online political communication, Martin Emmer et al. (2012) argue that citizens' political communication is rooted in everyday habits and approved sources. How stable are habitual patterns of this kind? Does the euro crisis affect them? Or, in contrast, does the crisis barely impinge on the European public connection, as shown in our analysis of print press coverage (cf. chapter 4)?

To answer these questions, we first have to consider our analytical statement that these three kinds of European public connections are rooted in habitual everyday practices. In a constructivist perspective, habit is more than repetition and routine. In fact, while the stabilisation and sedimentation of media-related practices are of paramount importance in citizens' everyday communication repertoires (Couldry 2012: 53), *habit* implies a certain dynamism. We understand habitualised public connections to be individual orientation structures oriented towards public issues. These orientation structures are both influenced by individual experiences and skills as well as by contextual dimensions, such as political environments (Knoblauch 2003: 8). Therefore irritations or challenges do not necessarily question habitualised practices in a fundamental way. Based on this definition of habit, any possible influence of the euro crisis does not merely concern the extent to which citizens feel affected by the euro crisis. It is also a matter of influence on habitualised political communication repertoires and the European public connections rooted in this.

The starting point for such an analysis is a general finding that resonates with our research results in the previous chapter on online interaction in internet forums. When in our interviews we asked about citizens' overall understanding of Europe, the issue of the euro crisis was not prompted by our questions. Nevertheless, across all the six countries studied, most of the interviewees raised this issue. When discussing the euro crisis in the interviews, a point constantly reiterated was how far our interlocutors felt activated by the crisis. But what does such 'activation' mean in practice? To answer this question we have to move on in two stages: First, we will characterise how this activation happens; second, we will distinguish two forms of possible activation.

Relatedness and activation

First of all, the euro crisis is a meaningful event for all interviewees that mention it. This holds implications for their political communication repertoires and hence their European public connections. What happened during the crisis was an intensification of political communication, activating the communication repertoire. This is not necessarily the same as politicisation, a consequence that is otherwise discussed as an influence on citizens of the euro crisis (Eder 2014; Roose 2015). Moreover, it does not necessarily entail an improvement in the quality of information. However, the crisis is an irritation that, as soon as citizens feel somehow affected by it, results in intensification of their search for and use of related sources, including the possibilities of communicating about the crisis in interpersonal communication.

Such 'relatedness' with respect to the euro crisis can be different. Some citizens report personal experience of the crisis, for example, by loss of savings or employment. Others express their concern with the uncertain consequences of the crisis. And finally, there are citizens that are affected when they feel pressure to investigate the crisis. Overall, we notice a shared assumption that the euro crisis is a meaningful event for citizens that might in a direct or indirect way affect their personal lives. This results in activation: the breaking up of hitherto habitualised forms of European public connection. Since worries and anxieties about the euro crisis will be discussed in more detail in chapter 7, we present at this point our insights through examples that illustrate the perceived relatedness in respect to the euro crisis across the three types of European public connection with varying intensities. More crucial is that citizens usually relate concern directly to their political communication repertoires.

The case of Dorothea Prenz provides an example of a noticing public connection. Dorothea is 68 years old and retired, but occasionally works as a cleaning lady. The range of her political communication repertoire is rather limited and dominated by television. She prefers daily soaps to political information. While Dorothea detected the euro crisis as a political event, she was at first not interested in it: 'Greece and stuff [. . .] I mean I deal with it, and then I also [. . .] slur over it again' (Dorothea Prenz, 68, GER). However, Dorothea reports that, later, she became communicatively involved in the euro crisis. As the crisis went on, she eventually began to talk about the latest TV news on Greece. And when she met her friends in the weekly choir session the crisis became a topic there. All were concerned that 'actually the funds get back' and that for Germany the crisis 'is also very expensive'. In her case, it was direct communication with her peers that pushed Dorothea to deal with the consequences of the euro crisis. Also other interviewees with a rather limited political communication repertoire report the stimulation of conversation with peers. For example, the Polish farmer Edyta Rolny discussed the issue with her neighbour:

> Well, in Greece, I have the impression that they do not really want to work, all these Greeks. Probably they are not so [. . .] we have talked about this from time to time, our neighbour has come here and said that they were all loafers! (Edyta Rolny, 33, PL)

Both ladies share their limited interest in politics, but nevertheless became interested in the euro crisis through peers and thus activated. And it is interesting to note that both remember precisely these moments of activation in their social surrounding. As Edyta puts it, it became a problem 'not to talk so much about politics with people'.

People with a centred European public connection also became activated by the euro crisis. However, here the activation is at least partly related to their topic of relevance. This said, the euro crisis is something that causes questions and uncertainty. Angélie Toulon, for instance, a student of agronomy, strives to understand the situation by reading 'articles about the crisis'. And she continues: 'I think it's very complicated to really understand what is going on in the crisis, because I do not have any economic education. [. . .] But sometimes I understand something and just one second later I do not understand anything anymore. It's very complicated' (Angélie Toulon, 21, F). In a similar way Jessica Price, a 50-year-old university project manager from London, says: 'It's just way too complicated and unwieldy for most people to understand. You know, what you get of the news is, the more you know the less you understand.' (Jessica Price, 50, UK). It is this feeling of complication that activates both of them to look for further information.

We notice such a perceived relatedness and activation also for interview partners that have a multi-perspective European public connection. The Italian-French Roberto Zero (25, F), for example, expresses his anxiety about the consequences of the crisis by asking 'the big question' of 'what happens if the crisis cannot be solved'. And he continues, 'this unsettles me a lot, and therefore I try to follow developments'. Bela Maschmann, the young artist from Berlin, pursues a more pragmatic approach. He states that there is no escape from an engagement with the current problems Europe faces:

Well, if we talk about Europe, clearly, it is obvious how Germany
relates to Europe and Italy relates to Europe and therefore also
Germany and Italy relate. It is also good, on the other hand, because
what else should we do? Basically, yes, it's okay that there is Europe
and that the countries somehow try to cope. But suddenly one is confronted with such a thing [the euro crisis, the authors], maybe with
things that you did not expect for Germany this way any more, like
in the near future. And suddenly there you have the problem again.
(Bela Maschmann, 32, GER)

A further example is Ludwik Reiter, a professor for computer science
in Radom, Poland. He compares the economic, cultural and religious
dimensions of Europe. While he supports Europe as an economic model,
he is sceptical about processes of 'Americanisation' and 'the decline of
religious values' (Ludwik Reiter, 65, PL), which he relates to the political union. With regard to the euro crisis, Ludwik is concerned that 'this
will be carried over here, to the local situation in the country' (Ludwik
Reiter, 65, PL). Having a wide-ranging, digitally dominated political
communication repertoire he tries to find answers to his questions by
reading various online sources:

Lately, I particularly read what I was interested in, which is the history of Greece and, you know, the question of the financial crisis
and all these solutions with demonstrating, who is it who really
has a lock on the situation [. . .] why for example the German and
the French behave this way, creating these specific funds. (Ludwik
Reiter, 65, PL)

Altogether these examples demonstrate that, irrespective of their kind
of European public connection, our interview partners recognise the
euro crisis, understand it as meaningful for them and start to reflect this
based on their political communication repertoires. It is this moment
which we call activation. Beyond the usual routines of everyday political
communication, the euro crisis becomes a special focus of attention. In
this sense, the euro crisis must be regarded as an opportunity to adjust or
at least to (re-)consider an existing European public connection.

Intensification and extension of political communication repertoires

If we consider how activation takes place, we notice two patterns:
'intensification' and 'extension' of political communication repertoires

(cf. Table 6.2.) Intensification means a temporal deepening of already existing forms of communication. Extension means a temporal addition of forms of political communication. Here we need to be very careful in analysing our data within this processual perspective on euro crisis-related change. This is because our interviews were all completed during the same period of time and we do not have data that would allow a systematic before and after comparison of the euro crisis. Therefore, our entire analysis of these two patterns is based on statements made by our interviewees regarding their impression of what changed through the euro crisis. While we have to handle this kind of data with care, there are some indications that an intensification and extension of political communication repertoires can result in a leap from one kind of European public connection to another. There are examples where activation, at least temporarily, appears to turn a noticing or centred European public connection into a multi-perspective one.

Let us start by discussing the intensification of political communication repertoires. German housewife and part-time dietician Anita Berger is an illustrative example. Anita, whose political communication repertoire is dominated by the local newspaper, explains that she usually does not have much time for her daily reading. However, during the euro crisis she was annoyed with herself that she 'simply did not read through these whole articles about Greece' (Anita Berger, 44, GER). Being activated by the crisis, she changed this and started to read at least one article per day more carefully. Other interviewees, such as Angélie Toulon, also intensified their readings and started to 'read as much as I can' (Angélie Toulon, 21, F).

Sławomir Kaszubski gives another example of intensification in his media diary. Sławomir lives as a retired farmer in the rural North of Poland in a small house on his family's farm, the farm now being run by his son. Formerly, Sławomir had been an important public figure in his village, with a position comparable to a mayor. Today, he has a lot of time and a vital interest in politics. For instance, he follows

Table 6.2 Patterns of citizens' communicative activation

Intensification of Political Communication Repertoires	Deepening communication repertoires, e.g. integrating further newspaper sections, participation in production, intensifying direct communication, etc.
Extension of Political Communication Repertoires	Adding of new media and forms of political communication, e.g. Facebook groups, buying other newspapers, etc.

the economic situation of various European nation states and compares them. He refers to a noticing European public connection, but the euro crisis has led him to develop a tendency to a multi-perspective European public connection. This is based on a rather narrow political communication repertoire, dominated by television, which has become intensified during the euro crisis.

The excerpts from his media diary illustrate the intensification of Sławomir's communication repertoire during the euro crisis (see Figures 6.10–6.12). After watching the news, he regularly discusses recent political events with his family (see Figure 6.11). Then the next day, he notes that he had already begun to follow the news in the morning (see Figure 6.12). We even find here certain moments of extension. In addition to the usual public TV channel, he also watches the news from the private TV station *Polsat*. The extent to which Sławomir searches for more information and wishes to extend his perspective on the euro crisis is striking.

This provides some insight into the meaning of extension of political communication repertoires. It is not only a more intensive use of the previous media and an intensive communication along established forms, but also a temporal addition of new media and forms of political communication to an established political communication repertoire. This represents an enrichment of a person's habitual political communication repertoire. He adds further blogs to this:

> Recently, there's another blog I that I really like. The guy who writes it is Chris Delos, ehm, who is, an economist. [. . .] He's quite good in explaining concepts and so to try to understand what is going on in Europe, in Greece, in the European crisis, I've been reading that quite a lot. (Dennis Cooper, 29, UK)

The same is the case for Bo Falck, a young Danish political scientist, who extends his political communication repertoire by reading the 'financial crisis stuff' in additional newspapers: 'when there are important issues that so to speak burn or so, then it happens that I read more newspaper [. . .] specific newspapers [. . .] well, those of which one thinks that they are quality newspapers' (Bo Falck, 29, DK).

How can we interpret statements like these? First of all, we consider them as examples of the degree to which the euro crisis temporally changes habitualised political communication repertoires by a process of activation having two possible characteristics: intensification and extension of the political communication repertoire. We understand this as a way of coping with the communicative challenge of understanding a

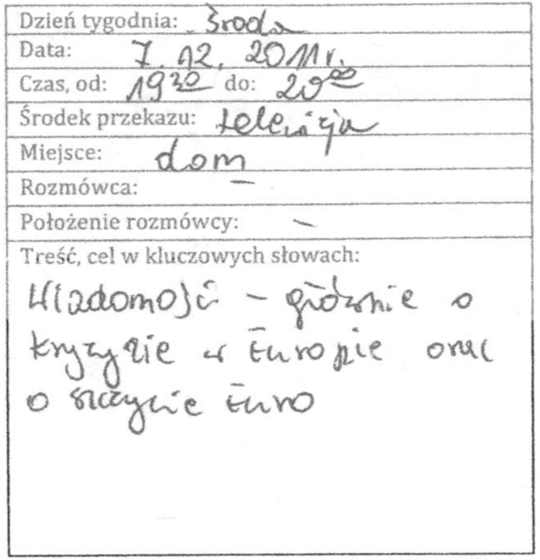

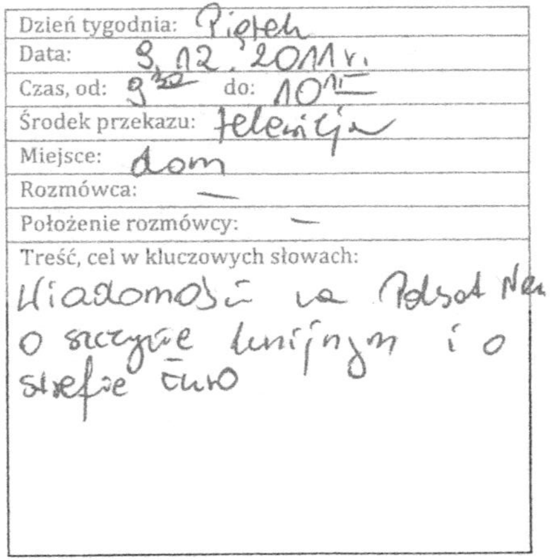

Dzień tygodnia: Piątek
Data: 8.12.20MVb
Czas, od: 9³⁰ do: 10¹⁵
Środek przekazu: telewizja
Miejsce: dom
Rozmówca: —
Położenie rozmówcy: —
Treść, cel w kluczowych słowach:
Wiadomości na Polsat News o szczycie unijnym i o strefie euro

Figure 6.12 Media diary of Sławomir Kaszubski (65, PL) – 'Friday, December 9th, from 9.30 to 10.15 am, at home, news on *Polsat* News on the European summit and the Euro zone'

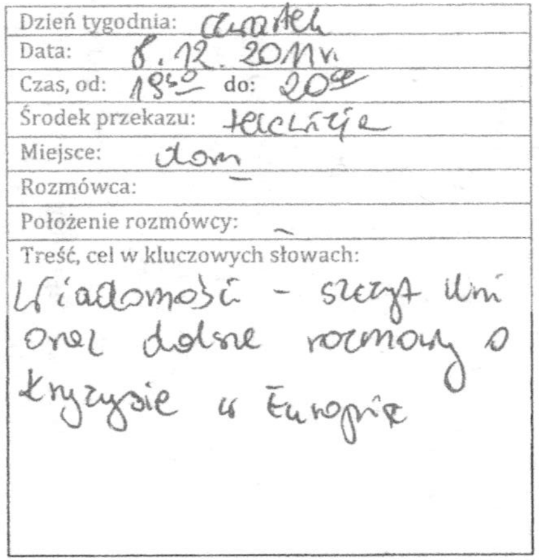

Dzień tygodnia: Czwartek
Data: 8.12.20MVb
Czas, od: 19³⁰ do: 20⁰⁰
Środek przekazu: telewizja
Miejsce: dom
Rozmówca: —
Położenie rozmówcy: —
Treść, cel w kluczowych słowach:
Wiadomości – szczyt Unii oraz dalsze rozmowy o kryzysie w Europie

Figure 6.11 Media diary of Sławomir Kaszubski (65, PL) – 'Thursday, December 8th, from 7.30 to 20 pm, TV, at home, news – European summit as well as follow-up talks on the crisis in Europe'

Dzień tygodnia: Środa
Data: 7.12.20MVb
Czas, od: 19³⁰ do: 20⁰⁰
Środek przekazu: telewizja
Miejsce: dom
Rozmówca: —
Położenie rozmówcy: —
Treść, cel w kluczowych słowach:
Wiadomości – głównie o kryzysie w Europie oraz o szczycie euro

Figure 6.10 Media diary of Sławomir Kaszubski (65, PL) – 'Wednesday, December 7th, from 7.30 to 20 pm, TV, at home, news – mainly on the crisis in Europe as well as the European summit'

euro crisis that interviewees feel impinges on their lives. As Lena Müller from Austria puts it, the euro crisis is an 'issue that concerns everybody'. Because of that, she became 'very, very active'. Being active means from her point of view that she 'personally started to search about the topic, thus was not only informed by others, but informed myself' (Lena Müller, 18, AT). She here expresses an intensifying as well as extending move in relation to her political communication repertoire: While Lena usually takes note of political news by following Facebook and the recommendations of her peers, she became active and started to search for more information on her own.

Therefore, activation – whether involving intensification or extension of the political communication repertoire – means the temporary suspension of aspects of habitualised political communication practices. In this, the euro crisis is like other important political events. Susanne Kramer (33, GER), for example, usually takes note of public issues by talking with her boyfriend, who has a deeper interest and is therefore better informed by his media use. However, when it came to the Fukushima nuclear incident, she was activated and her political communication repertoire was intensified for a period. Other possible events might be important elections, as with Tonja Hellesen (27, DK). She was activated by the last Danish national elections so much that she 'followed this [media coverage] really very much on [her] computer'. Her neighbour who was a candidate for the conservative-liberal party Venstre stimulated this activation. Wars might also trigger activation. British interviewee Ismael Brooker, for example, reports how his already wide-ranging political communication repertoire became extended and how he himself actively started to look for solid information during the time of the Iraq war. He visited the website *antiwar.com* on a daily basis and even wrote a letter to Al Gore in order to express his critical opinion about the action of the British government during the Iraq war.

7
Challenging Europe: Understanding and Solving the Euro Crisis

Having in the previous chapter explored how citizens in Europe are connected to the European public sphere and how they are involved in the process of the communicative construction of Europe, we now focus on the euro crisis as a specific moment of activation. We ask how a *legitimate* Europe is constructed in the citizens' perspective on the euro crisis. As we have already seen, the euro crisis represents a meaningful moment for European citizens, provoking significant changes in their communicative practices and thereby activating hitherto established forms of public connection (cf. chapter 6). The euro crisis is a potential moment of challenge for public connections, because citizens begin to question and re-negotiate the legitimacy of the EU. We argue that the euro crisis does not represent a serious risk for the European public sphere and its legitimacy but, in contrast, mobilises communicative constructions. It becomes a reason to discuss and reflect on the process of the communicative construction of Europe with respect to its legitimacy.

Against this background, the aim of this chapter is to examine the 'communicative construction of a legitimate EU' from the citizens' perspective. Taking the case of the euro crisis as an example and building on our in-depth interviews, network maps and media diaries with 182 citizens from six EU countries (cf. details in chapter 6 and in the appendix), we elaborate different patterns of construction. First of all, there are patterns indicating how people construct their understanding of the euro crisis. Secondly, there are patterns that we call 'legitimation constructions of Europe', pointing to a bigger picture of a future Europe that citizens consider legitimate and capable of overcoming the euro crisis. Since we conducted our fieldwork in late 2011, when the euro crisis had its first peak and a possible withdrawal of Greece from the eurozone was discussed, our interviewees often refer to the 'Greek crisis'.

Interestingly, our analysis from a transcultural perspective brings these transnational patterns to the fore, but does not point to national differences or stratification-related differences in the interviewees' statements. In other words, citizens' constructions of their understandings of the euro crisis as well as their legitimation constructions of Europe, seem to be truly transnational and are most plausibly rooted in a European culture of political discourse.

With the term 'legitimation constructions of Europe' we refer to the work of Peter L. Berger and Thomas Luckmann, who understand legitimation as a social construction emerging in communicative processes (cf. chapter 2). In their book *The Social Construction of Reality*, Berger and Luckmann (1967) elaborate a concept of legitimation that is rooted in and established by social practices: 'The function of legitimation is to make objectively available and subjectively plausible' (Berger/Luckmann 1967: 110) the so far established institutional order. The process of legitimation encompasses two forms of communicative practices: 'explanations' and 'justifications' (Berger/Luckmann 1967: 111). While firstly 'institutional order [is explained] by ascribing cognitive validity to its objectivated meanings', it is secondly justified 'by giving a normative dignity to its practical imperatives' (Berger/Luckmann 1967: 111). Hence, according to them, legitimation always encompasses both cognitive and normative elements, so that legitimation is not just a matter of *values*, but always implies *knowledge* as well (Berger/Luckmann 1967: 111). In other words, the process of legitimation articulates why one action should be performed and not another, and moreover explains 'why things *are* what they are', so that "knowledge" precedes "values" in the legitimation' (Berger/Luckmann 1967: 111) process. There is, thirdly, what Berger and Luckmann call the shift to 'symbolic universes', or what we call 'legitimating narrations', as reference points for the communicative construction of legitimacy. Such narrations 'integrate different provinces of meaning and encompass the institutional order in a symbolic totality, [. . .] [so that] the sphere of pragmatic application is transcended once and for' (Berger/Luckmann 1967: 113). The construction of legitimating narrations as a step in the legitimation process is characterised by the fact that the object of legitimation is no longer necessarily directly acknowledged, but integrated into a bigger picture.

Applied to our example of the euro crisis, we find both, explanations and justifications, as well as the construction of legitimating narrations or legitimation constructions. First, we observe that our interviewees across all countries try to understand and make sense of the euro crisis, that is, in Berger's and Luckmann's words, try to explain and justify the euro crisis and its mechanisms. At this point we are confronted with 'perplexity', 'anxiety' and 'speculations'. Second, we find different ideas of how to overcome the euro crisis. Here, our interview partners do not only discuss possible ways to solve and overcome the euro crisis, but they also delineate pictures of a future EU that they conceive to be legitimate and worth living in. In particular, from our interviews we extract four constructions of a legitimate Europe: 'Europe of nations', 'Europe of welfare and solidarity', 'Europe of economic cooperation' and the 'United States of Europe'. Interestingly, these ideas of a legitimate EU are discussed in the context of the euro crisis, but they do not necessarily refer (any longer) to the euro crisis or to the EU's euro crisis politics as an object of legitimation. Rather, they refer to a somewhat bigger picture of what a legitimate EU could look like.

Before presenting our findings, we wish to make clear that we do not initiate our analysis by defining the core character of the euro crisis. Having in mind the very general statement by Antonio Gramsci (1971: 178) as well as our reflections in chapter 2, that euro crisis is a process of struggle that includes its definition. We want to focus in detail on the people's communicative construction of the euro crisis in Austria, Denmark, France, Germany, Poland and the United Kingdom. Consequently, we ask: How do the people as European citizens construct the euro crisis? And how do they construct a legitimate Europe within such a frame?

7.1 Understanding the euro crisis: perplexity, anxiety and speculations

With regard to the first bundle of patterns pointing to understandings of the euro crisis, including explanations and justifications, we find the articulation of perplexity, anxiety and speculation. Across Europe, interviewed citizens construct the euro crisis as a serious matter. Their communicative activation becomes visible in their attempts to understand and make sense of it. When articulating their disorientation, the pattern of understanding characteristically widens: first of all, from wondering about how it all begun and what is going on; to second, worrying about effects on both their personal lives and the future of Europe; and third, speculation about the complex nature of the euro crisis. A 50-year-old University project manager from London says: 'It's just way too complicated and unwieldy for most people to understand. You know, what you get off the news is, the more you know the less you understand'

(Jessica Price, 50, UK). Similarly, a young man from France articulates his anxiety about the consequences of the euro crisis by stating that 'the big question is what happens if the euro crisis cannot be solved', and he continues, 'this unsettles me a lot, and therefore I try to follow the developments' (Roberto Zero, 25, F).

Perplexity: grasping the euro crisis

Above all, the interviewees are puzzled by the euro crisis. They construct it as complex in its economic and political nature, and difficult to understand in detail. In trying to understand the euro crisis and its impact, the interviewees rely on the information they acquire via the media they use as well as their everyday interchange with friends and family. In this whole process of appropriation, they relate this information back to their everyday lives, as well as to what they perceive as a broader European context.

For example, Amina Zündler, a 28-year-old woman from Austria who works as a manager on cultural projects, perceives the Greek crisis as bewildering and states that she cannot understand: 'How can a whole country fail?' In her eyes, the economic aspects of the euro crisis are obscure and opaque, so that she feels completely mystified. A young woman from Germany also wonders about the impact of a whole country going bankrupt: 'For me this is just too abstract to imagine what that actually means' (Leonie Stiesing, 26, GER). Similarly, a 50-year-old woman from London states 'that this whole sort of economic mechanism is just too complicated for anybody to understand now. [. . .] you know, the top economic brains in the world don't know how to fix it. And [. . .] governments are just incapable of knowing what to do about it' (Jessica Price, 50, UK). Ludwik Reiter, a 65-year-old professor of computer science from Poland, says that he was trying to understand 'who really determines the game [. . .]. Why, for example, do Germany and France behave in the way they do behave?' And he continues to wonder: 'Why do Merkel and Sarkozy do it in this and not in any other way?' Similarly, Dennis Cooper, aged 29 and a political science student from North London, states: 'The European financial crisis, I've been following that quite a bit. I think I don't know nothing about, I don't know anything about economics' (Dennis Cooper, 29, UK). To resolve this deficit, he follows media reporting on the financial crisis. He tries to find out more about the euro crisis, mostly online – via *BBC News*, *Twitter* and blogs such as the blog of Chris Delow, an economist who writes a lot about the financial crisis and the problems in Greece.

Likewise, for Angelie Toulon, a 21-year-old French student of agronomy, the euro crisis reveals both that the topic is very complicated and that she simply is not educated in economics. To compensate for this, she tries to understand what is going on and what the impact of the euro crisis might be by following the reporting of *Le Monde* – her favourite newspaper that she receives for free at her faculty. However, she does not always succeed: 'Sometimes I understand something and one second later I don't understand anything anymore' (Angelie Toulon, 21, F).

Another way of dealing with the uncertainty is to talk about the euro crisis within one's circle of friends and family. Here, we hear from French retired pharmacist Karlotta Sapon, aged 65, that she is presently talking about it a great deal with her husband, as the euro crisis is 'the big, our big worry' (Karlotta Sapon, 65, F). For Stéphane Trufon, aged 27, a psychologist living in Paris, it is his girlfriend who turns out to be his personal expert in this matter, as she studies International Relations.

To summarise, the interviewees share the experience that their common knowledge of economic topics proves insufficient when it comes to such a complex matter as the euro crisis. One approved but not always sufficient way to remedy this is to stick with media coverage; another way is to make use of personal networks and in this way to satisfy the need to talk about the euro crisis.

Anxiety: worrying about the future

The interviewees are very much concerned about the possible impact of the euro crisis. On the one hand, their worries are on a personal level, insofar as they articulate anxiety about rising unemployment rates, the risk of inflation and depreciation of their savings. On the other hand, in the interviewees' eyes the whole EU project is at stake. Regarding the EU's *raison d'être* first and foremost as an instrument for creating and maintaining peace, an economically flagging EU might once more result in terror and war.

When it comes to the personal lives of our interviewees, the euro crisis turns out to be an important topic of conversation in the family circle. For example, the 50-year-old Briton Jessica Price talks about how her family feels directly affected by the euro crisis: '[M]y daughter has just finished her undergraduate degree and then my auntie's son has as well, so we worried about finding jobs. [. . .] Ehm, you know, they're both looking for jobs and not finding it very easy not to pass on your mind at the moment' (Jessica Price, 50, UK). Similarly, the 21-year-old student Steven Corner from Plymouth in Southern England, states that the euro crisis 'does impact my family [. . .] as my mother might lose the house' (Steven Corner, 20, UK). However, worrying about the personal impact of the euro crisis is not limited to job-related threats, but is also threatening in terms of money. Herbert Sennenberger, a 65-year-old retired design draughtsman from Austria, who fears that the euro crisis might lead to inflation, something that he rather associates with his parent's generation's experiences: 'Even if we returned to gold, then I'd give a gold dollar for a kilogramme of bread, and the gold is all gone either way' (Herbert Sennenberger, 65, AT). Besides worries about every day basic needs such as food, there is also concern about financial investments. French interviewee Karlotta Sapon and her husband, for example, fear that the money they have invested in the stock exchange might be endangered by the euro crisis too.

Besides personal worries, the interviewees are also concerned about the future of the EU. Here, the spectrum of worries varies from non-specific concerns, as we hear from Jacques Ardèche, a 64-year-old French manager, from Angelie Toulon, who finds it hard to view the future of the EU optimistically, or Stéphane Trufon, who, in the light of the euro crisis, does not expect the EU to get anywhere. In this sense, Simon Gärtner, a 37-year-old gardener from Germany, states that he recently followed a discussion about Germany returning to the *Deutsche Mark* which made him 'angry, because I feel that the European spirit is in danger' (Simon Gärtner, 37, GER). These general doubts about the impacts of the euro crisis and the chances of overcoming it are reflected in perceptions of the euro crisis as characterised by the diversity of the EU's many different cultures, as the Austrian student of agriculture and nutrition science Kilian Wedekind, aged 26, puts it.

However, our interviewees do not totally agree as to what extent the excitement over the EU crisis is in fact appropriate: While some say that the euro crisis draws too much attention, others are troubled by the idea that the euro crisis might be even more serious than we see at first sight. For example, 23-year-old Maria Rudler, an Austrian student of political economics, complains that due to the euro crisis, other issues like foreign affairs, the environment and cultural matters are being obscured. Another interviewee, the previously mentioned gardener Simon Gärtner rather suspects that politicians even stoke conflicts like xenophobia and the risk of terror in order to distract from the actual dimensions of the financial crisis. For a third interviewee, Danish pensioner Bjørn Æby, aged 64, a former coppersmith, the implications of the euro crisis are not at all clear yet. Despite the fact that he does not feel affected personally, since he considers himself economically secure, he perceives the euro crisis as 'the worst thing he has experienced in Europe in his whole life' (Bjørn Æby, 64, DK). So far as he has noticed, some people in Denmark are already affected by the euro crisis and feel 'uncomfortable' with that. His greatest fear is that some other EU member states from Eastern Europe might join Greece and Italy in their financial problems. Eventually, the separation of a few or more countries from the eurozone would lead to chaos. It is this ultimate, almost apocalyptic scenario that plagues some of our interviewees. For example, 25-year-old agricultural engineer Roberto Zero from France wonders what would happen if no solution to the euro crisis can be found: 'Everything can collapse, dissolve, and this makes me very uneasy' (Roberto Zero, 25, F). Likewise, Hilde Haltenberger, an Austrian retired sales assistant, aged 56, hopes 'that the whole thing will not collapse' (Hilde Haltenberger, 56, AT). Or, as another Austrian pensioner, the former nurse Friede Kerner, aged 59, puts it: She is worried that 'something even worse might break out, something like war' (Friede Kerner, 59, AT).

As we have seen, it is common for our interviewees to be worried about the euro crisis. Both the extent and the cause of their concern nevertheless vary: from the individual to the collective level, from a general feeling of discomfort to fundamental fear for Europe's future.

Speculations: how the euro crisis came about

Although the interviewees construct the euro crisis as something that is hard to understand, they do not shy away from speculation about its causes. The explanations they present all presume that economic problems are predictable and, to some extent, avoidable. Either the failure lies with national misgovernment or with the EU system. At first glance, this conviction seems inconsistent with the impression that the interviewees are confused by the euro crisis, as we argued above. But a closer look reveals that both attitudes coexist, inasmuch as our interviewees try to overcome their disorientation by constructing individual explanations. We have identified three approaches to speculation about the euro crisis: involving an economic perspective, a focus on national misgovernment and the structure of the EU.

One way of reasoning about the euro crisis is to consider it from an economic perspective. For example, 58-year-old jobless Frenchman Lucas Almenos from Marseille states that the problem is that the banks, rather than the politicians, govern the world. Noah Moulin, a 28-year-old stock broker engineer from Paris, works in the financial industry himself. In the course of his daily work he 'watch[es] the financial markets breaking down'. He 'notice[s] many billions, billions and billions being transferred in order to help Greece, or to help Portugal' (Noah Moulin, 28, F). His opinion is that the Greeks, for instance, do in fact need help. The explanation he offers is that Greece should not have the euro – in his view, small countries with a generally weak economy need financial flexibility. In his eyes, the euro is unsuited to the Greek economy. Another interviewee, Kurt Binder, a 60-year-old pensioner from Germany, insists that the euro crisis is an economic crisis originating in the US. He considers that the euro crisis has no relation to the euro in particular or the EU in general. We find even less concrete guesswork in the case of 33-year-old Danish street newspaper-seller Anders Hansen, who suspects that 'someone' is keeping hold of the 'cash box' and that one needs to 'make him give back the money not only to Greece, but to Europe as a whole' (Anders Hansen, 33, DK). Characteristic for this approach is a focus on economic aspects only, allowing the complex issue of the EU financial crisis to be more easily understandable, but at the same time reduced to a simplification.

A second explanatory approach involves systemic aspects of the euro crisis relating to the national and historic context. Here we have, for example, Lone Søndergaard, a 24-year-old Danish student of education, who states that the Greek financial crisis does not necessarily have anything to do with the EU, except that Greece is situated in the middle of Europe geographically. On the contrary, she regards the whole problem as being caused by misgovernment on the part of Greek politicians. Responsible for this misgovernment are, in turn, the people of Greece. Max Rost, a 33-year-old Austrian electrician, makes the very same argument and suspects the euro crisis to be caused by national political 'disorder' (Max Rost, 33, AT). Another Danish interviewee, Mads Jespersen, a 51-year-old architect, admits that it is a problem if the Greeks are not willing to pay their taxes. Nevertheless, one has to ask why they refuse to do so. In his view, he continues, it is all based on mistrust of 'the central power', referring to Greece's recent experience of military dictatorship. On the basis of this, Mads Jespersen considers the Greeks to have every reason to fear that their taxes would not contribute to the collective good. Characteristic of this set of explanations is that they treat the euro crisis as based upon failures of national – Greek – politicians, condoned by the people of Greece for all too long. Therefore from this perspective, responsibility if not delinquency lies within the national field.

A third prevalent explanatory approach is that it is the EU itself that either caused the euro crisis or at least proved insufficiently effective in sheltering weaker member states from its effects. For example, Edgar Davies, a 71-year-old consultant from the UK, regards the euro as a disaster. Consequently, he expects the EU to 'go down the drain' (Edgar Davies, 71, UK) and predicts that the euro will be withdrawn. From Danish interviewee Poul Omegn, a 44-year-old sales promoter who is currently unemployed, we learn that the EU had recently grown too big too fast with respect to the Eastern enlargement of the EU. Mads Jespersen, the architect from Denmark, has a remarkable narrative regarding Greece's accession to the EU: Greece was assisted by the EU in manipulating its economic data. The objective, he suspects, had been to support the young democracy, and he concludes that the supervening political intention was to 'woo them into the warmth'. Another interviewee, 65-year-old French pensioner Clément Sapon, contests that the euro crisis would not have affected Greece and Portugal so much 'if there had been a European economic government providing harmonisation [. . .] – Taxes, expenditures, laws, and tolls need to be harmonised' (Clément Sapon, 65, F). Fabrice Girard, a 45-year-old French consultant, adds: 'We don't have a European defence policy, no European economic union, there's no one who represents us against the global lobby. Well, and now we face the disaster, as it is us who have to solve Greece's problems now. [. . .] We don't have a European government, and this is the catastrophe' (Fabrice Girard, 45, F). Here, we find hints of the interviewees' ideas about how the euro crisis might be overcome. Contrary to assigning blame to the national level, as presented above, it is characteristic of this approach to perceive the euro crisis as a consequence of systematic failure within the EU system. Statements vary, however, on the question of whether we should disestablish or intensify the structure of the EU, an issue upon which we will focus later.

We have presented a spectrum of speculation regarding the background of the euro crisis, ranging from a focus on economic aspects, to a national-systemic or an EU-systemic perspective on the complex issue of the euro crisis. Relating these findings back to the multi-segmented character of the European public sphere (cf. chapters 2, 3 and 4), we have to make clear once more that the patterns elaborated in this chapter do not point to national differences, nor to stratification-related differences. Hence, we cannot detect specific patterns that are primarily promoted by, for example, German interviewees. Moreover, we cannot find stratification-related differences suggesting that 'higher educated' people promote, for example, an economic perspective when speculating about the reasons for the euro crisis. Within the general pattern of understanding the euro crisis, there are references to the interviewees' conception of how the euro crisis could be overcome, as well as outlines of a legitimate Europe. We will now turn to this.

7.2   Overcoming the euro crisis: legitimation constructions of Europe

While the euro crisis, and the economic problems of Greece in particular, leaves our interviewees at a loss, worries them and makes them
consider its interrelations, they do not confine themselves to trying to
understand the euro crisis, but also propose solutions that might lead
Europe out of the euro crisis. Here we observe a shift to legitimation
constructions on the part of legitimating narrations. Activated by the
euro crisis, our interviewees do not only discuss possible solutions for
overcoming it, but they also outline different pictures of a future legitimate Europe and EU. These legitimation constructions are not confined
to the euro crisis as such or to specific political decisions with regard to
the euro crisis, but often refer to a broader picture of a legitimate EU.
From our analysis, we distinguish four legitimation constructions:

1. Europe of nations
2. Europe of economic cooperation
3. Europe of welfare and solidarity
4. United States of Europe

The interviewees who envisage a Europe of nations picture the EU as
a composition of sovereign national states and national cultures. They
favour 'national crisis solutions', emphasise Greece's national responsibility to solve 'its' problems on its own and reject the idea of helping
them out financially. A young Danish woman, a student of education
living in Copenhagen, emphasises that Greece has 'made its bed, and
now must lie on it' as 'there is no money to be grabbed' from the other
EU member states (Lone Søndergaard, 24, DK).

Interviewees emphasising the Europe of economic cooperation as the
key aspect of the EU consider intensified collaboration among EU member states on economic questions as the best way to push forward the
European integration process, as well as the EU's global position in general and overcoming the current financial crisis in particular. Our interviewees underline that the existence of effective economic government
would have helped to solve or even prevent the euro crisis in advance.
For instance, Daniel Weaver, a 49-year-old freelance financial consultant from England, states that 'without central money control' the EU is
'gonna have problems'.

According to the third legitimation construction that some of our
interviewees articulate, Europe must be marked by absolute solidarity.
These interviewees depict a EU of welfare and solidary in which the

member states work together as equal partners and help each other out, no matter what the economic situation looks like in the different countries, because otherwise 'there is no point in the EU at all' (Louis Barney, 21, UK). 'European solutions' are supported for the euro crisis.

The fourth legitimation construction that can be extracted from the interviewees' statements is a suggestion of a United States of Europe. By seeing the euro crisis as a 'crossroads' leading either to a 'European federal state', a 'separation' of the EU member states or remaining at the 'status quo', some interviewees postulate their 'ideal conception' as one leading to the 'United States of Europe' (Manuel Vechter, 19, AT). Only by fostering a European integration process corresponding to the US model might the EU become a real Union of Europeans, and solve its current and future economic problems.

For example, Fabrice Girard, a French freelance business consultant who lives in Paris but commutes to London for one week per month, regrets that only two political actors are visible in the euro crisis. The two political actors taking responsibility and visibly fostering political solutions are Angela Merkel, the German chancellor, and Nicolas Sarkozy, the then-French president: 'It is a shame that they [Merkel and Sarkozy] are doing this job alone, that there are no other countries who feel responsible to act. The others, they just twiddle their thumbs and watch, they just watch' (Fabrice Girard, 45, F). Nevertheless, he admits, it 'would be much more complicated to discuss all this with 15 or even 27 member states'. In a similar vein, some Danish interviewees like Faris Hom, a young man with family roots in Somalia who is currently preparing to be a taxi driver, states 'there are many countries [in the EU] that don't help. I think if everyone had helped like Angela Merkel does, then this problem here would have been solved a long time ago' (Faris Hom, 25, DK). And Poul Omegn, the unemployed sales promoter from Copenhagen, misses 'official EU politicians' acting as strong crisis managers: 'Rompuy [head of the European Council] does not act as a visionary, he doesn't do anything. There is always Angela Merkel, Berlusconi and Sarkozy' (Poul Omegn, 44, DK).

Beyond these perceptions and evaluations of national and European politicians acting or not acting in order to overcome the actual euro crisis, the interviewed citizens' reactions to the crisis is analysed in the following with regard to different legitimation constructions reaching far beyond merely a solution to the euro crisis.

Europe of nations

Interviewees articulating the legitimation construction of a Europe of nations underline the necessity in a future Europe of maintaining the cultural specificities as well as the national political sovereignty of every EU member state. Regarding the maintenance of every member state's individuality, 65-year-old Herbert Sennenberger from Austria states that 'one can absolutely be in the EU but nonetheless keep its individuality'. Also Agron Krisonic, a young man from Austria jobbing in a betting shop, emphasises that 'Although the peoples of Europe are our sister peoples, at the same time they are different from us. So we are each in our own family, and it's good how it is' (Agron Krisonic, 19, AT). Similarly, 49-year-old Daniel Weaver from England wants to preserve national differences in Europe: 'I would hope, I really want that the individual countries maintain their own identities. [. . .] I don't want, if I look at England now, like I said, every high street looks the same, it'd be very sad if every country started to look the same. I like the idea of going to France and everyone speaking French or going to Italy and everyone is speaking Italian. Umm, so I like the idea of distinct countries, so I think it helps'. In all, it is the plurality of cultures in Europe that our interviewees consider unique and worth preserving. As Fabrice Girard from France puts it: Europe is 'a cultural power that builds on a very rich mosaic' of national cultures as well as on 'very specific and diverse national cultures' (Fabrice Girard, 45, F).

Beyond these constructions of a legitimate EU emphasising the positive and enriching aspects of the cultural diversity in Europe, some of our interviewees point to certain aspects of EU institutions' political functioning that they regard as defective. For example, the EU's political institutions are regarded as inefficient, too expensive, sometimes even unnecessary. Anna Merkel from Germany emphasises that she thinks all EU magistrates are unnecessary. In her view, national governments are sufficient for relevant political problems: 'We don't need them [the EU politicians]. We don't need ten EU magistrates per blue-collar worker' (Anna Merkel, 64, GER). In a similar way, Heide Lehmann – also from Germany – emphasises: 'Well, for me, I don't need a unified Europe. That is, actually every country could continue working on its own, and we don't need such a EU, even though the governments want that' (Heide Lehmann, 50, GER). And as Radek Kerski from Poland speculates, Switzerland did well by not joining the EU, 'because they do not want to deal with these European Union idiots'. In comparison with the EU 'the [the Swiss people] have good income, a clean and beautiful country, loads of money [. . .]. And what about the EU? Breakdown in Germany, Denmark, market breakdowns everywhere' (Radek Kerski, 30, PL). As the quotations show, our interviewees regard the maintenance of national sovereignty as a very important aspect of a future legitimate Europe.

Other interviewees do not primarily emphasise the political sovereignty of every EU member state or the redundancy of the EU as political instance. Rather, they underline the contribution of single nation states to the political decision-making of the EU. Wilhelm Bergmann, for example, highlights Germany's pioneering task with regard to the exit from nuclear and fossil-fuel energy, and thinks it seminal for the other EU member states: 'What I like very much in Germany is that we are a nation that is making a difference in Europe. [. . .] We have to convince the other European countries, or rather, all the countries in the world that nuclear energy does not have any future in the long run' (Wilhelm Bergmann, 66, GER).

In the context of the legitimation construction of a Europe of nations, our interviewees reflect on the euro crisis too. Yet, it is the crisis situation that has activated people's communicative constructions about the future of a legitimate EU that they consider capable of overcoming the euro crisis and worth living in. Our interviewees who think in terms of a Europe of nations predominantly argue for national solutions to the euro crisis. In their view, it is above all maladministration, combined with corruption and unreasonableness, that has played a major role in the case of the euro crisis in general and Greece's economic problems in particular. Consequently, our interviewees consider it rational to let every aggrieved party solve their own problems. For example, the above-mentioned 65-year-old Herbert Sennenberger, a retired draughtsman from Austria, uses the term 'dissoluteness' when emphasising that Greece 'crept into the EU by faking facts'. He compares Greece, Germany and Austria to neighbouring families, with two of them being hard workers and one of them being dissolute and having squandered all his money. Against this background, he cannot approve supporting Greece; for him, it is not only the fault of the Greek politicians and banks, but it is also the upper class that 'has cheated on the state'. Quite similarly, Ismael Brooker, a former engineer who migrated to the UK from Lebanon in the 1960s and now runs a coffee shop in Richmond near London, tends to see each EU member state as responsible for its own economic problems, so that the EU should not help Greece as long as it continues to pursue 'wrong' policies. He compares Greece to a child who always spends all its pocket money and should therefore not be given any more money:

You know when you're raising kids [. . .], you give them pocket money; you have five kids, and one guy saves, [. . .] but one guy is a big spender and when the big guy spends money, you say, ok have some more. So it's not gonna fix his problem, and the same with Greece, it's not gonna fix anything. They don't care [. . .]. In my opinion this is what I think of the matter, why bring these countries, Lithuania for example, all these countries, why bring them around? (Ismael Brooker, 62, UK)

In line with these assignments of national responsibility, many of our interviewees say they are not willing to transfer 'their' national taxes to Greece. For example, Kurt Binder, a German pensioner from a small town in central Germany, does not trust Greece to handle European injections of cash responsibly. He fears that in consequence 'the German taxpayers have paid for it, and will in the end be burned one way or another' (Kurt Binder, 60, GER). In a similar vein, Ismael Brooker states 'every single man is paying more taxes, because they [EU] didn't let them [Greece] go' (Ismael Brooker, 62, UK).

From the interviewees' statements it becomes obvious that excluding the EU member state Greece from the eurozone may be considered to be a radical, but nevertheless conceivable consequence and solution. For example, Lisa O'Connor, a 62-year-old woman living in a rented castle in South Denmark and working as an arts and music manager, avers that one should 'send them to hell, sorry, them down in Greece. Well, if they do not stick to the rules we have here in the EU, then it's over, it simply is' (Lisa O'Connor, 62, DK). Similarly, the eastern German Joachim Gerke is obviously niggled that 'a whole country is flagging just because it is not able to, uhm, govern itself and to budget responsibly [. . .]. I cannot understand that there is still more and more money being invested into this country' (Joachim Gerke, 46, GER). A somewhat double-edged attitude, whether the European community generally should interfere with national sovereignty or not, can be observed in the case of Danish cleaning lady Lina Rendersen, who on the one hand refuses the EU's right to 'dictate Danish interests', but on the other hand expects Greece to let the EU assume responsibility for crisis management, 'because if they want something from us, then they also have to give something' (Lina Rendersen, 58, DK).

It has become obvious that we find the legitimation construction of a Europe of nations across all six countries in our sample. Appreciation of the maintenance of national cultures and identities in Europe as well as the perception of malfunctioning and therefore unnecessary European political institutions is not typical for certain countries in our sample. And moreover, the construction of a Europe of nations is promoted by citizens from all classes within the countries, as well as by well-educated and less-educated people. Again, we are confronted with a truly transnational pattern here.

Altogether, a national solution to the euro crisis is mostly shared by our interviewees, assigning national responsibility to Greece. As a consequence, it is up to the Greek government to solve the problems they created by national economic or political maladministration. Some of our interviewees even consider Greece's exclusion from the EU as a conceivable alternative. These national crisis solutions correspond to the legitimation construction of a Europe of nations. As we have shown, this legitimation construction does not only encompass specific solutions to the euro crisis. Rather, the euro crisis as a moment of activation for people's communicative constructions of Europe provoked our interviewees to articulate their visions of a legitimate EU – an EU that builds on the power of diverse national cultures and regards national political sovereignty to be an important feature.

Europe of economic cooperation

A second legitimation construction that we extract from the interviews points to a Europe of intensified economic cooperation between the member states, sometimes even to the creation of European economic government to improve and guarantee the stability of the EU common market. Activated by the euro crisis, the interviewees highlight the necessity of pushing forward European integration on the economic level as the first priority. As they point out, this would be the only way to solve current financial problems in Europe comprehensively and efficiently. In this sense, 25-year-old Charlie Willis from England, an usher in a London theatre, envisages the cutback of trade barriers in the EU: 'I feel it [the EU] should be more economic, just like, free trading and stuff first'. Also Luke Smith, a 59-year-old former teacher who owns a coffee shop in Northern England, thinks that the EU's main task 'is about economic free trade and really freedom for the people to work wherever they want in Europe' (Luke Smith, 59, UK). In a similar vein, Daniel Weaver, a 49-year-old freelance financial consultant who lives just outside London, argues that the EU needs 'economic strength because jobs are going to China and India, and that's why we need to have a strong economic design'. He continues: 'The main reason we need Europe is probably politically and economically. I mean politically with a small p, I don't mean, I'm not sure what the benefit would be of a United, you know, republic of Europe [. . .]. I think we need economic strength because jobs are going to China and India, and that's why we need to have a strong economic design' (Daniel Weaver, 49, UK).

Other interviewees state that the EU must be improved with regard to its institutional functioning in solving economic problems. We refer here to a statement already quoted from Fabrice Girard, the French business consultant. He regrets that there is currently 'no European Economic Union [. . .]. There is no European government, and this is the catastrophe. Europe, the next Europe that we will construct, must above all be political, so that the national governments will dissolve' (Fabrice Girard, 45, F). Also, the above quoted Daniel Weaver states that 'the EU needs central monetary control since this whole thing [the EU] seems a bit ill-conceived'. And: 'If you've got countries like Greece and Germany, with Greece trying to run similar economic models and such, and you don't have central money control, then you're gonna have problems' (Daniel Weaver 49, UK). Clément Sapon from France even goes a step further and asks for an 'economy that is like a *governance*' and that this 'economic governance would be European' (Clément Sapon, 65, F). Only then might EU member states really be forced to keep their national economies healthy. As Germany's Kurt Binder, aged 60, states that like Greece, 'Germany once had new indebtedness that was too high in relation to the European treaty agreement.' As a consequence, 'we [the Germans] received a letter of warning and have been threatened with penalties. However, these penalties have never been applied.' This could be changed with European economic governance, since then these penalties 'would be enforced'. With regard to the situation in Greece, he continues that EU economic governance could instruct Greek politicians to push austerity measures.

Summing up, the legitimation construction of a Europe of economic cooperation emphasises the stability of the European common market as the highest good for the future of Europe. Accordingly, our interviewees favour the improvement of economic cooperation between member states or even argue for the establishment of a proper European economic government. In our interviewees' perspective, European economic government should have the authority to enforce necessary austerity measures in case of future economic problems in the EU countries. Again, we cannot find national or stratification-related differences with regard to this legitimation construction. Hence, it is interviewees from all our researched countries that favour this construction, regardless of their level of education or social standing.

Europe of welfare and solidarity

In contrast to the legitimation constructions of national cultures and economic cooperation, other interviewees favour a Europe of welfare and solidarity. With regard to the euro crisis, they clearly argue for a solution on a European level, which they underscore by the argument of absolute solidarity, owing to humanitarian considerations and the postulate of European community. In this argument, we identify a strong commitment to the essential *raison d'être* of the EU, as taken for granted by these interviewees: 'The Greek crisis can be seen as the European time of reckoning' (Mads Jespersen, 51, DK). The legitimation construction of a Europe of welfare and solidarity points to the improvement of solidarity amongst the EU member states as well as to the establishment and maintenance of welfare for all citizens in Europe. Christine Hauschild from Germany, for example, underlines the importance 'of a political instance offering a secure frame to people, so that they are secured in case they lose their jobs, that they are covered by health insurance and that they receive a pension' (Christine Hauschild, 42, GER). Similarly, 36-year-old Sophie Clifton from England imagines a EU where 'no one [. . .] was living in poverty as such'. And Steven Corner, from Southern England states that he likes the idea of a united Europe 'working towards problems as an entire continent, I love that'. But in order to realise this idea, solidarity amongst the Europeans must be improved: 'I don't think we communicate enough with each other [. . .]. We see what's happening in other countries and don't do enough to help each other' (Steven Corner, 20, UK).

As our interviews show, the legitimation construction of a Europe of welfare and solidarity encompasses not only solidarity amongst European citizens and EU member states, but also the improvement and protection of humane and equal life chances for all people in Europe. In this context, our interviewees mention social protection systems, gender equality and the protection of human rights – for Europeans, and especially for migrants and refugees who want to take up residence in Europe.

Taking the euro crisis, and especially the Greek crisis, as an example, our interviewees consider it to be a human imperative or a natural consequence of Greece's EU membership to show *solidarity* – regardless of the claimed guilt of the Greek national government. Speaking of the Greeks as the 'bankrupt Greeks', the Austrian interviewee Fritz Kantler, who himself tries to make a living more or less unsuccessfully as a returned globetrotter with neither education nor employment, says this is unfair, since he considers the Greek people to be 'quite hard-pushed' (Fritz Kantler, 61, AT). In this sense, 21-year-old Louis Barney, living at his parent's house in Southern England and studying history and political science at the University of Plymouth, states quite emotionally:

'What's the point of being in [the EU] if you're not getting that [finan-cial] protection. It's necessary to help each other out. It's important for them [the Greeks] to know you want them to be back'. He continues, arguing that every EU member state 'has to give something back at some point', because the community makes it natural to help each other out and not to split up as soon as problems arise. As a consequence, 'every-one has gotta tighten their belts, and keep hoping. [. . .] The EU should be kept together [. . .] instead of splitting up and going back to say the Deutschmark or the Franc. [. . .] So just keep the economy strong and stick to it really' (Louis Barney, 21, UK).

Likewise, 52-year-old Pole Barbara Szymańska, a cleaning lady in Warsaw, supports common European endeavours to overcome the euro crisis – even though she says that she does not 'know what will be later, how we will have to pay off, how our children will feel'. In a similar vein, 37-year-old biologist Simon Gärtner, who works as a gardener in a public park in the Northern German city of Bremen, argues that Greece should stay in the EU: 'Europe as a whole deserves it to see this through.' With regard to Europe as a political community, the Danish unemployed salesman Poul Omegn characterises the current euro crisis as a European 'litmus test'. According to him, the question at stake is 'whether the European team spirit actually works' (Poul Omegn, 44, DK). Consequently, he is in favour of absolutely sticking together in the EU – otherwise it would be like refusing help to a family member. It is this reciprocal help that the EU stands for. Nevertheless, financial help for Greece would in the end also be beneficial for the sponsoring body – as the example of the Marshall plan after World War II has shown, said Poul Omegn, explaining that: 'This steel company will in the end profit from the fact that Greece gets financial help – because they will buy its steel products'.

The extreme position of unconditional European solidarity – not only in times of euro crisis – is what Austrian agricultural and nutritional stu-dent Kilian Wedekind of Vienna advocates. He even condemns national politicians who, promoting themselves in national elections, abuse the Greeks and their problems by saying, 'We pay, we pay, we pay [for them] and in the end we do not get anything back.' In principle, 'countries who perform badly economically have to be supported' (Kilian Wedekind, 26, AT). Similarly, British 50-year-old university project manager Jessica Price argues that politicians should not stigmatise countries like Greece now: 'I think we gotta be prepared not to stigmatise countries that are, have been performing badly economically. I think we've gotta be care-ful that the stronger countries don't bully the weaker countries. I think we've got to put everything in historical atrocities that have happened, ehm, in these countries'. She goes on to state that even though 'there doesn't seem to be any real leadership' in the euro crisis, it would be problematic to have one single country taking over this leadership:

> We don't want to reach the point where one country has too much power in Europe. Because that has always been dangerous in the past. Ehm, but I think we've got to [. . .] appreciate that despite being in the EU the constituent member countries are very different and very unique. And they're not all gonna fit this one-size fit sort of type concept. [. . .] You know, Germany and France have had strong, [. . .] I mean, Germany has got an amazingly strong economy, ehm, you know, most countries in the EU never gonna match Germany in its efficiencies and strong economy. It's just never gonna happen. [. . .] I think it's a bit rich for countries in Europe telling, you know, telling Greece what to do at this time, because you know, Greece has never been a strong economy and there are others, other economies in Europe that are a bit dysfunctional as well. And, ehm, I just don't think they should be punished in this way, I just think this whole thing is problematic. [. . .] Ehm, I feel really sorry for Greece. (Jessica Price, 50, UK)

Similar to Jessica Price's expression of sympathy with Greece, other interviewees state their concern as well. For example, Austrian Fritz Kantler, aged 61, living in 'precarious' circumstances having been out of regular work for decades, expresses his 'appreciation and sympathy for the people' in Greece. From his perspective, those people are 'in big difficulties [. . .], because the economic system, ehm, this is just horrible on the human level'. He associates his sympathy with the Greek people with his own stigmatisation as a 'longhair and, eh, eh anti-social' (Fritz Kantler, 61, A).

With regard to the legitimation construction of a Europe of welfare and solidarity, it is important to highlight once again that this construction is a transnational phenomenon. That is, we find the articulation of a Europe of welfare and solidarity in every country of our sample and with regard to every level of education or social standing amongst our interviewees. Activated by the euro crisis and taking the euro crisis as an example, our interviewees strongly argue for solidarity with Greece. In sum, our interviewees foster the idea of solidarity and social protection not only for whole countries, but also for migrants, refugees and poor people in Europe.

United States of Europe

The fourth legitimation construction articulated by our interviewees promotes the idea of a United States of Europe as a vision for the future legitimacy of Europe in general and as a solution to the euro crisis in particular. The interviewees' statements are strongly bound up with a call for the extension of European cooperation at the institutional level. Activated by the euro crisis and by seeing the euro crisis as a 'crossroads' leading either to a 'European federal state', a 'separation' of the EU member states or remaining at the 'status quo', Austrian political science student Manuel Vechter, aged 19, postulates his 'ideal conception' leading to the 'United States of Europe'. Similarly, Roberto Zero, a Frenchman aged 25, 'hopes that [. . .] the crisis allows Europe to foster integration even more'.

Often, our interviewees favour a United States of Europe oriented to the US model. Fostering the European integration process in such a direction would, in the perspective of our interviewees, help to overcome the euro crisis and prevent similar crises in the future. The loss of political power and sovereignty for every EU member state is regarded as a necessary precondition for this. Like Manuel Vechter, 30-year-old Tamara Tannhäuser from England states: 'What I'd love to see is something where Europe becomes a bit more like the US model', so that the member states are 'economically and financially a bit more interlinked with each other [. . .], that it's just a bit more stable within the EU' (Tamara Tannhäuser, 30, UK). Our interview partners justify their wish for more political integration at the EU level with both emotional and rational arguments. The emotional arguments point to the dream of a unified and peaceful Europe, so that our interviewees consider the idea of the United States of Europe just 'great', as Leonie Stiesing, aged 26 from Germany states. She continues: 'I like the idea [of the United States of Europe] a lot, because we would be closer together in Europe, there wouldn't be these hostilities between the different countries any more [. . .]. The United States of Europe, that sounds great to me!' (Leonie Stiesing, 26, GER). Similarly 66-year-old Wilhelm Bergman and 62-year-old Gerhard Deichen, also from Germany, underline that the United States of Europe would not only be a 'great dream' but could also help to avoid stultifying conflicts and power struggles between member states. 'All these disputes, for example the conflict between the Croats and Serbs as well as the conflict in Kosovo, all these would not exist anymore' (Wilhelm Bergmann, 66, GER). By promoting the United States of Europe as a dream, our interviewees also reject an economic orientation as the only reason for supporting the EU. Peter Auermann, business manager in the field of renewable energy, complains about the primarily economic orientation of the EU: 'Well, I don't like this economic course and the idea that the market will regulate everything [. . .]. I think the political integration of the EU must proceed – in the direction of the United States of Europe' (Peter Auermann, 29, AT).

Rational argument for the promotion of the United States of Europe often points to the economic and powerful strength of a unified Europe in the global context. Wilhelm Bergmann from Germany, for example, states that the idea of the United States of Europe 'encompasses all European countries [. . .]. Only as a unified Europe we can face economically powerful countries like China or India and America' (Wilhelm Bergmann, 66, GER).

As regards the crisis situation, our interview partners think that fostering the development of European integration towards a United States of Europe is the best way of overcoming the euro crisis, securing the future of Europe. Michael Mahdbauer from Austria, a 35-year-old administrative officer, states that it becomes obvious right now in the euro crisis, 'that the EU in its current construction is not that good and must continue to change [. . .] towards a European political union, into the direction of/ that would mean the end of the single European member states.' In a similar vein, Fabrice Girard from France laments that the absence of a United States of Europe has caused the financial 'catastrophe', because 'the problems of Greece must be solved, and there is only Angela Merkel and Nicolas Sarkozy taking care of it whilst the other member states turn their backs on the problem. [. . .] There is no European government, and that's the catastrophe. Europe, the next Europe that we build, must be a political union above all, so that the national governments move into the background' (Fabrice Girard, 45, F).

Summing up, the interviewees favouring the legitimation construction of the United States of Europe regard the euro crisis as a crossroads challenging the future of Europe. They emphasise their vision of a future Europe, integrating in a way that brings it closer to a United States of Europe, as a solution to the euro crisis and to the challenges of a globalised world with strong global players like the US, China or India. At this point, our interviewees indeed reflect on and approve the fact that the realisation of this idea means a loss of national sovereignty for every single EU member state. Once again, it is worth noting that the legitimation construction of the United States of Europe does not predominate in particular countries from our sample. This construction, though, appears across all countries and – similarly to all other legitimation constructions – across all social strata.

7.3   Transnational patterns: citizens' engagement with a legitimate Europe

Using the example of the euro crisis as a moment of activation in citizens' communicative constructions, our analyses have brought to light different patterns of understanding of the euro crisis, as well as different patterns of legitimation constructions of Europe. As in the previous chapter on citizens' European public connections, we have applied a transnational perspective. We have extracted transnational patterns that appear across all six countries in our sample. By highlighting the transnational perspective, we underline the fact that there is no radical difference between countries in the sense that German citizens, for example, would only favour the legitimation construction of a Europe of nations, including national solutions for the Greek crisis and the euro crisis. We find instead all patterns throughout the sample of our interviewees in all countries. And even more so, we find all patterns for all social strata and levels of education within the sample of interviewees.

Following Peter L. Berger's and Thomas Luckmann's conception of legitimation processes, we first looked at our interviewees' understandings of the euro crisis, including the effort to explain and justify the euro crisis. Here, our analysis showed that citizens try to make sense of the euro crisis by articulating perplexity, anxiety and speculation about the consequences and further development of the euro crisis. Secondly, we looked at the interviewees' legitimation constructions of Europe that often evolved from their reflections on possible solutions for the euro crisis and include a very broad vision of a future Europe they can imagine living in. The idea of a Europe of nations highlights not only the value of and the need to preserve the cultural diversity in Europe, but also the political sovereignty of every single EU member state. With regard to the euro crisis, our interviewees emphasise that countries like Greece who face severe financial difficulties should solve 'their' economic problems on their own, claiming that they have produced these difficulties themselves as a consequence of economic and political maladministration and corruption. Interviewees emphasising the idea of a Europe of economic cooperation either promote the improvement of economic cooperation between EU member states or the creation of European economic government to regulate financial and economic matters, and thereby protect the stability of the European market. Our interviewees consider that it is only by improving economic cooperation in the EU that the current and potential future economic crisis could be solved or prevented. In contrast to these first two legitimation constructions, the interviewed persons promoting a Europe of welfare and solidarity underline the need to look after each other in the EU, to improve and secure social welfare and, consequently, show solidarity with member states facing serious economic problems. Our interviewees favouring a Europe of welfare and solidarity prefer European ways out of the euro crisis: solidarity with Greece because of the fact that Greece is after all part of the European community and the community spirit ought to be to support each other, especially in times of difficulties. Interviewees who support the idea of a United States of Europe think in terms of improvements at the European institutional level, as well as a deepening of European integration to create better EU political instruments for managing and overcoming the euro crisis. Altogether, our analysis demonstrates that reflection on the euro crisis is not just an elite debate on the part of well-known intellectuals, but also a prominent topic of everyday discourse.

The existence of a fundamental anchoring of a European orientation persists through times of the euro crisis and across the multi-segmented European public sphere. This does not necessarily mean that there will be no criticism of the EU and of its crisis management. Nonetheless, fundamental legitimation of the European idea seems to be evident in spite of the euro crisis and in the form of the four different legitimation constructions of Europe extracted from our interview material.

How do we evaluate research results like these? In our view, two points are striking. First, our analysis demonstrates that the euro crisis in general, and the serious economic problems in Greece in particular, are a matter of great concern to interviewees across Europe. The question of whether the euro crisis is perceived as a threat to the EU and will possibly end with the breakup of the EU remains an open one, and is discussed ambivalently. However, the more striking point is that our interviewees are primarily involved in a shared discourse about the euro crisis. Irrespective of their construction of how the euro crisis should be overcome, this involvement is the core point. In the perspective of pragmatic concepts of citizenship and the public sphere (Dewey 1927; Lingenberg 2010a: 49f.), our interviewees position themselves as European citizens insofar as they construct the euro crisis as a problem affecting their own lives. In some cases, this kind of citizenship might be highly situational and framed negatively. However, if it is only situational positioning in critique, it remains a momentary positioning as a European citizen who is affected by the euro crisis and therefore has a certain understanding of it and often also wishes to articulate ideas of how to overcome the euro crisis.

Second, our transcultural analysis demonstrates the high degree of complexity in the contradictions of the euro crisis. We cannot work in terms of national patterns of euro crisis constructions, such that, for example, interviewees from Germany or the United Kingdom articulate only the 'national way' as a way out of the crisis for Greece. The patterns according to which the euro crisis will be overcome are found right across Europe. Nor do we find stratification-related patterns of crisis construction. This said, once more it becomes obvious that Europe is not only segmented in relation to nations or classes, but there are also transnational patterns of segmentation and transnational patterns of a shared sense of belonging and responsibility – as our analysis of citizens' understandings and constructions of a legitimate Europe have shown.

Reflecting on our analysis, there is a suggestion that this euro crisis might again result in a deepening of European integration at the level of citizens, as they seem to share an understanding of the present euro crisis as a common crisis in Europe. And in the event of a fundamental legitimation of the European idea remaining (cf. Hepp et al. 2012), there might be also a common solution – either in the form of the European way or another new way of re-negotiated European cooperation – and the result might be a strengthening of citizenship through the euro crisis. But this remains a matter of speculation.

8
Conclusion: The Contested Communicative Construction of Europe

In this conclusion, we will now tie the overall argumentation together. We present some general reflections on the present status of what we have called the communicative construction of Europe. Europe signifies the emergent European society with the EU as its political institution. As shown in chapter 2, we do not want to reduce Europe and the EU to a semiotic phenomenon by emphasising the aspect of communicative construction. By contrast, communicative construction has to be understood as one aspect of a multidimensional process of social construction. It is however a highly important aspect: When it comes to making sense and constructing the meaning of Europe and the EU, this is articulated in communication processes. We have shown the patterns of these processes through our long-term empirical research, combining a variety of social science methods at different levels of analysis: newspaper analysis over 30 years, newsroom studies, an analysis of online interaction in internet forums and audience studies. This research involves six countries studied with a transcultural perspective: Austria, Denmark, France, Germany, Poland and the United Kingdom.

We understood the European public sphere not as a replica of a national one, but as a transnational and transcultural communicative space that is 'thickened' by communication across national public spheres. This happens by shared monitoring of activity in Brussels and the EU (Europeanisation by vertical transnational connectivity), a mutual observation and discursive exchange (Europeanisation by horizontal transnational connectivity), a rapprochement of public communication on Europe and the EU (Europeanisation by transnationally converging discourse), and an articulation of a shared European identity and belonging (Europeanisation by transnational collective belonging). However, the European public sphere is not placed in a cultural vacuum, but rooted in what we called cultures of political discourse, meaning cultural patterns of political communication. These patterns point to a multi-segmented European public sphere: Despite Europeanisation, national segmentation prevails. This is caused by, among other things, national cultures of political discourse, rooted in national political traditions. However, across the countries studied, we noticed a transnational segmentation. This stems from a shared stratification in European national societies and in Europe as a whole. The study of the practices of journalists, public discourse, the intertwined online and offline practices of citizens, and the communicative construction of Europe has to take note of this complexity of multi-segmentation.

Following recent public and academic discussions, today's euro crisis is typically considered as a decisive point in this process. However, there are many different ways to understand the euro crisis. There are critical positions that regard the euro crisis as a considerable strain for Europe and the EU. As a consequence, the communicative construction of both should be discontinued. For more optimistic approaches, the euro crisis is a 'tipping point' (Eder 2014: 221) for people to take action (again). In normative terms, the communicative construction of Europe should become more oriented to the people.

In sum, the euro crisis is an expression of the contested character of the communicative construction of Europe. Or put differently, the communicative construction of Europe is not a linear process, but has its ups and downs, contradictions and conflicts. It is about a shared communicative *struggling* about the character of a *possible* 'European society' (Vobruba 2012: 263). The outcome is still pending and contested. Like other crises before it, the euro crisis – at least in its present stage – does not mean that this process of communicative construction breaks down. However, the euro crisis is a political incident which makes the different positions in this process of communicative construction apparent and therefore communicatively negotiable. The empirical studies we presented show that media are of great importance here, which is why we consider the euro crisis to be a 'mediatised conflict', a conflict in which media have an 'active performative involvement and [play a] constitutive role within' (Cottle 2006: 9).

From this perspective, new kinds of question emerge: questions concerning the relevance of the euro crisis for the long-term process of constructing Europe communicatively. We studied a variety of research issues and presented our findings in the previous chapters. Here we want to go one step further and relate these more phenomenologically driven research issues to four more fundamental questions concerning the present stage of Europe's development:

1. Are we witnessing an emerging European culture of political discourse that might provide a firm basis for a European public sphere also in times of crisis?
2. Could the euro crisis push up towards a more unified European public sphere, which could overcome its multi-segmentation?
3. Might the euro crisis lead us towards more engaged European citizens?
4. Do we partake in a movement towards the communicative construction of a more legitimate Europe?

Of course, these questions are far-reaching. Far from being speculative, however, we now take up these fundamental questions to pursue the possible trajectories of change to which the results of our transcultural investigations point.

Towards a European culture of political discourse?

Bernhard Peters proposed that each more or less stable public sphere is based on a culture of political discourse that is part of its 'social and cultural foundation that extends well beyond the framework of media markets and media organisations' (Peters 2008: 246). If we want to use this as an empirical indicator, the question is: To what degree does a European culture of political discourse emerge around the euro crisis? This discussion is particularly of interest if we relate it back to our findings in chapter 3 on journalists' practices and their roots in cultures of political discourse. While this emphasised the re-articulation of national cultures of political discourse and the transnational segmentation through stratification-related cultures of political discourse and the connected types of addressing audiences, we can change the perspective by asking: Is there any indication of an emerging European culture of political discourse that might provide a sustainable foundation for a European public sphere?

In the light of our empirical analysis, we, first of all, note contradictory developments. How journalists deal with the national domain and address their readership helps us understand the multi-segmented character of the European public sphere. On the one hand, we encounter more or less stable national patterns in journalists' practice. It is not only that the nation itself is the main reference point of the journalists' work. Additionally, across the member states, the articulation of this nationalisation is different. Journalists are part of their national cultures of political discourse and continuously re-articulate these cultures. On the other hand, we find transnational patterns of addressing audiences. We distinguished between the analyst, ambassador, reporter and caterer. These different transnational modes of addressing audiences are a manifestation of segmented cultures of political discourse. This helps us to understand the segmentation of the European public sphere across countries.

However, when we move to our question of whether a European culture of political discourse is emerging, our data begin to speak in a different way. A basic European culture of political discourse seems to be emergent. In journalists' practices we notice rudimentary cultural patterns that understand this way. In the everyday activity of most journalists, Europe is a shared and accepted horizon of meaning; this horizon does not replace the nation, but transcends it. Also the forms of country-specific practices and orientations of nationalisation are the same Europe-wide. National embedding and transnational contextualisation, hierarchisation, routinisation of the transnational, the horizons of information-seeking and the research networks are at root of journalists' practices across all countries studied in the same way.

It would be an intellectual mistake to consider these forms to be detached from content, from their social and cultural references. Form and content have to be thought of together. We cannot separate forms of practice from the content of activity, which in this case is related to different nationalities. However, it is striking that we can capture a deeper level of European similarities that we can use as an indicator of elements of a shared culture of political discourse. Various aspects trigger such an emergent culture of political discourse: a shared long-term history of cultural exchange, common political problems that are subject to common discussion and solution and increasingly deeper contact between journalists in Europe, partly mediated by correspondents in Brussels.

According to our findings, not only are journalistic professional standards comparable across Europe (Heikkilä/Kunelius 2006; Mancini 2008; Offerhaus 2011; Örnebring 2011; Schudson/Anderson 2009), but an emerging European culture of political discourse at all levels forms the basis for the journalists' everyday practices and is re-articulated by them. This European culture of political discourse is much less distinct than are those which are national and stratification-related. Also, the peculiar character of this European culture of political discourse can only be described in a comparison to other 'geocultural regions' (Hepp 2015: 93),

Latin America for instance (García Canclini 2001: 97–109). However, if we take the shared patterns we described as expressions of a rudimentary European culture of political discourse, it also helps us to understand why, in the tensions of the euro crisis, the communicative construction of Europe does not collapse. There seems to be a shared transnational cultural foundation for the European public sphere.

Further proof of this interpretation can be found when we extend our perspective to our research results from audiences. These are comparable to what we show for journalists. Analysing political communication repertoires and the European public connections of citizens across countries, we discussed social positioning, that is, a re-articulation of social stratification in certain images of class position. We described the re-articulation of the local and national as a context for the appropriation of media coverage on Europe and the EU. We see this as citizens' references to national and stratification-related cultures of political discourse. Our audience research also examined three kinds of European public connection: a noticing, a centred and a multi-perspective one. These variants of European public connection rest on different political communication repertoires that were not suspended by the euro crisis, but activated by it.

Again, we must be very careful when interpreting these results. We do want to argue that some aspects are indicators of a shared European culture of political discourse. Having at least a noticing European public connection seems to be something that is expected of people living in Europe, however limited this noticing might be. And if a person is highly interested in one topic or issue, again it seems to be expected that this issue be considered at least partly in relation to Europe and the EU. This becomes manifest in the centred European public connection. Finally, being highly politically interested in and oriented to a critical political discourse – which is the case for people with a multi-perspective European public connection – there seems to be the expectation that this interest at least somehow relates to Europe and the EU. These are the points we would like to consider as expressions of an emerging European culture of political discourse with respect to the people as a European 'citizen audience' (Lingenberg 2010b).

If we consider results like these, it is evident that a European culture of political discourse lacks the stability of a national or even a stratification-related culture. However, there are some indicators that a European culture of political discourse is in the process of emerging and that the euro crisis did not prevent this process. While the communicative construction of Europe remains a contested, open and therefore uncertain project, at least we notice the possibility of a stabilising cultural foundation.

Towards a more unified European public sphere?

Regarding the euro crisis, there is a second question: Are we moving towards a more unified European public sphere, or is the euro crisis an obstacle to such movement? Given the uncertainty of future developments it is hard to say anything definite on this. However, our empirical investigation offers some preliminary insights; here our long-term content analysis and the research on citizens' interactions in online forums are helpful.

If we consider our content analysis of qualitative, tabloid and regional newspapers for the period from 1982 to 2013, the following research result is striking: A multi-segmented European public sphere was formed by the end of the 1990s and it was not broken up by the euro crisis. To capture the empirical insights of our content analysis, we used the idea of a plateau: The Europeanisation of national print coverage took place in the 1990s and reached a certain level between the years 1996 and 2003 in the run-up to the European eastern-enlargement. First, in 1996 the plateau of horizontal Europeanisation was achieved, then in 2003 the plateau of vertical Europeanisation. Taking the example of Poland, we could demonstrate how latecomers quickly moved on to this plateau through 'catch-up Europeanization' (Kleinen-von Königslöw/Möller 2009: 101). Triggered by EU membership, the Europeanisation of print coverage in Poland quickly achieved patterns of Europeanisation comparable with other, older member states.

Reaching the plateau does not imply uniformity. While transnational references to other European countries are quite stable over time, references to speakers from different countries fluctuate. Being on the plateau means that a certain level is maintained. Maybe this metaphor of the plateau is the best possible shorthand for the impact of the euro crisis, involving a change of print media coverage, but not a change that challenged the level already reached. As we demonstrated, there was across all countries a temporary recession in the share of references to each other in 2008. This was not, however, very marked, and in 2013, the level was even higher. This higher level in 2013 could mean that there was intensified discussion among European speakers reflected in the coverage on the euro crisis. Nevertheless, this intensified discussion did not challenge the multi-segmented character of the European public sphere, something that is also demonstrated in other studies (cf. most recently

Koopmans 2015; Risse 2015a). The European public sphere was and remains multi-segmented.

As our content analysis demonstrates, the national segmentation of the European public sphere remains stable during the euro crisis, as did stratification-related segmentation with reference to some types of media outlet. However, the degree of national segmentation is uneven between countries. While France and Germany show a considerable degree of Europeanisation, the British press has a much lower share for European institutions and actors and a high level of reference to domestic institutions and actors. Austria and Poland, latecomers to the EU, as well as Denmark, fall somewhere in between. This represents a quite stable degree of national segmentation in a longitudinal perspective and also during the euro crisis – for our long-term content analysis reaching from 1982 to 2013. In sum, while the European public sphere did not fragment during the euro crisis, its national and stratification-related segmentation did not diminish either. As with the overall plateau, the multi-segmented character seems to be quite stable.

To understand the dynamics involved here, it is helpful to consider our analysis of interaction in online forums. Here we could demonstrate how far the euro crisis serves as a reference point for citizens' discourses in online forums. Again we find a multi-segmented character for the European public sphere. As our hyperlink analysis demonstrated, the internet's transnational potential is only weakly exploited. Transnational possibilities for the kind of communication in which users engage in direct horizontal exchange are limited. Users normally meet each other across nationalities in transnational forums. However, since the differences between national and transnational forums seem to be limited to the discussion of nationality in transnational forums, the distinction between transnational and national forums are also only of limited relevance. Instead, the commonalities in the constructions of the euro crisis and of Europe are apparent. Does the national segmentation of online forums actually hinder the emergence of a European public sphere and the communicative construction of Europe?

We argue that interaction in the forums can be relation-orientated (focused on building and maintaining relations between those involved) or issue-orientated (focused on the issue of the euro crisis). Three points are emphasised as the main results of our research: First, users express their observations on, evaluations of, thoughts on and contemplations about the euro crisis. Second, these observations build the basis for users creating, expressing and maintaining relations towards each other on the grounds of their engagement with the euro crisis. Third, these relations often take the form of conflict, especially when citizens' understandings of the euro crisis and of Europe diverge.

What we see here is a *contested* communicative construction of Europe: People share Europe and the EU as a point of reference. They are involved in an engaged – and sometimes negative – discourse about Europe and its future within and after the euro crisis. However, if we follow the theoretical considerations outlined in chapter two, this does not necessarily imply a negative impact on the construction of a European society. Indeed, if there is shared ground, such conflictual discourse keeps the communicative construction of Europe going, opposing understandings of it being negotiated through conflict. As a consequence, the outcome is *not* a unified European public sphere, but a conflictual one. Nonetheless, this kind of conflict is constitutive for the communicative construction of Europe.

An additional point of interest is the complexity of conflict in our data. National differences are not the sole necessary basis for conflict. There are certainly conflicts in the online forums arising from arguments out of national interest. However, a great deal of conflictual argument takes place across the nations. Other lines of conflict are political affiliation, ideas of adequate economic models, and attributions of blame and responsibility for or solutions to the euro crisis.

If we take these research results altogether, we find a more complex response to our question concerning the possibility of a more unified European public sphere. There are at least two points we should consider.

First, an egalitarian European public sphere might be a normative goal, depending on the normative model used (Lunt/Livingstone 2013). But if we consider a public sphere more empirically, as a thickened space of political communication, such normative ideas might be limited. A degree of shared references and exchange is necessary. This is the plateau the European public sphere reached between 1996 and 2003, a plateau that was not placed in question by the euro crisis. However, after reaching this plateau, variations in Europeanisation remain common as well, while multi-segmentation persists. Here the contradictory character of the European public sphere is not so different from national public spheres. The latter are also segmented, for example, regionally (Kleinen-von Königslöw 2010a) or by class and gender (Fraser 1993; Husband 2000; Negt/Kluge 1993). Since there is such segmentation in national public spheres it is no surprise that the more complex thickening of a European public sphere is no different.

Second, an egalitarian and harmonic European public sphere could be considered problematic. So long as we understand the process of constructing Europe communicatively to be ongoing and the definition of Europe as a possible transnational society still in the making, it is only to be expected that the construction process has a conflictual character. At this point, our research results are striking, since the research on online forums in particular demonstrates that lines of conflict are not merely national or related to stratification. Lines of conflict are also normative, regarding the kind of Europe that is desired and needed. This is especially the case when people express themselves as citizens within the multi-segmented European public sphere, as also demonstrated by the analysis of our interviewees' different constructions of legitimation.

We might answer the question concerning the possibility of further unification of the European public sphere as follows: A plateau in the European public sphere was reached and this was not threatened by the euro crisis. However, being at this plateau neither means empirically that an egalitarian and harmonious communicative space exists, nor would this be the adequate interest from a normative point of view. Since the definition of Europe as a transnational society and of the EU and its institutions is still open, the contested character of the European public sphere seems to remain necessary.

Towards more engaged European citizens?

Our third question refers to citizens' perspectives on the European public sphere. Does the euro crisis result in an increasingly engaged European citizenry? In recent research this is quite a common thesis, 'politicisation' being discussed as one consequence of the euro crisis (cf. for example Checkel/Katzenstein 2009; Eder 2014; Risse 2015b). Our research into online forum discussions might point in this direction. However, if we discuss in more detail the results of our audience study, matters become more complex.

To deal with this complexity, we took up the concept of public connection, reflecting engagement more as a gradual phenomenon than a binary idea – that one is either engaged or not. Having a European public connection means a joint 'orientation to a public world where matters of shared concern are, or at least should be, addressed' (Couldry et al. 2007b: 3). Therefore, having a European public connection represents a certain concern for Europe which makes up an individual part of the European 'citizen audience' (Lingenberg 2010b: 53). While this does not imply engagement in a more narrow sense, it is an important precondition for further engagement in Europe and the EU.

There are different ways of having a European public connection and we differentiate three fundamental kinds of European public connection: the noticing, the centred and the multi-perspective ones. On the basis of diverse samples of interviewees from Austria, Denmark, France, Germany, Poland and the United Kingdom, it was evident that all had a certain understanding of what is going on in Europe and felt in the same way concerned by this.

Linking this general insight to the euro crisis, we captured an activating role for the crisis. Activation means the intensification or extension of the political communication repertoires on which the European public connection of a person is based. This activation is rooted in the diffuse and somewhat undefined feeling of being affected by the euro crisis, though many of the persons interviewed could not explain this in any detail. This said, an activation of the political communication repertoire could result in a temporarily deeper European public connection or even a temporary switch from a noticing to a (partly) centred or multi-perspective European public connection. This intensified communicative engagement with Europe and the EU means a deeper everyday involvement in the process of the communicative construction of Europe. This is not necessarily politicisation, if we mean by that approaching Europe and the EU from a political point of view. Given the everyday perspective, the point of view can also be very different, reflecting practically the consequences of the euro crisis for one's own situation.

This brings us to the way in which interviewees tried to make sense of the euro crisis. Across the countries studied, as well as across various European public connections, we find three patterns: first perplexity, which means that people try to make sense of the crisis; second anxiety, involving worry about the future; and third speculation, reflecting on how the crisis came about. All of these three patterns are possibly linked to further politicisation, but not necessarily. In contrast, they might also be linked to an increased distancing from European politics.

At a high level of engagement are those citizens who became active in the online forums that we studied. Here our methodology imposed a limit. Since our aim was to investigate online interactions *in situ* – how they occur in forums – we have no interview data relating to this. Political engagement could only be reconstructed on the basis of activity within the forums. Nevertheless, we can make some important points.

First of all, being active in such a forum involves engagement, since it implies not only following public discourse about Europe and the EU, but registering in the forum and then interacting there. Second, discussion of the euro crisis is a relevant form of activity. The persons involved in online discussion of the euro crisis often and in many forums either express disapproval and rejection, or support and agreement regarding other comments on the euro crisis. Users repeatedly position themselves towards to each other with reference to the euro crisis.

Here again, we note that nationality is not the only or even the most important line of difference in the forums. Diversity in the different construction processes of the euro crisis and of Europe is founded upon differences in general (political) positions with reference to ideas of a future Europe or political or ideological affiliations, rather than with respect to nation states, or with respect to the national and transnational context of this discussion.

We argue that the euro crisis was an incident that had an activating role for citizens. This activation possibly relates to further politicisation, but not necessarily. Activation means taking part in the contested communicative construction of Europe in a more intensive or extensive way. People as citizens bring to this process the deep-rootedness of their perspectives on Europe and the EU in their everyday lives. Hence citizens' European public connections are quite different from what might be expected of politicians or journalists: just noticing, reflecting what something means for the everyday life; centred on a topic important in the everyday world; or multi-perspective, while these different perspectives are also closely connected to experiences in everyday life. The important role for an activated European citizen audience is to bring these everyday perspectives into the contested process of constructing Europe communicatively. And with the present changes in the media environment, they can more easily voice their opinions within this public discourse.

Towards the communicative construction of a more legitimate Europe?

Our fourth and final question refers back to the normative points we raised at the beginning of this chapter. What do our findings mean for the legitimation of the EU as the major political institution of Europe and for the possible emergence of a European society? Are we on the way towards the communicative construction of a more legitimate Europe? Much has been written on the legitimation deficit of the EU, as discussed in chapter 2. Our argument there was that we should rethink legitimation within the framework of communicative constructivism.

Different voices express legitimation, which is not just a matter of agreement or disagreement. One should therefore focus on the character of this legitimation.

Using ideas taken from Peter L. Berger and Thomas Luckmann (1967), we argued that legitimation is in essence a kind of narration, which explains and justifies an institutional order – quite often in a highly symbolic way. However, how far citizens share the communicative constructions that dominate the mediated public discourse remains an open question. Their everyday communicative constructions of legitimacy are quite different.

Across the countries that we studied, we found basic agreement with the European idea. While there might be great differences over politics or the present euro crisis, the basic idea of Europe – the idea of a common heritage, of the necessity of peace, freedom and cooperation – is shared. This is a basic legitimatising foundation for Europe; the legitimate character of this society and the EU as its political institution remaining open.

The kind of citizens' constructions of a legitimate Europe that we find within our data is striking. Activated by the euro crisis, our interviewees do not only discuss possible solutions to resolve the crisis. They also outline different ideas of what a legitimate Europe might be. These legitimation constructions are not confined to the euro crisis as such or to specific EU political decisions with regard to the euro crisis, but often involve a broader picture of a legitimate Europe. In our analyses, we distinguished four legitimation constructions. First a Europe of nations, wherein a legitimate Europe is thought to be a loose association of largely independent nation states with specific national cultures. These states are understood to be the main units of responsibility. Second, there is the construction of a Europe of economic cooperation. In this case, a legitimate Europe and EU still consist of independent states, but which cooperate intensively with each other to attain a better position in an economically globalised world. The third construction is that of a welfare and solidarity Europe. Here, member states work together as equal partners and assist each other, no matter what the economic situation. Finally, there is the construction of the United States of Europe. Here, a legitimate Europe and EU would be deeply integrated in much the same way as the United States of America is. In all of these versions, citizens are part of a contested communicative construction of a legitimate Europe.

Even more contested is the question of specific EU politicians and EU politics. This is where we found the highest level of disagreement in our data, for interviews as well as online forums. Here we find many critical

statements: EU regulations are seen as contradictory, national representatives at the EU are considered to be second-rate, the EU bureaucracy is
described as ineffective and so forth.

We can consider these findings in greater detail trough contextualising them in a legitimation pyramid (cf. Figure 8.1). This idea helps to
capture the different constructions of legitimation and their contested
character. First of all and across our whole sample, the European idea
is unquestioned by citizens. This is the basis upon which the communicative construction of Europe takes place. More contested are the
four constructions of a legitimate Europe. At this point, we see differences and conflicts between the constructions of a Europe of nations,
a Europe of economic cooperation, welfare and solidarity Europe, and
a United States of Europe. Because of the contradictory definitions of
the character of a European society, as well as the ordering of its EU
institutions, debate and conflict is only to be expected. Finally, the most
contested and partly 'precarious' area (Nullmeier et al. 2010: 186–221) is
represented by current EU politicians and the politics in which they are
engaged. To put it pointedly, the more concrete the statements of our
interviewees are with regard to EU politics and politicians, the lower is
the level of legitimation.

From this it becomes evident that we should think about European
legitimation in a different manner than has been done in previous media
and communication research. Legitimation is not just the outcome of a
functional European public sphere made by EU politicians, their public relations officers and journalists, and measured by the normative

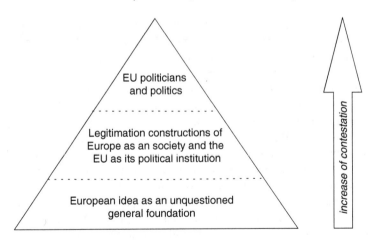

Figure 8.1 The European legitimation pyramid

expectations of a national public sphere. Rather, it is the result of highly complex and contradictory processes of communicative construction in which people have an active role, which is increasingly supported by online platforms and the associated possibilities for citizens to engage in these communicative constructions. This is one of the main reasons why European legitimation takes various forms and differences of degree. To disagree with certain politicians or politics, or even to disagree with certain constructions of a legitimate Europe, does not necessarily mean denying the existence of European legitimation. We must look very carefully at the particular point of reference for each attribution of legitimation. This will enable us to understand legitimation as part of a far-reaching and contested process of constructing Europe communicatively.

Within this process, we understand the present euro crisis analytically as a magnifier: a politically important incident that renders the underlying processes visible and therefore empirically accessible. Analytical reference to the euro crisis enables us to provide a tentative answer to fundamental questions concerning the communicative construction of Europe. Communicative construction is still rooted in different national and stratification-related cultures of political discourse. But we notice some indicators for an emerging European culture of political discourse that might make the European public sphere sustainable. Given differences in cultures of political discourse, the European public sphere remains multi-segmented. However, it has reached a certain plateau, where the euro crisis represents an issue but not a challenge to shared political discourse. It cannot be said that every citizen was politicised by the euro crisis. But the crisis had a certain activating role for them, rooted in their everyday life. And finally, we noticed the complexity in the legitimation of Europe and of the EU. We conclude that Europe as a society and the EU as its political institution remain an open-ended and contested project.

To sum up this research in one sentence: We are in the midst of a process involving the contested and open-ended communicative construction of Europe. It is worth recalling once more what the sociologist Georg Vobruba (2012) wrote about Europe. He argued that the present situation of Europe presents an excellent opportunity for analysing the social construction of a society. This makes us think of what a society is, as well as strive to understand how the process of articulation of a society takes place. The core argument of our book is that we should understand such a process not only as European integration as it is described from an institutional perspective. It is at least to the same extent a process of communicative construction.

We notice the open-endedness of this process in everyday media coverage, in online-discussions and in our conversations about Europe. Because of this open-endedness it is no wonder that this book cannot come to a final conclusion, if we understand by this a description of the final result of this process of communicative construction. To expect this would be to misunderstand our overall research objective. Our aim was to describe the fundamental patterns in the contested process of communicative construction, in and across a group of selected typical countries in Europe: Austria, Denmark, France, Germany, Poland and the United Kingdom. While many European countries have been omitted, we hope to have offered an understanding of the fundamental patterns of communicative construction – and that this book represents an empirically rooted, critical reflection of an ongoing social and cultural challenge.

Appendix: On Methodology

This appendix summarises all the methodological information relevant to an understanding of the empirical research on which our book *The Communicative Construction of Europe* is based: the newsroom studies and semi-structured interviews with journalists (chapter 3, Appendix A), the standardised longitudinal, cross-media and cross-country content analysis (chapter 4, Appendix B), the online interaction analysis (chapter 5, Appendix C), and the qualitative audience research (chapters 6 and 7, Appendix D). It describes samples, the coding processes and the coding schemes. The basic idea of our research was not just to realise a country comparison of processes of Europeanisation. Rather, it is driven by the critique of 'methodological nationalism' (Beck 2006; Wimmer/Glick Schiller 2002), which in our case means looking for 'transcultural patterns' and 'processes of transcultural communication' within countries, as well as national differences between them (Hepp 2015: 22–28). For additional information about our methodology and further material (guiding questions for the semi-structured interviews, codebook, lists and schemes of categories, and so on), please consult our website http://www.europeanpublicsphere.org.

All research was conducted across a broad and diverse country sample, encompassing Austria, Denmark, France, Germany, Poland and the United Kingdom. The idea behind this sample is to investigate how Europe is communicatively constructed within the countries that build 'its financial core'. The countries were chosen in order to include sufficient variation in the power, size and length of EU membership of a country. Austria and Denmark are comparatively small member states, dwarfed by France, the United Kingdom and Poland as larger and more powerful countries, as well as by Germany, which, with a population of 82 million and a per capita GDP of 35,479 euros, is the biggest economy in the EU. Together with France it is also a founding member of the European community, joined by the United Kingdom and Denmark in 1973, and, more recently, by Austria (1995) and Poland (2003). Including latecomer Poland in the sample also enables us to explore various processes of political communicative construction in Europe both before and at the time of the euro crisis.

Appendix A   Design of the newsroom studies

To grasp the forms of multi-segmentation of the European public sphere by the re-articulation of cultural patterns in the everyday activity of journalists, we conducted qualitative newsroom studies in the six European countries under study, aiming at a description of cultural patterns in the production of EU and European foreign news in relation to both national and transnational commonalities. The studies were undertaken synchronously in autumn 2008 and consisted of interviews with EU and foreign news editors, chief editors, and the foreign correspondents of 23 quality, tabloid and regional papers; network maps that the interviewed journalists drew up with regard to their professional contacts; participatory observations of two newsrooms per country over three to five work days; and the research diaries of each researcher. The research was conducted by project members as well as two additional researchers who were employed especially for carrying out the newsroom studies in Denmark and the United Kingdom, as well as a German student assistant. Katharina Kleinen-von Königslöw realised the newsroom study in Austria, Swantje Lingenberg in France, Johanna Möller in Poland, Sune Blicher in Denmark, Gabriel Moreno in the United Kingdom, and Michael Brüggemann and Stefanie Trümper in Germany. The interviews encompass EU and foreign editors, chief editors, and correspondents – in all 36 interviews per country (cf. Table 3.1. in chapter 3 for further details on the interviewed journalists; Quandt 2008 for reflecting the approach of newsroom observation, Hannerz 2004 for a general ethnographic approach, in his case on foreign correspondents).

The selection criteria for the newspapers

The quality papers are the two leading papers with regard to the sold print run with a high reputation among political, intellectual and economic elites, with extensive reporting on foreign and EU issues, and with different political orientations. The boulevard paper is one of the two papers with the highest circulation. And the regional paper is one of the three regional papers with the highest circulation that is not situated in the country's capital. However, newsroom observation could not in all cases be conducted over three to five working days. At the German *BILD*, as well as the French *Le Parisien*, newsroom observation was done for only one working day and for the German *FAZ* only half a working

Table A.1 Newspaper sample newsroom studies

	Austria	Denmark	France	Germany	Poland	United Kingdom
Quality paper	*Die Presse* (103,000) *Der Standard* (100,000)	*Politiken* (110,000) *Berlingske Tidende* (125,000)	*Le Monde* (358,000) *Le Figaro* (344,000)	*FAZ* (363,000) *SZ* (534,000)	*Gazeta Wyborcza* (411,000) *Rzeczpospolita* (157,000)	*The Times* (686,000) *Financial Times* (448,000)
Regional paper	*Kleine Zeitung* (289,000)	*Jydske Vestkysten* (72,000)	*Ouest France* (764,000)	*WAZ* (580,000)	*Dziennik Zachodni* (82,000)	*Manchester Evening News* (82,000)
Tabloid paper	*Kronen Zeitung* (891,000)	*Ekstra Bladet* (90,000)	*Le Parisien/ Aujourd'hui* (534,000)	*Bild* (4,100,000)	*Fakt* (495,000)	*Daily Express* (727,000)

Note: Sold print run of the papers in brackets, data as of February 2008, rounded to the nearest thousand. Source: ÖAK, DO, Mediadaten, OJD, ABC, ZKPD day. The British tabloid papers denied any access to their newsroom for observation, so that the British data refer to the interviews with journalists as well as the newsroom observations at *The Times* and the *Financial Times*. The Austrian tabloid paper also denied access to their newsroom for observation, so that the second newsroom observation in Austria was done at the regional paper. Table A.1 gives an overview of the newspaper sample.

The methodological approach of 'triangulation' (Flick 2004) of interviews, participatory observations and network maps corresponds to the 'ethnographic miniatures' described by Bachmann and Wittel (2006). By combining research instruments, we gained interpretive access to the field and got an impression of the interplay of journalistic practices in their respective cultural context.

Data analysis

The material was coded following grounded theory methodology and analysed from a transcultural perspective (Glaser/Strauss 1967; Hepp 2009, 2015). The aim was to discover national specifics by country-specific comparison, pointing to national political discourse cultures and, moreover, exploring transnational patterns of journalistic news production involving outlet-type specific cultural forms, that is, stratification-related political discourse cultures. We identified five practices of nationalisation that journalists in all countries share, but articulate in different ways in each country. With regard to journalists' practices of addressing audiences, we found four transnational types. The nationalisation practices have been extracted with the help of the following categories: the preferred topics of the journalists as well as their ways of constructing the importance of reporting on the EU; the importance of reporting on EU countries; and the importance of reporting on other foreign news. At a second level 'axial coding' (Strauss/Corbin 1997: 123) of the sections of our interview and observation data coded by the categories above, we identified four patterns of nationalisation in the journalists' practices: national embedding, transnational contextualisation, national hierarchisation and transnational ritualisation. The transnational modes of addressing audiences have been extracted with the help of the following categories: the journalists' image of their audience, the journalists' self-conception, the attributed significance and attitude towards the EU, the attributed significance of other EU-countries and the world, as well as the aforementioned nationalisation practices. The four modes of addressing audiences are: analyst, ambassador, reporter and caterer.

Table B.1   Newspaper sample with number of coded articles, sampling period, selection of articles and sample size

	Quality paper (N = 7,164)	Regional paper (N = 17,545)	Tabloid paper (N = 14,049)
Germany	Frankfurter Allgemeine Zeitung (N = 1,276)	Westdeutsche Allgemeine Zeitung (N = 1,988)	Bildzeitung (N = 4,225)
France	Le Monde (N = 912)	Ouest France (N = 2,271)	Le Parisien/ Aujourd'hui (N = 1,814)
United Kingdom	The Times (N = 1,186)	Manchester Evening News (N = 2,966)	The Sun (N = 4,091)
Austria	Die Presse (N = 1,082)	Kleine Zeitung (N = 1,817)	Kronenzeitung (N = 3,610)
Denmark	Politiken (N = 1,078)	Jydske Vestkysten (N = 3,093)	Ekstra Bladet (N = 2,709)
Poland	Gazeta Wyborcza (N = 1,630)	Dziennik Zachodni (N = 1,914)	Super Express (N = 1,096)
Transnational	*Financial Times Europe* (N = 1,670)		
Sampling periods	1982, 1989, 1996, 2003, 2008, 2013 – two constructed weeks per year		
Selection of articles	All *discursive* articles, for example: • Editorials/Commentaries • Interviews • Contributions from external authors • News analysis and background articles		
Sample size	**N = 38,758 articles** **N = 40,428 articles (including *Financial Times Europe*)**		

Appendix B   Design of the newspaper content analysis including main structure of the codebook

The content analysis is based on a selection of quality, regional and tabloid newspapers within the countries researched. The idea of the sample was to gain typical access to the processes of political communication within the respective countries (cf. Table B.1). Across these countries, the *Financial Times Europe* was selected as a newspaper that represents the European level.

Criteria for newspaper and articles selection

The reason for taking newspaper outlets to investigate the content level of the European public sphere was twofold. First, reaching back to the beginning of our research, quality newspapers were typically understood as the most transnationalised media outlets. This means that processes of Europeanisation can first be registered with reference to them. Second, newspapers are also easily accessible retrospectively (unlike television news). It was only through the investigation of newspapers that the form of long-term research we planned to do became possible. Through this, we could also take into account the EU's long-term development, including leading events like the establishment of the single market in the 1980s, the move towards political union in the 1990s, the introduction of the euro and the enlargement in the 2000s, up to the triggering of the current euro crisis in 2008. For each year in the sample (1982, 1989, 1996, 2003, 2008 and 2013), two constructed weeks were created. For each day in these constructed weeks, the edition of one quality, tabloid and regional paper per country was selected.

The principle selection of discursive articles was based on formal criteria that were the same for all newspapers. However, taking country- and newspaper-related particularities into account, we developed additional criteria for the selection of discursive articles.

According to our focus on political and societal discourses in quality newspapers, all articles in the political section were potentially taken into account. Thus, all potentially relevant articles for selection and coding came from sections or categories like politics, reports of the day, background and opinion. As in regional newspapers, socio-political discourse could also be found in the regional section, so articles in the political and regional section were also considered. Since tabloids generally do not differentiate between thematic subdivisions, it was up to the coder to distinguish which pages contain potentially relevant articles for selection and coding. While the introductory pages were basically open for choice, obviously cultural, sports and other pages to the back of the newspaper were excluded.

The codebook in brief

Since the codebook has already been published in the methodological appendix of our previous publication (Wessler et al. 2008: 200–220), we scale it down here to a brief textual description. Beside several formal categories such as date of publication, length of the article, mode of presentation and so on, the codebook contains five groups of categories for analysing the articles' content: (1) references to authors and speakers, (2) references to countries, (world) regions and political institutions,

(3) references to topics, (4) discursive references and citations and (5) references to collective identities.

All relevant variables could be coded several times within an article (for example country reference 1, 2, 3 up to a predefined maximum of numbers), while each value was not to be coded more than once (for example country reference 14 = United Kingdom), even if one country or a speaker was mentioned several times (for example Angela Merkel is directly quoted three times, but coded only once). Variables of identification were handled differently. Here, identical we-references and identical references to collective identities were coded as often as they were mentioned.

Authors and speakers were generally coded by their societal function (for example David Cameron, Prime Minister) and their national origin (David Cameron, United Kingdom). Furthermore, we differentiate between individual actors (David Cameron), and collective actors like institutions (the British Government), political parties, groups and so on that can be quoted directly and indirectly by the journalist. This distinction is essential in order to observe the degree of personalisation within the news coverage. Authors and speakers that have multiple functions (for example Tony Blair, Prime Minister and President of the European Council in 2005) or multiple references to their country of origin were coded in their first-mentioned function respectively origin (for example an interview with a scientist from Harvard of Egyptian-descent would be coded as American, if it is first mentioned that she comes from Harvard; she would have been coded as Egyptian if the descent is referred to first). In the frame of transnational politics within the EU, the UN or other transnational organisations, political actors generally reference national and transnational levels at the same time. If their nationality is not explicitly mentioned, they are coded as transnational (for example Nicolas Sarkozy, President of the European Council, would be coded as transnational, whereas the Spanish commissioner Joaquín Almunia' would be coded as Spanish). If journalists change here within the article for stylistic reasons, actors are coded as first introduced (for example, 'Nicolas Sarkozy, President of the European Council, pronounced at the summit (. . .). The Frenchman emphasized [. . .]'). The journalist was neither coded as author nor as speaker, since in the first case the variable author exclusively concentrated on the set of media-external authors, and in the second case every statement would have needed to be considered as a direct or indirect self-quotation. Only with judgements of we-identities and collective identities can journalists be identified as sources.

Among references to countries, (world) regions, and political institutions, we differentiated between primary and secondary references. This is important in order to gain an insight into which countries and political institutions are at the centre of political debate and which are marginal. Moreover the proportions of primary and secondary references can show how news about foreign countries or transnational organisations is treated within the domestic context of the newspaper. Should it turn out that the EU is mostly mentioned as a secondary reference, this is a clue for a nationalisation of European politics. Primary references are those countries, regions or institutions that are explicitly mentioned in the heading, the prefix or in the first paragraph of the text. In exceptional cases, when a country is mentioned in the first paragraph, but is evidently not the main country of the article, the country that was named first was coded as the secondary reference. If cities like Brussels or New York were mentioned and the article clearly did not address Belgium or the US, but rather seats of the EU or the UN, they were coded as the corresponding institutions. With regard to world regions, the coder should code a clear territorial reference and should not be mistaking it for collective identities such as the West, the Africans or political institutions such as the EU for the region Europe.

The coding of topics provides information about the similarity of public discourse agendas. We coded a general topic and when the EU, EU actors or EU issues were addressed, and the EU policy fields touched upon were also coded. For the general topic, the main theme or the central focus of an article was applicable. The decision about the topic that sets the dominant framing of the issue was not always easy, since topics usually overlap. The most important clue for coding the main topic was the heading and the first paragraph. Further orientation was given by terms that were frequently mentioned within the article. As far as possible, only one topic should have been selected for coding and only on rare occasions a second or third topic. In contrast to that, even the most incidental reference to EU policy fields was coded if issues had a link to the EU.

A speaker is somebody whose position is directly and indirectly quoted. Only speech acts (something somebody has said, asked, expressed) were coded and not someone's action (something decided, abolished, adopted, prevented). Statements from documents (for example laws, directives, studies) could also be coded for a speaker when they could be related to their individual or collective author.

The last category of variables dealt with different types of identification, since speaker can refer to the question of 'Who are we?' and 'Who are the others?'. So we assumed that references to collective identities were marked by self-identification of the speaker on the one hand (we-references) and by addressing external collectives on the other hand (references to collective identities). A we-reference could be noticed if personal pronouns like we, us or our appeared in the article. The use of terms like 'the Germans', 'the Europeans', 'the Muslims' or 'the West' was an indicator for referring to national or cultural communities. Attention had to be paid to the fact that 'the Germans' should be coded as a collective identity only when the German population – the German people and not the German governance – was referred to. For each we-reference and for each collective identity, we coded function and origin of the speaker.

The coding procedure

The newspaper articles were coded by a total of 48 coders over the 12 years of research. Prior to the coding, several generations of coders were trained for two weeks, both on the identification of discursive articles and on the application of the coding scheme. As some of the authors were part of the coding team in addition to student coders, the quality of the coding could be checked continuously and problematic categories could be discussed directly with the research team. Newspapers were distributed on the basis of the language competencies of the coders (about 50% of the coders were native speakers) and each paper had at least two different coders in each coder generation. For each generation of coders, a reliability test was performed at the beginning of the coding period in order to check whether any revisions of the coding schemes were necessary and to improve the consistency of the coding (cf. for example Wessler et al. 2008: 204f. for quality papers; cf. Offerhaus et al. 2014 for regional papers). All relevant variables – references to political institutions, countries, speakers, topics, we-identities and collectives identities – could be coded several times within an article. In the last coder generation, the coder reliability of content related variables reached an average value of 0.97 according to Holsti's formula. With 97 per cent accordance, the intercoder reliability was highly satisfactory. The coding of topics, with a value of 0.87, turned out to be the most problematic variable.

Appendix C   Design of the analysis of hyperlink networks and the interaction analysis

With the analysis of citizens' communication about the euro crisis in online comment forums, we aimed at gaining insights into the social processes of the European crisis situation from a citizens' perspective. Focusing on the transnational comparison of citizens' communicative practices led to insights about nationally and culturally segmented, or transnationally and transculturally shared processes of citizens' communicative constructions of Europe and the European Union in the context of the euro crisis. The methodological approach here was two-fold. First, the span of citizens' political communication on the internet was mapped with an analysis of hyperlink networks of political web-sites within our six research countries. The technological potential of the internet, furthermore, allowed us to also identify a transnational European dimension in citizens' political communication on the inter-net. Second, the perspective was then shifted towards the level of citizens' actual communicative practices in their online comments on the euro crisis. In order to assess the processes of communicatively constructing images of the euro crisis, Europe and the European Union, we conducted an interaction analysis of citizens' online comments. A transnational comparative perspective guided our interest throughout the analysis.

Analysis of hyperlink networks

According to classical forms of network analysis, a node's prominence can be determined by its position within an encompassing network (Wasserman/Faust 2007: 172). If one conceptualises websites as such nodes, which are connected to each other through incoming and out-going hyperlinks, it becomes possible to evaluate a website's position within the emerging hyperlink architecture of the web. Through the analysis of hyperlink structures, it is, then, possible to identify central and peripheral online services in the web's structure (Stegbauer/Rausch 2006), which offer a space for citizens to communicate about – for example – issues such as the euro crisis.

With the help of a webcrawler (Govcom.org Foundation (2015); Issue Crawler software; Amsterdam: Govcom.org, http://www.issuecrawler. net; Rogers 2010), we conducted an issue-specific analysis of hyperlink networks to achieve an overview of the central political online services for each research country and for a transnational European level. For that purpose, we selected a list of starting points consisting of the most important political websites for each research country and for Europe. This list was assembled through search engine results, blog rankings and the *Alexa top site ranking* to include the quantitatively most impor-tant political websites. These contained mostly news media sites and political blogs (professional and non-professional, journalistic and non-journalistic) and to a much lesser extent websites from institutions for political education, government sites etc.

From these starting points, the web crawler catches all the outgo-ing and incoming links in a procedure involving several steps, eventu-ally building a network of interlinked websites. One needs to consider that because of this procedure, a network of hyperlinks necessarily remains highly situational and highly dependent on its starting points. Furthermore, the attempt to visualise and map the non-physical structure of interlinked websites is necessarily fragmentary and already out of date the moment it is conducted (Packwood 2004). Despite these limitations of the mapping procedure, such an analysis of hyperlink networks provides a general overview of the central political websites for each country in the sample and for Europe.

Our aim was to identify the range of websites constituting the political web for each country in the sample and how those websites connect towards each other. These networks, then, do not only reflect a website's traffic or ranking in a Top 100 blog list (data, which were among others used for assembling the lists for the webcrawler), but rather portrays the broader realm of central political websites for each country in which people can realise their connection to a political public sphere. Furthermore, and very importantly for questions of a European public sphere, these maps allow the distribution of political websites within or across national boundaries to be assessed, as we have described in detail in chapter 5.

Sampling of online forums and material collection for the interaction analysis

To identify the communicative practices through which citizens engage in the communicative construction of Europe in their online discussion of the euro crisis, we drew a forum sample based on the results from the analysis of the hyperlink networks. From the list of central political websites from each country as well as from the transnational European level, we selected a number of websites on which users were able to comment in online forums. The analysis of the hyperlink networks revealed that a number of different political services were important for the countries in the sample. That is why forums from news media, from blogs as well as several *Facebook* accounts, were chosen as a pre-set filter for selecting online forums for the further analysis. For each category (blog, news media, *Facebook* account), we conducted a distinct selection process. Our general aim was to identify websites with a relatively high degree of activity (based on user comments). We anticipated that websites with a high degree of activity generally would need to be quite visible and, therefore, intensely embedded in the political hyperlink networks. At the same time, we acknowledge that rankings like the ones we applied and used within the forum selection process are necessarily subjective and often opaque. However, they are helpful in assessing a websites' relevance and traffic to some degree and, for that reason, allow us to make a preliminary judgement on the level of anticipated user activity.

The basis for the graphical display of the hyperlink networks is the data on the incoming and outgoing links between URLs that the web crawler caught during its crawl. We outputted a ranked actor list (by page), which listed URLs along the quantity of a webpage's incoming hyperlinks from other URLs in the network. Having mapped the range and scope of the hyperlink networks, we were in the forum selection process primarily interested in identifying the quantitatively most embedded websites for each category. Therefore, we first selected the websites of news media and blogs separately from the actor list for each crawl. For the URLs selected in that way, we then had to verify their general political focus, which led to the exclusion of for example blogs on specific political issues (for example, internet policy, media watch blogs and so on). We also deleted URLs from this list which did not incorporate an online forum in which users could publish their comments or websites whose forum was not actively used. For the remaining URLs, we gathered additional ranking data from more data-rich rankings such as the *Alexa top site ranking* or national blog rankings, in order to confirm and validate their quantitative centrality as a political website. Generally, rankings from different sources corresponded quite well with each other. Therefore, based on the new ranking of URLs created in this manner, it was easy to select the highest-ranked blog and news media for each country. If two different blogs or news media were listed at the top of the *Alexa top site ranking*, a national blog ranking and our own actor list, we selected the URL that incorporated the more active forum based on the number of comments.

As social networking sites, *Facebook* and *Twitter* appeared to be the most important websites in the networks. We aimed at including *Facebook* accounts in our analysis, since compared with *Twitter*'s restriction to 140 characters, we anticipated more adequate comment material for our planned analysis of citizens' interpersonal communication (although we are not implying that communication on *Twitter* is not relevant for citizens' political communication). As the web crawl does not provide detailed data on which accounts and pages within *Facebook* are quantitatively central in the field of political *Facebook* pages, we looked for the *Facebook* pages of all the blogs and news media websites from the actor list that the crawl had delivered. For all of these *Facebook* pages, we then collected the number of *Likes* that they had received and ranked them accordingly. However, during that process, we had already noticed that there was in general not much action on the *Facebook* pages of the bloggers from our networks. So we decided to only look at the *Facebook* pages of news media, which are usually treated as extensions and distribution

Table C.1 Online forum selection based on the analysis of hyperlink networks and contextual data

	Blog	News media	Facebook
GER	Spiegelfechter *www.spiegelfechter.com*	Spiegel Online *www.spiegel.de*	Bild *www.facebook.com/bild* Spiegel Online *www.facebook.com/spiegelonline*
DK	Berlingske Blogs *blogs.berlingske.dk*	Politiken *politiken.dk*	Politiken *www.facebook.com/politiken* Ekstra Bladet *www.facebook.com/ekstrabladet*
F	Sarkofrance *sarkofrance.blogspot.de*	Libération *www.liberation.fr*	Le Monde *www.facebook.com/lemonde.fr* Libération *www.facebook.com/Liberation*
UK	Guido Fawkes *order-order.com*	The Guardian *www.guardian.co.uk*	BBC *www.facebook.com/bbcnews* The Guardian *www.facebook.com/theguardian*
AT	FS Misik *derstandard.at/r6114/FS-Misik*	Der Standard *derstandard.at*	Kurier *www.facebook.com/www.KURIER.at* Der Standard *www.facebook.com/derStandardat*
PL	Stary Salon24 *lubczasopismo.salon24.pl/kasandra*	Gazeta Wyborcza *wyborcza.pl*	Gazeta Wyborcza *www.facebook.com/wyborcza* Fakt *www.facebook.com/faktpl*
EU	Charlemagne *www.economist.com/blogs/charlemagne*	Financial Times *http://www.ft.com/*	Financial Times *www.facebook.com/financialtimes* The Economist *www.facebook.com/TheEconomist*

platforms of the original news media website. As there is usually less activity on the *Facebook* pages compared with the original news media website (concerning numbers of articles and therefore also of comments) we selected two *Facebook* pages of news media for each country.

As Table C.1 demonstrates, for some countries we selected a blog which is closely related to the news medium that was sampled for the analysis. In general, we were aiming to identify blogs that were independent from other news outlets, but were unable to do so; especially in the smaller countries Austria and Denmark, where we could not find a very active blogosphere on general political topics. That is why we selected the blog *FS Misik* by the independent Austrian journalist Robert Misik, which is published on a weekly basis on the website of the Austrian paper *Der Standard*. For Denmark, we selected the blog section on the website of one of the biggest news media in the country *Berlingske*, where journalists of the newspaper but also external authors publish blog posts. Likewise, the selection of an independent blog for Europe proved to be problematic, but the blog *Charlemagne,* part of the *The Economist,* proved to be central.

Interaction analysis

Starting from the sampled forums, users' online comments were selected during one week (25 June until 2 July 2012) around one of the EU Council's summits. This summit was selected for the period of sampling because of the European-wide media attention it received. Beforehand, the summit was already being portrayed as a decisive moment for the management and solution of the euro crisis. Therefore it became a transnationally staged media crisis event, which first of all ensured sufficient reporting on the euro crisis during the week of sampling. Secondly, its portrayal as a decisive moment in the crisis' development created the summit as a moment of transformation in which – most likely – citizens would be observing the situation and trying to come to an understanding of it.

During that timeframe, all articles were selected for analysis that were published on the starting page of the selected websites and that contained the search string 'EU', 'euro' or any other variation of the word 'Europe' in the respective languages. These articles – mostly written by journalists or bloggers – were labelled as primary inputs in the context of this study, since they represent the first point of reference for the users, who were later commenting on these articles. Continuing from these primary inputs, all the comments – here labelled as secondary inputs – that users published in the following three days after the first publication of the primary input were then selected and sampled for the interaction analysis.

The assembled sample of users' online comments in the discussion of Europe in the context of the euro crisis was qualitatively analysed with an interaction analysis. Such an approach is partly based on the principles of conversation analysis (Antaki et al. 2006; Gibson 2009; Steensen 2014; Stommel/Meijman 2011), but it also takes into account the media specificities (Hepp 2012: 14) that the online environment of the comment forums entails. It is used to identify forms of interaction in users' online comments through identifying typical communicative practices in the forums. The analysis can be traced back to ethnomethodological approaches (Garfinkel 1967), as it starts from the general assumption that users' online interactions are not arbitrary but evolve along a specific interaction order, as Erving Goffman (1983) called it. The aim of the interaction analysis is to identify elements of this interaction order in the online comment forums through identifying the communicative practices that are typical for the specific communicative situation and space of the online forums. These communicative practices can then be assembled to describe typical forms of interaction that users are commonly producing in their online interactions. These forms of interaction are a way of approximating the processes of communicative construction taking place in the forums.

For this qualitative analysis, the study started with a selection of comment threads from the overall sample. Following the principle of theoretical sampling from grounded theory (Glaser/Strauss 1967), more and more diverse comment threads were being included in the coding. In order to include the most diverse sample of comment threads, a matrix was designed that considered the thematic variation of the primary input (Europe and domestic politics, supranational European politics, common foreign and security policy, USA and EU, and so on), the type of primary input (news item, commentary, interview, guest article and so on), the length of the comment thread (from a couple up to several hundred comments), and the date of the primary input's publication. Through this procedure we identified and analysed 125 comment threads, which led to the analysis of 6,201 comments in total (cf. Table C.2).

Appendix D Design of the qualitative audience research including scheme of categories

The qualitative audience study provides the basis for the analyses in chapter 6, on public connections to a European public sphere and their

Table C.2 Sample of comment threads for the interaction analysis

No.	Country	Forum	Primary Input	Publ. date	Coded secondary inputs
1	GER	FB Bild	Teil-Niederlage beim EU-Gipfel: Merkel spaltet Europa/ Was sagt ihr zum Einknicken Merkels beim EU-Gipfel	30 June 2012	242
2	GER	FB SpOn	Euro-Gipfel. Italien und Spanien siegen im Verhandlungspoker.	1 July 2012	56
3	GER	FB SpOn	Perfekte Lösungen brauchen lange	25 June 2012	35
4	GER	FB SpOn	EU-Wachstumsrhetorik. Der Mogelpakt	26 June 2012	14
5	GER	FB SpOn	Interview mit Georg Soros: 'Deutschland wird gehasst werden.'	26 June 2012	72
6	GER	FB SpOn	Euro-Krise: Europas Mächtige treten an zum Streit-Gipfel.	27 June 2012	17
7	GER	Spiegelfechter	Krise der Institutionen	1 July 2012	127
8	GER	Spiegelfechter	Irrfahrt im Fiskalsturm	26 June 2012	81
9	GER	Spiegelfechter	Demokratie, Austerität und die zwei Europas.	28 June 2012	32
10	GER	Spiegelfechter	Zypern - ein weiteres Opfer der Finanzkrise	29 June 2012	90
11	GER	Spiegel	Alle Hoffnungen ruhen auf dem Plan der Vier	25 June 2012	33
12	GER	Spiegel	Warum die Bürger über Europa abstimmen sollen	26 May 2012	96
13	GER	Spiegel	Merkel lässt Monti abblitzen	28 June 2012	100
14	GER	Spiegel	Die Klügere gab nach	29 June 2012	60
15	GER	Spiegel	Der Rettungsfonds wird kein Selbstbedienungsladen	30 July 2012	100
16	GER	Spiegel	Syrischer General flieht in die Türkei	28 June 2012	44
17	EU	Charlemagne	A delicate proposal	26 June 2012	110
18	EU	Charlemagne	Less Disunion	29 June 2012	85
19	EU	Charlemagne	Europe on the rack	30 June 2012	124
20	EU	FB Financial Times	Why Mario Monti needs to speak truth to power	25 June 2012	157
21	EU	FB Financial Times	12% rise for top bankers	26 June 2012	144
22	EU	FB Financial Times	Yet again the EU is about to hold a summit	26 June 2012	43
23	EU	FB Financial Times	It's EU summit day	27 June 2012	6

24	EU	FB The Economist	The moral core	24 June 2012	12
25	EU	FB The Economist	Gloom in Polderland	25 June 2012	6
26	EU	FB The Economist	Powerful as well as dangerous	25 June 2012	139
27	EU	FB The Economist	A delicate proposal	26 June 2012	11
28	EU	FB The Economist	Tumbling towards the summit	26 June 2012	6
29	EU	FB The Economist	When the chips are down	26 June 2012	7
30	EU	FB The Economist	Angela's vision	27 June 2012	33
31	EU	FB The Economist	The rube goldberg solution	27 June 2012	17
32	EU	FB The Economist	Keeping it real	29 June 2012	14
33	EU	FB The Economist	Victory in football, self-defeat in summit	29 June 2012	19
34	EU	FB The Economist	Less Disunion	30 June 2012	5
35	EU	Financial Times	Cameron considers EU referendum	1 July 2012	31
36	EU	Financial Times	How to shift Germany out of can't do mode	25 June 2012	170
37	EU	Financial Times	The political test facing the Euro	28 June 2012	22
38	EU	Financial Times	EU plan to rewrite Eurozone budgets	26 June 2012	89
39	EU	Financial Times	More questions than answers after the summit	29 June 2012	76
40	F	Sarkofrance/ Chroniques de Juan	Politique: trois visage d'un premier jour de juillet	1 July 2012	4
41	F	Sarkofrance/ Chroniques de Juan	Le chiffre de la semaine: 130 millards d'Euro	24 June 2012	5
42	F	Sarkofrance/ Chroniques de Juan	Pouvoir d'achat: 2012 . . . L'année perdu . . . Par Sarkozy?	28 June 2012	7
43	F	Sarkofrance/ Chroniques de Juan	269ème semaine politique: Hollande à l'offensive, l'UMP cherche ses valeurs	30 June 2012	9
44	F	F3 Le Monde	Athêne aurait triché	24 June 2012	44
45	F	F3 Le Monde	La périlleuse présidence européene de Chypre	26 June 2012	14
46	F	FB Le Monde	A Bruxelles Hollande veut que	28 June 2012	32
47	F	FB Le Monde	Paris s'apprête à recevoir Aung San Suu Kyi	28 June 2012	8
48	F	FB Le Monde	Un compromis a été trouvé	28 June 2012	7

(continued)

Table C.2 (Continued)

No.	Country	Forum	Primary Input	Publ. date	Coded secondary inputs
49	F	FB Libération	Europe trop tard	27 June 2012	37
50	F	FB Libération	A la une de Libération	29 June 2012	115
51	F	FB Libération	La nuit où le Sud	29 June 2012	24
52	F	Libération	Chypre appelle l'Europa à l'aide	25 June 2012	60
53	F	Libération	Ioula Timochenko	25 June 2012	8
54	F	Libération	Les choses vont bien entre Français et Allemands	28 June 2012	123
55	F	Libération	Promesses	28 June 2012	95
56	F	Libération	Au sommet de Bruxelles	26 June 2012	56
57	F	Libération	La nuit où le Sud	29 June 2012	141
58	UK	FB BBC	The baby box returns to Europe	26 June 2012	109
59	UK	Guido Fawkes	Read Guido in the daily star Sunday	1 July 2012	120
60	UK	Guido Fawkes	Make your mind up time	26 June 2012	48
61	UK	Guido Fawkes	Farage batters van Rompuy	3 July 2012	147
62	UK	Guido Fawkes	Full text of Tory MPs letter to Cameron	28 June 2012	62
63	UK	Guido Fawkes	50 cross party MPs urge Lansley against plain packs	29 June 2012	89
64	UK	Guardian	Cyprus seeks Eurozone bail-out	25 June 2012	158
65	UK	Guardian	Leaders draft federal plan to save the eurozone	26 June 2012	100
66	UK	Guardian	Eurozone crisis live	29 June 2012	122
67	UK	Guardian	Cameron pledges referendum if EU demands more power	30 June 2012	97
68	UK	Guardian	The Euro – rebuilding Rome in a day	30 June 2012	95
69	AT	FB Kurier	Mehr Macht für EU in Brüssel	1 July 2012	2
70	AT	FB Kurier	Merkel ist tough und klug	2 July 2012	2
71	AT	FB Kurier	Österreicher trauen Faymann die Bewältigung nicht zu	25 June 2012	2
72	AT	FB Kurier	George Soros	27 June 2012	3
73	AT	FB Kurier	Mehr Macht der EU	27 June 2012	2
74	AT	FB Kurier	Eurozone beschließt Bankenaufsicht	29 June 2012	2

75	AT	FB Kurier	Kritik an Merkel	30 June 2012	1
76	AT	FB Standard	Freie Binnengrenzen	25 June 2012	2
77	AT	FB Standard	Zypern stellt Antrag auf EU-Hilfen	25 June 2012	5
78	AT	FB Standard	Einserkastl Europa	29 June 2012	2
79	AT	FB Standard	Merkel beugt sich Druck von Italien und Spanien	29 June 2012	2
80	AT	FS Misik	Angela Merkel, die gefährlichste Frau der Welt	1 July 2012	145
81	AT	FS Misik	Terror der Ökonomie	24 June 2012	191
82	AT	Der Standard	Kampf um Reisefreiheit	24 June 2012	50
83	AT	Der Standard	Europa ohne Euro wäre Rückschritt	25 June 2012	38
84	AT	Der Standard	Den Finanzmärkten droht der Kollaps	26 June 2012	100
85	AT	Der Standard	Nur eine Stabilitätsunion kann den Euro retten	26 June 2012	85
86	AT	Der Standard	Ein Lob für Faymann und Spindelegger	27 June 2012	55
87	AT	Der Standard	Europa für Stammtische	27 June 2012	34
88	AT	Der Standard	Märkte prügeln Eurounion herbei	29 June 2012	131
89	AT	Der Standard	Merkel knickt vor Spanien und Italien ein	29 June 2012	97
90	DK	Berlingske Tidende	Er det danske formandskab en success?	24 June 2012	5
91	DK	Berlingske Tidende	Europas skabneuge	24 June 2012	5
92	DK	Berlingske Tidende	Red Europa	26 June 2012	28
93	DK	Berlingske Tidende	Staatminister skader danske interesser	26 June 2012	4
94	DK	Berlingske Tidende	Uklædeligt EU-lurepasseri	27 June 2012	6
95	DK	Berlingske Tidende	Vigtigt Signal	29 June 2012	95
96	DK	FB Ekstra Bladet	EU-afstemning	27 June 2012	18
97	DK	FB Politiken	Have a nice weekend	29 June 2012	50
98	DK	Politiken	Frankrig og Europa er hinandens forudsaetninger	25 June 2012	2
99	DK	Politiken	Danmark må lade sig hæge af fremtidens EU	26 June 2012	4
100	DK	Politiken	Vil du stemme om de danske EU-forbehold	26 June 2012	13
101	DK	Politiken	EU-toget kører uden Danmark	27 June 2012	31
102	DK	Politiken	Danmark skal holde sig til, når Europa rykker	28 June 2012	20
103	DK	Politiken	Forbeholdene er ikke nok	29 June 2012	3
104	DK	Politiken	Thorning håner det danske sprog	29 June 2012	74

(continued)

Table C.2 (Continued)

No.	Country	Forum	Primary Input	Publ. date	Coded secondary inputs
105	DK	Politiken	Branden er slukket	30 June 2012	3
106	DK	Politiken	Krisen i europæisk økonomi	30 June 2012	2
107	DK	Politiken	Nej-floj har vundet slaget om Europa	30 June 2012	15
108	PL	FB Fakt	Wow! To mote byc cenna informacja	29 June 2012	3
109	PL	Gazeta Wyborcza	Mlodzi wybieraja wies, bo dzieki UE latwiej sie tam dorabiaja niz w miescie	1 July 2012	21
110	PL	Gazeta Wyborcza	Ziobro u Rymanowskiego: Euro to porazka rzadu, taka okazja sie nie powtorzy	1 July 2012	41
111	PL	Gazeta Wyborcza	Berlin odrzuca sugestie Obamy w sprawie pomocy dla strefy euro	25 June 2012	1
112	PL	Gazeta Wyborcza	Nikt nie bedzie zrzucal Europie dolarow z helikoptera	25 June 2012	47
113	PL	Gazeta Wyborcza	Rzad Hiszpanii oficjalnie zwrocil sie do eurolandu o pomoc dla banku	25 June 2012	2
114	PL	Gazeta Wyborcza	Media: Merkel przeciwna euroobligacjom, 'poki zyje'	26 June 2012	3
115	PL	Gazeta Wyborcza	Cypr prosi o pomoc Miedzynarodowy Fundusz Walutowy	27 June 2012	2
116	PL	Gazeta Wyborcza	W zamoznej Europie niektorzy wciaz sa glodni	27 June 2012	4
117	PL	Gazeta Wyborcza	Dzis kolejny szczyt UE, jako uratowac strefe euro	28 June 2012	9
118	PL	Gazeta Wyborcza	Litewski Sejm ratyfikowal europejski pakt fiskalny	28 June 2012	1
119	PL	Gazeta Wyborcza	Przyszedl czas na Federacje Europejska	28 June 2012	3
120	PL	Gazeta Wyborcza	Tusk: Polska nie zlozy deklaracji ws. Unii bankowej i podatku FTT	28 June 2012	2
121	PL	Gazeta Wyborcza	Premierze, jak zyc po Euro	29 June 2012	43
122	PL	Gazeta Wyborcza	Europa sie zmienia az dziw	30 June 2012	13
123	PL	Gazeta Wyborcza (Głos Rydzyka)	Europoseł w Radiu Maryja: Handel dziecmi dla homoseksualistow w Holandii	26 June 2012	120
124	PL	Stary Salon 24	Eurokoko	29 June 2012	42
125	PL	Stary Salon 24	Powrot	30 June 2012	54

activation in the euro crisis context, and for chapter 7, with a focus on European legitimation constructions. Within this part of our study, we investigated in an open manner the way citizens obtain information on, communicate about and participate in discussions on Europe; in other words, their access to a European public sphere, how they appropriate the discourses of this public and, based on this, how they (re)act to it in their everyday life. The study was realised in the aforementioned six EU countries Austria, Denmark, France, Germany, Poland and the United Kingdom, using qualitative interviews with approximately 30 interviewees per country. In sum, 182 European citizens were interviewed. The interviews included a half-standardised questionnaire on the citizens' socio-demographic background, and qualitative network maps for the interviewees' illustrations of their communication repertoires and communication networks. In addition, the interviewees were asked to fill in media diaries over a period of one week. Illustrative examples of the network maps and media diaries can be found in chapter 6. The fieldwork was conducted from September to December 2011, a period when discourses surrounding the euro crisis had a first peak. For this reason, comments on the euro crisis, and Greece in particular, were frequent.

Sample of interview partners

The selection of our interview partners was oriented towards the model of 'theoretical sampling' as developed by the grounded theory methodology (Glaser/Strauss 1967: 45–77). This made it possible to sample in relation to our broadening and deepening theoretical understanding. However – and at this point we had to break with the fundamental approach by Glaser and Strauss – comparing six countries, it was impossible to realise jointly all the collecting, coding and analysing of the data. For practical reasons, we had to limit our fieldwork to the duration of three months in total. This is the reason why we understand our approach only as oriented by the strategy of theoretical sampling and not as a one-to-one realisation.

In essence, in each of the researched countries we were looking for the most divergent cases with regard to age, education, income and living context. Table 6.1 (cf. chapter 6) illustrates the final sample of 182 European citizens with regard to these criteria. Beyond these rather formal criteria, the three interviewers considered whether different viewpoints, approaches or issues in the context of the general research interest in public connections to Europe and communication repertoires would arise during the interviews. As the interviewees were chosen during the fieldwork in the respective countries, we were able to directly

Table D.1 Interviewees' sample for the audience study

Interviewee (pseudonym)	Age	Interviewees' context	Interview place
AUSTRIA			
Manuel Vechter	19	Student of political science, participates in Model United Nations, a simulation of the work of the UNO	Vienna
Maria Rudler	23	Student of political economics, lives with her boyfriend in an anonymous neighbourhood	Vienna
Cornelia Sucher	56	Learning counsellor, associated with the Waldorf community, interested in basic income grant as an alternative welfare system	Hietzing, suburb of Vienna
Kilian Wedekind	26	Student of agriculture and nutrition science, develops a system for self-sufficiency	Vienna
Melanie Hitzler	38	Business administrator, carrying trade, attached to her cats and animals in general, has a girlfriend from the North of Germany and therefore frequent holidays there	Leopoldsdorf, village near Vienna, in Lower Austria
Ilja Hecker	29	Freelance software engineer, highly interested and engaged in local alternative projects (social, economic, . . .)	Vienna
Fritz Kantler	61	Returned globetrotter, unemployed, unskilled, who tries to support people with even fewer chances, volunteers in a freestore	Vienna
Peter Auermann	29	Business manager, renewable energies, holding a doctor's degree in economics/social sciences, returned to his local community to spend his life together with his family there	Settlement near Wels, Upper Austria
Max Rost	33	Electrician, highly active in training children in his local football club	Steinbach, village in Upper Austria
Friede Kerner	59	Retired nurse, has worked in Africa for some years, engages for peace and is against nuclear energy	Settlement near Wels, Upper Austria
Kristina Huber	24	Trainee in a steelworks, has recently been to Mexico for a study sojourn	Linz, Upper Austria

Note: One entry appears to be a person who is worried about his personal belongings (associated with the Kilian Wedekind row).

Name	Age	Description	Location
Felix Denkmeier	26	Locksmith and actor, agitates against 'the media' and 'the politicians', thinks a lot of local communities and relies especially on his friends	Pettenbach, village in Upper Austria
Hilde Haltenberger	56	Early retired sales assistant, had been abroad as a young adult, always wanted to travel and live in other countries, but decided to stay in her home region and to comply with her desire by integrating it into her work, where she could make use of her foreign language skills	Settlement near Wels, Upper Austria
Edeltraut Riedel	52	Seamstress by trade, currently working as a kindergarten assistant after a long period of preoccupation as a housewife and mother	Settlement near Wels, Upper Austria
Amina Zündler	28	Manager for cultural projects, Carinthian Slovene, network of journalists, politicians and other related elites, had established language courses for asylum-seekers, an – initially – award-winning initiative that was later made impossible	Klagenfurt, Kärnten
Karl Autelberg	52	Writer, solitary, taken with Marxist ideas while dismissing their implementation through respective political parties, watches the people around him intensively but does not seek interaction with them	Klagenfurt, Kärnten
Herbert Sennenberger	65	Retired draughtsman, prefers harmony both on a personal level and on the level of society/politics	Walddorf, village on the periphery of Klagenfurt, Kärnten
Rüdiger Genzmer	51	Radiographer, interested in theatre	Klagenfurt, Kärnten
Samir Sirani	48	Heating engineer, immigrated from Iran (then Persia) as a young adult, lives with his family in a middle-class residential area	Klagenfurt, Kärnten
Tobias Odmayr	28	Unemployed, unskilled, college dropout who has returned to his home village, interested in the development of the gold price, occupies himself with computer role-playing, volunteer in the auxiliary fire brigade	Greifenburg, village near Spittal, Kärnten
Franz Wellinghaus	63	Retired elementary school teacher, competent with the computer, teaches – on an informal basis – other people to use it	Greifenburg, village near Spittal, Kärnten
Hubert Panzer	50	Secondary school teacher, likes to ride his motorcycle	Greifenburg, village near Spittal, Kärnten

(continued)

Table D.1 (Continued)

Interviewee (pseudonym)	Age	Interviewees' context	Interview place
Carola Dudersdorf	41	Pharmacist, currently mostly occupied with her young children, interested mainly in her domestic duties and local events	Settlement west of Innsbruck, Tyrol
Irene Hiebler	38	Social worker, currently on parental leave, family roots in Bosnia	Vienna
Agron Kirsonic	19	Jobs in a betting shop, dropped out from three apprenticeships, family roots in Bosnia	Vienna
Ute Neidler	22	Draughtsperson, concentrates on her local network with her family and her boyfriend, leaves the field of politics to her father and her boyfriend, assuming that she is not well-read about these issues	Traiskirchen, village south of Vienna, in Lower Austria
Helmar Klinker	48	Trainer and moderator, contacts with politicians and journalists, perceives himself as part of civil society, which for him is everyone who stands up for something	Graz, Styria
Michael Mahdbauer	35	Administrative officer, family roots in Germany, tries to get as many perspectives of media coverage via the use of a smartphone app which he uses to read articles from various countries, if he can understand the language	Village near Graz, Styria
Lena Müller	18	Pupil, lives in her mother's household, previously dedicated her time to anime/manga and, more recently, identifies more with online gaming	Suburbs of Vienna
Zahra Yezemin	20	Attending job-creating measures, Muslim, immigrated from Turkey as a child	Vienna
DENMARK			
Mette Kongebjær Engholm	24	Musician and teacher of music, highly appreciates security (personal and national), reluctant to advocate for something, as this might rebound on her negatively and put her career at risk	Ballerup, suburb of Copenhagen, Sealand
Anne Solveig Dybegaard	49	Church vocalist, quite withdrawn and contemplative	Copenhagen, Sealand
Bo Falck	29	Recently graduated student of politics, active in various informal projects in the fields of theatre, politics, music, film.	Copenhagen, Sealand

Name	Age	Description	Location
Lasse Drengenbjerg	21	Student of economics at the CBS, jobs in a hippie-like soup bar	Copenhagen, Sealand
Poul Omegn	44	Sales promoter, currently unemployed, holds both liberal, conservative and even left wing positions	Brøndby, suburb of Copenhagen, Sealand
Jelena Frydshøj Helsbæk	67	Retired graphic designer, immigrated from former Czechoslovakia as a young adult, experienced Denmark as very open and liberal, in contrast to her country of origin	Brøndby, suburb of Copenhagen, Sealand
Bjarke Kristensen	49	Forestry worker and landowner, perceives all political aspects explicitly from the perspective of his profession	Gl. Stenderup, village in the south of Fyn
Astrid Hyllegaard	43	Teacher, different political orientation (very left wing) than her husband (more conservative), which frequently leads to intensive but productive discussions	Countryside in the middle of Fyn
Lisa O'Connor	62	Arts and music manager, not interested in chitchatting with her neighbours, focuses more on superordinate issues	Castle on the countryside in the middle of Fyn
Marja Kestrupsholm	70	Retired farmer, who does community service in an archive for local history and teaches computing for the elderly	Gl. Stenderup, village in the south of Fyn
Sigurd Birk Vandelmose	65	Former blacksmith, night-watchman and church vocalist	Faaborg, small town in the south of Fyn
Bjørn Æby	64	Early retired coppersmith, formerly highly active in training handball, in recent years turned to playing golf and maintains much of his network there	Munkebo, village in the north of Fyn
Signe Hæselbjerg	43	Business manager of a handicraft business, always busy, frequent business trips in Denmark but also abroad in Europe and in the Middle East	Håstrup, village nearby Faaborg, south of Fyn
Bente Kallesen	67	Retired nurse, still active doing community service with elderly people	Kerteminde, village in the north of Fyn
Karen Tøjdsholm	22	Trainee in a young fashion boutique, has gained a new perspective on her country/Europe during a round-the-world-trip, looks at politics from the fashion perspective	Odense, major city in the middle of Fyn
Lina Rendersen	58	Cleaning lady, unskilled, backs her family besides her challenging job	Rural settlement in the south of Fyn
Sanne Hellebæk	18	Stock keeper in a supermarket, unskilled, occupied with her daily struggles	Håstrup, village nearby Faaborg, south of Fyn

(continued)

Table D.1 (Continued)

Interviewee (pseudonym)	Age	Interviewees' context	Interview place
Lone Søndergaard	24	Student of education, adopted from Korea as a baby, volunteer in a street project	North of Copenhagen, Sealand
Mads Jespersen	51	Architect and hostel keeper, open/liberal, sets a high value on sustainability and environmental issues	Amager, Copenhagen, Sealand
Kjeld Hjemkjær	25	Homeless and unemployed/unskilled, occupied with his life, not interested in politics	Copenhagen, Sealand
Faris Hom	25	Preparing to be a taxi driver, immigrated from Somalia as a child, has moved around a lot in the past years in Europe, Asia/Middle East, Africa	Copenhagen, Sealand
Anders Hansen	33	Street newspaper seller, unskilled, homeless, focuses on the needs of people with difficult means	Copenhagen, Sealand
Jasper Kristensen	55	Allround handyman, autodidact, rejects EU/politicians in general, appreciates his local and informal network	Christiania, Copenhagen, Sealand
Tonja Hellesen	27	Care assistant, unskilled, focuses on her daily life, protests against close-down of a school in her rural area, commutes for shopping across the Danish-German border	Rinkenæs, village in the south of Jutland
Helge Svensen	40	Foreman in a locksmith's, many German colleagues, commutes for shopping across the Danish-German border	Ullerup, village in the south of Jutland
Lotte Lillebjerg	34	Storekeeper, trained farmer, currently on parental leave	Ullerup, village in the south of Jutland
Mikkel Poul Karstensen	32	Vocational counsellor and student of theology, strong Christian belief	Mørke, small village north of Aarhus, middle of Jutland
Linnea Sign Holmbjerg	27	Kindergarten worker, currently on maternity leave	Aarhus, middle of Jutland
Zuzan Aril	19	Voluntary service in a congregation, Assyrian Christian, immigrated with her family as a child	Aarhus, middle of Jutland
Pelle Kristiansen	22	Social education worker in training	Aarhus, middle of Jutland

FRANCE			
Angelie Toulon	21	Student of agronomy, shares a flat with other students in Southern Paris, hails from Rouen in West France, plans an Erasmus year in Spain	Paris
Jaques Ardèche	64	Director of a small company in the field of pharmaceutical congresses, loves arts, museums and concerts, well situated family background	Paris
Roberto Zero	25	Agricultural engineer, lives in Mannheim (Germany), but regularly returns to Paris to see his girlfriend, Italian father, French mother	Paris
Stéphane Trufon	27	Psychologist, identifies strongly with Paris, hails from West France, did a lot of backpacking (Russia, Vietnam etc.)	Paris
Victor Mattelart	56	Director of a small company in the publishing sector, identifies strongly with Paris	Paris
Arielle Filou	32	Project manager, shares a flat with a friend, lived in Germany for three years, family roots in Germany	Paris
Karlotta Sapon	65	Retired pharmacist, moved from Paris to a small village with her husband, has three daughters, seven grandchildren	Abondant, small village in central France
Clément Sapon	65	Pensioner, moved from Paris to his place of birth with his wife Karlotta	Abondant, small village in central France
Inès Marquis	45	French teacher, lives in Marseille, speaks several languages, lived in Germany for two years, studied in Paris	Aix-en-Provence, South of France
Marielle Gispon	30	Physics teacher, lives with her husband and two-year-old daughter in a small village, identifies strongly with South of France	Le Crès, small village east of Montpellier
Julien Hermès	61	Doctor in the local hospital, born in Dakar (Africa), migrated to France at the age of 18	Valence, South-Eastern France
Fabrice Girard	45	Freelance business consultant, lives and works one week per month in London, lived in Switzerland for a year	Paris
Emma Albert	35	Assistant in the purchasing department of a small fashion company, lives in a suburb in southern Paris	Paris
Florence Bompard	37	Housewife, mother of four children, used to work as a PR assistant, lived abroad for eight years (USA and Norway)	Nantes, Western France

(continued)

Table D.1 (Continued)

Interviewee (pseudonym)	Age	Interviewees' context	Interview place
Paul Bompard	43	Controller at the French consulate general, worked and lived together with his wife Florence and his four children for eight years abroad (USA and Norway)	Nantes, Western France
Susan Filou	38	Housewife, mother of three children, holds a French and a German passport, trained confectioner	Nantes, Western France
Charlotte Maison	35	Biologist at a local meat factory, grew up near Paris, building a house for herself, her partner and their daughter	La Ménitré, small village in Western France
Fabrice Maison	35	Project manager for the city council, identifies strongly with the region, building a house for himself, his partner Charlotte and their daughter	La Ménitré, small village in Western France
Martin Fleur	63	Pensioner, continues working as a consultant for the company he was employed at, well-situated family background	Paris
Pierre Artis	56	Professor of pharmacy, lives in West France and commutes to Paris for work	Paris
Pauline Miró	42	Engineer, lives with her husband and their two children in a Parisian suburb, loves concerts and making music	Paris
Sylvie Corona	25	Jobless, recently graduated in history and political science, lives with her mother in a Parisian suburb	Paris
Théo Perrier	29	History teacher, lives together with his German girlfriend	Paris
Madaleine Crespel	50	Piano teacher, mother of two children, migrated from Ukraine to France 12 years ago, lives with her French husband in a Parisian suburb	La Frette-sur-Seine, small town in the north of Paris
Cécil Dubiel	39	Sales manager for a news agency, trained agricultural economist, graduated in Marketing, travelled the world for one year	Paris
Fréderic Baisnée	24	Accounting clerk at the French railway company, identifies strongly with his home town Paris	Paris
Amélie Lamarque	25	Doctoral student of history, shares a flat with another student	Antony, small town in the south of Paris
Yves Loire	30	Supply teacher of history, lives in his parents' house in Versailles	Versailles, small town in the west of Paris

Name	Age	Description	Location
Noah Moulin	28	Stock broker at a bank, born and raised in South of France, studied in the UK	Paris
Claudine Mattieu	32	Freelance legal adviser, regularly travels to Paris for work	Montpellier, South of France
Lucas Almenos	58	Jobless, born in Marseille, lived for several years in Algeria, moved to Paris with his wife and two sons a couple of years ago	Paris
GERMANY			
Christine Hauschild	42	Foreign language secretary, employed in public service administration, constantly improves her language skills and travels regularly	Bremen, city in Northern Germany
Simon Gärtner	37	Environmental biologist, currently gardener in a public park, identifies strongly with the multicultural and low-to-middle-income district he lives in.	Bremen, city in Northern Germany
Dietmar Lange	60	Retired offset-printer, strong engagement in leftist and environmental activities within the 1968 leftist movement, experiments with engaging in local politics for the green party, trainer of a local soccer team	Bremen, city in Northern Germany
Gerhard Deichen	62	Retired chief executive of a public transport company, travels globally and engages in numerous NGOs despite a recent heart transplantation	Bremen, city in Northern Germany
Susanne Kramer	33	Early-retired and unemployed former cook, fears her approaching move to a larger city as well as too much information on actual politics, interested in cartoons and arts	Bremen, city in Northern Germany
Marianne Becker	40	Long-term unemployed, failed her final exam as a bakery salesperson, depends on social security benefits, dreams of possessing a car	Bremen, city in Northern Germany
Leonie Stiesing	26	Student of biology, well-situated family background, has studied abroad, lives in a shared flat with international students and expresses her support of Europe	Bremen, city in Northern Germany
Anja Gerber	31	Clerical employee about to apply for more fulfilling job, closely related to her family and their local surroundings in a small village nearby Bremen.	Bremen, city in Northern Germany
Karsten Hinze	31	Project manager in a company that coordinates concert ticket sales, writes for music magazines and blogs occasionally.	Bremen, city in Northern Germany

(continued)

Table D.1 (Continued)

Interviewee (pseudonym)	Age	Interviewees' context	Interview place
Anita Berger	44	Trained dietician, working as a cook after long parental leave, strong ties to her family, the local Catholic church and the Münsterland region	Coesfeld, small town in Western Germany
Markus Kleimann	37	Employed in IT management, trained fowarding agent, following his training in a large company he returned with his family, a Canadian wife and two children, to his home village	Klein-Gerau, village suburb of Frankfurt
Wilhelm Bergmann	66	Retired employee in public service, engages in various civil projects and activities – among others as a volunteer in a national census, as a member in a local running team and skat (card-playing) club	Taunusstein, a village near Wiesbaden, South-Western Germany
Sabine Deterding	33	Nurse on parental leave, continues living in her home town, stems from a well-off family, now struggles with economic challenges	Obertshausen, middle-size Frankfurt suburb
Anna Merkel (with participation of her husband Juri)	64	Cleaning lady and her husband, a retired truck driver, both stem from an ethnic group of Germans in Siberia, came to Germany for a better life	Witten, a city in the Ruhrgebiet agglomeration, Western Germany
Heide Lehmann	50	Housewife with two late-teenage sons at home, middle-class family, former office and legal assistant	Witten, a city in the Ruhrgebiet agglomeration, Western Germany
Christoph Lehmann	20	(The above) Heide Lehmann's son, chemical laboratory assistant in training, continues living at home, shares a passion for old timers with his father and brother	Witten, a city in the Ruhrgebiet agglomeration, Western Germany
Corinna Imhof	47	Both on sick leave and jobless, former hairdresser, cosmetician and office clerk, is about to lose the house she grew up in and lives with her family due to financial problems	Witten, a city in the Ruhrgebiet agglomeration, Western Germany

Name	Age	Description	Location
Joachim Gerke	46	Clerk, working for a company that delivers goods to building centres, spends most of his working time in the car, spends every free minute with his little daughter	Linum, village in Brandenburg, East Germany
Constantin Zielke	25	Trained in fishery, returned to living at home after working as a construction worker in Denmark, now employed in an integral nature reserve, head of the local youth fire brigade	Linum, village in Brandenburg, Eastern Germany
Lara Bamberger	31	Public servant, working for the Federal Ministry of Transport, in charge of supervising the implementation of EU development programmes, currently on parental leave, cannot imagine living anywhere else than Berlin	Berlin
Yvonne Rauch	22	Works occasionally as a cleaning lady while also training as a social assistant, very modest financial resources, expecting her first baby	Berlin
André Kopp	25	Cleaning worker, specialised in hospital cleaning, boyfriend of (the above) Yvonne Rauch, low income, gave up smoking hash for his girlfriend and future family	Berlin
Paul Unger	42	Lecturer, teaching German in Erasmus student classes, has working experience in Central Eastern European countries, travels a lot, engages in civic and cultural projects	Berlin
Bela Maschmann	32	Artist, lives under quite rough conditions in the storage room of his shared studio, reports to avoid social contacts	Berlin
Kurt Binder	60	Retired manager of sewing company, trained tailors for the company's production in Southern Europe, financially independent, strongly engaged in a local shooting club, part-time hunter	Bielefeld, Western Germany
Dorothea Prenz	68	Originally trained as a laundry worker, has been a housewife for many years, now works as a cleaning lady to upgrade her modest retirement pension, engages in a local church choir	Bielefeld, Western Germany
Jana Kaminski	18	Pupil in 11th grade, lives at home in middle-class conditions, Polish family background, interested in the anarchist movement	Osterholz-Scharmbeck, small town in Northern Germany

(continued)

Table D.1 (Continued)

Interviewee (pseudonym)	Age	Interviewees' context	Interview place
Idris Hartmann	18	Stems from a Turkish-German family, currently jobless, finished secondary modern school, spends his time on *Facebook*, chilling and playing soccer	Berlin
Arnim Pollmann	69	Retired fireman, strong bonds to his local surrounding, travels regularly	Berlin
Christian Bauer	20	Agriculturalist in training, very low regular income, lives partly with his employer and his family	Koblenz, South-West Germany
POLAND			
Kamila Sasnal	21	Soldier from a family of soldiers and student of medicine, lives together with her little son, parents and grandparents, travels regularly to Germany and the USA	Otwock, village in the Warsaw suburb
Janusz Ruchniewicz	24	Student of history, interested in theatre and arts, lives with his grandmother due to limited financial means, travels to his family's residence near Cracow regularly	Warsaw
Marcin Cichocki	31	Monk and priest, living in a comparably large Dominican community, stems from a family of academics in Northern Poland, PhD in theology	Warsaw
Beata Szarek	58	Works in a cloakroom at the University of Warsaw, very limited financial means, takes care of her sick husband, always lived in Warsaw	Warsaw
Barbara Szymańska	52	Trained sales assistant, now working as a cleaning lady for upper-class families, lives with her husband and two teenage sons in a tiny apartment in the centre of Warsaw.	Warsaw
Marlena Gruzińska	29	Finished her German studies a couple of years ago, commutes for her job with a large German travel company from her family home to Warsaw.	Kobyłka, little town near Warsaw
Karla Goszyk	68	Retired accountant, assists others in official affairs on an occasional basis in order to augment her income, shares her house with a large number of pets	Radom, town in the center of Poland

Name	Age	Description	Location
Ludwik Reiter	65	Professor of computer science, identifies strongly with traditional family background, was engaged as a local politician in the past	Radom, town in t... of Poland
Arkadiusz Hawajski	44	Sales manager, identifies strongly with the Catholic Church and the PiS party	Radom, town in the ce... of Poland
Gabriela Klich	32	Research assistant at the University of Gdańsk, holds a PhD in economics, mainly concentrates on her academic career and her two little daughters	Czaple, dormitory suburb of Gdańsk, Northern Poland
Magdalena Gwosdek	33	Young mother and teacher, specialised in assisting disabled children, organises youth camps in European countries	Gdańsk, city in Northern Poland
Dagmara Ptaszek	28	Assistant in the local heritage administration of historical monuments, cannot realise her travelling dreams due to her very low income, learns a number of languages to recompense	Częstochowa, town in Southern Poland
Grzegorz Samochowiec	54	Became comparably wealthy by running a micro business dealing with car tyres, strong bonds to his hometown Cracow	Cracow
Wojciech Budlewski	52	Has been working occasionally as a construction worker, due to a recent eye operation now at home, lives with his family in a one-room apartment	Cracow
Agnieszka Alpińska	30	Works as an assistant to the executive board of a large German company after finishing her German studies, settling into her newly acquired apartment after her recent marriage.	Warsaw
Radek Kerski	30	Identifies strongly with Warsaw's former workers' district Praga, where he lives and successfully runs a car workshop, maintains some contacts to the local underworld	Warsaw
Marzena Pikarska	48	Jurist, now working as a self-employed law consultant to internet companies, recently bought a house of her own, values classic humanitarian education	Warsaw
Tadeusz Silnicki	24	Student of engineering and former Polish champion of weightlifting, focused on building a successful life, aiming at a well-paid job, an own apartment, a representative car and a family.	Warsaw
Mariola Nierubca	26	Trained librarian, currently jobless, confesses to be not really interested in working, rather aims at being a housewife, self-perception as a 'real' and original Warsawian	Warsaw

(continued)

Table D.1 (Continued)

Interviewee (pseudonym)	Age	Interviewees' context	Interview place
Bogdan Barań	25	Skilled logistics worker, his dream of buying his own apartment will probably remain out of reach, his passion and hobby is cooking	Piaseczno, dormitory suburb of Warsaw
Paweł Pronobis	60	Commutes from his home village in the south-eastern Polish mountains to work as a lawyer in Warsaw during the week, well-educated, traumatised by his family's experiences in WWII	On the train, from Warsaw to Lublin, Eastern Poland
Horacy Ogrodnik	62	Garden engineer, successfully runs a farm that experiments with agricultural seeds within the network of an international company, travels globally, nevertheless strongly values his local surrounding	Nałęczów, health resort near Lublin, Eastern Poland
Monika Gajdowicz	62	Tailor, lives in very modest circumstances, is a strong believer and meanwhile bitterly disappointed with the ambiguous attitudes of Polish Catholic priests, loves to follow soap operas	Palikije, settlement near Lublin, Eastern Poland
Marlena Szczapa	18	Pupil, preparing for her final school exams, bored by Grójec, spends her rare free time biking or going on shopping trips to Warsaw	Grójec, small town near Warsaw
Greta Dzielska	18	Pupil, preparing for her final school exams, best friend of (the above) Marlena Szczapa with whom she spends most of her free time.	Grójec, small town near Warsaw
Bogdana Kruczaj	56	Works as a legal consultant and regularly engages in taking care of her grandchildren, strong faith, media repertoire mainly consists of religious media.	Cracow
Ryszard Golczyk	58	Early-retired shipyard worker, identifies strongly with the Kashubian region, breeds and keeps pigeons, engagement in the Polish pigeon society and exceptional interest in European soccer	Rumia, village near Gdynia, Northern Poland
Danuta Szerszyńska	38	Trained seamstress, now housewife and mother of two children, identifies strongly with the Kashubian region and the Catholic Church, her husband works abroad, so she gets to know 'the world' through his eyes	Kczewo, settlement in the Kashubian region, Northern Poland
Maciej Szerszyński	22	Nephew of (the above) Danuta Szerszyńska, lives in his parents farmhouse, used to commute to Sopot for a job in a car workshop, now works on an occasional basis	Kczewo, settlement in the Kashubian region, Northern Poland

Name	Age	Description	Location
Edyta Rolny	33	Took over a farm from her parents which she now runs with her husband, disappointed with the EU subsidies which did not improve her financial basis, but complicated daily business	Bartoszylas, village in Northern Poland
Sławomir Kaszubski	65	Retired farmer from a family with a long tradition in farming, lives in a small house on his family's areal, takes over representative functions when it comes to public affairs in his village	Bartoszylas, village in Northern Poland
UNITED KINGDOM			
Trisha Mahin	24	Marketing Assistant, moved to Bristol six months ago, shares a flat with three young women, travels to her family's house in Yorkshire regularly	Bristol, South England
John Campbell	58	Homeless, used to work as a cleaner, has no contact to his sister who lives in North London	London
Edgar Davies	71	Retired engineer, still assists his former company for which he worked longer periods in Saudi Arabia	London
Elizabeth Hamilton	53	Holds a BA in English Literature	
Lisa Harvey	58	Trained teacher, works as a manager in a hairdresser's shop, hails from Ireland	Hampstead, small suburb in the north of London
Oliver Cox	30	Waiter in a fish restaurant, working-class family background, lives together with his French girlfriend	Richmond, small town in the west of London
Eva Celik	42	Owner of a small clothes shop, hails from Turkey, strongly identifies with her Turkish neighbourhood community	Richmond, small town in the west of London
Daniel Weaver	49	Freelance financial trader and statistics trainer, graduated in natural sciences	London
Louis Barney	21	Graduated in English Literature recently, currently jobless, shares a flat with his girlfriend and other students	Wimbledon, suburb in the south of London
Charlotte Miller	36	Nurse, politically active in local groups in the field of charity, spent a year working and travelling in New Zealand	London

(continued)

Table D.1 (Continued)

Interviewee (pseudonym)	Age	Interviewees' context	Interview place
Ismael Brooker	62	Owner of a small coffee shop, former engineer, hails from Lebanon, migrated to the UK in the 1960s, politically active against the Iraq war	Richmond, small town in the west of London
Heather Turner	28	Logistics manager at the British ministry of defence, shares a flat with three young women, family roots in Manchester	Bristol, West England
Amber Johnson	29	Architect, born in South Africa (South African mother), grew up in a small village in South East England, strong identification with the UK	Bristol, West England
Julia Riley	25	Project manager, shares a flat with three young women, family roots in Somerset (South West England)	Bristol, West England
Alexander Spring	27	Biologist, owner of a small event agency, strong identification with his home town Bristol	Bristol, West England
Dennis Cooper	29	Political scientist (BA), worked for a think tank, politically active in the Labour party, currently studying political science (MA)	London
Jessica Price	50	Project Manager at the University, family roots in India, politically active in the field of environmental protection	London
Sophie Clifton	36	Elementary school teacher, hails from Australia, lived in England for 12 years, shares her house with a friend	London
Tamara Tannhäuser	30	Marketing Assistant, born in England, grew up in Germany, where her parents and sister live, studied in Holland, Belgium, Spain and Australia	London
Rebecca Brix	20	Student of social work, shares a flat with other students, family roots in London	Plymouth, South England
Steven Corner	20	Student of history and political science, lives together with his mother, strong identification with his home town Plymouth	Plymouth, South England
Charlie Willis	25	Works as an usher in a small theatre, lives together with his parents, family background characterised by narrow circumstances	London

Name	Age	Description	Location
Scarlett Koronis	54	Social worker at a college, lives separated from her husband in a small house with her 19-year-old daughter	Sowerby Bridge, small village in Yorkshire
Nicole Koronis	19	Insurance agent, lives together with her mother (the above) Scarlett	Sowerby Bridge, small village in Yorkshire
Jamie Plotter	24	Political scientist, voluntary worker in an Oxfam bookshop, earns his living by looking after a handicapped boy	Leeds, Midlands England
Luke Smith	59	Retired teacher, owner of a small coffee shop that he does not run for profit but for meeting young people and organising concerts	Leeds, Midlands England
William Porter	63	Pensioner, works for 1–2 days per week in a second-hand bookshop, has been politically active in the city council	Leeds, Midlands England
Nancy Warner	53	Owner of a small bed and breakfast business, lives separated from her husband and her two sons, online games play a major role in her free time	York, East Midlands England
Jack Whistler	36	IT supporter of the local archaeological charity, identifies strongly with his hometown and region, has travelled only twice abroad	York, East Midlands England
Megan Fraser	27	Saleslady in a local bookshop, hails from Scotland, moved to York four years ago, identifies strongly with Scotland	York, East Midlands England

contrast the cases and vary them with regard to these two sets of criteria in the course of the on-going research. Following this procedure, we collected the aforementioned 182 cases. The table above (cf. Table D.1) introduces the interviewees in more detail by providing a short description for each of them.

Design of the audience study

The fieldwork in the six countries was conducted in two phases of six weeks from September to December 2011. Each of the three researchers investigated two countries, while engaging in a shared interpretative discourse among the research team. The data collection in each of the citizens' cases was composed of five elements: first, a qualitative semi-structured interview; second, her or his drawing of the communicative means that she or he refers to as well as the social network she or he felt surrounded by; third, a semi-quantitative questionnaire collecting some basic socio-demographic data; fourth, a media diary filled out by the interviewees for one week; and finally, fifth, an interview report completed by the researchers shortly after concluding the interview, considering the core research questions.

The qualitative semi-structured interviews with European citizens were at the centre of the audience study. Having a general interest in their view on Europe and/or the EU, media appropriation and public engagement in mind, we asked our interviewees about their personal life and biography, their media use and communicative networking, their possible access to the national and (mainly by that) European public sphere, their participation in the European public sphere, as well as their political identification and understanding of political legitimation. In order to stay as close as possible to the interviewees' interpretations, the interviews were conducted in their respective mother tongues. Depending on the interviewees, the interviews took between half an hour and three hours.

During the conversations, the interviewees were asked to draw two network maps: one related to their media use and another one sketching their personal network. A network map provides space for the interviewees' individually perceived mediated and social surroundings. A simple cross in the middle, labelled 'me', indicates that the respective interviewee should consider herself or himself at the centre and locate herself or himself with regard to media used or social settings. As the examples in chapter 6 show, these illustrations are up to the interviewee and thus take very different shapes. While some interviewees draw a hierarchy of the media they find more or less important in their communication repertoire, others organise them with regard to the time they regularly spend with them. Also with regard to social networks, the drawings vary considerably. Whereas some, for instance, refer to the quality of relationships with single persons as close or distant, others organise their network maps with respect to the social groups in which they see themselves involved. The network maps fulfil a double function. In the first place, we were interested in gaining an overview over the mediated communication and social context the interviewees would situate themselves in. At the same time, as we could repeatedly observe, drawings significantly stimulated the ongoing and continuously recorded conversation. Often, interviewees suddenly remembered situations where Europe and the EU had played a role and felt more at ease to talk about it.

Third, every interview session was accomplished by completing a semi-quantitative questionnaire, composed of two elements. Firstly, the interviewees were asked to provide some basic information regarding their age, professional position, educational background, language skills and approximate income. Secondly, we asked them to scale the significance various contexts had for them, including their actual local surroundings, their place of origin, their region and/or federal state, their country, and Europe. In addition, the interviewees were free to mention additional contexts, such as their membership in an association, their family and so on. Each of these contexts was assessed on a scale ranging from 1 to 5, with 1 being of minor and 5 being of high importance. Again, we were not mainly interested in the numbers, but in stimulating the interviewees to comment on their contextual embeddedness. In consequence, we took care that the conversation while filling out the questionnaire was also recorded.

Anja documents the following: 'Day of the week: Sunday, Date: . . . , Time: from 5.20 to 7 pm, media: computer, internet, location: study, communication partner: . . . , location of communication partner: . . . , content/intention in short: checked mail, looked for information regarding the upcoming job interview, sent unsolicited job application via mail, senseless browsing around on *Facebook* (only wasted time) (left); day of the week: Sunday, Date: . . . , Time: from 7 to 10 pm, medium: television, location: living room, communication partner: boyfriend, location communication partner: living room, content/intention in short: zapping around during dinner, from 8.15 pm onwards *Tatort* [a famous German crime series, the authors] (as every Sunday).'

In addition, citizens were asked to fill out a media diary, documenting their media use during the course of one week. Figure D.1 provides an illustrative example of a typical media diary. The interviewees

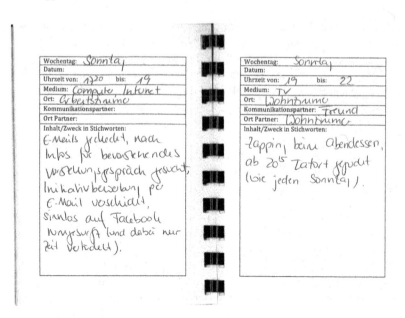

Figure D.1   Representative page from the media diary filled out by Anja Gerber (31, GER)

Table D.2   General categories

Category groups	Categories
Legitimation constructions	[Citizens' Europe] [Democratic Europe] [EU of national cultures] [Exit options] [Transparency] [United States of Europe] [EU of welfare and solidarity] [Other constructions]
Values	[Solidarity] [Peace Welfare and Fairness] [Human rights] [Freedom (to move)] [Cultural diversity] [Participation] [Strength] [Efficiency] [Transparency] [Security] [Progress] [Environmental protection] [Sovereignty] [Cultural openness] [Integrity] [Trust] [Dignity] [Education] [Specialist knowledge]
Symbols	[Boundaries] [State symbolism] [Bureaucracy] [Currency] [Representatives] [Development programmes] [Food] [Historical events] [Art] [Sport] [Language]
Actors	[Political institutions] [Politicians] [Consultants/Lobby] [Administration] [Population] [Media] [NGOs]
Experiences	[Historical events] [Political decisions] [Actions of fellow citizens] [Establishment] [Experiences of mobility]
Basic political attitude	[Indifferent] [Disillusioned] [Overtaxed] [Active] [Interested]
Identification	[Local identification] [National identification] [European identification] [Class related identification] [Topic related identification]

Table D.3 'Appropriating Europe' – typology of the public connections

Category groups	Categories
Communicative participation	[Social commitment] [Aesthetic commitment] [Political commitment]
Appropriated media	[Letter] [Book] [Chat] [Email] [Television] [Landline telephone communication] [Movies/Series] [Cinema] [Mobile telephone communication] [Music] [Radio] [Online telephone communication] [Short messages] [Social Network Sites] [Social Web] [Digital Games] [WWW] [Print] [Software] [Photography]
Reflection on communication	[Media biography] [Representation of network] [Media specificities] [Daily and weekly behaviour] [Communication risks] [Loss of infrastructure] [Media manipulation]
Interaction	[Intermediary of interactions] [Discussion of media] [Habitualisation] [Modality and frequency]
Frame of communication	[Purchase] [Public] [Information] [Enjoyment] [Work] [Education] [Relationship]

documented when, where and with whom they used media and provided a short text to illustrate their intention in so doing. Besides gaining a better overview over the respective communication repertoires, more specifically the intention was also to find out more about which media were used for political communication, especially with regard to Europe and EU-related issues.

Finally, directly following the talk, the interviewers documented the interview situation and characteristic patterns that came up during the interview by means of a post-interview protocol. The main objective of this interview protocol was to reflect both on the whole interview process, for example things that were unintentionally left-out or misleading communicative dynamics, and on the further process of sampling. As outlined above, the intent was to collect a highly diverse sample that, beyond various socio-demographic criteria, considered differences in citizens' public connections with Europe and politics in general.

Data analysis

The interviews were transcribed and – together with the network maps and media diaries – analysed following coding procedures suggested by grounded theory (Glaser/Strauss 1967; Strauss/Corbin 1997). This implies a multi-step process: first an 'open coding' of the data, then an 'axial coding' that searches for the interrelation of the analytical categories and finally a 'selective coding' that rounds off the theory (cf. Tables D.2 and D.3). We performed this analysis in a transcultural perspective (Hepp 2015: 22–28; Hepp/Couldry 2009). Without the data first being aggregated on a national-territorial basis, our interview data was compared with one another. In this way, we obtained a system of categories that describes not simply national differences, but more general common factors and differences in cultural patterns. This approach makes a greater complexity of analysis possible and paves the way for the identification of cultural thickenings that can assume very different forms.

References

Adam, Silke (2007): Symbolische Netzwerke in Europa. Der Einfluss der nationalen Ebene auf europäische Öffentlichkeit. *Deutschland und Frankreich im Vergleich*. Köln: Halem.

AIM Research Consortium (2006): *Understanding the logic of EU reporting in the mass media. Analyses of EU media coverage and interviews in editorial offices in Europe*. Dortmund: Projektverlag.

AIM Research Consortium (ed.) (2007): *Reporting and managing European news. Final report of the project adequate information management in Europe 2004–2007*. Dortmund: Projektverlag.

Almond, Gabriel A./Verba, Sidney (1963): *The civic culture. Political attitudes and democracy in five nations*. Princeton: Sage Publications.

Anderson, Benedict (1983): *Imagined communities. Reflections on the origins and spread of nationalism*. New York: Verso.

Ang, Ien (1991): *Desperately seeking the audience*. London and New York: Routledge.

Angouri, Jo/Wodak, Ruth (2014): 'They became big in the shadow of the crisis'. The Greek success story and the rise of the far right. *Discourse & Society*, 25(4), 540–565.

Antaki, Charles/Ardévol, Elisenda/Núñez, Francesca/Vayreda, Agnès (2006): 'For she who knows who she is'. Managing accountability in online forum messages. *Journal of Computer-Mediated Communication*, 11(1), 114–132.

Axel Springer Media Impact (2015): MA 2015 Pressemedien I, www.reichweiten. de, date accessed 20 January 2015.

Bach, Maurizo/Lahusen, Christian/Vobruba, Georg (eds.) (2006): *Europe in motion. Social dynamics and political institutions in an enlarging Europe*. Berlin: Edition Sigma.

Bachmann, Götz/Wittel, Andreas (2006): Medienethnografie. In: Ayaß, Ruth/Bergmann, Jörg (eds.): *Qualitative Methoden der Medienforschung*. Reinbeck bei Hamburg: Rowohlt, pp. 83–219.

Baden, Christian/Springer, Nina (2014): Com(ple)menting the news on the financial crisis: The contribution of news users' commentary to the diversity of viewpoints in the public debate. *European Journal of Communication*, 29(5), 529–548.

Baisnée, Olivier (2002): Can political journalism exist on an EU level? In: Kuhn, Raymond/Neveu, Erik (eds.): *Political journalism. New challenges, new practices*. London and New York: Routledge, pp. 108–128.

Baisnée, Olivier (2006): Understanding EU news production logics. Norms, channels and structures of reporting Europe from Brussels. In: AIM Research Consortium (ed.): *Reporting and managing European news*. Bochum: Projektverlag, pp. 25–43.

Barker, Rodney (2001): *Legitimating identities. The self-representations of rulers and subjects*. Cambridge: Cambridge University Press.

Barry, Andrew (2001): *Political machines: Governing a technological society*. London and New York: The Athlone Press.

Beck, Ulrich (1987): Beyond status and class. Will there be an individualized class society? In: Meja, Volker/Misgeld, Dieter/Stehr, Nico (eds.): *Modern German sociology*. New York: Columbia University Press, pp. 340–355.

Beck, Ulrich (1996): *The reinvention of politics: Rethinking modernity in the global social order*. London: Polity Press.

Beck, Ulrich (2000): *What is globalization?* London and Cambridge: Blackwell Publishers.

Beck, Ulrich (2006): *Cosmopolitan vision*. Cambridge and Malden: Polity Press.

Beck, Ulrich (2014): *German Europe*. Cambridge: Polity Press.

Beck, Ulrich/Beck-Gernsheim, Elisabeth (2001): *Individualization. Institutionalized individualism and its social and political consequences*. London and New Delhi: Sage.

Bennett, W. Lance/Lang, Sabine/Segerberg, Alexandra (2015): European issue publics online: The cases of climate change and fair trade. In: Risse, Thomas (ed.): *European public spheres. Politics is back*. Cambridge: Cambridge University Press, pp. 108–137.

Berger, L. Peter/Luckmann, Thomas (1967): *The social construction of reality. A treatise in the sociology of knowledge*. London: Penguin.

Berkel, Barbara (2006): *Konflikt als Motor europäischer Öffentlichkeit. Eine Inhaltsanalyse von Tageszeitungen in Deutschland, Frankreich, Großbritannien und Österreich*. Wiesbaden: VS.

Best, Heinrich (2011): The elite-population gap in the formation of political identities. A cross-cultural investigation. *Europe-Asia Studies*, 63(6), 995–1009.

Billig, Michael (1995): *Banal nationalism*. London, Thousand Oaks and New Delhi: Sage.

Bird, S. Elizabeth (2011): Are we all producers now? *Cultural Studies*, 25(4–5), 502–516.

Bjur, Jakob/Schrøder, Kim C./Hasebrink, Uwe/Courtois, Cédric/Adoni, Hanna/ Nossek, Hillel (2014): Cross-media use – Unfolding complexities in contemporary audiencehood. In: Carpentier, Nico/Schrøder, Kim C./Hallett, Lawrie (eds.): *Audience transformations. Shifting audience positions in late modernity*. New York: Routledge, pp. 15–29.

Blöbaum, Bernd/Bonk, Sophie/Karthaus, Anne/Kutscha, Annika (2010): Das Publikum im Blick. Die veränderte Publikumsorientierung des Journalismus seit 1990. *Journalistik Journal*, No. 1, 33–35.

Böckenförde, Ernst W. (1991): *Staat, Verfassung, Demokratie: Studien zur Verfassungstheorie und zum Verfassungsrecht*. Frankfurt am Main: Suhrkamp.

Bohman, James (2007): *Democracy across borders. From dêmos to dêmoi*. Cambridge and London: MIT Press.

Bolin, Göran (2006): Visions of Europe: Cultural technologies of nation-states. *International Journal of Cultural Studies*, 9(2), 189–206.

Boomgaarden, Hajo G./De Vreese, Claes H./Schuck, Andreas R. T./Azrout, Rachid/ Elenbaas, Matthijs/Van Spanje, Joost H. P./Vliegenthart, Rens (2013): Across time and space. Explaining variation in news coverage of the European Union. *European Journal of Political Research*, 52(5), 608–629.

Boomgaarden, Hajo G./Vliegenthart, Rens/De Vreese, Claes H./Schuck, Andreas R. T. (2010): News on the move. Exogenous events and news coverage of the European Union. *Journal of European Public Policy*, 17(4), 506–526.

Bourdieu, Pierre (2010): *Distinction. A social critique of the judgement of taste*. London and New York: Routledge.

Breen, Richard/Luijkx, Ruud/Müller, Walter/Pollak, Reinhard (2010): Long-term trends in educational inequality in Europe: Class inequalities and gender differences. *European Sociological Review*, 26(1), 31–48.

Breeze, Ruth (2014): Perspectives on North and South: The 2012 financial crisis in Spain seen through two major British newspapers. *Discourse & Communication*, 8(3), 241–259.

Brüggemann, Michael (2008): *Europäische Öffentlichkeit durch Öffentlichkeitsarbeit? Die Informationspolitik der Europäischen Kommission.* Wiesbaden: VS.

Brüggemann, Michael (2011): Journalistik als Kulturanalyse: Redaktionskulturen als Schlüssel zur Erforschung journalistischer Praxis. In: Jandura, Olaf/Quandt, Thorsten/Vogelgesang, Jens (eds.): *Methoden der Journalismusforschung.* Wiesbaden: VS, pp. 47–66.

Brüggemann, Michael (2012): Transnationale Kulturen des Journalismus. Praktiken journalistischer Themenfindung im Vergleich. *Medien & Kommunikationswissenschaft*, 60 (Sonderband Nr. 2, *Grenzüberschreitende Medienkommunikation*), 76–92.

Brüggemann, Michael/Schulz-Forberg, Hagen (2008): Towards a pan-uropean public sphere? A typology of transnational media in Europe. In: Wessler, Hartmut (ed.): *Transnationalization of public spheres.* Basingstoke and New York: Palgrave Macmillan, pp. 78–94.

Bruns, Axel (2008): *Blogs, Wikipedia, second life, and beyond: From production to produsage.* Berlin: Peter Lang.

Brunsdon, Charlotte/Morley, David (1978): *Everyday television: Nationwide.* London: BFI.

Bruter, Michael (2005): Citizens of Europe? The emergence of a mass European identity. Basingstoke and New York: Palgrave Macmillan.

Burke, Peter (1978): *Popular culture in early modern Europe.* Aldershot: Wildwood House.

Calhoun, Craig (ed.) (1992): *Habermas and the public sphere.* Cambridge: MIT Press.

Canclini, Nestor (2001): *Consumers and citizens. Globalization and multicultural conflicts.* Minneapolis and London: University of Minnesota Press.

Carpentier, Nico (2011): *Media and participation. A site of ideological-democratic struggle.* Bristol: Intellect.

Chadwick, Andrew (2013): *The hybrid media system: Politics and power.* Oxford: Oxford University Press.

Checkel, Jeffrey T./Katzenstein, Peter J. (2009): The politicization of European identities. In: Checkel, Jeffrey T./Katzenstein, Peter J. (eds.): *European identity.* Cambridge: Cambridge University Press, pp. 1–25.

Cohen, Robin/Kennedy, Paul (2000): *Global sociology.* Basingstoke: Palgrave.

Colin, Crouch (2004): *Post-democracy.* Cambridge: Polity Press.

Corcoran, Farell/Fahy, Declan (2009): Exploring the European elite sphere. The role of the 'Financial Times'. *Journalism Studies*, 10(1), 100–113.

Corner, John (2000): Influence. The contested core of media research. In: Curran, James/Gurevitch, Michael (eds.): *Mass media and society.* London: Routledge, pp. 376–397.

Cottle, Simon (2006): *Mediatized conflicts: Understanding media and conflicts in the contemporary world.* Maidenhead: Open University Press.

Cottle, Simon (2009): Global crises in the news. Staging new wars, disasters, and climate change. *International Journal of Communication*, 3, 494–516.

Couldry, Nick (2010): *Why voice matters. Culture and politics after neoliberalism.* London and Thousand Oaks: Sage.

Couldry, Nick (2012): *Media, society, world. Social theory and digital media practice.* Cambridge and Malden: Polity Press.

Couldry, Nick/Hepp, Andreas (2013): Conceptualising mediatization: Contexts, traditions, arguments. *Communication Theory*, 23(3), 191–202.

Couldry, Nick/Langer, Ana I. (2005): Media consumption and public connection. Towards a typology of the dispersed citizen. *Communication Review*, 8(2), 237–257.

Couldry, Nick/Livingstone, Sonia M./Markham, Tim (2007a): Connection or disconnection? Tracking the mediated public sphere in everyday life. In: Butsch, Richard (ed.): *Media and public spheres*. Basingstoke and New York: Palgrave Macmillan, pp. 28–42.

Couldry, Nick/Livingstone, Sonia M./Markham, Tim (2007b): *Media consumption and public engagement. Beyond the presumption of attention*. Basingstoke and New York: Palgrave Macmillan.

Cross, Mai'a K. Davis/Ma, Xinru (2013): EU crises and the international media. *ARENA Working Paper*. ARENA, Centre for European Studies, University Oslo, 3, pp. 1–37.

Cross, Mai'a K. Davis/Ma, Xinru (2015): EU crises and integrational panic. The role of the media. *Journal of European Public Policy*, 22(8), 1053–1070.

Curran, James/Fenton, Natalie/Freedman, Des (2012): *Misunderstanding the Internet*. London: Routledge.

Curran, James/Park, Myung-Jin (eds.) (2000): *De-westernizing media studies*. London and New York: Routledge.

D'Haenens, Leen (2005): Euro-vision. The portrayal of Europe in the quality press. *Gazette: The International Journal for Communication Studies*, 67(5), 419–440.

Dahlgren, Peter (1992): Introduction. In: Dahlgren, Peter/Sparks, Colin (eds.): *Journalism and popular culture*. London, Thousand Oaks and New Delhi: Sage, pp. 1–23.

Dahlgren, Peter (2004): Theory, boundaries and political communication. The uses of disparity. *European Journal of Communication*, 19(1), 7–18.

Dahlgren, Peter (2005): The public sphere: Linking the media and civic cultures. In: Rothenbuhler, Eric W./Coman, Mihai (eds.): *Media anthropology*. Thousand Oaks, London and New Delhi: Sage, pp. 318–327.

Dahlgren, Peter (2006): Doing citizenship: The cultural origins of civic agency in the public sphere. *European Journal of Cultural Studies*, 9(3), 267–286.

Dahlgren, Peter (2013): *The political web: Media, participation and alternative democracy*. Basingstoke and New York: Palgrave Macmillan.

De Vreese, Claes H. (2001): Europe in the news. A cross-national comparative study of the news coverage of key EU-events. *European Union Politics*, 2(3), 283–307.

De Vreese, Claes H. (2003): *Framing Europe. Television news and European integration*. Amsterdam: Aksant.

De Vreese, Claes H./Boomgaarden, Hajo G. (2006): Media effects on public opinion about the enlargement of the European Union. *Journal of Common Market Studies*, 44(2), 419–436.

De Vreese, Claes H./Boomgaarden, Hajo G. (2009): A European public sphere. Media and public opinion. In: Salovaara-Moring, Inka (ed.): *Manufacturing Europe. Spaces of democracy, diversity and communication*. Göteborg: Nordicom, pp. 117–128.

Delors, Jacques/Solana, Javier/Beck, Ulrich/Cohn-Bendit, Daniel et al. (2012): Let's create a bottom-up Europe. *The Guardian*, http://www.guardian.co.uk/commentisfree/2012/may/03/bottom-up-europe/print, date accessed 2 December 2012.

Deuze, Marc (2002): National news cultures. A comparison of Dutch, German, British, Australian and US journalists. *Journalism & Mass Communication Quarterly*, 79(1), 134–149.

Dewey, John (1927): *The public and its problems*. New York: Holt.

Downey, John/Koenig, Thomas (2006): Is there a European public sphere? The Berlusconi-Schulz case. *European Journal of Communication*, 21(2), 165–187.

Downey, John/Mihelj, Sabina/König, Thomas (2012): Comparing public spheres. Normative models and empirical measurements. *European Journal of Communication*, 27(4), 337–353.

Dreßler, Angela (2008): *Nachrichtenwelten. Hinter den Kulissen der Auslandsberichterstattung. Eine Ethnographie*. Bielefeld: Transcript.

Du Gay, Paul/Hall, Stuart/Janes, Linda/Mackay, Hugh/Negus, Keith (1997): *Doing cultural studies. The story of the Sony walkman*. London: Sage.

Eder, Klaus (2000): Zur Transformation nationalstaatlicher Öffentlichkeit in Europa. *Berliner Journal für Soziologie*, 10(2), 67–184.

Eder, Klaus (2009): A theory of collective identity. Making sense of the debate on a 'European identity'. *European Journal of Social Theory*, 12(4), 427–447.

Eder, Klaus (2014): The EU in search of its people: The birth of a society out of the crisis of Europe. *European Journal of Social Theory*, 17(3), 219–237.

Elvestad, Eiri/Blekesaune, Arild (2008): Newspaper readers in Europe. A multilevel study of individual and national differences. *European Journal of Communication*, 23(4), 425–447.

Emmer, Martin/Wolling, Jens/Vowe, Gerhard (2012): Changing political communication in Germany. Findings from a longitudinal study on the influence of the internet on political information, discussion and the participation of citizens. *Communications*, 37(3), 233–252.

Eriksen, Erik O./Fossum, John E. (eds.) (2002): *Democracy in the European Union. Integration through deliberation?*. London and New York: Routledge.

Esser, Andrea (2002): The transnationalization of European television. *Journal of European Area Studies*, 10, 13–29.

Esser, Frank/Strömbäck, Jesper (eds.) (2014): *Mediatization of politics. Understanding the transformation of Western democracies*. Basingstoke and New York: Palgrave Macmillan.

Fairclough, Norman (1995): *Media discourse*. London, New York, Sydney and Auckland: Edward Arnold.

Favell, Adrian (2008): *Eurostars and Eurocities: Re movement and mobility in an integrating Europe*. Malden: Blackwell.

Favell, Adrian/Recchi, Ettore (2011): Social mobility and spatial mobility. In: Favell, Adrian/Guiraudon, Virginie (eds.): *Sociology of the European Union*. Basingstoke: Palgrave Macmillan, pp. 50–75.

Fehmel, Thilo (2014): Konflikttheorie und Gesellschaftsbildung. *Serie Europa – Europe Series*, 1, 1–23.

Firmstone, Julie (2008): Approaches of the transnational press to reporting Europe. *Journalism*, 9(4), 423–442.

Flew, Terry (2009): The citizen's voice. Albert Hirschman's Exit, Voice and Loyalty and its contribution to media citizenship debates. *Media, Culture & Society*, 31(4), 978–995.

Flick, Uwe (2004): *Triangulation. Eine Einführung*. Wiesbaden: VS.

Foret, François (2009): Symbolic dimensions of EU legitimization. *Media, Culture & Society*, 31(2), 313–324.

Forst, Rainer (2015): Öffentlichkeit und Macht. Im Gedenken an Bernhard Peters. In: *TransState Working Papers, 186*, http://www.sfb597.uni-bremen.de/pages/pubApBeschreibung.php?SPRACHE=de&ID=228, date accessed 20 April 2015.

Fotopoulos, Takis (2010): Greece: The implosion of the systemic crisis. *The International Journal of Inclusive Democracy*, 6(1), http://www.inclusivedemocracy.org/journal/vol6/vol6_no1_takis_Greece_the_implosion_of_the_systemic_crisis.htm, date accessed 20 April 2015.

Foucault, Michel (1970): *The order of things*. New York: Pantheon Books.

Fraser, Nancy (1993): Rethinking the public sphere. A contribution to the critique of actually existing democracy. In: Robbins, Bruce (ed.): *The phantom public sphere*. London and Minneapolis: University of Minnesota Press, pp. 1–32.

Fraser, Nancy (2007): Transnationalizing the public sphere. On the legitimacy and efficacy of public opinion in a post-westphalian world. *Theory, Culture & Society*, 24(4), 7–30.

Fuchs, Dieter (2011): European identity and support for European integration. In: Lucarelli, Sonia/Cerutti, Furio/Schmidt, Vivien A. (eds.): *Debating political identity and legitimacy in the European Union. Interdisciplinary views*. London and New York: Routledge, pp. 55–75.

García Canclini, Néstor (2001): *Consumers and citizens. Globalization and multicultural conflicts*. Minneapolis and London: Minnesota University Press.

Garfinkel, Harold (1967): *Studies in ethnomethodology*. Englewood Cliffs: Prentice-Hall.

Gattermann, Katjana (2013): News about the European Parliament. Patterns and external drivers of broadsheet coverage. *European Union Politics*, 14(3), 436–457.

Georgakopoulou, Alexandra (2014): Small stories transposition and social media. A micro-perspective on the 'Greek crisis'. *Discourse and Society*, 25(4), 519–539.

Gerhards, Jürgen (1993): Westeuropäische Integration und die Schwierigkeiten der Entstehung einer europäischen Öffentlichkeit. *Zeitschrift für Soziologie*, 22(2), 96–110.

Gerhards, Jürgen (2000): Europäisierung von Ökonomie und Politik und die Trägheit der Entstehung einer europäischen Öffentlichkeit. In: Bach, Maurizio (ed.): *Die Europäisierung nationaler Gesellschaften*. Westdeutscher Verlag: Opladen, pp. 277–305.

Gerhards, Jürgen (2001): Missing a European public sphere. In: Kohli, M./Novak, M. (eds.): *Will Europe work? Integration, employment and the social order*. London and New York: Routledge, pp. 145–158.

Gerhards, Jürgen/Hans, Silke (2014): Explaining citizens' participation in a transnational European public sphere. *Comparative Sociology*, 13(6), 667–691.

Gerhards, Jürgen/Lengfeld, Holger/Häuberer, Julia (2014): The EU crisis and citizens support for a European welfare state. In: *Berlin Studies on the Sociology of Europe*, No. 30. Berlin: Freie Universität Berlin, pp. 3–24.

Gerhards, Jürgen/Offerhaus, Anke/Roose, Jochen (2009): Wer ist verantwortlich? Die Europäische Union, ihre Nationalstaaten und die massenmediale Attribution von Verantwortung für Erfolge und Misserfolge. In: Pfetsch, Barbara/Marcinkowski, Frank (eds.): *Politik in der Mediendemokratie, PVS-Sonderheft*. Wiesbaden: VS Verlag, pp. 529–558.

Gibson, Will (2009): Intercultural communication online: Conversation analysis and the investigation of asynchronous written discourse. *Forum: Qualitative*

Research, 10(1), Art. 49, http://nbn-resolving.de/urn:nbn:de:0114-fqs0901493, date accessed 21 April 2015.

Giddens, Anthony (1984): *The constitution of society. Outline of the theory of structuration*. Berkeley: University of California Press.

Giddens, Anthony (2012): In Europe's dark days, what cause for hope? *The Guardian*, Wednesday, 25 January 2012, http://www.guardian.co.uk/world/2012/jan/25/anthony-giddens-europe-dark-days-hope/print, date accessed 1 December 2012.

Giddens, Anthony (2014): *Turbulent and mighty continent*. Cambridge: Polity.

Glaser, Barney G./Strauss, Anselm L. (1967): *Discovery of grounded theory. Strategies for qualitative research*. Chicago: Aldine Transaction.

Gleissner, Martin/de Vreese, Claes H. (2005): News about the EU Constitution. Journalistic portrayal of the European Union Constitution challenges and media. *Journalism*, 6(2), 221–242.

Goffman, Erving (1983): The interaction order. American Sociological Association, 1982 Presidential Address. *American Sociological Review*, 48(1), 1–17.

Golding, Peter (2008): European journalism and the European public sphere. In: Bondebjerg, Ib/Madsen, Peter (eds.): *Media, democracy and European culture*. Bristol: Intellect Books, pp. 121–133.

Govcom.org Foundation (2015): *Issue Crawler software*. Amsterdam, available at http://issuecrawler.net

Gramsci, Antonio (1971): *Selection from the prison notebook*. London: Lawrence & Wishart.

Gripsrud, Jostein (2007): Television and the European public sphere. *European Journal of Communication*, 22(4), 479–492.

Gripsrud, Jostein/Murdock, Graham (eds.) (2015): *Money talks: Media, markets, crisis*. Bristol: Intellect.

Gurevitch, Michael/Levy, Mark R./Roeh, Itzhak (1997): The global newsroom: Convergences and diversities in the globalization of television news. In: Dahlgren, Peter/Sparks, Colin (eds.): *Communication and citizenship*. London: Routledge, pp. 195–216.

Habermas, Jürgen (1984): *The theory of communicative action*. Boston: Beacon Press.

Habermas, Jürgen (1989): *The structural transformation of the public sphere: An inquiry into a category of bourgeois society*. Cambridge: MIT Press.

Habermas, Jürgen (1996): *Between facts and norms*. Cambridge: MIT Press.

Habermas, Jürgen (2011): *Zur Verfassung Europas: Ein Essay*. Berlin: Suhrkamp.

Habermas, Jürgen (2012): *The crisis of the European Union: A response*. Cambridge: Polity.

Hahn, Julia/Mok, Kathrin/Roessler, Patrick/Schmid, Michaela/Schwendemann, Nicolas (2008): Mediated events in political communication. A case study on the German European Union Council presidency 2007. *Communications: The European Journal of Communication Research*, 33(3), 333–352.

Hahn, Oliver/Rosenwerth, Karen K./Schröder, Roland (2006): News Management zwischen Europa-PR und EU-Journalismus. Theoretische Überlegungen zu einem effizienten transnationalen Kommunikationskonzept. In: Langenbucher, Wolfgang/Latzer, Michael (eds.): *Europäische Öffentlichkeit und medialer Wandel*. Wiesbaden: VS, pp. 286–295.

Hahn, Oliver/Schröder, Roland/Dietrich, Stefan (2008): Journalistische Kulturen. Forschungstypologie und Aufriss. In: Hahn, Oliver/Schröder, Roland/Dietrich, Stefan (eds.): *Journalistische Kulturen. Internationale und interdisziplinäre Theoriebausteine*. Köln: Halem, pp. 7–30.

Hall, Stuart (1973): Encoding and decoding in television discourse. In: *Occasional Papers, 7*, Centre for Contemporary Cultural Studies, Birmingham, pp. 1–12.

Hall, Stuart (1997): The centrality of culture: Notes on the cultural revolutions of our time. In: Thompson, Kenneth (ed.): *Media and cultural regulation*. London: Sage, pp. 207–238.

Hallin, Daniel C./Mancini, Paolo (2004): *Comparing media systems: Three models of media and politics*. Cambridge: Cambridge University Press.

Hallin, Daniel C./Mancini, Paolo (eds.) (2012): *Comparing media systems beyond the Western world*. Cambridge: Cambridge University Press.

Hanitzsch, Thomas/Hanusch, Folker/Mellado, Claudia/Anikina, Maria/Berganza, Rosa/Cangoz, Incilay/Coman, Mihai/Hamada, Basyouni/Hernandez, María E./ Karadjov, Christopher D. (2011): Mapping journalism cultures across nations: A comparative study of 18 countries. *Journalism Studies*, 12(3), 273–293.

Hannerz, Ulf (2004): *Foreign news: Exploring the world of foreign correspondents*. Chicago: Chicago University Press.

Hasebrink, Uwe (2015): Kommunikationsrepertoires und digitale Öffentlichkeiten. In: *Communicative Figurations, Working Paper No. 8*, available at http://www. kommunikative-figurationen.de/fileadmin/redak_kofi/Arbeitspapiere/CoFi_ EWP_No-8_Hasebrink.pdf, date accessed 20 April 2015.

Hasebrink, Uwe/Domeyer, Hanna (2012): Media repertoires as patterns of behaviour and as meaningful practices. A multimethod approach to media use in converging media environments. *Participations. Journal of Audience & Reception Studies*, 9(2), 757–779.

Hasebrink, Uwe/Herzog, Anja (2009): Mediennutzung im internationalen Vergleich. In: Hans-Bredow-Institut (ed.): *Internationales Handbuch Medien*. Baden-Baden: Nomos, pp. 131–154.

Hasebrink, Uwe/Jensen, Klaus B./Van den Bulck, Hilde/Hölig, Sascha/Maeseele, Peter (2015): Changing patterns of media use across cultures. A challenge for longitudinal research. *International Journal of Communication*, 9, 435–457.

Hasebrink, Uwe/Lampert, Claudia (2012): Onlinenutzung von Kindern und Jugendlichen im europäischen Vergleich. Ergebnisse der 25-Länder-Studie 'EU Kids Online'. *Media Perspektiven*, 12, 635–647.

Hasebrink, Uwe/Popp, Jutta (2006): Media repertoires as a result of selective media use. A conceptual approach to the analysis of patterns of exposure. *Communications*, 31(2), 369–387.

Heidenreich, Martin (2014): Eurokrisen und Vergesellschaftung. Die krisenhafte Europäisierung nationaler Fiskalpolitiken. Eine Einführung. In: Heidenreich, Martin (ed.): *Krise der Europäischen Vergesellschaftung? Soziologische Perspektiven*. Wiesbaden: VS, pp. 1–28.

Heikkilä, Heikki/Kunelius, Risto (2006): Journalists imagining the European public sphere: Professional discourses about the EU news in ten countries. *Javnost – The Public*, 12(4), 63–80.

Heikkilä, Heikki/Kunelius, Risto (2008): Ambivalent ambassadors and realistic reporters: The calling of cosmopolitanism and the seduction of the secular in EU journalism. *Journalism*, 9(4), 377–397.

Hepp, Andreas (2009): Transculturality as a perspective: Researching media cultures comparatively. *Forum: Qualitative Social Research*, 10(1), http://nbn-resolving.de/urn:nbn:de:0114-fqs0901267, date accessed 1 January 2009.

Hepp, Andreas (2012): Mediatization and the 'molding force' of the media. *Communications*, 37(1), 1–28.

Hepp, Andreas (2013): *Cultures of mediatization*. Cambridge: Polity Press.

Hepp, Andreas (2015): *Transcultural communication*. Malden: Wiley Blackwell.

Hepp, Andreas/Berg, Matthias/Roitsch, Cindy (2014): *Mediatisierte Welten der Vergemeinschaftung. Kommunikative Vernetzung und das Gemeinschaftsleben junger Menschen*. Wiesbaden: VS.

Hepp, Andreas/Brüggemann, Michael/Kleinen-von Königslöw, Katharina/Lingenberg, Swantje/Möller, Johanna (2012): *Politische Diskurskulturen in Europa. Die Mehrfachsegmentierung europäischer Öffentlichkeit*. Wiesbaden: VS.

Hepp, Andreas/Couldry, Nick (2009): What should comparative media research be comparing? Towards a transcultural approach to 'media cultures'. In: Thussu, Daya K. (ed.): *Internationalizing media studies. Impediments and imperatives*. London and New York: Routledge, pp. 32–47.

Hepp, Andreas/Couldry, Nick (2010): Introduction: Media events in globalized media cultures. In: Couldry, Nick/Hepp, Andreas/Krotz, Friedrich (eds.): *Media events in a global age*. London: Routledge, pp. 1–20.

Hepp, Andreas/Lingenberg, Swantje/Elsler, Monika/Möller, Johanna/Mollen, Anne/Offerhaus, Anke (2013): 'I just hope the whole thing won't collapse'. 'Understanding' and 'overcoming' the EU financial crisis from the citizens' perspective. In: *TransState Working Papers, No. 168*, Bremen: University of Bremen.

Hepp, Andreas/Lingenberg, Swantje/Möller, Johanna/Elsler, Monika/Mollen, Anne/Offerhaus, Anke (2012): Europe beyond crisis? Citizens' (re)actions on the multi-segmentation of the European public sphere. In: Morganti, Luciano/Bekemans, Léonce (eds.): *The European public sphere – From critical thinking to responsible action*. Brussels: Peter Lang, pp. 69–84.

Hepp, Andreas/Wessler, Hartmut (2009): Politische Diskurskulturen. Überlegungen zur empirischen Erklärung segmentierter europäischer Öffentlichkeit. *Medien & Kommunikationswissenschaft*, 57(2), 174–197.

Herrmann, Richard/Brewer, Marilynn B. (2004): Identities and Institutions. Becoming European in the EU. In: Hermann, Richard/Risse, Thomas/Brewer, Marilynn B. (eds.): *Transnational Identities. Becoming European in the EU*. Lanham: Rowman & Littlefield, pp. 1–24.

Herzog, Anja/Zingg, Matthias (2007): Media use and Euroscepticism in less educated groups. Paper presented at *IAMCR 2007*, Paris.

Hesmondhalgh, David (2006): Bourdieu, the media and cultural production. *Media, Culture and Society*, 28(2), 211–231.

Highfield, Timothy J. (2009): Which way up? Reading and drawing maps of the blogosphere. *Ejournalist*, 9(1), 99–114.

Hirschman, Albert (1970): *Exit, voice and loyalty: Responses to decline in firms, organizations, and states*. Cambridge: Harvard University Press.

Hix, Simon (2008): *What's wrong with Europe and how to fix it.* Cambridge: Cambridge University Press.

Hjarvard, Stig (2013): *The mediatization of culture and society*. London: Routledge.

Hohlfeld, Ralf (2005): Der missachtete Leser revisited. In: Behmer, Markus/Blöbaum, Bernd/Scholl, Armin/Stöber, Rudolf (eds.): *Journalismus und Wandel*. Wiesbaden: VS Verlag für Sozialwissenschaften, pp. 195–224.

Husband, Charles (2000): Media and the public sphere in multi-ethnic societies. In: Cottle, Simon (ed.): *Ethnic minorities and the media*. Buckingham: Open University Press, pp. 199–214.

Johnson, Richard (1986): What is cultural studies anyway? *Social Text*, 16, 38–80.

Joris, Willem/D'Haenens, Leen/Van Gorp, Baldwin (2014): The euro crisis in metaphors and frames: Focus on the press in the Low Countries. *European Journal of Communication,* 29(5), 608–617.

Kaina, Viktoria (2006): European identity, legitimacy, and trust. Conceptual considerations and perspectives on empirical research. In: Karolewski, Ireneusz P./ Kaina, Viktoria (eds.): *European identity. Theoretical perspectives and empirical insights.* Münster and Berlin: Lit-Verlag, pp. 113–146.

Kaitatzi-Whitlock, Sophia (2014): Greece, the eurozone crisis and the media: The solution is the problem. *Javnost – The Public,* 21(4), 25–46.

Kannengießer, Sigrid (2012): Transkulturelle Intrasektionalität als Perspektive in der geschlechtertheoretischen Migrationsforschung. In: Hausbacher, Eva/Klaus, Elisabeth/Poole, Ralph/Brandl, Ulrike/Schmutzhart, Ingrid (eds.): *Kann die Migrantin sprechen? Migration und Geschlechterverhältnisse.* Wiesbaden: VS, pp. 24–40.

Kantner, Cathleen (2004): *Kein modernes Babel. Kommunikative Voraussetzungen europäischer Öffentlichkeit.* Wiesbaden: VS.

Kantner, Cathleen (2015): National media as transnational discourse arenas. The case of humanitarian military interventions. In: Risse, Thomas (ed.): *European public spheres. Politics is back.* Cambridge: Cambridge University Press, pp. 84–107.

Karlsson, Martin (2012): Understanding divergent patterns of political discussion in online forums – Evidence from the European citizens' consultations. *Journal of Information Technology & Politics,* 9(1), 64–81.

Kaun, Anne (2012): Civic experiences and public connection. Media and young people in Estonia. In: *Örebro Studies in Media and Communication 14,* Södertörn Doctoral Dissertation 67.

Kaun, Anne (2014): 'I really don't like them!' – Exploring citizens' media criticism. *European Journal of Cultural Studies,* 17(5), 489–506.

Keller, Reiner (2012): Entering discourses. A new agenda for qualitative research and sociology of knowledge. *Qualitative Sociology Review,* 8(2), 46–75.

Kepplinger, Hans M. (2002): Mediatization of politics. Theory and data. *Journal of Communication,* 52(4), 972–986.

Kleinen-von Königslöw, Katharina (2010a): *Die Arenen-Integration nationaler Öffentlichkeiten. Das Beispiel der deutschen Öffentlichkeit.* Wiesbaden: VS Verlag.

Kleinen-von Königslöw, Katharina (2010b): Europe for the people. The Europeanization of public spheres in the tabloid press. In: Tréfás, David/Lucht, Jens (eds.): *Europe on trial: Shortcomings of the EU with regard to democracy, public sphere, and identity.* Innsbruck: Studien-Verlag, pp. 44–60.

Kleinen-von Königslöw, Katharina/Möller, Johanna (2009): Nationalisierte Europäisierung. Die Entwicklung der politischen Medienöffentlichkeit in Polen nach 1989. In: Dupuis, Indira (ed.): *Nordosteuropäische Geschichte in den Massenmedien. Medienentwicklung, Akteure und transnationale Öffentlichkeit.* Nordost-Archiv Band XVIII. Lüneburg: Nordost-Institut, pp. 101–131.

Kleinsteuber, Hans J./Rossmann, Thorsten (eds.) (1994): *Europa als Kommunikationsraum. Akteure, Strukturen und Konfliktpotenziale in der europäischen Medienpolitik.* Opladen: Leske + Budrich.

Knoblauch, Hubert (2003): Habitus und Habitualisierung. Zur Komplementarität von Bourdieu mit dem Sozialkonstruktivismus. In: Rehbein, Boike/Saalmann, Gernot/Schwengel, Herrmann (eds.): *Pierre Bourdieus Theorie des Sozialen. Probleme und Perspektiven.* Konstanz: UVK, pp. 187–201.

Knoblauch, Hubert (2013): Communicative constructivism and mediatization. *Communication Theory,* 23(3), 297–315.

Koopmans, Ruud (2015): How advanced is the Europeanization of the public sphere? Comparing German and European structures of political communication. In: Risse, Thomas (ed.): *Theorising communication flows within a European public sphere*. Cambridge: Cambridge University Press, pp. 53–83.

Koopmans, Ruud/Erbe, Jessica (2004): Towards a European public sphere? Vertical and horizontal dimensions of Europeanized political communication. *Innovation: The European Journal of Social Science Research*, 17(2), 97–118.

Koopmans, Ruud/Erbe, Jessica/Meyer, Martin F. (2010): The Europeanization of public spheres: Comparisons across issues, time, and countries. In: Koopmans, Ruud/Statham, Paul (eds.): *The making of a European public sphere: Media discourse and political contention*. Cambridge: Cambridge University Press, pp. 63–96.

Koopmans, Ruud/Pfetsch, Barbara (2006): Obstacles or motors of Europeanization? German media and the transnationalization of public debate. *Communications*, 31, 115–138.

Koopmans, Ruud/Statham, Paul (2010a): Theoretical framework, research design, and methods. In: Koopmans, Ruud/Statham, Paul (eds.): *The making of a European public sphere: Media discourse and political contention*. Cambridge: Cambridge University Press, pp. 34–59.

Koopmans, Ruud/Statham, Paul (eds.) (2010b): *The making of a European public sphere: Media discourse and political contention*. Cambridge: Cambridge University Press.

Koopmans, Ruud/Zimmermann, Ann (2003): Internet: A new potential for European political communication? In: Wissenschaftszentrum Berlin für Sozialforschung (ed.): *Veröffentlichungsreihe der Arbeitsgruppe 'Politische Öffentlichkeit und Mobilisierung'*. Berlin: WZB, pp. 1–25.

Koopmans, Ruud/Zimmermann, Ann (2010): Transnational political communication on the Internet: Search engine results and hyperlink networks. In: Koopmans, Ruud/Statham, Paul (eds.): *The making of a European public sphere: Media discourse and political contention*. Cambridge: Cambridge University Press, pp. 171–194.

Kraidy, Marwan M. (2005): *Hybridity, or the cultural logic of globalization*. Philadelphia: Temple University Press.

Krotz, Friedrich (2009): Mediatization: A concept with which to grasp media and societal change. In: Lundby, Knut (ed.): *Mediatization: Concept, changes, consequences*. New York: Peter Lang, pp. 19–38.

Krzyżanowski, Michał (2009): Europe in crisis? Discourses on crisis events in the European press 1956–2006. *Journalism Studies*, 10(1), 18–35.

Kunelius, Risto/Heikkilä, Heikki (2007): Mainstream journalism. Problems and potential of a European public sphere (EPS). In: AIM Research Consortium (ed.): *Reporting and managing European news. Final report of the project adequate information management in Europe 2004–2007*. Dortmund: Projektverlag, pp. 45–77.

Kutter, Amelie (2014): A catalytic moment: The Greek crisis in the German financial press. *Discourse & Society*, 25(4), 446–466.

Landerer, Nino (2013): Rethinking the logics: A conceptual framework for the mediatization of politics. *Communication Theory*, 23(3), 239–258.

Latour, Bruno (2007): *Reassembling the social: An introduction to actor-network-theory*. Oxford: Oxford University Press.

Lingenberg, Swantje (2006): The European public sphere and its audience. Citizens' participation in the European Constitutional debate. In: Bertelli, Dominique/Julia, Jean-Thierry (eds.): *Démocratie participative en Europe*. Toulouse: Corep, pp. 52–59.

Lingenberg, Swantje (2010a): *Europäische Publikumsöffentlichkeiten. Ein pragmatischer Ansatz*. Wiesbaden: VS Verlag.

Lingenberg, Swantje (2010b): The citizen audience and European public spheres: Exploring civic engagement in European political communication. *Communications*, 35(1), 45–72.

Lingenberg, Swantje/Möller, Johanna/Hepp, Andreas (2010): Doing nation. Journalistische Praktiken der Nationalisierung Europas. In: *TranState Working Papers, No. 140*, Bremen: CRS 597 Transformations of the State.

Livingstone, Sonia M. (2004): The challenge of changing audiences. Or, what is the audience researcher to do in the age of the internet? *European Journal of Communication*, 19(1), 75–86.

Livingstone, Sonia M. (2013): The participation paradigm in audience research. *The Communication Review*, 16(1–2), 21–30.

Lodge, Juliet/Sarikakis, Katharine (2013): Citizens in 'an ever-closer union'? The long path to a public sphere in the EU. *International Journal of Media & Cultural Politics*, 9(2), 165–181.

Lohner, Judith (2011): *Die Europäische Union in der Regionalpresse. Inhalte und journalistische Praxis aktueller Berichterstattung*. Berlin: Lit Verlag.

Luckmann, Benita (1970): The small life-worlds of modern man. *Social Research*, 37(4), 580–596.

Lundby, Knut (2014): Mediatization of communication. In: Lundby, Knut (ed.): *Mediatization of communication*. Berlin and New York: De Gruyter, pp. 3–35.

Lunt, Peter/Livingstone, Sonia M. (2013): Media studies' fascination with the concept of the public sphere: Critical reflections and emerging debates. *Media, Culture & Society*, 35(1), 87–96.

Machill, Marcel/Beiler, Markus/Fischer, Corinna (2006): Europe-topics in Europe's media. The debate about the European public sphere. A meta-analysis of media content analyses. *European Journal of Communication*, 21(1), 57–88.

Madianou, Mirca/Miller, Daniel (2012a): *Migration and new media. Transnational families and polymedia*. London and New York: Routledge.

Madianou, Mirca/Miller, Daniel (2012b): Polymedia. Towards a new theory of digital media in interpersonal communication. *International Journal of Cultural Studies*, 16(2), 169–187.

Maier, Michaela/Strömbäck, Jesper/Kaid, Lynda L. (eds.) (2011): *Political communication in European parliamentary elections*. Farnham and Burlington: Ashgate Publication.

Malik, Maja (2004): *Journalismus-Journalismus. Funktionen, Strukturen und Strategien der journalistischen Selbstthematisierung*. Wiesbaden: VS.

Mancini, Paolo (2005): Is there a European model of journalism? In: de Burgh, Hugo (ed.): *Making journalists: Diverse models, global issues*. London and New York: Routledge, pp. 77–93.

Mancini, Paolo (2008): Journalism culture. A multi-level proposal. In: Hahn, Oliver/Schröder, Roland (eds.): *Journalistische Kulturen. Internationale und interdisziplinäre Theoriebausteine*. Köln: Halem, pp. 149–167.

Mau, Steffen/Verwiebe, Roland (2010): *European societies. Mapping structures and change*. Bristol: Policy Press.

McLaren, Lauren M. (2006): *Identity, interests and attitudes to European integration*. Basingstoke and New York: Palgrave Macmillan.

Meijers, Maurits (2013): The euro-crisis as a catalyst of the Europeanization of public spheres? A cross-temporal study of the Netherlands and Germany. In: *LSE 'Europe in Question' Discussion Paper Series*. London: London School of Economics, pp. 1–35.

Meyen, Michael/Riesmeyer, Michael (2009): *Diktatur des Publikums. Journalisten in Deutschland*. Konstanz: UVK.

Meyer, Christoph O. (1999): Political legitimacy and the invisibility of politics: Exploring the European Union's communication deficit. *Journal of Common Market Studies*, 37(4), 617–639.

Meyer, Christoph O. (2005): The Europeanization of media discourse. A study of quality press coverage of Economic policy co-ordination since Amsterdam. *Journal of Common Market Studies*, 43(1), 121–144.

Meyer, Jan-Henrik (2010): *The European public sphere. Media and transnational communication in European integration 1969–1991*. Stuttgart: Steiner.

Michailidou, Asimina (2010): Vertical Europeanisation of online public dialogue: EU public communication policy and online implementation. In: Bee, Cristiano/Bozzini, Emanuela (eds.): *Mapping the European public sphere. Institutions, media and civil society*. Surrey: Ashgate Publishing, pp. 65–82.

Michailidou, Asimina/Trenz, Hans-Jörg (2010): Mediati(zi)ng EU politics. Online news coverage of the 2009 European Parliamentary elections. *Communications*, 35(3), 327–346.

Michailidou, Asimina/Trenz, Hans-Jörg/De Wilde, Pieter (2012): (W)e the peoples of Europe: Representations of the European Union polity during 2009 European Parliamentary elections on the internet. In: Evas, Tatjana/Liebert, Ulrike/Lord, Christopher (eds.): *Multilayered representation in the European Union. Parliaments, courts and the public sphere*. Baden-Baden: Nomos, pp. 215–232.

Mihelj, Sabina (2007): The European and the national in communication research. *European Journal of Communication*, 22(4), 443–459.

Möller, Johanna (2013): *Transkulturelle Öffentlichkeitsakteure. Grenzüberschreitende Gestaltungspotenziale in der deutsch-polnischen politischen Kommunikation*. Dissertation, University of Bremen.

Morley, David (1992): *Television audiences and cultural studies*. London and New York: Routledge.

Nederveen Pieterse, Jan (1995): Globalization as hybridization. In: Featherstone, Mike/Lash, Scott/Robertson, Roland (eds.): *Global modernities*. London, Thousand Oaks and New Delhi: Sage, pp. 45–68.

Negt, Oskar/Kluge, Alexander (1993): *Public sphere and experience. Toward an analysis of the bourgeois and proletarian public sphere*. Minneapolis: University of Minnesota Press.

Negus, Keith (2002): The work of cultural intermediaries and the enduring distance between production and consumption. *Cultural Studies*, 16(4), 501–515.

Neidhardt, Friedhelm (2006): Europäische Öffentlichkeit als Prozess. In: Langenbucher, Wolfgang R./Latzer, Michael (eds.): *Europäische Öffentlichkeit und medialer Wandel*. Wiesbaden: VS Verlag für Sozialwissenschaften, pp. 46–61.

Neverla, Irene/Schoon, Wiebke (2008): Europäischer Journalismus. Annäherung an eine vernachlässigte Dimension europäischer Öffentlichkeit. *Medien & Zeit*, 3, 18–30.

Nielsen, Rasmus K./Schrøder, Kim C. (2014): The relative importance of social media for accessing, finding, and engaging with news. An eight-country cross-media comparison. *Digital Journalism*, 2(4), 472–489.

Novy, Leonard (2013): *Britain and Germany imagining the future of Europe. National identity, mass media and the public sphere*. Basingstoke and New York: Palgrave Macmillan.

Nullmeier, Frank/Biegon, Dominika/Gronau, Jennifer/Nonhoff, Martin/Schmidtke, Henning/Schneider, Steffen (2010): *Prekäre Legitimitäten: Rechtfertigung von Herrschaft in der postnationalen Konstellation.* Frankfurt am Main: Campus Verlag.

Oberhuber, Florian/Bärenreuter, Christoph/Krzyzanowski, Michał/Schönbauer, Heinz/Wodak, Ruth (2005): Debating the European Constitution. On representations of Europe/the EU in the press. *Journal of Language and Politics,* 4(2), 227–271.

Offerhaus, Anke (2011): *Die Professionalisierung des deutschen EU-Journalismus. Institutionalisierung, Expertisierung und Inszenierung der europäischen Dimension im deutschen Journalismus.* Wiesbaden: VS.

Offerhaus, Anke (2012): Auslandskorrespondenten zwischen sachlicher Expertise und nationalem Vorurteil. Eine Gegenüberstellung von journalistischen Selbstaussagen und inhaltsanalytischen Befunden. *Medien & Kommunikationswissenschaft (Sonderband 'Grenzüberschreitende Medienkommunikation'),* 60, 93–114.

Offerhaus, Anke/Mollen, Anne/Hepp, Andreas (2014): Nationalizing Europe regionally – The Europeanization of public spheres in regional newspaper reporting and the 'crisis' in Europe. In: Stepinska, Agnieszka (ed.): *Media and communication in Europe.* Berlin: Logos Verlag, pp. 13–32.

Örnebring, Henrik (2009): Comparative European journalism. The state of current research. In: *Working Papers,* Reuters Institute for the Study of Journalism, pp. 1–22.

Örnebring, Henrik (2011): The two professionalisms of journalism. Journalism and the changing context of work. In: *Working Papers,* Reuters Institute for the Study of Journalism, No. 5, pp. 1–19.

Örnebring, Henrik/Jönsson, Anna M. (2004): Tabloid journalism and the public sphere: A historical perspective on tabloid journalism. *Journalism Studies,* 5(3), 283–295.

Ortner, Christina (2014): *Wie junge Erwachsene die EU sehen und was die Medien dazu beitragen. Zur Bedeutung medienvermittelter Erfahrungen für die Entwicklung von Orientierungen gegenüber der EU.* Baden-Baden: Nomos.

Packwood, Nicholas (2004): Geography of the blogosphere: Representing the culture, ecology and community of weblogs. In: Gurak, Laura/Antonijevic, Smiljana/Johnson, Laurie/Ratliff, Clancy/Reyman, Jessica (eds.): *Into the blogosphere: Rhetoric, community, and culture of weblogs,* http://blog.lib.umn.edu/blogosphere/geography_of_the_blogosphere.html, date accessed 14 April 2015.

Parkin, Frank (1972): *Class inequality and political order.* St. Albans: Paladin.

Paus-Hasebrink, Ingrid/Ortner, Christina (2009): Images of Europe from the bottom. The role of media for the attitudes towards Europe among socially disadvantaged groups. In: Garcia-Blanco, Iñaki/van Bauwel, Sofie/Cammaerts, Bart (eds.): *Media agoras. Democracy, diversity, and communication.* Cambridge: Cambridge Scholars Publishing, pp. 73–96.

Paus-Hasebrink, Ingrid/Ortner, Christina (2010): Zur Rolle der Medien bei der Konstruktion von Europabildern sozial Benachteiligter unter besonderer Berücksichtigung von Jugendlichen. In: Klaus, Elisabeth/Sedmak, Clemens/Drüeke, Ricarda/Schweiger, Gottfried (eds.): *Identität und Inklusion im europäischen Sozialraum.* Wiesbaden: VS, pp. 193–220.

Peter, Jochen/De Vreese, Claes H. (2004): In search of Europe. A cross-national comparative study of the European Union in national television news. *Press/Politics,* 9(4), 3–24.

Peters, Bernhard (2008): *Public deliberation and public culture*. Basingstoke and New York: Palgrave Macmillan.

Pfetsch, Barbara (2008): Agents of transnational debate across Europe: The press in emerging European public sphere. *Javnost – The Public*, 15(4), 21–40.

Pfetsch, Barbara/Adam, Silke/Eschner, Barbara (2008): The contribution of the press to Europeanization of public debates. A comparative study of issue salience and conflict lines of European integration. *Journalism*, 9(4), 465–492.

Pfetsch, Barbara/Esser, Frank (2012): Comparing political communication. In: Esser, Frank/Hanitzsch, Thomas (eds.): *Handbook of comparative communication research*. New York: Routledge, pp. 25–47.

Pfetsch, Barbara/Heft, Annett (2015): Theorising communication flows within a European public sphere. In: Risse, Thomas (ed.): *European public spheres. Politics is back*. Cambridge: Cambridge University Press, pp. 29–52.

Post, Senja/Vollbracht, Matthias (2013): Processing crisis news. Media coverage on the economy and public opinion after the financial crisis. *Zeitschrift für Marktwirtschaft und Ethik*, 2, 116–130.

Preston, Paschal (2009): An elusive trans-national public sphere? Connectivity versus journalism and news culture in the EU setting. *Journalism Studies*, 10(1), 114–129.

Preunkert, Jenny/Vobruba, Georg (2011): Die Eurokrise. Konsequenzen der defizitären Institutionalisierung der gemeinsamen Währung. *Arbeitsbericht des Instituts für Soziologie*, 57, 1–23.

Pye, Lucian W. (1968): Political culture. In: Sills, David L. (ed.): *International encyclopedia of the social sciences*. Basingstoke: Palgrave Macmillan, pp. 218–225.

Quandt, T. (2008): Methods of journalism research: Observation. In: Löffelholz, Martin/Weaver, David/Schwarz, Andreas (eds.): *Global journalism research: Theories, methods, findings, future*. Malden, Oxford and Carlton: Blackwell, pp. 131–142.

Raeymaeckers, Karin/Cosijn, Lieven/Deprez, Annelore (2007): Reporting the European Union: An analysis of the Brussels press corps and the mechanisms influencing the news flow. *Journalism Practice*, 1(1), 102–119.

Rafter, Kevin (2014): Voices in the crisis: The role of media elites in interpreting Ireland's banking collapse. *European Journal of Communication*, 29(5), 598–607.

Rasmussen, Terje (2013): Internet-based media, Europe and the political public sphere. *Media, Culture & Society*, 35(1), 97–104.

Reese, Stephen D. (2008): Theorizing a globalized journalism. In: Löffelholz, Martin/Weaver, Daniel (eds.): *Global journalism research: Methods, findings, future*. Malden: Blackwell Publishing, pp. 240–252.

Reinemann, Carsten (2003): *Medienmacher als Mediennutzer: Kommunikations- und Einflussstrukturen im politischen Journalismus der Gegenwart*. Köln: Böhlau.

Reus-Smit, Christian (2007): International crises of legitimacy. *International Politics*, 44(2), 157–174.

Riegert, Kristina (1998): *Nationalising foreign conflict*. Stockholm: University of Stockholm.

Risse, Thomas (2004): European institutions and identity change: What have we learned? In: Hermann, Richard/Risse, Thomas/Brewer, Marilynn B. (eds.): *Transnational identities: Becoming European in the EU*. Lanham: Rowman & Littlefield, pp. 247–271.

Risse, Thomas (2010): *A community of Europeans? Transnational identities and public spheres*. New York: Cornell University Press.

Risse, Thomas (2015a): European public spheres, the politicization of EU affairs, and its consequences. In: Risse, Thomas (ed.): *European public spheres. Politics is back.* Cambridge: Cambridge University Press, pp. 141–164.

Risse, Thomas (2015b): Introduction. In: Risse, Thomas (ed.): *European public spheres. Politics is back.* Cambridge: Cambridge University Press, pp. 1–25.

Risse, Thomas/Grabowsky, Jana K. (2008): European identity formation in the public sphere and in foreign policy. In: *RECON Online Working Paper 2008/04*, http://www.reconproject.eu/main.php/RECON_wp_0804.pdf?fileitem=50511948, date accessed 20 April 2015.

Rogers, Richard (2010): Mapping public web space with the Issuecrawler. In: Reber, Bernard/Broussard, Claire (eds.): *Digital cognitive technologies: Epistemology and the knowledge society.* London: ISTE, pp. 89–99.

Roose, Jochen (2015): Politisiert die Krise? Veränderungen bei der Diskussion EU-politischer Fragen in der Bevölkerung. In: Roose, Jochen/Rössel, Jörg (eds.): *Empirische Kultursoziologie.* Wiesbaden: Springer VS, pp. 425–454.

Rovisco, Maria (2010): One Europe or several Europes? The cultural logic of narratives of Europe-views from France and Britain. *Social Science Information Sur Les Sciences Sociales*, 49(2), 241–266.

Russ-Mohl, Stephan (2003): Towards a European journalism? Limits, opportunities, challenges. *Studies in Communication Science*, 3(2), 203–216.

Sarikakis, Katharine (ed.) (2007): *Media and cultural policy in the European Union.* Amsterdam: Rodopi.

Sarikakis, Katharine/Lodge, Juliet (2013): Citizens in 'an ever-closer union'? The long path to a public sphere in the EU. *International Journal of Media and Cultural Politics*, 9(2), 165–181.

Sarrica, Mauro/Fortunati, Leopoldina/O'Sullivan, John/Balcytiene, Aukse/Macgregor, Phil/Nuust, Vallo/Roussou, Nayia/Meso, Koldobika/Pereira, Xosé/De Luca, Federico (2010): The early stages of the integration of the internet in EU newsrooms. *European Journal of Communication*, 25(4), 413–422.

Sassen, Saskia (2008): *Das Paradox des Nationalen.* Frankfurt am Main: Suhrkamp.

Scharkow, Michael/Vogelgesang, Jens (2010): Effects of domestic media use on European integration. *Communications*, 35(1), 73–91.

Scharpf, Fritz W. (1999): *Regieren in Europa. Effektiv und demokratisch?* Frankfurt am Main and New York: Campus.

Scharpf, Fritz W. (2009): Legitimität im europäischen Mehrebenensystem. *Leviathan*, 37(2), 244–280.

Schlesinger, Philip (1993): Wishful thinking. Cultural politics, media, and collective identities in Europe. *Journal of Communication*, 43(2), 6–17.

Schlesinger, Philip/Deirdre, Kevin (2002): Can the European Union become a sphere of publics? In: Eriksen, Erik O./Fossum, John E. (eds.): *Democracy in the European Union: Integration through deliberation?.* London: Routledge, pp. 206–229.

Schranz, Mario/Eisenegger, Mark (2011): The financial crisis and the media: An analysis of newspapers in the United Kingdom, the United States and Switzerland between 2007 and 2009. In: Suter, Christian/Herkenrath, Mark (eds.): *World society in the global economic crisis.* Zürich and Münster: LIT Verlag, pp. 285–302.

Schrøder, Kim C. (2011): Audiences are inherently cross-media: Audience studies and the cross-media challenge. *Communication Management Quarterly*, 18(6), 5–27.

Schrøder, Kim C. (2014): News media old and new. *Journalism Studies*, 16(1), 60–78.

Schrøder, Kim C./Kobbernagel, Christian (2010): Towards a typology of cross-media news consumption. A qualitative-quantitative synthesis. *Northern Lights*, 8(1), 115–138.

Schrøder, Kim C./Phillips, Louise (2007): Complexifying media power. A study of the interplay between media and audience discourses on politics. *Media, Culture & Society*, 29(6), 890–915.

Schuck, Andreas R. T./De Vreese, Claes H. (2006): Between risk and opportunity. News framing and its effects on public support for EU enlargement. *European Journal of Communication*, 21(1), 5–32.

Schuck, Andreas R. T./De Vreese, Claes H. (2011): Finding Europe: Mapping and explaining antecedents of 'Europeanness' in news about the 2009 European Parliamentary elections. *Studies in Communication\Media (SCM)*, 2(1), 265–294.

Schuck, Andreas R. T./Vliegenthart, Rens/Boomgaarden, Hajo. G./Elenbaas, Matthijs/Azrout, Rachid/Van Spanje, Joost/De Vreese, Claes H. (2013): Explaining campaign news coverage. How medium, time, and context explain variation in the media framing of the 2009 European Parliamentary elections. *Journal of Political Marketing*, 12(1), 8–28.

Schuck, Andreas R. T./Xezonakis, Georgios/Elenbaas, Matthijs/Banducci, Susan A./De Vreese, Claes H. (2011): Party contestation and Europe on the news agenda: The 2009 European Parliamentary elections. *Electoral Studies*, 30(1), 41–52.

Schudson, Michael/Anderson, Chris (2009): Objectivity, professionalism, and truth seeking in journalism. In: Wahl-Jorgensen, Karin/Hanitzsch, Thomas (eds.): *The handbook of journalism studies*. New York and London: Routledge, pp. 88–101.

Schütz, Alfred/Luckmann, Thomas (1973): *Structures of the life-world*, Volume 1. Evanston: Northwestern University Press.

Simmel, Georg (1950): Conflict. In: Simmel, Georg (ed.): *The sociology of Georg Simmel*. Translated by Kurt H. Wolff. Glencoe: Free Press, pp. 13–17.

Statham, Paul (2007): Journalists as commentators on European politics. Educators, partisans or ideologues? *European Journal of Communication*, 22(4), 461–477.

Statham, Paul (2008): Making Europe news: How journalists view their role and media performance. *Journalism*, 9(4), 398–422.

Statham, Paul (2010a): Making Europe news: Journalism and media performance. In: Koopmans, Ruud/Statham, Paul (eds.): *The making of a European public sphere: Media discourse and political contention*. Cambridge: Cambridge University Press, pp. 125–150.

Statham, Paul (2010b): What kind of Europeanized public politics. In: Koopmans, Ruud/Statham, Paul (eds.): *The making of a European public sphere: Media discourse and political contention*. Cambridge: Cambridge University Press, pp. 277–306.

Statham, Paul/Trenz, Hans-Jörg (2013): *The politicization of Europe. Contesting the constitution in the mass media*. London and New York: Routledge.

Steensen, Steen (2014): Conversing the audience: A methodological exploration of how conversation analysis can contribute to the analysis of interactive journalism. *New Media & Society*, 16(8), 1197–1213.

Stegbauer, Christian/Rausch, Alexander (2006): *Strukturalistische Internetforschung: Netzwerkanalysen internetbasierter Kommunikationsräume*. Wiesbaden: VS.

Stommel, Wyke/Meijman, Frans J. (2011): The use of conversation analysis to study social accessibility of an online support group on eating disorders. *Glob Health Promotion*, 18(2), 18–26.

Storey, John (2003): *Inventing popular culture. From folklore to globalization*. Oxford: Blackwell.

Strauss, Anselm L./Corbin, Juliet (1997): *Grounded theory in practice*. Thousand Oaks: Sage.

Strömbäck, Jesper/Todal Jenssen, Anders/Aalberg, Toril (2011): The financial crisis as a global news event: Cross-national media coverage and public knowledge of economic affairs. In: Aalberg, Toril/Curran, James (eds.): *How media inform democracy. A comparative approach*. London: Routledge, pp. 159–175.

Taneja, Harsh/Webster, James G./Malthouse, Edward C. (2012): Media consumption across platforms. Identifying user-defined repertoires. *New Media & Society*, 14(6), 951–968.

Thomassen, Jacques (2007): Democratic values. In: Dalton, Russell J./Klingemann, Hans-Dieter (eds.): *The Oxford handbook of political behaviour*. Oxford: Oxford University Press, pp. 418–434.

Thompson, John B. (1995): *The media and modernity. A social theory of the media*. Cambridge: Cambridge University Press.

Thussu, Daya K. (ed.) (2009): *Internationalizing media studies*. London: Routledge.

Tomlinson, John (1999): *Globalization and culture*. Cambridge and Oxford: Polity Press.

Trenz, Hans-Jörg (2004): Media coverage on European governance. Exploring the European public sphere in national quality newspapers. *European Journal of Communication*, 19(3), 291–319.

Trenz, Hans-Jörg (2005): Die mediale Ordnung des politischen Europas: Formen und Dynamiken der Europäisierung politischer Kommunikation in der Qualitätspresse. *Zeitschrift für Soziologie*, 34(3), 188–206.

Trenz, Hans-Jörg (2009): Digital media and the return of the representative public sphere. *Javnost – The Public*, 16(1), 33–46.

Trenz, Hans-Jörg/Eder, Klaus (2004): The democratizing dynamics of a European public sphere. Towards a theory of democratic functionalism. *European Journal of Social Theory*, 7(1), 5–25.

Triandafyllidou, Anna/Wodak, Ruth/Krzyżanowski, Michał (eds.) (2009): *The European public sphere and the media: Europe in crisis*. Basingstoke and New York: Palgrave Macmillan.

Tsuneyoshi, Takao/Hashimoto, Akihiro/Haneda, Shoko (2012): Quantitative evaluation of nation stability. *Journal of Policy Modelling*, 34(1), 132–154.

Tzogopoulos, George (2013): *The Greek crisis in the media. Stereotyping in the international press*. Farnham: Ashgate.

Vaara, Eero (2014): Struggles over legitimacy in the Eurozone crisis. Discursive legitimation strategies and their ideological underpinnings. *Discourse & Society*, 25(4), 500–518.

Van de Steeg, Marianne (2010): Theoretical reflections on the public sphere in the European Union. A network of communication or a political community? In: Bee, Cristiano/Bozzini, Emanuela (eds.): *Mapping the European public sphere. Institutions, media and civil society*. Fanham and Burlington: Ashgate, pp. 31–45.

Van de Steeg, Marianne/Risse, Thomas (2010): The emergence of a European Community of communication insights from empirical research on the Europeanization of public spheres. In: *KFG Working Paper Series (Vol. 15)*. Berlin: Freie Universität Berlin.

Van Spanje, Joost/De Vreese, Claes H. (2014): Europhile media and eurosceptic voting. Effects of news media coverage on eurosceptic voting in the 2009 European Parliamentary elections. *Political Communication*, 31(2), 325–354.

Vetters, Regina (2007): Vor Ort in Europa. Ein Vergleich der EU-Berichterstattung deutscher Qualitäts- und Regionalzeitungen. *Medien & Kommunikationswissenschaft*, 55(3), 355–371.

Vobruba, Georg (2012): The social construction of the European society. *Current Perspectives in Social Theory*, 30, 263–279.

Vobruba, Georg (2013): Time horizons of transformation: Lessons from the German unification for the eurozone. In: *openDemocracy*, http://www.opendemocracy.net/georg-vobruba/timehorizons-of-transformation-lessons-from-german-unification-for-eurozone, date accessed 1 February 2014.

Vobruba, Georg (2014a): Gesellschaftsbildung durch die Eurokrise. In: Heidenreich, Martin (ed.): *Krise der Europäischen Vergesellschaftung? Soziologische Perspektiven.* Wiesbaden: VS, pp. 185–199.

Vobruba, Georg (2014b): The Europeanization of distributional conflicts within the euro crisis. In: Petropoulos, Nicholas P./Tsobanoglou, George O. (eds.): *The debt crisis in the eurozone. Social impacts.* Newcastle: Cambridge Scholars Publishing, pp. 23–31.

Volkmer, Ingrid (2008): Satellite cultures in Europe. Between national spheres and a globalized space. *Global Media and Communication*, 4(3), 231–244.

Volkmer, Ingrid (2011): The European public. Between national spheres and a deterritorialized space. Keynote address for the conference: *Media, communication & democracy. Global and national environments conference.* Melbourne: RMIT University, http://mams.rmit.edu.au/l09q0zubhb3j.pdf, date accessed 15 July 2015.

Walby, Sylvia (2007): Complexity theory, Systems theory, and multiple intersecting social inequalities. *Philosophy of the Social Sciences*, 37(4), 449–470.

Wasserman, Stanley/Faust, Katherine (2007): *Social network analysis: Methods and applications.* New York: Cambridge University Press.

Weaver, David/Löffelholz, Martin (2008): Questioning national, cultural, and disciplinary boundaries. A call for global journalism research. In: Löffelholz, Martin/ Weaver, David/Schwarz, Andreas (eds.): *Global journalism research: Theories, methods, findings, future.* Malden: Blackwell, pp. 3–12.

Weber, Max (1949): *On the methodology of the social science.* Glencoe: The Free Press of Glencoe.

Weber, Max (1972a): *Economy and society. A study in the integration of economic and social theory.* London: Routledge & Kegan Paul.

Weber, Max (1972b): *Wirtschaft und Gesellschaft. Grundriss der verstehenden Soziologie.* Tübingen: Mohr Verlag.

Weber, Max (1978): *Economy and society. An outline of interpretative* society, Volume I. Berkeley, Los Angeles and London: University of California Press.

Webster, James G./Ksiazek, Thomas B. (2012): The dynamics of audience fragmentation. Public attention in an age of digital media. *Journal of Communication*, 62, 39–56.

Weischenberg, Siegfried (2002): *Journalistik. Theorie und Praxis aktueller Medienkommunikation. Band 2: Medientechnik, Medienfunktionen, Medienakteure.* Opladen: Westdeutscher Verlag.

Welsch, Wolfgang (1999): Transculturality – The puzzling form of cultures today. In: Featherstone, Mike/Lash, Scott (eds.): *Spaces of culture. City, nation, world.* London: Sage, pp. 194–213.

Wessler, Hartmut (2008): Investigating deliberativeness comparatively. *Political Communication*, 25(1), 1–22.

Wessler, Hartmut/Peters, Bernhard/Brüggemann, Michael/Kleinen-v. Königslöw, Katharina/Sifft, Stefanie (2008): *Transnationalization of public spheres*. Basingstoke: Palgrave Macmillan.

Wiedebusch, Jutta (1989): *Selbstverständnis und Rezipientenbilder von Hörfunkjournalisten*. Frankfurt am Main, Bern, New York and Paris: Lang.

Wilke, Jürgen/Reinemann, Carsten (2007): Invisible second-order campaigns? A longitudinal study of the coverage of the European Parliamentary elections 1979–2004 in four German quality newspapers. *Communications. The European Journal of Communication Research*, 32(3), 299–322.

Willem, Joris/D'Haenens, Leen/Van Gorp, Baldwin (2014): The euro crisis in metaphors and frames. Focus on the press in the Low Countries. *European Journal of Communication*, 29(5), 608–617.

Williams, Raymond (1978): The press and popular culture. A historical perspective. In: Boyce, George/Curran, James/Wingate, Pauline (eds.): *Newspaper history. From the seventeenth century to the present day*. London: Constable, pp. 41–50.

Wilson, Richard W. (2000): The many voices of political culture: Assessing different approaches. *World Politics*, 52, 246–273.

Wimmer, Andreas/Glick Schiller, Nina (2002): Methodological nationalism and beyond. Nation-state building, migration and the social sciences. *Global Networks*, 2(4), 301–334.

Winker, Gabriele/Degele, Nina (2011): Intersectionality as multi-level analysis. Dealing with social inequality. *European Journal of Women's Studies*, 18(1), 51–66.

Wittel, Andreas (2006): Auf dem Weg zu einer Netzwerk-Sozialität. In: Hepp, Andreas/Krotz, Friedrich/Moores, Shaun/Winter, Carsten (eds.): *Konnektivität, Netzwerk und Fluss. Konzepte gegenwärtiger Medien-, Kommunikations- und Kulturtheorie*. Wiesbaden: VS, pp. 163–188.

Wodak, Ruth/Angouri, Jo (2014): Introduction to a special issue. From Grexit to Grecovery. Euro/crisis discourses. *Discourse & Society*, 25(4), 417–423.

Wodak, Ruth/Meyer, Michael (eds.) (2009): *Critical discourse analysis. History, agenda, theory, and methodology*. London, Thousand Oaks, New Delhi and Singapore: Sage.

Wodak, Ruth/Wright, Scott (2006): The European Union in cyberspace. Multilingual democratic participation in a virtual public sphere? *Journal of Language and Politics*, 5(2), 251–275.

Wodak, Ruth/Wright, Scott (2007): The European Union in cyberspace: Democratic participation via online multilingual discussion boards. In: Danet, Brenda/Herring, Susan C. (eds.): *The multilingual internet: Language, culture, and communication online*. Oxford and New York: Oxford University Press, pp. 385–407.

Wright, Scott (2007): A virtual European public sphere? The Futurum discussion forum. *Journal of European Public Policy*, 14(8), 1167–1185.

Zürn, Michael (2000): Democratic governance beyond the nation state. *European Journal of International Relations*, 6(2), 83–221.

Index

GPSR Compliance
The European Union's (EU) General Product Safety Regulation (GPSR) is a set
of rules that requires consumer products to be safe and our obligations to
ensure this.

If you have any concerns about our products, you can contact us on

ProductSafety@springernature.com

In case Publisher is established outside the EU, the EU authorized
representative is:

Springer Nature Customer Service Center GmbH
Europaplatz 3
69115 Heidelberg, Germany

www.ingramcontent.com/pod-product-compliance
Lightning Source LLC
LaVergne TN
LVHW050144060326
832904LV00004B/163